Illustrated Account of Chinese Characters

漢 字 圖 解

Illustrated Account of Chinese Characters

謝光輝 主編

Compiled By Guanghui Xie

三 聯 書 店 （香 港） 有 限 公 司

責任編輯　俞　笛
裝幀設計　吳冠曼

Illustrated Account of Chinese Characters
Compiled by Guanghui Xie

Original Simplified Chinese edition ©2001 Peking University Press
Complex Chinese edition ©2003 Joint Publishing (H.K.) Co., Ltd.
Published in Hong Kong
ISBN 978-962-04-2088-7

書　　名　漢字圖解
主　　編　謝光輝
出　　版　三聯書店（香港）有限公司
　　　　　香港北角英皇道499號北角工業大廈20樓
發　　行　香港聯合書刊物流有限公司
　　　　　香港新界大埔汀麗路36號3字樓
印　　刷　深圳中華商務安全印務股份有限公司
　　　　　深圳市龍崗區平湖鎮萬福工業區
版　　次　2003年3月香港第一版第一次印刷
　　　　　2016年3月香港第一版第七次印刷
規　　格　16開（184×235mm）704面
國際書號　ISBN 978-962-04-2088-7

本書原由北京大學出版社以書名《常用漢字圖解》出版，經由原出版者
授權本公司在除中國大陸以外地區出版發行。

前　言

　　漢字是世界上歷史最悠久、使用最廣泛的文字之一。它已經有了五六千年的發展歷史，現在有約佔全球人口四分之一的人在使用着它。漢字的起源和發展，與中華民族的文明緊密相關。它是中華傳統文化的基本載體，也是中華民族文化思想延伸、傳播和交流的基本工具，在中華民族悠久的歷史進程中起着極其重要的作用。可以這樣説，沒有漢字，就沒有中華民族光輝燦爛的文化。今天，漢字為全世界每一個華語華文的應用者所時刻不可或缺，在世界文化的發展中起着愈來愈重要的作用。

　　學習漢語，首先要解決的問題就是漢字。如何有效地學習漢字，是擺在語文研究工作者面前的一個首要解決的問題。

　　漢字是屬於表意體系的文字，字的形體與字義密切相關。因此，要了解漢字，首先就要掌握漢字形體結構的特點和規律。根據字形辨析文字的本義，並進而説明其引申義和假借義，是研究漢字的人必須遵循的基本原則。

　　研究漢字的形體構造，中國傳統文字學有"六書"之説。所謂"六書"，是指漢字構成和使用的六種方法，即象形、指事、會意、形聲、轉注和假借。從字形學的角度來看，象形、指事、會意、形聲可以説是漢字的構造方法，而轉注、假借則不過是用字之法。所以，過去認為"六書"是漢字的造字之法，其實是不確切的。不過，"六書"説基本上反映了漢字產生、發展的一般規律，它對正確了解和掌握漢字的構造原理及其使用規律，進而從根本上認識和把握每一個漢字的本來含義，具有指導性的意義。

　　1.象形　　所謂象形，就是像實物之形，也就是把客觀事物的形體描繪出來的意思。漢字多起源於圖畫文字。最初的漢字字形多是根據實物的形狀把它描畫出來的，這就是象形。不過，象形字和圖畫是有其本質性的區別的。象形字的寫法較圖畫大為簡化，往往只是實物形體的一個簡單輪廓（如日、月、山、川、人、大等），或某一具有特徵性意義的部份（如牛、羊等）。此外更主要的是，它必須和語言中表示概念的詞和語音結合起來，從而成為記錄語言的符號。隨着字形的不斷簡化和抽象化，後代的象形字的形體與造字之初大不相同。從甲骨文發展到現在的楷體，原來的象形字已經完全不象形了。實際上，它們已經失去了象形的意義，成了單純的書寫符號。

　　象形字要像實物之形，而語言中很多抽象的概念是無形可像的，是不能"畫成其物"的。這一必不可免的局限性制約了象形字的發展。所以在漢字中，象形字的數量並不多。但象形卻是漢字最基本的一種造字方法，是各種漢字形成的基礎：指事字的大部份是在象形字的基礎上增加指示符號造成的，會意字則由兩個或兩個以上的象形字組合而成，而形聲字實際也是兩個象形字（或會意字、指事字）的組合，只不過其中一個用來表示意義類屬，另一個用來代表讀音罷了。

2.指事 指事是一種用抽象的指示符號來表達語言中某種概念的造字方法。指事字的構成有兩種情形：一種是在象形字上添加指示符號構成的指事字，如刃、本、末等；另一種是由純抽象符號組成的指事字，如上、下、一、二、三等。

指事字在全部漢字中是數量最少的一種。這是因為，絕大多數字都不需要用指事的方法來造：要表示客觀的物體，可以用象形的方法，而要說明抽象的概念則可以採用會意或形聲。

3.會意 所謂會意，是把兩個或兩個以上的字組合在一起以表示一個新的意思。從結構上看，會意字是兩個或兩個以上的字的並列或重疊。從意義上講，它又是兩個或兩個以上字的意義的會合。如一個“木”字代表一棵樹，兩個“木”字組合在一起則代表成片的樹群（林），而三個“木”字則表示更大面積分佈的樹林（森）。又如“休”字，由“人”和“木”組成，表示人靠着大樹歇息的意思。

會意字是由兩個或兩個以上的象形字組合而成。它和象形字之間的根本區別在於：象形字是獨體的，而會意字則為合體。會意的方法與象形、指事比較起來，有很大的優越性。它既可以描繪具體的實物，也可以表達抽象的概念；不僅能描繪靜態的物貌，同時也能夠反映物體的動態。一個象形字，可以和很多其他的象形字組成不同的會意字；而同一個象形字，由於排列方式的不同，也可以組成不同的會意字。這樣，就大大提高了象形字的利用效率。所以，會意字的數量要比象形字和指事字多得多。在形聲造字法廣泛使用之前，會意是一種最主要的造字之法。只是在更先進的有標音成份的形聲字被普遍使用之後，它才退居次要的地位，甚至原有的會意字，也變成了形聲字，或為同音的形聲字所代替。

4.形聲 形聲字是由意符（形旁）和音符（聲旁）兩部份組成。其中意符表示形聲字本義所屬的意義範疇（或類屬），音符則代表形聲字的讀音。如以“木”為意符的形聲字“松”、“柏”、“桃”等都屬於樹木類，而以“手”為意符的“摧”、“拉”、“提”、“按”等都同手的行為動作有關。但在形聲字中，意符只能代表其意義範疇或類屬，不能表示具體的字義。它的具體字義是靠不同的讀音，也就是不同的音符來區別的。有些形聲字的音符既有表音的作用，又有表意的作用（如“娶”）。這就是所謂的“會意兼形聲”。但是就多數形聲字來說，音符只是表示讀音，和字義沒有必然的聯繫。如“江”、“河”二字，其中的“工”、“可”只代表讀音，和江、河的字義是毫無關係的。

　　形聲造字法進一步打破了象形、指事、會意的諸多局限，具有無可比擬的優越性。我們知道，世界上許多事物或抽象概念是很難用象形或會意的方法來表示的。比如"鳥"是鳥類的總稱，但是鳥的種類成千上萬，無法用象形或會意的辦法來一一加以區別。於是，就出現了形聲字：用"鳥"作為意符來表示鳥的總類，而用不同的音符來區別不同種類的鳥，如鴿、鶴、雞、鵲等。由此方法，就產生了大量的形聲字。愈到後代，形聲字的發展愈快，數量也愈多。據統計，在漢代的《說文解字》一書中，形聲字約佔收錄漢字總數的80％；宋代的《六書略》，形聲字佔了88％；清代的《康熙字典》達到90％；而在現在通用的簡化字中，形聲字更是佔了絕對的多數。

　　5.轉注　　轉注是"六書"中最多爭議的一個概念，歷來眾說紛紜，至今沒有定論。根據許慎《說文解字》的定義，所謂轉注字應該是指那些同一部首、意義相同、可以互相註釋的字。如"老"和"考"兩個字，都隸屬於老部，意義也相同。《說文解字》："老，考也。"又："考，老也。"說明它們之間是可以互相註釋的。

　　嚴格來講，轉註只不過是一種"訓詁"的方法。其目的在於解釋字義，即用"互訓"的辦法比較、說明字義，並不能因此造出新字來。因此，轉註不能算作是造字之法，而是一種用字之法。

　　6.假借　　假借也是一種用字之法。許慎給它的定義是"本無其字，依聲托事"，即借一個已有的字來表示語言中與其讀音相同或相近的詞。這種由於音同或音近而被借用來表示另外一個意義的字，就是假借字。它是借用已有的字來表示另外一個新的詞，並不能因此而產生一個新的字，所以也不能算是造字之法。

　　在早期文字中，假借字的數量是不少的。因為那時所造出來的文字數量不多，要用較少的字表達語言中眾多的概念，就必須採用同音假借的辦法，以擴大字的使用效率。如甲骨文的"自"是個象形字，其本義是指鼻子，借用來表示自己、自我的意思。又如甲骨文"來"字像麥穗形，本義指麥子，假借為來往之來。

　　本書定名為《漢字圖解》。所收錄的絕大部份都是常用字。少數字不大常用，但與同類字屬於一個系列，為使讀者有一個系統的認識，一並列出。在選字上，以象形、指事、會意字為主，亦雜有個別形聲字，主要是由早期的象形字或會意字轉變而來的形聲字。

　　按照科學的分類方法，我們把所收錄的漢字分別歸屬於人體、器具、建築、動物、植物、天文地理等幾大類。全書按義類排列，而每一類中又將意義相關的字排列在一起。通過這樣的分類和排列，能使讀者更清晰地了解早期漢字的造字規律和特點，即所謂的"近取諸身（人體），遠取諸物（器具、建築）"，"仰則觀象於天（天文），俯則觀法於地（地理），視鳥獸之文（動物）與地之宜（植物）"。

　　本義的解說，以古文字及文獻為根據，着重由字形結構說明本義，引申義及常用的轉義則隨文指明。部份條目後附有常見詞語，目的是幫助理解本義和常用義。書中每字配插圖一幅，以與文字說明相配合，通過生動活潑的漫畫形式，形象地展示由字形結構所反映出來的文字本義。

　　每個字根據本義及常用義加註拼音，字下面加【】的為相關的異體字。並選臨有代表性的古文字字形：甲骨文、金文、小篆、石鼓文、古璽等，以使讀者明瞭字形的源流及其演變的規律。

　　為便於讀者查檢，目錄後另附漢語拼音索引和筆畫索引。

謝光輝

1996 年 10 月於廣州暨南大學

Introduction

The Chinese script is one of the oldest and most widely used writing systems in the world. It has a history of five or six thousand years, and is used by about one fourth of the total population on the earth. The creation and evolution of Chinese characters is closely interwoven with the development of Chinese culture. Chinese characters are the basic carriers of the traditional Chinese culture and as an important tool for extending, spreading and exchanging ideas. They have played a tremendous role in the long history of the Chinese nation. One may well argue that without Chinese characters there would be no such splendid Chinese culture. In the world today, Chinese characters are not only indispensable to any Chinese user but also have an ever increasing important role to play in worldwide cultural development.

Anyone learning Chinese will have to learn the characters first. How to help learners master the characters efficiently, therefore, is a major task for Chinese language workers.

The Chinese script is an ideographic writing system, in which the form is related to the meaning directly. Hence the first step toward the mastery of Chinese characters is to learn the characteristics and regularity in their composition. It is a rule every student of Chinese characters must follow to base one's judgment of the original meaning of a character on its form, and only when that relation is clear can one go on to discuss its extended and shifted meanings.

In the study of the composition of Chinese characters, there is a traditional theory known as *Liu Shu* (six writings). That is there are six types of characters in terms of their composition: pictographs, indicatives, ideographs, phonetic compounds, mutual explanatories and phonetic loans. Strictly speaking only the first four refer to the ways to compose Chinese characters, the last two are concerned with the ways to use them. The traditional view that *Liu Shu* is a summary of the different ways of composing characters, therefore, is not very accurate. Nevertheless the theory *Liu Shu* is basically correct in revealing the general pattern in the creation and development of Chinese characters. It may help learners to better understand the composition of Chinese characters and their original meanings, and thence use them more accurately.

1. Pictographs　A pictograph is a depiction of a material object. Chinese characters mostly originaled from picture writing. In other words, most Chinese characters were originally pictures of objects. However there is a fundamental difference between pictographs and pictures: the former, usually rough sketches of objects (e. g. 日 "sun"，月 "moon"，山 "mountain"，

川 "river" ，人 "man" ，大 "big") or consisting of a characteristic part only (e. g. 牛 "ox" ，羊 "sheep"), are much simpler than the latter. More important is that pictographs are associated with definite meanings and pronunciations, and have become symbolic. And as a result of increasing simplification and abstraction, pictographs of the later ages are quite different from their originals. Compared with those in the Oracle-Bone Inscriptions, pictographs in the Regular Script are no longer picturelike. In a sense they are not really pictographic, but simply symbolic.

Pictographs are based on the external form of material objects, but the abstract concepts in language are formless, which renders it impossible to picture them. This impossibility inevitably hinders the growth of pictographs, and that is why their number is limited. However, pictography remains the most important method of composing Chinese characters. The others are only developments on this basis: indicatives are mostly formed by adding indicating signs to pictographs, ideographs are usually made up of two or more pictographs, and phonetic compounds are also composed of two pictographs (or ideographs or indicatives), except that one of them specifies the meaning while the other represents the pronunciation.

2. Indicatives　　Indication refers to the way to form abstract characters with indicating signs. There are two subtypes of indicatives: one is composed of a pictograph and an indicating sign, e. g. 刃(knife-edge),本(root),末(treetop); the other is composed purely of abstract signs, e. g. 上(on top of),下(underneath),一(one),二(two)and 三(three).

Indicatives account for the smallest percentage of Chinese characters. The reason is that for most characters there are simpler ways of composition: characters referring to material objects may be composed pictographically and those expressing abstract concepts may be composed ideographically or by way of phonetic-compounding.

3. Ideographs　　Ideographs are compounds, composed of two or more than two existing characters. In terms of structure, an ideograph is the composition of two or more characters side by side or one on top of another. In terms of meaning, an ideograph is also the composition of the meanings of its component characters. For example, a single character 木 stands for a tree, two trees together (林) refers to a group of trees — forest, and the character made up of three trees (森) means a place full of trees, a thick forest. And the character 休 consists of 人 (man) and 木 (tree), signifying that a man is taking a rest against a tree.

Ideographs are made up of two or more than two pictographs, hence they differ from each other in that the former are complex while the latter simplex. Compared with pictography and indication, ideography is more adaptable. Characters of various kinds may be composed in this way, whether they refer to material objects or express abstract concepts, depict static states or describe dynamic processes. The same pictograph may be used to form different ideographs with different pictographs, or with the same pictograph by appearing in different positions. Thus there are more chances of existing pictographs used in the composition of new characters. As a result there are much more ideographs than pictographs or indicatives in Chinese. Ideography was the most important way of composing characters before phonetic compounds became popular. It was only because phonetic compounds, with a phonetic component, are more convenient to use that the importance of ideographs decreased. Some ideographs were even changed into phonetic compounds, and some were replaced by phonetic compounds pronounced the same.

4. Phonetic compounds　　A phonetic compound consists of a radical and a phonetic. The radical indicates its semantic field and the phonetic its pronunciation. For example, phonetic compounds with 木 (tree) as the radical like 松 (pine), 柏 (cypress), 桃 (peach) are all names of trees; those with 手 (hand) as the radical like 推 (push), 拉 (pull), 提 (lift), 按 (press) all refer to actions performed by the hand. However the radical only shows the general semantic class of the character, not its specific meaning. The specific meanings of the characters sharing the same radical are differentiated by the phonetics they each have. The phonetics in some phonetic compounds may also be semantical, e. g. the phonetic 取 in 娶 is also meaningful in the sense of "take", hence the name ideographic-phonetic compounds. But as far as the majority of phonetic compounds are concerned, the phonetic is only phonetical, not semantical. For example, the phonetics 工 and 可 in 江 and 河 respectively are only indicative of their pronunciations, and have nothing to do with their meanings.

Compared with pictography, indication and ideography, phonetic compounding is more flexible. There are many objects and abstract ideas which are difficult to express through pictography or ideography. For example, 鳥 is the general term for birds, but there are tens of thousands types of birds in the world, and it is impossible to differentiate each of them by way of pictography or ideography. In contrast this is easily achieved in phonetic compounding by adding different phonetics to the radical 鳥, e. g. 鴿 (pigeon), 鶴 (crane), 雞 (chicken) and 鵠 (swan). Thus there is an enormous number of phonetic compounds in Chinese, and this number is growing larger and larger in the modern period. Statistics show that phonetic compounds accounted for 80% of the total characters in the *Origin of Chinese Characters* (Shuo Wen Jie Zi) of the Han Dynasty, 88% in *Aspects of the Six Categories of Chinese Characters* (Liu Shu Lüe) of the Song Dynasty, and 90% in *Kangxi* (K'ang-Hsi) *Dictionary* of the Qing Dynasty. In the modern simplified form currently in use, phonetic compounds make up an even larger percent.

5. Mutual explanatories

Mutual explanation is a most dubious concept in the theory of *Liu Shu*. Numerous definitions have been offered, but none of them is definitive. According to Xu Shen's definition in his *Origin of Chinese Characters*, mutual explanatories are those which share the same radical, mean the same and are mutually explainable. For example, the characters 老 and 考, both of the age radical (老) and meaning the same, are mutual explanatories. Thus the *Origin of Chinese Characters* says, "老 means 考" and "考 means 老".

Strictly speaking, mutual explanation is a way to explain the meaning of characters through comparison. There is no new character created in this way. Hence mutual explanation is not a way of composing new characters, but a way of using existing ones.

6. Phonetic loans

Phonetic loan is also a way of using existing characters. Xu Shen defined it as a character which is used in a new sense on account of its pronunciation. In other words, it is an internal borrowing on the basis of pronunciation: a character is used in a new meaning which is expressed by a similar sound in the spoken form. In this way an existing character has acquired a new meaning, but no new character is created. Phonetic loan, therefore, is not a way of composing Chinese characters either.

At the early stage, there were quite a few phonetic loans in the writing system. As the number of existing characters at that time was limited, many concepts had to be expressed by phonetic loans. For example, the character 自 in the Oracle-Bone Inscriptions was originally a pictograph and referred to the nose, but it is now used in the sense of "self" as a result of phonetic loan. The character 來 in the Oracle-Bone Inscriptions was also a pictograph, referring to the wheat, but is now used in the sense of "come" as a phonetic loan.

This book is entitled the *Illustrated Account of Chinese Characters*. The characters in the book mostly have a high frequency of use. A few characters, which are not as frequently used, are also included for the purpose of presenting a complete picture of the characters in the same series. In terms of composition type, most of the characters are pictographs, indicatives and ideographs. The few phonetic compounds included are developments of earlier pictographs or ideographs.

These characters are classified on the basis of their meaning into categories of the human body, implements, buildings, animals' plants, astronomy, geography, etc., under which there are specific classes, again based on the meaning. The arrangement of characters in this way is intended to help readers better understand the regularity and characteristics of character creation in the early stage, that is, people modelled the characters on all kinds of things, as close as the various parts of the human body and as distant as material objects like implements and buildings. In order to compose characters more rationally, they looked closely upward at the celestial bodies in the sky and downward at the configuration of the earth's surface. They observed the movements of animals and appearances of plants.

The original meaning of a character is determined in accordance with its form in ancient writing systems and its use in classical records. The emphasis is on the revelation of the relation between the original meaning and the shape of the character, the extended and shifted meanings are mentioned in passing. There are common expressions at the end of some entries to deepen readers' understanding of the charactere concerned. To show the original meaning of the characters more vividly, there is a picture, or rather a cartoon, accompanying the text for each character.

The phonetic transcription given shows how the character is pronounced when it is used in its original meaning or common meaning. Between the symbol 【 】, there are corresponding variant characters.We also emumerate the representative forms of the character in ancient writing systems, tracing it to its source. The ancient writing include 甲骨文 (the Oracle-Bone Inscriptions), 金文 (the Bronze Inscriptions), 小篆 (the Later Seal Character), 石鼓文 (the Stone-Drum Inscriptions) and 古璽 (ancient seals).

To facilitate readers' use of the book, there are two indexes after Contents, one is in the order of the number of strokes in a character and the other is in an alphabetical order of the characters in Pinyin.

Xie Guanghui

Jinan University, Guangzhou

October 1996

目錄 Contents

方括號內是相關的異體字。

The corresponding original complicated forms are enclosed in square brackets, and the variant forms in square brackets.

漢語拼音索引
Index in Pinyin

炙	529	州	621	主	659	斫	640	卒	384
陟	156	周	643	貯	281	酌	317	族	261
雉	509	帚	247	祝	310	子	58	俎	361
彘	472	冑	369	鑄	364	自	102	尊	314
中	257	朱	544	爪	120	字	60	左	122
眾	9	蛛	490	專	252	宗	415	坐	11
重	13	竹	537	隹	501	走	146		
舟	267	逐	473	屯	564	足	143		

筆畫索引 Index in Stroke-Number

繁體字、異體字統一按筆畫多少排列。筆畫數相同的接起筆的橫、豎、撇、點、折順序排列。筆畫數按新字形，如"即"算七畫，"華"算十二畫。

The Characters, whefher in Simplified, complicated or variant form, are att arranged in the order of their stroke-number. Those having the same stroke-number are arranged according to the first stroke, i. e. in the order of horizontal, vertical, left-falling stroke, dot and turning stroke.

The number of Strokes in a character is determined on the basis of its new form, e. g.即 is of seven strokes, and 華 is of twelve strokes.

[一至三畫] One to Three Strokes									
		土	630	中	257	弔	12	爪	120
		士	185	丹	438	引	213	父	192
		夕	600	之	150	心	164	牙	115
		大	28	尹	299	戈	173	牛	443
一	665	女	46	井	439	戶	429	犬	454
丁	251	子	58	介	218	手	119	王	184
人	3	寸	124	元	4	支	543	市	377
几	285	小	629	六	400	文	33	殳	196
刀	197	尸 [屍]	21	分	199	斗	356		
力	236	山	635	午	232	斤	191	[五畫] Five Strokes	
匕	358	川	617	卅	670	日	587		
十	668	工	253	友	125	曰	111		
卜	306	巾	376	及	136	月	598	且	308
下	667	干	225	反	127	木	538	丘	631
丈	256	弓	212	天	29	欠	105	主	659
上	666			夫	34	止	144	付	135
凡	346	[四畫] Four Strokes		天	31	比	5	令	412
刃	198			尺	10	毛	533	冉 [冄]	77
勺	358			屯	564	水	613	冊	303
口	104	不	563	廿	669	火	650	出	398

華	561	歲	183	寧	345	[十五畫]		霍	513
蛛	490	萬	489	寡	409	Fifteen Strokes		頤	75
貯	281	禽	230	實	284			龍	492
買	282	經	372	寢	403	彈	215	龜	494
進	515	聖	97	徹	331	憂	165	廩	422
開	435	葉	558	榮	562	暴	591	
閑	430	葬	27	漁	497	樂	294	[十七畫]
間	432	裔	385	疑	155	盤	347	Seventeen Strokes
隊	15	裘	383	盡	353	磊	639	
陽	634	解	532	監	93	輦	264	嬰	280
集	518	辟	194	睡	85	養	467	爵	320
雲	609	農	241	福	311	鬧	132	糞	245
須[鬚]	76	遊[游]	260	稱	498	魯	499	聲	100
飲	108	達	154	網	227	齒	116	臀	22
馭	464	雉	509	翟	508			臨	94
黍	580	雷	608	聞	96	[十六畫]		輿	265
黑	42	電	607	舞	44	Sixteen Strokes		簋[毀]	338
黽	472	零	611	蓋	355		
斝	321	鼎	324	賓	408	劓	203	[十八畫]
淼	624	鼓	290	邁	496	器	365	Eighteen Strokes
		鼠	486	鄙	425	奮	514	
		豐	336	需	612	學	65	彝	523
[十三畫]		黽	493	鳴	511	戰	180	瞿	507
Thirteen Strokes				鳳	505	燕	503	轟	99
		[十四畫]		齊	576	燎	652	舊	510
塊	243	Fourteen Strokes		箙	211	盥	351	蟲	487
嵩	637			耤	239	磬	297	豐	337
新	189	僕	20			穆	575	闖	463
彙	589	塵	484			縣	73	雙	521
會	343	夢	166			興	250	鞭	224
業	298						

以下各字未見於字目，而在相關的字裡講到。

The following is a list of characters, mentioned in relevant texts but not treated as separate entries.

人 體 類

Human Body

rén

古人關於人體形象的字造了很多，有正面站立的（大），有側面站立的（人），有躺着的（尸），有跪着的（卩），有女人形（女），有老人形（長），有小孩形（兒）等。古文字的人字，是一個側面而立的人形，它的本義即指人類，是所有人類的總稱。而凡以"人"字所組成的字，大都與人類及其行為狀態有關，如從、眾、伐、休、伏、保、介等。

甲骨文　　　　金文　　　　小篆

There are many characters based on the shape of a human body, e.g. 大 representing the frontal view of a man on his feet, 人 the side view of a man on his feet, 尸 a man lying down, 卩 a man on his knees, 女 a woman, 長 an old man, and 兒 a child. The character 人 in ancient writing systems presents the side view of a man on his feet. It is a general term, referring to all mankind. Characters with 人 as a component are all related to the human race and their behaviour, e.g. 從 (to follow), 眾 (many), 伐 (to attack), 休 (to rest), 伏 (to lie prostrate), 保 (to protect), and 介 (to interpose).

yuán

　　元字的本義就是人頭。早期金文中的元字，像一個側面而立的人形，而特別突出了人的頭部。這個頭部的形狀在甲骨文和後來的金文中簡化成一橫，而在橫上又另加一點，以指示頭在人體中的位置。元字由人的頭部之義又可引申為指事情的開頭，有開始、第一的意思，所以從前帝王改換年號的第一年就叫做元年，一年中的第一個月叫元月，一年的第一天叫元旦。把事情的開端叫做"元始"，所以元字又有本來、原先之義。

【元首】相當於俗語中的"頭兒"、"頭頭"，現在則用來專指一個國家的君主或最高領導人。

甲骨文　　　　金文　　　　小篆

The original meaning of 元 was "the head of a man". In the early Bronze Inscriptions, 元 looks like the side view of a man on his feet, with the head especially prominent. In the Oracle-Bone Inscriptions and late Bronze Inscriptions, the part signalling the head is simply a horizontal stroke, on top of which a dot is added to indicate the position of the head in a human body. From "the head of a man" have derived its extended meanings of "the beginning" and "the first". That is why when an emperor changes his reign title, the first year is called 元年. And the first month in a year is 元月, the first day is 元旦. The beginning of an event is 元始. In addition, 元 could mean "original", though the more usual character for it now is 原.

【元首】head of state

bǐ

古文字的比字，像一前一後緊靠在一起的兩個人形。它的本義為並列、靠近、緊挨；引申指比較、較量；又指勾結，用作貶義，如"朋比為奸"（互相勾結幹壞事）。

【比周】結黨營私，又指聯合、集結。

【比翼齊飛】翅膀挨着翅膀一齊飛翔，比喻夫妻的親密關係。

【比肩繼踵】形容人多擁擠。比肩，肩膀挨着肩膀；繼踵，腳尖碰腳跟。

甲骨文

金文　　　　　小篆

In ancient writing systems, the character 比 looks like two men standing together, one in front of the other. Its primary meaning, therefore, is "to stand side by side", "to get close to", from which have derived its extended meanings "to compare" and "to compete". And it can also mean "to gang up with", e.g. 朋比為奸 (to associate with for nicked purposes).

【比周】to collude with

【比翼齊飛】to pair off wing to wing; a devoted couple

【比肩繼踵】(lit.) shoulder against shoulder and toe after heel; to jostle each other in a crowd; be crowded closely together

cóng

古文字的從字，是一前一後兩個人形，像一個人在前面走，另一個人隨後跟從的樣子，其本義為跟隨、隨從。從字由跟從之義，引申為指聽從、歸順之義，又有參與其事的意思，如從軍、從政、從事等。

【從容】安逸舒緩，不慌不忙。

【從善如流】指能隨時聽從善言，或擇善而從。

甲骨文　　　　　金文　　　　　　小篆

In ancient writing systems, the character 從 looks like two men walking together, one in front of the other. Its primary meaning is "to follow", from which have derived the meanings "to heed" and "to obey". It can also mean "to be engaged in", e.g. 從軍 (to join the army), 從政 (to go into politics) and 從事 (to go in for).

【從容】calm; leisurely

【從善如流】to follow good advice as naturally as a river follows its course

bĕi

古文字的北字，像兩個人相背而立的樣子，其本義為相背、違背。軍隊打了敗仗，士兵相背四散而逃，所以北字又有敗、敗逃之義。此外，北又多借用為方位名詞，指北方，與南方相對。

【北面】舊時君接見臣，尊長接見卑幼，皆南面而坐，臣子或卑幼者則北向而立，故以北面指向人稱臣。拜人為師也稱北面。

| 甲骨文 | 金 文 | 小 篆 |

In ancient writing systems, the character 北 looks like two men standing back to back, hence its original meaning "to be contrary to". When an army suffered a defeat, the soldiers all ran for their lives with their backs toward each other, so the character 北 has come to mean "to be defeated" as well. In addition, 北 is also used as a locative, meaning "the north", opposite to 南 (the south).

【北面】(lit.) to face the north; to act as a subject to a ruler or as a pupil to a master (as the ruler or master usually faces the south when a subject or pupil comes to pay respect to him)

bìng

【併，並】

甲骨文、金文的并字，像兩人被連在一起的形狀。它的本義為合併，即聯合在一起的意思。并【並】字還可用作副詞，相當於"皆"、"都"的意思，又指一起、一齊。

【併力】齊心合力。

【併吞】兼併侵吞，即把別國的領土或別人的產業強行併入自己的範圍內。

【併日而食】兩天只能吃到一天的飯，形容家貧食不能飽。

甲骨文　　　　　金文　　　　　小篆

In the Oracle-Bone Inscriptions and Bronze Inscriptions, the character 并 looks like two men linked together. Its primary meaning is "to combine". But it may also be used as an adverb, meaning "all", "altogether" or "simultaneously".

【併力】 to pull together

【併吞】 to swallow up; to annex

【併日而食】 (lit.) to eat up one's daily ration every two
　　　　days to have only one meal a day out of
　　　　poverty

zhòng

甲骨文眾字，像烈日當空，很多人彎腰在地上勞動的樣子，真有點"鋤禾日當午"的味道。金文和小篆的眾字，上面的日變成了目，似乎像奴隸主的一雙牛似的大眼在監視一群奴隸勞動。因此，眾的本義當指成群的奴隸，引申為指眾人、大家、許多人，同時又泛指人或事物之多。

【眾生】泛指所有有生命的事物，包括人、動物和植物等，有時只指人和其他動物。

【眾口難調】指人多意見多，不易做到使人人滿意。

【眾志成城】眾人同心齊力，可以共築起一座城池。比喻心齊力量大。

甲骨文

金文

小篆

In the Oracle-Bone Inscriptions, the character 眾 looks like a picture in which many people are tilling the soil in the scorching sun. In the Bronze Inscriptions and Later Seal Character, the sun part on top changes into an eye part, as if the labourers were slaves working under the close surveillance of a slave owner. So the original meaning of 眾 was "masses of slaves", but it has evolved to mean a crowd of people, or simply, a large number (of people or of things).

【眾生】all living things, including human beings, animals and sometimes even plants

【眾口難調】It is difficult to cater for all tastes.

【眾志成城】Unity of will is an impregnable stronghold.

chǐ

尺是一種長度單位名稱。十寸為一尺，十尺為一丈。在古代，各種長度單位多以人體的部位為準則，如寸、尺、咫等。金文的尺字，是在一個人形的小腿部位加一個指示符號以表示一尺的高度所在。小篆尺字的結構方法相同，只是形體稍有變化罷了。尺的本義是指一種長度單位，引申為指一種量長度或畫線用的器具——尺子。

【尺寸】尺和寸都是小度量，引申為指少、短小、細微。又指法度、標準。

【尺度】計量長度的定制。又指標準。

【尺牘】長為1尺的竹片書信。

【尺短寸長】尺有所短，寸有所長，比喻每個人都有長處和短處。

金 文

小 篆

尺 is a measure of length, equal to ten 寸 or one tenth of 丈 in the Chinese System, and one third of a metre in the Metric System. In ancient times, these measures of length were based on the length of parts of a human body. In the Bronze Inscriptions, the character 尺 looks like a man with a sign on the shank, marking the length of 尺. In the Later Seal Character, the character has the same structure except some minor change in the shape. From its primary meaning has also derived the use of 尺 to refer to an instrument for measuring length －尺子 (ruler).

【尺寸】measurement

【尺度】yardstick, measure

【尺牘】(lit.) bamboo slips of one chǐ (尺) in length; letter

【尺短寸長】One chǐ (尺) may be too short in one case while one cùn (寸) may be long enough in another; Every person has his weak points as well as strong points.

zuò

坐，是指人臀部着地以支持體重的一種方式。《説文解字》中所錄 "古文" 的坐字，從二人從土，像二人面對面坐在地上之形。坐的本義為跪坐，引申為搭、乘之義。

【坐而論道】坐着空談大道理。

【坐井觀天】坐在深井中看天，比喻眼光狹小、看到的有限。

小篆

坐 means "to sit", especially "to sit on the ground". The character 坐 in the Ancient Script, as is recorded in the *Origin of Chinese Characters*, consists of two man parts and a ground part, signalling two men sitting face to face on the ground. The meaning "to travel by (a vehicle)" is one of its extended meanings.

【坐而論道】to sit talking about theories only (of a theorist who never applies his theory to practice)

【坐井觀天】to look at the sky from the bottom of a well; to have a very narrow view

diào

甲骨文、金文的弔字，像人身上纏帶矰（zēng，一種帶有長繩的短箭）繳之形。其本義不明。此字在金文中常用為叔伯之叔，典籍中則用為哀悼、慰問、撫恤之義，現在多用來作為懸掛的意思。

【弔古】憑弔古蹟，感懷舊事。
【弔唁】哀悼死者稱弔，安慰死者家屬稱唁。
【弔橋】舊時架設在城壕上可以起落的橋。
【弔民伐罪】撫慰人民，討伐有罪。

甲骨文　　　　金文　　　　小篆

In the Oracle-Bone Inscriptions and Bronze Inscriptions, the character 弔 looks like a man around whom winds a long rope with a short arrow at its head. Its original meaning is unclear. In the Bronze Inscriprions, 弔 was often used to refer to one's father's younger brother. In some ancient records, it was used in the sense "to express one's condolences, sympathies". Nowadays, however, it usually means "to hang (something)".

【弔古】to think of the ancients or ancient events
【弔唁】to offer one's condolences over the death of sb.
【弔橋】drawbridge; suspension bridge
【弔民伐罪】to condole the people and attack the guilty

zhòng

重是個會意字，早期金文的重，從人從東，像一個人背上扛着一個大包袱，非常吃力的樣子，表示所背的東西很沉重。稍後的金文重字，"人"與"東"兩形合併為一體，已看不出背物之意。小篆重字從壬從東，也是由金文演變而來的。總之，重的本義指重量，與"輕"相對；引申為厚重、嚴重、莊重等義。此外，重又可讀為 chóng，有重疊、重複的意思。

金文　　　　　小篆

重 is an ideograph. In the early Bronze Inscriptions, the character 重 consists of 人 and 東, like a man carrying a sack on his back strenuously, signalling that the sack is heavy. In the late Bronze Inscriptions, the two components 人 and 東 are combined, with no sign of a man carrying things on his back any more. The character 重 in the Later Seal Character, derivative from the Bronze Inscriptions, consists of 壬 and 東. In short, its primary meaning is "heavy", as against 輕 (light). Its extended meanings include "honest and kind", "serious" and "solemn". 重 can also be pronounced as chóng, meaning "to overlap" and "to repeat".

xiàn

　　臽為"陷"的本字。小篆的臽字，從人在臼中，臼像土坑、陷阱之形，表示人掉落土坑中的意思。所以，臽的本義為陷落、掉入，又指陷阱、土坑。

甲骨文　　　　　金 文　　　　　小 篆

臽 was the original form of 陷. In the Later Seal Character, the character 臽 looks like a man in a hole, signified by 臼. Its primary meaning is "to fall (into a hole)", but it can also be used as a noun, meaning "a hole", "a pitfall".

duì

隊為"墜（zhuì）"的本字。甲骨文隊字從阜從倒人（或倒子），像人從高高的山崖上掉落下來的樣子。金文隊字的人形換成了"豕"，所以到小篆時隊字就變成了從阜豕聲的形聲字。隊的本義為墜落，即由高處往下掉的意思。此字後來多借用為隊列、隊伍之義，故另選"墜"字來代替它的本義。

【隊列】排得整齊的行列。

【隊伍】指軍隊。又指有組織的群眾團體。

| 甲骨文 | 金文 | 小篆 |

隊 was the original form of 墜 (zhuì). In the Oracle-Bone Inscriptions, the character 隊 consists of a mound part and an upsidedown man part, signalling a man falling off a cliff. In the Bronze Inscriptions, the upside-down man part is changed into a pig part (豕). As a result, in the Later Seal Character, it becomes a phonetic compound with 阜 as the radical and 豕 as the phonetic. Its original meaning was "to fall down". This meaning, however, is now expressed by a later development 墜, as 隊 is usually used in the sense of "a file of people", "a contingent".

【隊列】a formation of people

【隊伍】troops; a contingent of people

hé

何字本是一個會意字。甲骨文、金文的何字，像一個人肩上扛着一把戈在行走的樣子；小篆訛變為從人可聲，成為形聲字。何的本義為負荷，讀 hè，即扛、揹的意思。此字後來多借用為疑問代詞（什麼、誰、哪裡）和副詞（多麼），它的本義則為"荷"字所取代。

金文　　　　小篆

The character 何 was originally an ideograph. In the Oracle-Bone Inscriptions and Bronze Inscriptions, the character 何 looks like a man marching with a dagger-axe on his shoulder. In the Later Seal Character it becomes a phonetic compound with 人 as the radical and 可 as the phonetic. Pronounced as hè, the original meaning of 何 was "to carry". But this meaning is now expressed by 荷, as 何 has come to be used as an interrogative pronoun or adverb, meaning "what", "who", "where", or "how".

yǒng

永是"泳"的本字。古文字的永字，像一個人在水中划行的樣子，本義為游、泳。此字後來多用為指水流長遠，又引申為長久、長遠之義，故另造"泳"字來代替它的本義。

【永久】長久，永遠。

【永恆】永遠不變。

【永垂不朽】指姓名、事蹟、精神等永遠流傳，不被磨滅。

甲骨文　　　　　金文　　　　　小篆

永 was the original form of 泳. In ancient writing systems, the character 永 looks like a man moving in the water, i.e. swimming. Later, this character came to be used in the sense of "a long river", and acquired the meaning of "for long". Its original meaning is now expressed by a new character 泳.

【永久】permanent; everlasting

【永恆】eternal; perpetual

【永垂不朽】to be immortal

qiāng

羌是中國古代西北地區的少數民族之一。其地風俗,以遊牧為業,其人則身穿羊皮衣,頭戴羊皮帽,帽上通常還有羊毛的裝飾。甲骨文羌字,正像一個頭戴羊毛裝飾的人形,有的人形脖子上還有繩索。這是因為羌人是當時漢族的敵人,在戰爭中常被漢人掠為俘虜、奴隸,甚至被當作祭品,所以常以繩索綑綁之。

甲骨文　　　　金文　　　　小篆

羌 is the name of a national minority in ancient China, who lived in the northwest in ancient times. They were a nomadic tribe, living on the sheep. They wore clothes and hats made of sheepskin, and there were often woolen decorations on the hats. In the Oracle-Bone Inscriptions, the character 羌 looks like a man with woolen decorations on the head. Sometimes, there is a rope round the neck. This is a reflection of a fact that the Qiang and Han were enemies then, and the Qiang people would be taken prisoner and tied up when they were defeated.

jìng

甲骨文和早期金文的競字，像兩個人一起並肩向前奔走之形，其本義為"互相爭逐而行"，如競逐、競走等；引申為"爭強"、"較量"之義，如競爭、競技、競賽等。

甲骨文　　　　　　　金　文　　　　　　　小　篆

In the Oracle-Bone Inscriptions and early Bronze Inscriptions, the character 競 looks like two men running shoulder to shoulder. Its primary meaning is "to strive to go ahead of sb. else", e.g. 競逐 (compete and pursue), and 競走 (a heel-and-toe walking race). Its extended meanings include "to compete" (競爭) and "to contest" (競賽).

pú

甲骨文的僕字，像一個人手捧畚箕的樣子：其中人形的頭上從辛。辛是古代刑具，表示該人是受過刑的戰俘或罪人；人形的臀下有尾毛，是對奴隸的一種侮辱性裝飾；箕上的幾點代表塵土，表示鏟土揚塵的意思。因此，僕字的本義是指手捧箕具從事家務勞動的奴隸，即奴僕、僕人。

【僕從】舊時指跟隨在主人身旁的僕人。

甲骨文

金 文

小 篆

In the Oracle-Bone Inscriptions, the character 僕 looks like a man holding a winnowing pan. The part atop the man's head is 辛, an instrument of torture, signalling that the man is a prisoner of war or criminal, who has been put to torture. The tail at the buttocks of the man is a sign of insult. The dots above the winnowing pan represent the dust to be rid of. So the primary meaning of 僕 is "a slave who winnows or does other chores", e.g. 奴僕 (servant), and 僕人 (domestic servant).

【僕從】a footman; a retainer

shī

【屍】

甲骨文、金文的尸字，均像一仰躺的側視人形，本義為尸體，即人死後的軀體，所以小篆和楷書尸字都在尸下加死字以表義。古代祭祀時，代死者受祭。象徵死者神靈的人被稱為"尸"，一般以臣下或死者的晚輩充任。後世祭祀改為用牌位、畫像，不再行用尸的制度。

【尸祝】尸，代表鬼神受享祭的人；祝，傳告鬼神言辭的人。又指立尸而祝禱之，表示崇敬。

【尸位素餐】空佔着職位，不做事而白吃飯。

甲骨文

金文

小篆

In the Oracle-Bone Inscriptions and Bronze Inscriptions, the character 尸 looks like a man lying on his side. Its primary meaning is "a corpse", "a dead body", that is why in the Later Seal Character and Regular Script there is the character 死 (dead) under 尸. In ancient times, the man who in the name of the dead accepted the sacrifice and worship at sacrificial rites was called 尸. Later the custom was changed. A memorial tablet or portrait of the dead was used instead. So this meaning is no longer current.

【尸祝】(lit.) the man representing the dead and the master of ceremonies; to select a man to represent the dead and pray to him

【尸位素餐】to hold down a job without doing a stroke of work

tún

臀，即髀，指人體後面兩股的上端和腰相連接的部份。甲骨文的臀字，是在人形的臀部加一指事符號以指示臀的位置。造字方法與"身"、"肱"等字相同。

甲骨文

小篆

臀 means "buttocks". In the Oracle-Bone Inscriptions, the character 臀 looks like a man with a sign marking the position of the buttocks, similar to the composition of many other characters, such as 身 (body) and 肱 (the upper arm).

wěi

遠古時代，人們為了獵取野獸，頭上戴着獸角，臀部接上一條尾巴，裝扮成野獸的樣子以便靠近它們。後來這獸角和尾巴逐漸變成了裝飾，在慶典活動時戴着它跳舞。甲骨文的尾字，正像一個人在臀部下繫一條尾巴狀的飾物，其本義是指動物的尾巴，引申為末尾和在後面的意思。

【尾隨】指在後面緊緊跟隨。

【尾大不掉】比喻下屬勢力強大，無法指揮調度。現在也比喻機構臃腫，不好調度。

甲骨文

小篆

In ancient times, people would dress up like wild animals, wearing horns on the head and attaching a tail at the buttocks, in order to get close to them and catch them. Later on these horns and tails became ornaments, people danced with these things on at ceremonies. In the Oracle-Bone Inscriptions, the character 尾 looks like a man with an ornamental tail at the buttocks. Its primary meaning is "the tail of an animal", from which have derived its uses to refer to the end of something or something at the back.

【尾隨】to tail after; to follow at sb.'s heels

【尾大不掉】a leadership rendered ineffectual by recalcitrant subordinates; too cumbersome to be effective

niào

　　甲骨文尿字，像一個側立的人形，身前的三點代表激射的尿線，表示人站着撒尿的意思。小篆尿字從尾從水，構字方式與甲骨文不同，但意義相同。所以尿字的本義為撒尿，又指尿液。

甲骨文　　　　　　　　小篆

In the Oracle-Bone Inscriptions, the character 尿 looks like the side view of a man, and there are three dots in front standing for the urine passed from the body. In the Later Seal Character, the character 尿 is composed, differently from that in the Oracle-Bone Inscriptions, of 尾 (tail) and 水 (water). But they mean the same, i.e. "to urinate", or as a noun, "urine".

shǐ

甲骨文屎字，像一個蹲着的側面人形，人形臀部下的幾個小點代表從人肛門出來的排泄物。表示人拉屎的意思。因此，屎的本義指糞便。

【屎詩】指拙劣的詩作。《通俗篇·藝術》："今嘲惡詩曰屎詩。"

甲骨文

In the Oracle-Bone Inscriptions, the character 屎 looks like the side view of a man squatting. The dots under the buttocks stand for the excrement passed from the body. Hence 屎 means "excrement", "dung" or "droppings".

【屎詩】an extremely bad poem

SǏ

甲骨文死字，左邊是一垂首跪地的人形，右邊的歹表示死人枯骨，像活人跪拜於死人朽骨旁默默弔祭的樣子，特指死亡、生命結束之義。由於死去的東西不會動，所以僵硬的、不靈活的東西也稱為"死"，如死板（不靈活）、死氣沉沉（形容氣氛不活潑或精神消沉不振作）；再引申為堅決之義，如死心塌地（形容打定主意，決不改變）。

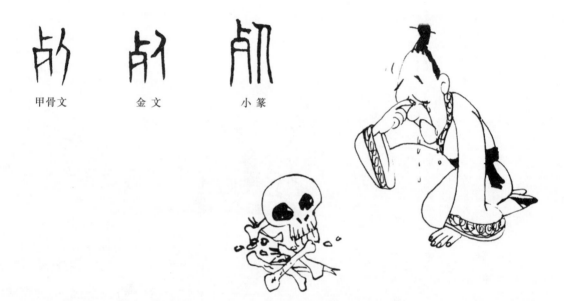

| 甲骨文 | 金文 | 小篆 |

In the Oracle-Bone Inscriptions, the left side of the character 死 looks like a man on his knees lowering his head, and the 歹 on the right stands for the skeleton of a dead man. This is a picture of the living mourning on his knees over the dead. Hence its meaning "to die", "to be dead". As anything dead will not be able to move, 死 is also used for things which are stiff, inflexible, e.g. 死板 (rigid), 死氣沉沉 (lifeless), from which derives its meaning "to be determined", e.g. 死心塌地 (to be dead set on).

zàng

小篆的葬字，中間為"死"，上下從草，表示人死後把屍體埋於荒郊野地的意思。所以葬的本義是指掩埋屍體，如埋葬、安葬；又泛指處理死者遺體，如火葬、海葬等。

【葬送】指掩埋死者、出殯等事宜，引申為斷送、毀滅之義。

小篆

In the Later Seal Character, the character 葬 has a dead part (死) in between two grass parts (草), signalling that a dead man is buried in a wilderness of weeds. Hence the primary meaning: to bury the dead. But it can also be used in a more general sense to refer to the ways to dispose of the dead, e.g. 火葬 (cremation), and 海葬 (sea-burial).

【葬送】(1)to bury the dead (2) to ruin

dà

古文字的大字，是一個兩手平伸、兩腳分開正面而立的人形。大的本義指大人，即成年人或有地位的人；後來引申指在面積、體積、數量、力量、強度等方面超過一般或超過所比較的對象，與"小"相對。

【大度】氣量寬宏能容人。

【大局】整個的局面，整個的形勢。

【大庭廣眾】人多而公開的場合。

【大智若愚】指有智慧有才能的人，不炫耀自己，外表好像愚笨。

甲骨文　　　金文　　　小篆

In ancient writing systems, the character 大 looks like the frontal view of a man with the hands stretched out and the legs apart. Originally it referred to an adult or a man of position. But now it refers to anything greater in size, volume, number, strength, hardness, etc., as opposed to 小 (small).

【大度】magnanimous and tolerant

【大局】overall situation

【大庭廣眾】(before) a big crowd; (on) a public occasion

【大智若愚】A man of great wisdom often appears slow-witted

tiān

天和元一樣，都是指人的頭部。早期甲骨文和金文的天字，像一個正面而立的人形，而特別突出了人的頭形。和元字一樣，這個頭形後來也簡化成一橫，有的也在橫上加一點指示頭部所在。天的本義為人頭或頭頂，引申為指頭頂以上的天空，還可以用來泛指自然界。凡自然生成的事物均可稱為"天"，如天文、天氣、天險、天然等。現在則把一晝夜之內的時間也稱為"一天"，如一整天、今天、明天等。

【天下】天空之下，指我們人類生活的空間。

【天子】古人認為天是有意志的神，是萬物的主宰，是至高無上的權威，因而把天稱作"天神"、"上帝"，而把統治人間的君王稱為"天子"，即上天之子。

| 甲骨文 | 金文 | 小篆 |

Similar to 元, 天 originally meant the head of a man. In the early Oracle-Bone Inscriptions and early Bronze Inscriptions, the character 天 looks like the frontal view of a man with the head especially prominent. Also like what happened to 元, this head was later simplified into a horizontal stroke, on which sometimes there was a dot to signal the position of the head. 天 originally meant the head of a man, or the top of the head, but it has gradually come to mean the sky above the human head, and even more generally the whole natural world. Anything that comes naturally may be called 天, e.g. 天文 (astronomy), 天氣 (weather), 天險 (natural barrier), and 天然 (natural). Nowadays, 天 also means "day", e.g. 一整天 (the whole day), 今天 (today), and 明天 (tomorrow).

【天下】 land under heaven; the world

【天子】 the Son of Heaven; the Emperor

wú

吳，是古代的國名和地名。西周初年，泰伯居吳（在今江蘇無錫市梅里），後世興盛稱王，是為吳國，至公元前 **475** 年為越國所滅。其地在今江蘇一帶。該地以陶器、鐵器等手工製造業而聞名。古文字的吳字，像人肩扛器皿（陶器之類）之形，是對陶器等手工製造者的形象描繪。吳字用作國名或地名，大概與該地人民善於製作陶器有關。

甲骨文　　　　　　金文　　　　　　小篆

吳 is a name of a place, also used as a name of a state or kingdom in ancient times. In the early Zhou Dynasty, 泰伯, a son of the then king, came to live in 吳 (now known as 梅里 in Wuxi, Jiangsu Province). His descendants became powerful and established the first state named by 吳, which was destroyed by 越 (a state in present-day Zhejiang and Fujian) in 475 b.c. The State of Wu occupied an area centred around Jiangsu, a place well known for its handicrafts, such as earthware and ironware. That perhaps is the reason why the character 吳 in ancient writing systems looks like a man holding a piece of pottery on his shoulder.

yāo

甲骨文、金文的夭字，本像一個人奔跑時甩動雙臂的樣子，其本義即指人奔跑的樣子。小篆形體發生訛變，夭字變成人頭傾側屈折之形，其意義也隨之改變，即表示屈曲、摧折之義，又引申為指人早死，即少壯而死。

【夭折】短命早死。

【夭斜】歪斜，婀娜多姿的意思。

【夭矯】屈伸自如，形容人的縱恣之貌。

【夭桃穠（nóng）李】本指艷麗爭春的桃李，又比喻少女年輕美麗。

金文

小篆

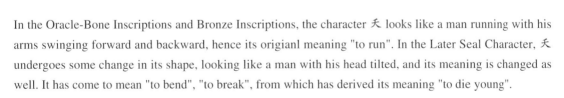

In the Oracle-Bone Inscriptions and Bronze Inscriptions, the character 夭 looks like a man running with his arms swinging forward and backward, hence its origianl meaning "to run". In the Later Seal Character, 夭 undergoes some change in its shape, looking like a man with his head tilted, and its meaning is changed as well. It has come to mean "to bend", "to break", from which has derived its meaning "to die young".

【夭折】to die young

【夭斜】(of a woman's bearing) gracefully aslant

【夭矯】(lit.) to bend and stretch the limbs freely; to let oneself go

【夭桃穠（nóng）李】(of a girl) as beautiful as a peach or plum in blossom

jiāo

古文字交字像一個人兩腿交叉的樣子，其本義是交叉、交錯的意思，引申為連接、結交、互相等義，如交界、交涉、交情、交心、交易、交流等。

甲骨文　　　　　金 文　　　　　小 篆

In ancient writing systems, the character 交 looks like a man with his legs crossed, hence the primary meaning "to cross", "to interlock". Its extended meanings include "to link" and "to associate with", e.g. 交界 (to have a common border), 交涉 (negotiate), 交情 (friendship), 交心 (to open one's heart to), 交易 (transaction), and 交流 (to exchange).

wén

　　"文"是個象形字。甲骨文和金文的"文"字,像一個正面站立的人形,人形的胸部刺畫着花紋圖案。這其實就是古代"文身"習俗的形象描繪。所以"文"字本來的意思是指身上刺有花紋的人,又有花紋、紋理的意思。後來才引申出文字、文章、文化、文明等眾多的意義。

甲骨文

金文

小篆

文 is a pictograph. In the Oracle-Bone Inscriptions and Bronze Inscriptions, the character 文 looks like the frontal view of a man with a tattoo on his chest. Hence the character 文 originally meant "a man with tattoos", from which have derived the meanings of "a decorative pattern" or "lines". Its uses in words like 文字 (characters; script; writing), 文化 (culture), 文章 (article), and 文明 (civilization) are all later developments.

fū

按照古代禮制，男子到了二十歲，就要束髮加冠，表明他已經是成年人。夫字從大從一，"大"為人，"一"表示用來束髮的簪子。甲骨文、金文的夫字，像一個束髮插簪的人形，它的本義即指成年男子。男子成年始成婚配，故"夫"可引申為指丈夫，即女子的配偶，與"婦"、"妻"相對；成年始服勞役，故夫又指服勞役或從事某種體力勞動的人，如漁夫、農夫等。

【夫人】舊時對別人妻子的敬稱，現多用於外交場合。

【夫子】古代男子的尊稱，又指學生對老師的尊稱。

甲骨文

金 文

小 篆

In ancient times, it was a custom for a man of twenty to have his hair held together and to put on a hat, to show that he had reached manhood. The character 夫 consists of 大 and 一, the former meaning "man", and the latter representing the hair clasp which does the holding. In the Oracle-Bone Inscriptions and Bronze Inscriptions, the character 夫 looks like a man with his hair held together by a hair clasp. Its primary meaning, therefore, is "adult man". As a man is allowed to get married only after he has reached adulthood, 夫 also means "husband", in opposition to 婦 (woman) or 妻 (wife). An adult man would also have to serve as a forced labourer in ancient times, so 夫 is also used in the sense of "forced labourer", and more generally, any type of labourer, e.g. 漁夫 (fisherman) and 農夫 (farmer).

【夫人】wife, esp. on formal occasions

【夫子】a respectful form of address to a man, esp. a teacher, in ancient times

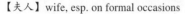

yì

亦是"腋（yè）"的本字。古文字的亦字，像一個正面站立的人形，兩臂之下的兩個點是指事符號。表示這裡就是腋下。後來亦字多被借用為虛詞，相當於"也"的意思。因此，只好另造了一個從月（肉）夜聲的"腋"字來代替亦的本義。

【亦步亦趨】比喻自己沒有主張，或為了討好，每件事都順從別人，跟着人家走。

甲骨文

金文

小篆

亦 was the original form of 腋 (yè, armpit). In ancient writing systems, the character 亦 looks like the frontal view of a man with two dots under the arms showing the position of the armpits. As 亦 later came to be used as a function word, equivalent to 也 (too), another character 腋, with 月 (肉, meat) as the radical and 夜 as the phonetic, was invented to replace 亦 for its original meaning.

【亦步亦趨】to ape sb. at every step; to blindly follow suit

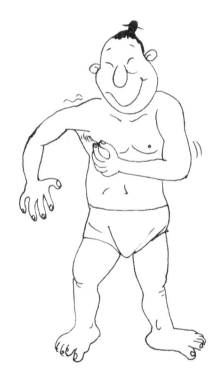

jiā

古文字的夾字，像左右兩個小人攙扶着中間一個大人的樣子，本義為夾持，即從左右相持，引申為輔佐之義。此外，夾還可以指兩者之間的空隙，如夾縫、夾道等；又可以指裡外兩層，如夾衣、夾被等。

【夾註】書中正文中間的小字註釋。

【夾帶】以不應攜帶的物品雜入他物之中，希圖蒙混。又舊時考生應試，私帶書籍等文字資料入場，叫夾帶。

【夾輔】在左右輔佐。

甲骨文　　　　　金 文　　　　　小 篆

In ancient writing systems, the character 夾 looks like two small men supporting a big man in the middle, hence the primary meaning "to help from the sides" or "to assist". In addition, it is used in the sense of "space between two things", e.g. 夾縫 (a space between two adjacent things) and 夾道 (passageway). And it can also be used to refer to things made up of two layers, e.g. 夾衣 (a traditional Chinese coat with a thick lining) and 夾被 (a quilt without the padding material in between).

【夾註】interlinear notes

【夾帶】to carry secretly; notes smuggled into an examination hall

【夾輔】to assist

甲骨文、金文的立字，像一個正面站立的人形，人的腳下一條橫線代表地面，表示一個人站立在地面之上。所以立的本義就是站，引申為樹立、設置、建立等義，如立功、立法、立威等。此外，古代君王即位也稱"立"。

【立竿見影】竿立而影現。比喻收效很快。

甲骨文　　　　　金　文　　　　　小　篆

In the Oracle-Bone Inscriptions and Bronze Inscriptions, the character 立 looks like the frontal view of a man on his feet, with a line underneath signalling the ground, hence the primary meaning "to stand". "to set up" and "to establish" are its extended meanings, e.g. 立功 (to do a deed of merit), 立法 (to make a law), and 立威 (to build up one's prestige). In ancient times, the ascending of a new emperor to the throne was also called 立.

【立竿見影】Set up a pole and one sees its shadow; to get instant results

wèi

位字從人從立，本義當指人所站立的位置，特指帝王諸侯的王位及大臣爵次、位次，所以《說文解字》："列中庭之左右謂之位。"位字還引申為指人的身份、地位，又泛指方位、位置。

【位望】地位和聲望。

【位子】人所佔據的地方，座位。

甲骨文

金文

小篆

The character 位, consisting of 人 (man) and 立 (to stand), refers primarily to the place where a man stands, and the office of a king or the rank of a minister in particular. Thus the *Origin of Chinese Characters* says, "The position at court in which a man stands is known as 位". It is also used to refer to the capacity and status of a person, or more generally, to the location of anything.

【位望】fame and position

【位子】place, seat

ti

金文的替字，像兩個人一上一下之形，表示替換、接替之意。所以替字的本義為更換、接替、替代，引申為廢棄，衰敗之義。

【替人】接替的人。

【替身】替代別人的人，多指代人受過的人。

【替天行道】代行上天的旨意。多指除暴安良，拯救蒼生之意。

金 文

小 篆

In the Bronze Inscriptions, the character 替 looks like two men in an arrangement of one upper than the other, signalling that one is to take the place of the other. Hence the character 替 primarily means "to replace", "to substitute for", from which have derived the senses "to discard" and "to be on the decline".

【替人】replacement

【替身】scapegoat; stand-in

【替天行道】to uphold justice on behalf of Providence

měi

在古代，人們為了狩獵，往往在頭上戴上獸角或羽毛做成的裝飾，以便接近禽獸。後來這種獸角或羽毛逐漸成為裝飾品，戴在頭上成為美的標誌。這就是甲骨文和早期金文美字的來歷。後代美字從羊從大，即是由此演變而來，表示頭戴羊角（或羊毛）為美。因此，美字的本義是指人的裝束漂亮好看，引申指人的容貌、聲色、才德或品格的好，同時還可用來指食物味道的甘美。

甲骨文　　　金 文　　　小 篆

In ancient times, people would wear horns or feathers on their heads in order to get close to wild animals and catch them. Later on horns and feathers of this type became decorations to be put on the head as a sign of beauty. This is the origin of the character 美 in the Oracle-Bone Inscriptions and Bronze Inscriptions, from which derived the later form of 美, consisting of 羊 (sheep) and 大 (man). That is to say a man with sheep horns (or wool) on the head is regarded as beautiful. So, originally 美 meant the beautiful decorations of a person. Its use to refer to the looks, talents or virtue of a person is a later development. And its sense has also been extended to cover the delicious taste of food.

yāng

甲骨文、金文的央字，像人用扁擔挑物之形，擔物時人在扁擔中間，所以央字有中間之義，如中央（即中間）。央字又有窮盡的意思，如長樂未央。此外，央還有懇求之義，如央求。

甲骨文　　　　　金文　　　　　小篆

In the Oracle-Bone Inscriptions and Bronze Inscriptions, the character 央 looks like a man carrying something with a bamboo pole. As the things are hung from the two ends of the carrying pole, and the man is in the middle, the character 央 has the primary meaning of "middle", e.g. 中央 (central). But 央 can also mean "end", e.g. 長樂未央 (happy without end). Another extended meaning of 央 is "to ask earnestly", e.g. 央求 (to beg; to plead).

hēi

金文的黑字，像一個被煙火熏烤的人，大汗淋漓、滿面污垢的樣子。它的本義指被火熏黑，引申為泛指黑色，與"白"相對。黑色暗淡，故黑字引申為指黑暗，即昏暗無光的意思；又引申為指隱祕的，不公開的。

【黑白】黑色與白色。比喻是非、善惡。

【黑幫】泛指地下祕密組織或其成員。

【黑市】暗中進行不合法買賣的市場。

【黑甜鄉】指夢鄉。形容酣睡。

【黑白分明】比喻是非嚴明，處事公正。

甲骨文

金文

小篆

In the Bronze Inscriptions, the character 黑 looks like a man sweating with heat from a fire and blackened with smoke from it. It is primarily used to refer to something blackened by smoke, and more generally, to anything that is black in colour, as against 白 (white). The colour of black is dim, so 黑 is also used in the sense of darkness, from which derive the further extended meanings of "secret" and "covered".

【黑白】black and white; right and wrong; good and evil

【黑幫】sinister gang

【黑市】black market

【黑甜鄉】dreamland; to sleep soundly

【黑白分明】with black and white sharply contrasted; in sharp contrast

yí

夷，是古代漢族對邊遠少數民族和外國人的通稱。在古代，漢族以華夏為中心，蔑視和虐待其他民族，常把他們抓來當作奴隸或作為祭祀時的犧牲品。甲骨文和金文中的夷字，多用"尸"字來代替，顯然含有鄙視侮辱的意思。而金文夷字又有作一正面人形被繩索五花大綁之形，則是表示把少數民族抓來做奴隸或犧牲品的意思。

金 文

小 篆

夷 in ancient times was a general term for the national minorities in remote areas and foreigners. At that time the Han people regarded their own land as the centre, and despised and tyrannized other nationalities, who were often used as slaves or sacrifices. In the Oracle-Bone Inscriptions and Bronze Inscriptions, these people were often referred to as 尸 (corpse), showing open contempt for them. On the other hand, the character 夷 in the Bronze Inscriptions looks like the frontal view of a man tied up with ropes, signalling that he has been captured and is used as a slave or sacrifice.

wǔ

甲骨文舞字，像一個手持樹枝（或飄帶）翩躚起舞的人形，本義指舞蹈。此字後來由於多被借用為有無之無，所以金文的舞字特意加上辵旁表示舞蹈的動作，小篆以後則普遍加雙腳形。這樣，舞與無就不再容易混淆了。而舞字除舞蹈之義外，還含有舞動、戲弄等義，如揮舞、舞弄等。

甲骨文

金 文

小 篆

In the Oracle-Bone Inscriptions, the character 舞 looks like a man dancing with branches or ribbons in hand, hence the primary meaning "to dance". As this character was often used in the sense of 無 ("without"), in the Bronze Inscriptions, a component 辵 signalling the use of legs, was added to emphasize its primary meaning. In the Later Seal Character, on the other hand, a part representing two legs was added. So that 舞 and 無 would no longer be confused. In addition, the character 舞 can also mean "to wave" (舞動) and "to wield (swords and spears)" (舞弄).

chéng

傳說上古時代，有一位聖人叫有巢氏。他教人們在樹上構木為巢，作為居住的場所，用以躲避野獸和洪水的侵襲。這種在樹上居住的方式，被稱為"巢居"。它是一種非常原始的生活方式。甲骨文、金文的乘字，就是一個人爬在樹頂上的形象，是巢居生活的形象寫照。因此，乘的本義為爬樹，引申為爬、登、乘坐之義（如乘車、乘船、乘馬等）。

| 甲骨文 | 金文 | 小篆 |

It is said that in the remote ages, there was a sage called You Chao (Nester), who taught people to build nests on trees for homes, so as to protect themselves from the attacks of wild animals and floods. This primitive way of life, to dwell on tress, is known as nesting. In the Oracle-Bone Inscriptions and Bronze Inscriptions, the character 乘, in the shape of a man on top of a tree, is a vivid description of nesting. Hence the original meaning of 乘 was "to climb trees", from which have derived its extended meanings "to climb", "to ascend" and "to ride", e.g. 乘車 (to take a bus), 乘船 (to travel by boat) and 乘馬 (to ride a horse).

nǚ

女

女，指女性，與男性相對。在古代，女性地位低下。體現在字形上，甲骨文的女字像一個雙膝跪地的人形，兩手交叉垂下，一副低眉順眼、卑恭屈服的樣子。後代的女字，漸漸地由跪變立，但屈腿彎腰，仍是一副柔順的姿態。

甲骨文

金文

小篆

女 means "female", opposite to 男 (male). In the old days, the female had a very low social status, and this is reflected in the form of the character 女. In the Oracle-Bone Inscriptions, this character looks like a woman on her knees, with her arms lowered and crossed, a show of complete subservience. In the later writing systems, the kneeling woman stands up, but her waist and legs are bent, still a posture displaying her meek and mild nature.

mǔ

古文字的母字，像一個斂手屈膝的女子，胸部的兩點代表突出的乳房。母的本義當指成年生育過的女子，又特指母親。由母親一義，母字又被用作女性尊長的通稱，如伯母、祖母等。因為母能生子，所以母字也可以引申為指事物的本源。此外，母也泛指動物的雌性，如母雞、母牛等。

甲骨文　　　　　金文　　　　　小篆

In ancient writing systems, the character 母 looks like a woman on her knees, with her arms crossed in the front, and there are two dots on the chest representing the breasts. 母 primrily refers to a woman who has children, i.e. mother. From this sense, has derived its use as a general term for senior females in the family, e.g. 伯母 (aunt), 祖母 (grandmother); and even more generally for all female animals, e.g. 母雞 (hen) and 母牛 (cow). As mothers are able to produce the young, 母 may also be used in the sense of "origin".

měi

甲骨文的每字，像一個斂手腹前跪坐地上的女子，她的頭上插戴着花翎錦羽一類的裝飾。金文的字形略有變化，即在原來女字中間加兩點表示乳房，女字變成母字，仍是代表女性。女人頭戴羽翎，男人頭戴獸角（如美字），在古人眼中就是一種美的象徵，所以每字的本義是指婦女之美。每和美字的構造方法相近，表達的意義也相近，只不過一個是指女性之美，一個代表男性之美。後來"美"行而"每"廢。每字被借用來作虛詞，表示"往往"、"時常"、"每次"、"逐一"等義，它的本義也就很少有人知道了。

甲骨文

金 文

小 篆

In the Oracle-Bone Inscriptions, the character 每 looks like a woman on her knees, with her arms crossed in the front, and there are ornamental plumes on her head. In the Bronze Inscriptions, the shape of the character is changed, with two dots representing the breasts added. In other words, the lower part changes from the component 女 into 母, though the meaning is not changed, as it still signifies the female. In ancient times, it was a sign of beauty for a woman to have plumes on her head, similar to a man wearing animal horns on the head (as in the character 美), so 每 originally was used to refer to the beauty of a woman, The characters 每 and 美 were composed in the same way and had similar meanings, except that the former was used for women while the latter for men. Later on, the use of 美 spread and 每, in the sense of beauty, fell into disuse. It has come to be used as a function word instead, signalling "frequently", "every" or "each". And few people nowadays know its original meaning.

yāo

要為"腰"的本字。金文的要字，下面的"女"代表人形，"女"上的部份代表人的腰部，上面是兩手叉腰狀。小篆的要字，像一個人雙手叉腰站立的樣子，較之金文更為形象。要的本義為腰，後多借用為求、取等義，如要求、要挾等。腰在人體的中樞位置，所以要有樞要的意思，讀yào，引申為重要之義，又指重要的內容，如綱要、要點等。

甲骨文

金 文

小 篆

要 was the original form of 腰. In the Bronze Inscriptions, the lower part of the character, 女, stands for a human being, and the upper part looks like two hands on the sides, hence it refers to the waist of a person. In the Later Seal Character, the character 要, more picturelike than in the Bronze Inscriptions, looks like a person with arms akimbo. Though the original meaning of 要 was "waist", it is more usually used in the senses "to demand" and "to ask", e.g. 要求 (to demand), 要挾 (to coerce). As the waist occupies the central position in a human body, 要 pronounced as yào, also takes on the sense of "key position", from which have derived its senses of "important", "the main points" or "essentials".

qiè

古代通常把戰俘和罪犯充當奴隸，以供役使。古文字的妾字，從女從辛，其中辛是一種刑具，表示這是一個受過刑罰的女奴隸。因此，妾的本義是指女奴隸，又引申為指小妻，即正妻之外的小老婆。此外，妾又是舊時女子自稱的謙詞。

甲骨文　　　　金 文　　　　小 篆

In ancient times, prisoners of war and criminals were often used as slaves to do forced labour. The character 妾 in ancient writing systems consists of 女 (woman) and 辛 (an instrument of torture), signalling that this is a woman slave, who has been put to torture. So the original meaning of 妾 was a woman slave. The use of 妾 in the sense of concubine is an extended meaning. In the past, the character was also used by women as an expression of self-depreciation.

nú

古代的奴隸，多為在戰爭中抓來的俘虜和從別的部落中擄掠的人口。古文字的奴字，像一隻大手抓住一個女子的形狀，其本義當指女奴、婢女，又泛指奴隸。

【奴婢】喪失自由被剝削作無償勞動的人。通常男稱奴，女稱婢。

【奴役】把人當做奴隸使用。

【奴顏婢膝】形容低聲下氣，諂媚奉承的樣子。

金文　　　　小篆

In ancient times, slaves were usually prisoners of war or civilians captured from other tribes. In ancient writing systems, the character 奴 has the shape of a big hand in possession of a woman, hence its meaning "woman slave", "servant-girl", or more generally, slave of any type.

【奴婢】(lit.) man slave and woman slave; servant

【奴役】to enslave

【奴顏婢膝】subservient; servile

qī

妻指的是男子的配偶，相當於口語中的老婆、太太。古文字的妻字像一個人用手（又）抓住女人的頭髮。這實際上就是古代搶婚習俗的形象描繪。搶婚習俗曾經在原始社會風行，即某一部落的男子可以到另一部落中間去搶掠女子為妻。這種習俗在後代雖然被取消，但強搶民女為妻的野蠻現象卻還是時有發生。在古代，妻既然是指搶來的老婆，其社會地位之低下是不言而喻的。

甲骨文

小篆

妻 refers to the spouse of a man, i.e. his wife. In ancient writing systems, the character 妻 looks like a man getting hold of a woman's hair. This is in fact a vivid description of the practice of marriage by capture at that time: a man would go to another tribe and abduct a woman as his wife. Since the wife was obtained by force, she would naturally have no position at home at all. It is only in civilized societies, where equality between men and women is a major concern, that wives are no longer taken by force.

hǎo

古人崇尚多子多福的觀念，又提倡孝道，認為"不孝有三，無後為大"。因此，衡量一個女子的好壞首先是以其能否生育為標準的。好字從女從子，是表示婦女生育而有子的意思。婦女有子能生兒育女，就是好。好字用作形容詞，有美和善的意思，與"壞"相對。又可讀作 hào，用作動詞，表示喜歡、喜愛之義，如好奇、嗜好等。

【好處】指對人或事物有利的因素。又指使人有所得而感到滿意的事物。

【好（hào）逸惡勞】喜歡安逸，厭惡勞動。

甲骨文　　　　金文　　　　小篆

In the traditional view, more children meant more happiness. And people were urged to observe filial piety, according to which among the three sins of an unworthy descendant, not to have any children was the worst. So the first requirement of a good woman was to be able to bear children. The character 好 consists of 女 (woman) and 子 (child), signalling that for a woman to bear children constitutes what is good. The character 好, as an adjective, has the senses of "good" and "kind" , as against 壞 (bad). It can also be used as a verb, pronunced as hào, meaning "to like" , "to love" , e.g.好奇 (to be curious) and 嗜好(to have a liking for).

【好處】good; benefit; advantage

【好 (hào) 逸惡勞】to love ease and hate work

qǔ

娶字是個會意兼形聲的字。娶字從取從女，表示把女子取過來成親的意思；同時，取字又表示娶字的讀音，所以它又是一個從女取聲的形聲字。娶的本義是指男子娶妻結婚，與"嫁"相對。

甲骨文　　　　　小篆

娶 is both an ideograph and a phonetic compound. It consists of 取(to get) and 女 (woman), meaning to take a woman to wife. The component 取 at the same time serves as the phonetic, in which case, 女 is seen as the radical, it thus is also a phonetic compound. 娶, for a man to get married with a woman, is opposite to 嫁, for a woman to get married with a man.

shēn

甲骨文的身字，像一個腹部隆凸的人形，其本義當指妊娠，即婦女身懷有孕的意思。身又指人或動物的軀體、身體，引申指自身、自我，又引申為親自之義。凡從"身"的字，大都與人的身體有關，如躬、躲、躺、軀等。

【身份】人在社會上的地位、資歷等。

【身世】人生的經歷、遭遇。

【身教】以自己的實際行動，對人進行教育。

【身體力行】親身體驗，努力實行。

甲骨文　　　　　　金文　　　　　　小篆

In the Oracle-Bone Inscriptions, the character 身 looks like a woman with a round abdomen, hence its primary meaning: to be pregnant. 身 also means the body of a human being or animal, with its extended meanings of "oneself", "personally" or "in person". Characters with 身 as a component all have to do with the body, e.g. 躬 (to bend forward; to bow), 躲 (to hide), 躺 (to lie down) and 軀 (the human body).

【身份】social status; capacity; identity

【身世】(bitter) experience; (hard) lot

【身教】to teach others by one's example

【身體力行】to earnestly practice what one advocates

yùn

　　甲骨文的孕字，像一個大腹便便的側面人形，人的腹中有"子"，表示懷有身孕的意思。小篆字形訛變，不但腹中之"子"跑了出來，而且"人"形也已變樣，最後演變成楷書從乃從子的"孕"字。孕的本義為懷胎、生育，一般是指在母體中孳養嬰兒的胚胎，後也比喻在既存事物中培養出新生事物。

【孕育】懷胎生育，引申為庇護撫育。

甲骨文

小 篆

In the Oracle-Bone Inscriptions, the character 孕 looks like the side view of a human body with 子 in the abdomen, signalling she is pregnant. In the Later Seal Character, the shape of the character is changed. The 子 inside the abdomen comes to the outside and the "human being" also changes its form, ending up as an ideograph consisting of 乃 and 子 in the Regular Script. This character primarily means "to be pregnant", "to breed", but it is also used metaphorically to refer to the development of new things out of the existing ones.

【孕育】to be pregnant; to breed

yù

甲骨文、金文的育字，像一個婦女正在生育的形狀：女人形的下部一個頭朝下的"子"形，像嬰兒剛從母體中分娩出來的樣子；"子"下的三點，則表示產子時流出來的胎液。字形為"毓"字。育的本義為生育，即生孩子，引申為撫養，培養之義。

【育齡】在年齡上適合生育的階段。

甲骨文　　　金文　　　小篆

In the Oracle-Bone Inscriptions and Bronze Inscriptions, the character 育 looks like a woman in the process of giving birth to a baby. Under the part signalling a woman, there is the component 子 with its head down signalling the newborn baby. The three dots underneath the baby signal the liquid coming along with it. The primary meaning of 育 is to give birth to, but it is also used in the senses "to rear", "to raise" and "to bring up".

【育齡】the right age to bear child

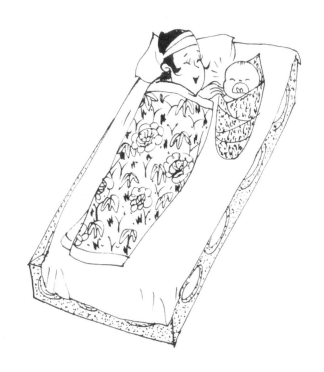

ZǏ

甲骨文、金文的子字,均像一個頭大身小的嬰孩形象,主要有兩種表現方式:一是新生嬰兒裹在襁褓之中雙手亂動的樣子;一像小孩雙腳立地而突出表現其頭髮稀疏、腦囟未合的特徵。因此,子字的本義是指嬰兒,引申為指子嗣,即兒女。子又借用為干支名,是十二地支的第一位。漢字中凡從"子"的字,大都與嬰孩或子嗣有關,如孩、孫、孝、孕、字等。

【子弟】子與弟。相對"父兄"而言。又是對後輩的通稱,指子姪。

【子夜】夜半子時,即夜十一時至翌晨一時之間。

【子城】附屬於大城的小城,如內城及附郭的月城等。

甲骨文

金文

小篆

In the Oracle-Bone Inscriptions and Bronze Inscriptions, the character 子 looks like a baby with a big head and a small body. In some writings, the baby in swaddling clothes is waving its arms. In others, the baby is on its feet, with very little hair and the fontanelles are not closed yet. The character 子 refers to baby, and descendants in general. But it is also used as a name of the first of the twelve Earthly Branches, a traditional Chinese system of sequence. Characters with 子 as a component most have to do with the baby or descendant, e.g. 孩 (child), 孫 (grand child), 孝 (filial piety), 孕 (to be pregnant) and 字 (〔derivative〕character).

【子弟】 sons and younger brothers; juniors

【子夜】 midnight

【子城】 inner city

rǔ

甲骨文乳字，像一人胸前乳頭突出，又雙臂抱子讓他吮吸奶水的形狀，其本義為餵奶、哺乳，即以乳汁餵嬰兒，又指吃奶。乳字由吃奶之義，引申為泛指飲、喝，如"乳血餐膚"；由餵奶之義又引申為指奶汁、乳房；再由哺乳嬰兒之義引申為產子、生育之義，又指剛生育過的或剛生下的、幼稚的。

【乳母】被僱為別人哺育嬰兒的婦女。

【乳虎】指育子的母虎。又指幼虎。

【乳臭未乾】口中還有奶氣，指其幼稚。

甲骨文　　　　　　小篆

In the Oracle-Bone Inscriptions, the character 乳 looks like a woman with nipples standing out and a baby in her arms, hence the primary meaning: to breastfeed a baby. From this primary meaning derives the meaning of sucking or drinking in general, e.g. 乳血餐膚 (to suck blood and eat flesh). Its extended meanings include "milk", "breast", "to give birth to", and even "one who has just become a mother" or "newborn".

【乳母】 wet nurse

【乳虎】 mothering tigress; newborn tiger

【乳臭未乾】 to still smell of one's mother's milk; to be young
　　　　　　 and inexperienced

zì

　　"字"的構形,上部一個寶蓋頭(宀)代表房子,下面一個子字表示嬰兒。嬰兒在屋內,表示生育之義,引申為養育、滋生、孳乳等義。古人把最早產生的獨體象形字稱為"文",而把由兩個或兩個以上的獨體字組合而成的合體字叫做"字"。因為合體字是由獨體的文孳乳衍生出來的,所以稱"字"。後世"文"、"字"不分,多以"字"來作為文字的通稱。

金 文　　　　　小 篆

The character 字 consists of a house part (宀) and a baby part (子).In other words, it signals that there is a baby in a house, hence its original meaning of "giving birth to" and extended meanings of "raising" and "multiplying". In ancient times, the monadic pictographs were known as 文, while those made up of two or more monads were known as 字, in the sense that they were derivatives from monads. Nowadays, however, the two characters are no longer distinguished in this way, and 字 has become the general term for characters, or writing.

bǎo

　　嬰兒初生，不能行立，如何護理，實非易事。常見的辦法是把嬰兒抱在胸前或揹在後面。甲骨文和早期金文的保字，像一個人把嬰兒放在背上並伸出一隻手在後面加以保護的樣子，後來這隻手形與人形分裂，變成右下的一點，為了平衡，又在子字的左下增加一點，原有象形意味就蕩然無存了。總之，保字的本義相當於"抱"，引申為護理、撫養、養育之義，進一步引申為保護、保祐、守衛等義。

甲骨文

金　文

小　篆

A newborn baby, unable to stand on its own feet and walk, has to be put under the care of the adult. Usually the baby is carried in the arms or on the back. In the Oracle-Bone Inscriptions and early Bronze Inscriptions, the character 保 looks like a man carrying a baby on his back, with an arm stretched out to prevent it from falling. In other writing systems, the arm part is separated from the man part and becomes a dot on the right. To redress the balance. another dot is added on the left, resulting in a total destruction of the original picturelike image. In short, the original meaning of 保 was the same as 抱,i.e. to hold in the arms. The meanings "to take care of", "to raise" and "to bring up" are its earlier extended meanings, and "to protect", "to guard" and "to defend" are its later extended meanings.

ér

　　古文字的兒字，像一個嬰兒的形狀：身小頭大，囟門尚未閉合。《說文解字》："兒，孺子也。……像小兒頭囟未合。"所以兒的本義即指兒童。在古時，男稱兒，女稱嬰，但籠統而言皆稱兒。

【兒女】子女。又指青年男女。

【兒戲】兒童遊戲。又比喻做事不認真，處事輕率有如小兒嬉戲。

【兒女情】指男女戀愛或家人之間的感情。

甲骨文

金文

小篆

In ancient writing systems, the character 兒 looks like a baby with a big head and a small body, and the fontanelles are not closed yet. The *Origin of Chinese Characters* says, "兒 means baby. …like the fontanelles which have not been closed yet." Hence the primary meaning of 兒 is "little child." In ancient times, a boy was called 兒, and a girl 嬰.But this distinction was not always kept and 兒 could sometimes refer to children of both sexes.

【兒女】 sons and daughters

【兒戲】 child's play; to trifle with

【兒女情】 love between young man and woman

sūn

孫字從子從系，子是小兒形，系是繩索形，繩索有繫聯之義，表示子孫連續不斷之義。孫的本義指孫子，即兒子的兒子，也泛指孫子以後的各代，如曾孫、玄孫。

甲骨文　　　　金 文　　　　小 篆

The character 孫 consists of 子 and 系.The former looks like a child and the latter is in the shape of a rope signalling connection. Hence the character 孫 signifies children in succession. 孫 primarily refers to the son of a son, i.e. grandson, but it is also used for the later generations, e.g. 曾 孫(great grandson) and 玄孫 (great great-grandson).

jiāo

古代"撲作教刑"（以棍棒作為教學的工具），用肉體的刑罰來督導學習，所謂"不打不成材"。這種"棍棒政策"的教育就很生動地表現在教字的字形上。古文字的教字，右邊像人手持教鞭（或棍棒），左邊一個"子"表示兒童，"子"上的兩個叉代表算數的籌策（小木棍或草桿），所以教字的本義為督導兒童學習，引申為指導、培育、訓誨等義。

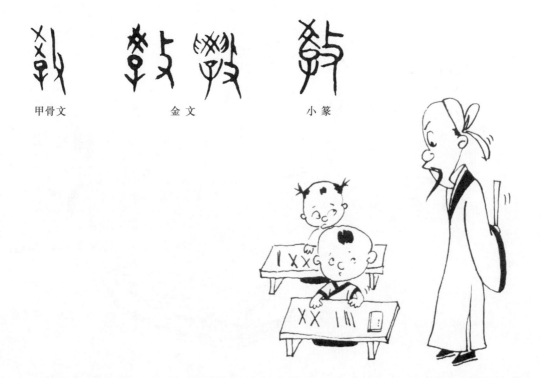

甲骨文　　　　　　金 文　　　　　　小 篆

In ancient times, corporal punishment was a commonplace in education. The rod was regarded as a necessary instrument for teaching, as the saying goes "Spare the rod and spoil the child". The composition of the character 教 is a picturelike reflection of this practice. In ancient writing systems, its right part looks like a man holding a rod while the left is made up of 子 (child) and two crosses above representing counters for addition and subtraction. So the primary meaning of 教 is "to urge pupils to study", and it is more generally used in the senses of "giving guidance", "educating" and "teaching".

xué

學是一個會意字。甲骨文的學字，像人雙手擺弄籌策（小木棍或草桿）來算數的樣子；金文增加一個"子"，表示是兒童在學習算數。因此，學字的本義即為學習、仿效；引申為指學問、學說、知識等，如"品學兼優"（人品和學問都很優秀）；又可以用來指人學習的場所，即學校。

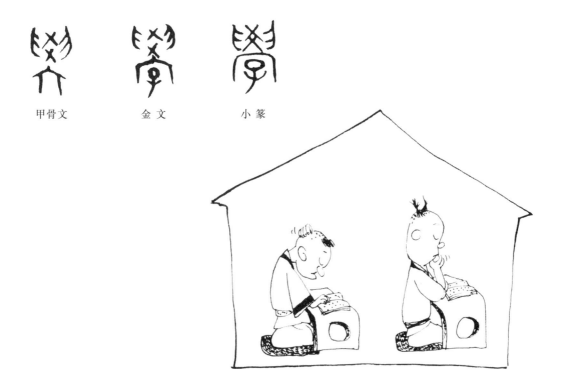

甲骨文　　　金文　　　小篆

學 is an ideograph. In the Oracle-Bone Inscriptions, the character 學 looks like a man setting counters in order to learn to do sums. In the Bronze Inscriptions, the component 子 is added to make it clear that it is a child who is learning to count. So its primary meaning is "to learn", and the senses of "learning", "theory" and "knowledge" are its extended meanings, e.g. 品學兼優 (of both good character and scholarship). It can also be used to refer to the place where one learns, i.e. school.

zhǎng

甲骨文、金文的長字，是一個手拄枴杖的老人形，而特別突出其長髮飄飄的特徵。長字的本義是老人，引申為指尊長，即輩份大、職位高的人，又指首領。用作動詞，長字又有生長、滋長、增長、成長等義。此外，長還可讀為cháng，為長短之長，引申為長遠、長久等義。

甲骨文	金文	小篆

In the Oracle-Bone Inscriptions and Bronze Inscriptions, the character 長 looks like an old man with a walking stick in hand, and the long hair is especially noticeable, hence the primary meaning: old man. Its extended meanings include "senior" (older or of higher rank) and "chief". When it is used as a verb, it means "to grow", "to develop" and "to increase". 長 can also be pronounced as cháng, meaning "long".

lǎo

甲骨文、金文的老字，像一個彎腰駝背、老態龍鍾的老人手拄枴杖的樣子。老的本義即指老人，即年歲大的人；引申為指年歲大的，與"少"或"幼"相對；又指陳舊的，與"新"、"嫩"相對。

【老當益壯】年紀雖老，但志氣更高，幹勁更大．

【老謀深算】周密的籌劃，深遠的打算，形容辦事精明老練。

甲骨文　　　　　　金文　　　　　　小篆

In the Oracle-Bone Inscriptions and Bronze Inscriptions, the character 老 looks like an old doddering man, back bent and a stick in hand, hence its primary meaning: a man of old age. Its extended meanings include "old in age" contrasted with 少, 幼 (young), and "belonging to past times", contrated with 新 (new) or 嫩 (tender).

【老當益壯】old but vigorous

【老謀深算】circumspect and farseeing; experienced and astute

xiào

孝是中國古代封建社會所崇奉的道德標準之一。舊時稱善於侍奉父母為"孝"。古文字的孝字，上部是一個彎腰駝背白髮飄飄的老人形，下邊的子代表小孩，表示小孩攙扶老人的意思。敬重老人，幫助老人，這正是孝道的具體表現之一。孝又指居喪，即在尊長死後一定時期內要遵守一定的禮俗。

【孝子】指孝順父母的人。又指父母死後居喪的人。

【孝順】盡心奉養父母，順從父母意志。

【孝敬】把物品獻給尊長，表示敬意。

甲骨文　　　金　文　　　小　篆

孝, filial piety, was one of the old moral concepts in Chinese feudal society, according to which children should be obedient to their parents at any time. In ancient writing systems, the character 孝 is made up of two parts: the upper part representing an old man with a long white hair and a bent back, and the lower part a child. The child is under the old man, suggesting that the former is helping the latter. To respect and help the old is one of the contents of filial piety. 孝 can also mean to observe certain codes of behaviour during the mourning period of one's seniors.

【孝子】(1) worthy descendants (2) those who are in the mourning period of their parents

【孝順】to show filial obedience

【孝敬】to give presents (to one's elders or superiors) to show one's respect

yīn

金文的殷字，像人手持一根針形的器具往一個腹部膨大的
人身上刺扎之形，表示醫治疾病之義。殷的本義為醫治，引申
為治理、定正之義。此外，殷還有盛大、眾多、富足等義。

【殷實】富足。

【殷聘】盛大的聘禮。指古代諸侯遣使互相訪問，以敦睦邦交之禮。

【殷切】深厚而急切。

【殷勤】熱情而周到。也指親切的情意。

金 文　　　　　　小 篆

In the Oracle-Bone Inscriptions and Bronze Inscriptions, the character 殷 looks like a man giving an acupuncture treatment to a patient who has a swollen belly. Hence the original meaning of "medical treatment", from which derive the meanings "to treat" or "to adjust." In addition, 殷 also means "grand", "great number of" and "well-off".

【殷實】well-off; substantial

【殷聘】rich presents brought by diplomats from another state to promote friendship in between

【殷切】ardent; eager

【殷勤】eagerly attentive; solicitous

xià

　　古文字夏字，像一個挺胸叉腰、四肢健壯、高大威武的人形，其本義指高大威武之人，引申為指物之壯大者。古代漢族自稱為"夏"，又稱"華夏"。中國第一個朝代稱為夏朝，而現在的夏字多作為姓氏使用。此外，夏又用作季節名，是春夏秋冬四季的第二季。

【夏令】夏季的節令。

【夏曆】即農曆，也稱陰曆。其制始於夏代。夏正建寅，以正月為歲首，故名。

金　文

小　篆

In ancient writing systems, the character 夏 looks like a big man of strong limbs, who sticks out his chest with the hands on the sides. In ancient times, the Han people called themselves by the name 夏, or 華夏. The first dynasty in the Chinese recorded history is known as the Xia Dynasty. But nowadays the character 夏 is usually used as a surname. In addition, it is also used for the second season of the year, i.e. summer.

【夏令】summertime

【夏曆】the traditional Chinese calendar; the lunar calendar

yè

甲骨文的頁字，像一個頭部特別突出的人形，其本義即指人頭。許慎《説文解字》："頁，頭也。"頁字現多借用為葉，特指書冊中的一張，也指紙的一面，如冊頁、活頁等。在漢字中，凡由頁字所組成的字又大都與頁的本義"人頭"有關，如頸、項、額、頂、鬚等。

甲骨文　　　　　金 文　　　　　小 篆

In the Oracle-Bone Inscriptions, the character 頁 looks like a man with an enormous head, hence the original meaning: the head of a man. Thus Xu Shen says in his *Origin of Chinese Characters,* " 頁 means head". Nowadays, however, the character 頁 is usually used in the sense of leaf, especially as a sheet of paper in a book, or one side of a sheet–page, e.g. 冊頁 (an album of paintings or calligraphy) and 活頁 (loose-leaf). But characters with 頁 as a component most have to do with its original meaning of "head", e.g. 頸(neck), 項 (nape of the neck), 額 (forehead), 頂 (crown) and 鬚 (beard).

shǒu

　　甲骨文首字是一顆頭顱的形象，但這個頭形並不大像人類的頭，而是更像獸類（如猿猴）的頭。金文的首字則只用一隻眼睛和頭髮來作為頭部的象徵符號。因此，首的本義是指人或其他動物的頭。由頭的意義引申，首字有首領之義，即指一群之長，又引申為指事物的開始、第一、最高等義，如首屆、首席、首當其衝、首屆一指等。

甲骨文

金 文

小 篆

In the Oracle-Bone Inscriptions, the character 首 is in the shape of a head, though it is more like a monkey's head than a man's. In the Bronze Inscriptions, the character 首 uses an eye and some hair to represent the head. So the primary meaning of 首 is a head, of a man or any animal. From this meaning derive the extended meanings of "leader", "beginning", "the first" and "the highest", e.g. 首屆(the first session),首席(chief),首當其衝 (to be the first to be affected〔by a disaster, etc.〕; to bear the brunt), and 首屆一指 (to come first on the list; to be second to none).

xiàn

縣是"懸"的本字。金文的縣字,左邊的木代表樹或木杆,用一根繩子把一顆人頭懸掛在樹或木杆上,表示梟首示眾的意思。小篆縣字形體略有變化,其左為倒"首",右為"系",也是懸掛人頭之義。所以,縣的本義為懸掛人頭,梟首示眾,引申為弔、懸、繫(jì)掛之義。縣字後來借用為地方行政區劃名稱,故另造"懸"字來代替它的本義。

金文

小篆

縣 was the original form of 懸. In the Bronze Inscriptions, the character 縣 is made up of a tree on the left and a head hanging from it with a rope on the right. In the Later Seal Character, the shape of the character has undergone some change. The left is an upside-down 首 (head), and the right 系 (to link). But it keeps the original meaning: "the hanging of a head" or "to chop off a head and hang it ". The more general sense of the hanging of anything is its extended meaning. As 縣 came to be used as a name of an administrative area — county later, a new character 懸 was created to take its place for the original meaning.

miàn

甲骨文的面字，外部是一張臉的輪廓，中間有一隻大眼睛，它的本義即指人的臉。不過在古代，臉和面的含義是有所不同的。臉，最初指頰，即眼與顴骨之間；而面則指整個頭部的前面部份。所以面字可引申為泛指前面，又指物體的外表、表面。現又借指麵粉義。

【面目】面貌。也泛指事物的外貌。

【面壁】面向牆壁。又佛教稱坐禪為面壁，謂面向牆壁，端坐靜修。

【面面相覷】相視無言。形容緊張驚懼、束手無策之狀。

甲骨文

小篆

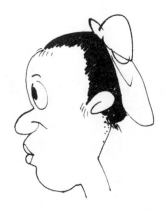

In the Oracle-Bone Inscriptions, the character 面 has a big eye inside an outline of a face, hence the primary meaning: face. However, in ancient times, 臉(nowadays meaning the same as面)and 面 meant differently. 臉 referred to the part between the eye and cheekbone on either side of the face, while 面 referred to the whole of the front of a head. That is why 面 can also be used for anything that is in the front, or in the outside. In addition it can mean "flour".

【面目】 facial features; appearance

【面壁】 (1) to face the wall (2) (Buddhism) to sit in meditation

【面面相覷】 to look at each other in speechless despair

yí

頤，是指人臉的頰、腮部位。甲骨文的頤字，像臉的頰、腮部位之形；有的在腮部畫有鬍鬚；楷書則更加"頁"旁，以表示頤在人的頭面範圍。頤字除指人面的頰、腮之外，還可用作保養之義，如頤養。

【頤指氣使】不說話而用面部表情來示意，形容有權勢的人的傲慢神氣。

甲骨文　　　　　　小篆

頤 refers to the part of face known as cheek in English. In the Oracle-Bone Inscriptions, the character looks like the cheek of a face; in some of them there are even strokes representing whiskers. In the Regular Script, the part 頁, signalling head, is added, to show that 頤 is part of a head. Apart from this sense, 頤 can also mean "to keep fit", e.g. 頤養（to take care of oneself）.

【頤指氣使】 to order people about by gesture; to be insufferably arrogant

xū

【鬚】

古代男子以鬚眉稠秀為美。金文的須字，正像人面有鬚的樣子，其本義指鬍鬚。須字在後來多假借為"需"，有需要、必需、應當等義。

【鬚眉】鬍鬚和眉毛。舊時指男子。

【須臾】指時間上的片刻。佛教把一日一夜分為三十須臾。

【須彌芥子】須彌，佛教傳說中的山名。芥子，即芥菜之籽。把龐大的須彌山納於微小的芥子之中，比喻不可思議。

金文

小篆

In ancient China, men were proud of their beautiful thickness beard and eyebrow. In the Bronze Inscriptions, the character 須 looks like a face with beard, hence its primary meaning "beard". But it has come to take on the senses of "need", "must" and "should" as well.

【鬚眉】beard and eyebrow; male

【須臾】moment; instant

【須彌芥子】(Buddhism)to put Mount Xumi inside a mustard seed; unthinkable; incredible

rǎn

【髯】

冉是"髯"的本字，即鬍髯的意思。古代髭、髯有別，髯的本義是指頰毛，髭則指下巴上的鬍子。古文字的冉字，正像面部兩頰旁邊髯毛下垂的樣子。冉字由髯毛下垂引申為柔弱、垂下之義。而冉冉連用，則有慢慢、漸漸之義。

【冉冉】漸進的樣子。又柔弱下垂之狀。

甲骨文　　　　　　金 文　　　　　　小 篆

冉 was the original form of 髯, referring to whiskers, sometimes to beard (known as髭) as well; though they were strictly kept apart at the beginning, 髯 referring to hair on the cheeks and 髭 to that on the chin. In ancient writing systems, the character 冉 looks like hair growing on the two cheeks of a man's face. As whiskers are soft and hang down, the character 冉 has also taken on the senses of "soft" and "to hang down". And two 冉 used together means"slowly"and"gradually".

【冉冉】slowly; gradually

ér

金文的而字，像人頰下鬍髮飄拂的樣子，其本義當指下巴上的鬍毛，今人則多稱鬍子或鬍鬚。而字後來多借用為代詞，相當於汝、你、你們；又借為連詞，有和、及、才、就、並且等多種含義和作用。其本義反而少為人知了。

【而已】語末助詞，僅止於此，相當於口語中的"罷了"。

【而立】《論語・為政》："子曰：吾十有五而志于學，三十而立。"後因稱三十歲為"而立"之年。

甲骨文　　　　金文　　　　小篆

In the Bronze Inscriptions, the character 而 looks like the beard on the chin fluttering in the wind, hence the original meaning "beard". However this meaning is now usually expressed by 鬚. And the character 而 has come to be used instead as a pronoun, meaning "you"; or as a conjunction, meaning "and", "but", "if", etc.

【而已】 that is all; nothing more

【而立】 thirty years of age (from Confucius, who says, according to the *Analects,* "I set out to learn the moral codes of Zhou at fifteen and was able to conform to them at thirty".)

nài

耐是古代一種剃去鬍鬚的輕微刑罰。耐字從而從寸，"而"是鬍鬚，"寸"為手，表示用手除去鬍鬚之義。此字後多借用為忍受、禁得住之義，本義遂不再行用。

【耐久】指能經久。

【耐煩】忍受麻煩。

小篆

In ancient times, 耐 referred to a light form of punishment: to shave off the beard. The character 耐 consists of 而 and 寸, the former meaning beard and the latter hand, hence the meaning to take away beard by hand. However, the character has gradually come to be used in the sense "to tolerate" and "to bear", and its original meaning is no longer current.

【耐久】lasting long; durable

【耐煩】patient

méi

甲骨文、金文的眉字，均像人眼上有眉毛之形，其本義即為眉毛。小篆以後眉字形體略變，原字的象形成份就逐漸減弱了。

【眉目】眉毛和眼睛，泛指容貌，後又指一件事情的頭緒、條理。

【眉睫】眉毛和眼睫毛，比喻近在眼前。

【眉批】眉在人臉五官的上端，所以凡在上面的往往稱為"眉"，比如書頁的上端稱"書眉"，而在書眉部份加上批語，就叫做"眉批"。

甲骨文

金 文

小 篆

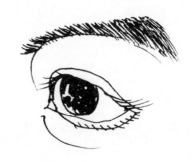

In the Oracle-Bone Inscriptions and Bronze Inscriptions, the character 眉 looks like either a man with his eye and eyebrow especially prominent, or is made up of simply an eye and eyebrow, hence the meaning "eyebrow". Since the time of the Later Seal Character, however, the character 眉 has undergone some change in its shape, and become less pictorial.

【眉目】eyebrow and eye; facial features; logic; sequence of ideas

【眉睫】eyebrow and eyelashes; sth. immediately before the eye; urgent

【眉批】notes and commentary at the top of a page

mù

目字是個象形字。甲骨文、金文的目字,是一隻非常逼真的眼睛之形。它的本義即指眼睛,引申為動詞,是以目視物,即看的意思。目又可用來指魚網的網孔(俗稱"網眼"),引申為指條目、細目等。漢字中凡從"目"之字,都與眼睛及其作用有關,如看、眉、相、瞪、瞥等。

【目送】以眼光相送。

【目前】眼前,現在。

【目錄】按次序編排以供備考的圖書或篇章的名目。

【目空一切】形容驕傲自大,甚麼都看不起。

甲骨文

金文

小篆

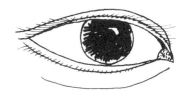

目 is a pictograph. In the Oracle-Bone Inscriptions and Bronze Inscriptions, the character 目 is a vivid description of an eye. It was only used as a noun at the beginning, but later also used as a verb, meaning to see things with the eye. The character 目 can also be used to refer to the holes of a fishnet, i.e. meshes, from which sense derive the senses of "clauses (of a document)", "entries (of a dictionary)" and "spicific items". Characters with 目 as a component all have to do with the eye and its function, e.g. 看 (to look at), 眉 (eyebrow), 相 (to appraise), 瞪 (to stare) and 瞥 (to shoot a glance at).

【目送】to watch sb. go

【目前】at present; now

【目錄】table of contents

【目空一切】to consider everybody and everything beneath one's notice

zhí

甲骨文的直字，為目上一條直線，表示目光直視的意思。許慎《説文解字》：“直，正視也。”因此，直的本義為直視、正視，引申為成直線的（與“曲”相對）、垂直（與“橫”相對）、正直、公正、直爽、直接等義。

【直觀】用感官直接接受的，直接觀察的。

【直截了當】（言語、行動等）簡單爽快。

【直言無諱】直率而言，無所隱諱。

甲骨文

小篆

In the Oracle-Bone Inscriptions, the character 直 has the shape of an eye with a straight line above it, signalling "to look straight ahead". Xu Shen says in his *Origin of Chinese Characters*, "直 means to look squarely at". Hence the original meaning of 直 was "to look straight ahead", "to look squarely at", from which have derived its extended meanings of "straight (opposite to 曲, bent)", "vertical (opposite to 橫, horizontal)," "honest", "fair-minded", "frank" and "direct".

【直觀】 directly perceived through the senses

【直截了當】 straightforward

【直言無諱】 to call a spade a spade

mín

古代的奴隸主為了強迫奴隸勞動，防止他們造反，往往採取極其殘酷的鎮壓手段：或給他們戴上沉重的腳鐐手銬，或用繩索套着他們的脖子，或砍（或鋸）去他們的一隻腳，或用錐子刺瞎他們的眼睛。甲骨文、金文的民字，正像以錐刺眼之形，其本義原指奴隸；引申為指被統治者，其中包括奴隸和平民；後也泛指普通的群眾、老百姓。

金文　　　　　小篆

In the old days, slave owners used extremely cruel methods to force slaves to work and to stop them from rebelling, e.g. to shackle them with heavy metal chains, to tie them together with ropes round their necks, to chop off one of their legs or to blind them with an awl. In the Oracle-Bone Inscriptions and Bronze Inscriptions, the character 民 has the shape of an eye being pricked with an awl. So it was originally used to refer to slaves, but gradually its meaning was broadened to cover all the ruled, including freemen. Hence its present-day sense: common people.

máng

盲字是個會意兼形聲的字，從亡從目，亡即無，表示眼中無眸的意思，此外，亡又代表這個字的讀音。《説文解字》："盲，目無牟（即眸）子。"目中無眸子就看不見東西，是為瞎，所以盲的本義為瞎，為失明。

【盲目】眼瞎，比喻沒有見識，認識不清。

【盲從】不問是非地附和別人；盲目隨從。

【盲動】沒經考慮，沒有明確目的就行動。

【盲人摸象】形容對事物沒有全面了解，固執一點，亂加揣測。

璽 文

小 篆

The character 盲 is both an ideograph and a phonetic compound. It consists of 亡(without)and 目 (eye),signalling an eye without the pupil. On the other hand, 亡 is also its phonetic, representing its pronunciation. Xu Shen says in his *Origin of Chinese Characters,* " 盲 means an eye without the pupil". An eye without the pupil will not be able to see things, hence its primary meaning "blind".

【盲目】blind; unable to tell one thing from another clearly

【盲從】to follow blindly

【盲動】to act rashly

【盲人摸象】like the blind men trying to size up the elephant;
to take a part for the whole

shuì

　　睡字從目從垂，是個會意字，表示垂頭閉目休息的意思。《説文解字》："睡，坐寐也。"所以睡的本義指坐着打瞌睡，又泛指睡覺、睡眠。

【睡鄉】即夢鄉，入睡後的境界。

【睡魔】人疲乏時，急遽欲睡，詩文中比方由於魔力催促，稱為睡魔。

小篆

The character 睡 is an ideograph. It consists of 目 (eye) and 垂 (to hang down), signalling to rest with one's head lowered and eyes closed. Xu Shen says in his *Origin of Chinese Characters,* "睡 means to sit dozing". Hence its original meaning was to sit dozing, but it has come to be used in the more general sense "to sleep".

【睡鄉】dreamland

【睡魔】(lit.) sleep demon; sleepness; drowsiness

xiàng

相字從木從目，是個會意字，表示用眼細細觀賞樹木外形之義。相的本義是指觀察事物的外表以判斷其優劣，引申為指人或事物的外觀形貌。此外，相字還有輔助之義，又用作官名，特指宰相。相又可讀xiāng，相共、交互之義，也表示一方對另一方有所動作。

【相術】指觀察人的形貌，預言其命運的一種方術。

【相貌】即容貌，指人的面部模樣。

【相（xiāng）得益彰】指互相配合，更能顯出好處。

甲骨文　　　　金　文　　　　小　篆

The character 相 is an ideograph. It consists of 木 (tree) and 目 (eye), signalling to look at the trees carefully. The primary meaning of 相 is to judge whether something is good by looking at its appearance. Later it came to mean the appearance, looks, of people or things. Besides, the character 相 can also mean to assist, and can be used as the name of a minister who assists the emperor. 相 pronounced as xiāng refers to the same actions performed by two or more than two parties and their influences on each other.

【相術】(lit.) the skill to judge sth. by its appearance; the tricks used by fortune-tellers

【相貌】facial features; looks

【相(xiāng)得益彰】each shining more brilliantly in the other's company; to bring out the best in each other

kàn

看是個比較晚出現的會意字，在甲骨文和金文中還未發現。小篆的看字，從手在目上，像手搭涼棚往遠處眺望之形。因此，看的本義為遠望，引申為觀察、注視之義，再引申為探望、訪問之義。

【看台】供觀望的高台。

【看待】對待。

【看法】對客觀事物所抱的見解。

【看風使舵】比喻跟着情勢而轉變方向，即隨機應變。多用作貶義。

小篆

看 is a relatively new ideograph. It did not appear in the Oracle-Bone Inscriptions or Bronze Inscriptions. In the Later Seal Character, the character 看 consists of 手 (hand) and 目 (eye), signalling to look into the distance in the shade formed by a hand atop the eye. Hence its primary meaning to look far into the distance. But its meaning has gradually been extended to observing and watching, and even further to visiting the sick, or visit in general.

【看台】bleachers; stand

【看待】to look up on; to treat

【看法】a way of looking at a thing; view

【看風使舵】(derog.) to trim one's sails; to adapt oneself to circumstances

wàng

"望"本是個會意字。甲骨文的"望"，是一個人站在一個高出地面的土墩上翹首遠看的形狀；金文"望"字增加月形，表示"舉頭望明月"的意思。因此，"望"的本義為"仰觀"、"遠看"；而登高遠望有等待之意，故又可引申出"期望"、"希盼"等義。小篆以後，"望"字形體發生變化，原來代表眼睛的"臣"被"亡"（表示讀音）所代替，"望"字即由會意字變成了形聲字。

甲骨文

金文

小篆

望 was originally an ideograph. In the Oracle-Bone Inscriptions, the character 望 looks like a man raising his head and looking into the distance on a mound. In the Bronze Inscriptions, there is also the part 月 (moon) on the upper righthand, signalling to raise one's head and look at the moon. Hence the primary meaning of 望 is "to look up at" and "to look into the distance". As to look into the distance on a mound suggests expectation, 望 has also come to mean "to expect" and "to hope". Since the time of the Later Seal Character, the character 望 has undergone some change in its shape: the part representing eye 臣 is replaced by 亡 to indicate its pronunciation, resulting in a phonetic compound.

jiàn

古文字的見字，是人形之上一隻大眼，眼形非常突出，像一個人張眼凝神而視的樣子。見的本義為看見，指眼睛觀看物體而有所感覺。由此引申，則耳之所聞、心之所悟均可稱之為"見"，如聽見、見識、見解等。此外，見還常借用為助動詞"被"，表示被動。

【見地】見解、見識。

【見效】發生效力。

【見笑大方】指知識淺陋，為有道者譏笑。今多用為謙辭。

【見義勇為】見正義之事而勇於作為。

【見微知著】從事物的細微跡象，認識其實質和發展的趨勢。

甲骨文

金文

小篆

In ancient writing systems, the character 見 looks like a man with a big eye on the top, suggesting a man is staring at things. The primary meaning of 見 is to see , to sense something by the power of sight. Later on the sensing of something by other organs also came to be known as 見, e.g. 聽見 (to hear), 見識(knowledge)and 見解 (opinion). Besides,見 can also be used as an auxiliary, expressing passive voice.

【見地】insight; judgment

【見效】to become effective

【見笑大方】to be laughed at by the professionals

【見義勇為】ready to take up the cudgels for a just cause; never hesitate to do what is righteous

【見微知著】From the first small beginnings one can see how things will develop.

xiàn

金文的限字，左邊的"阜"像高丘形，右邊是一張目反顧的人形，表示一個人回頭向後看，但被高丘阻擋視線，無法極目遠眺。限的本義為阻擋、阻隔，引申為限制，又指界限。此外，限字還可當門檻講，因為門檻本身就有限制、界限之義。

【限定】在數量、範圍等方面加以規定。

【限度】範圍的極限；最高或最低的數量或程度。

【限期】指定日期，不許超過。又指指定的不許超過的日期。

金 文

小 篆

In the Bronze Inscriptions, the character 限 has a hill part on the left and a part depicting a man looking back on the right, suggesting that the man's sight is blocked by a hill and he is unable to look into the distance. So the primary meaning of 限 is "to block", "to obstruct", from which derive its senses "to limit" and "boundary". Besides, 限 can also be used to refer to the threshold, as it is a limit to the outsider.

【限定】to set a limit to

【限度】limit; limitation

【限期】deadline

chén

臣字最初的本義指男性奴隸或俘虜。如《尚書》中所説：凡是奴隸，"男曰臣，女曰妾。"引申為泛指下賤僕役之人。甲骨文、金文的臣字，像一豎起的眼睛。因為奴隸在主人面前不能抬頭平視，只能俯首仰視，所以成豎目。以豎目代表奴隸，即卑恭、屈服之人，所以臣又有臣服、屈服之義。在奴隸、封建君主制時代，從各級官員到普通老百姓，都是帝王君主的奴僕，在君主面前均自稱為"臣"。

甲骨文

金文

小篆

The original meaning of 臣 was man slave or captive. Thus *Shang shu* (the Book of History)says, of slaves, "the male is called 臣 and the female 妾". From this meaning has derived its use to refer to servants. In the Oracle-Bone Inscriptions and Bronze Inscriptions, the character 臣 looks like a vertical eye. The reason is that at that time slaves were not allowed to raise their heads and look level ahead before their owners. They had to lower their heads and look upwards, hence the eye became vertical. As a vertical eye suggests submission and obedience, the character 臣 has also come to be used in these senses. In the old days all the people, including officials of various ranks, were subjects of the sovereign, so they all called themselves 臣 in front of the latter.

WÒ

臥字從人從臣，臣為豎目形，人低頭俯視則目豎，從金文臨、監二字所從的臥字來看，均為俯身而視形。所以臥字的本義為俯伏、趴下，引申為仰躺、睡下的意思。

【臥具】枕席被褥等臥室用具的統稱。

【臥病】因病躺下。

【臥薪嚐膽】形容人立志報仇雪恥，因此刻苦自勵，不敢安逸。

小篆

The character 臥 consists of 人 (man) and 臣 (vertical eye), signalling a man lowering his head and looking upwards. In the Bronze Inscriptions, the character 臥, as shown in both 臨 and 監, has the shape of a man lowering his head and looking upwards. Hence the primary meaning of 臥 is to lie prostrate, later it also came to mean to lie on one's back, or to sleep.

【臥具】bedclothes

【臥病】to be confined to bed with an illness

【臥薪嚐膽】to sleep on brushwood and taste gall; to undergo self-imposed hardships so as to strengthen one's resolve to wipe out a humiliation (from the story of Gou Jian, King of Yue, who splept on brushwood and tasted gall every day after his country was conquered by the State of Wu in 494 B. C. and eventually took revenge in 475 B. C. by destroying Wu in return)

jiān

在古代沒有發明鏡子之前，人們若想看到自己臉面的樣子，就只有一個辦法，即用水來照。甲骨文的監字，像一個人跪在水盆（皿）邊，張眼向下看的樣子，表示人利用盆中之水照看自己模樣的意思，所以監字的本義為臨水自照，即自己看自己。由自己看自己引申為觀察別的人或事物，故監又有監視、監督之義。

甲骨文

金 文

小 篆

In ancient times when mirror was not yet invented, there was only one way for a man to see his own face, that is to look at one's reflection in the water. In the Oracle-Bone Inscriptions, the character 監 looks like a man staring at a basin on his knees, suggesting that the man is looking at his reflection in the water. Hence the original meaning of 監 was to look at oneself in the water, from which derive the meaning to observe other people and things, e.g. 監視 (to supervise; to watch)and 監督 (to superintend; to control).

lín

金文的臨字，像人俯視眾物之形。小篆的臨從臥從品，臥像俯視人形，其下為禮物，其會意與金文同。因此，臨的本義指俯視，引申為面對、降臨、到、及等義，又引申為指統管、治理。

【臨時】到事情發生之時。又指一時、暫時。

【臨渴掘井】感到渴了才掘井，比喻平時沒有準備，臨時才想辦法。

【臨淵羨魚】比喻只有空想和願望，而不去實幹，就無濟於事。

金 文

小 篆

In the Bronze Inscriptions, the character 臨 looks like a man looking down at many things. In the Later Seal Character, it consists of 臥 and 品, the former representing a man looking down and the latter presents, meaning the same as that in the Bronze Inscriptions. The original meaning of 臨 was to look down at things, but it has taken on the extended meanings of facing, befalling, arriving, and even those of governing and ruling later on.

【臨時】(1)at the time when sth. happens (2) temporary; provisional

【臨渴掘井】not to dig a well until one is thirsty; not to make timely preparations

【臨淵羨魚】to stand on the edge of a pool and idly long for fish; not to take practical steps to achieve one's aims

ěr

甲骨文、金文的耳字，正像一隻耳朵之形，本義即指耳朵。耳是人和動物的聽覺器官，故凡從"耳"的字，都與耳朵及其聽覺有關，如聞、聶、取等。

【耳目】指見聞。又指替人刺探消息的人。

【耳食】比喻不善思考，輕信傳聞。

【耳濡目染】形容經常在一起，聽得多了看得多了之後，無形之中會受到影響。

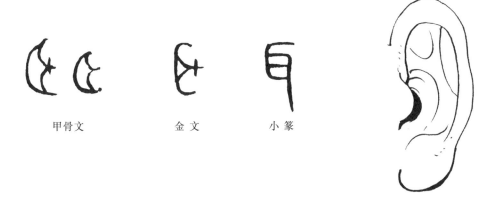

甲骨文	金文	小篆

In the Oracle-Bone Inscriptions and Bronze Inscriptions, the character 耳 looks just like an ear, hence the meaning: ear. The ear is the organ of hearing in human beings and animals, so characters with 耳 as a component all have to do with ear and its function of hearing, e. g. 聞 (to hear), 聶 (to whisper) and 取 (to cut off an ear).

【耳目】(1) what one sees and hears; information (2) one who spies for sb. else

【耳食】credulous (of hearsay)

【耳濡目染】to be imperceptibly influenced by what one constantly sees and hears

wén

甲骨文的聞字，像一個人豎起耳朵正在聚精會神地聽着什麼東西的樣子。小篆聞字從耳門聲，門也可以是個義符，似乎可以理解為一耳貼在門外偷聽別人說話。聞的本義為聽、聽見，又指所聽到的事情、消息，如新聞、奇聞，引申為指見聞、知識。此外，聞字還有"嗅"的意思，如"聞香下馬"。

【聞風喪膽】聽到一點風聲就嚇破了膽。形容對某種力量極端恐懼。

【聞一知十】形容聰明，善於類推。

甲骨文

金文

小篆

In the Oracle-Bone Inscriptions, the character 聞 looks like a man pricking up his ears. In the Later Seal Characer, 聞 has 耳 (ear) as its radical and 門 (door) as its phonetic. But 門 can also be ideographic, and the character 聞 seen as such means to put one's ear to the door of another in order to hear what is said inside, i.e. to eavesdrop. The primary meaning of 聞 is to listen, to hear, but it can also be used in the extended meanings for what has been heard e.g. 新聞 (news), 奇聞 (something unheard-of); and even for what one knows by way of seeing and hearing e.g. 見聞 (knowledge). In addition, 聞 can also mean to smell, e.g. 聞香下馬 (to dismount from a horse at the smell of fragrance).

【聞風喪膽】to become terror-stricken at the news

【聞一知十】to draw inferences about other cases from one instance; to learn by analogy

shèng

甲骨文、金文的聖字，像一個人站着聽人說話的樣子。其中的口表示有人在說話，而人形頭上的耳朵特別突出，則表示聽力極佳的意思。所以，聖字的本義指聽覺靈敏，又有聰明睿智、百事通達之意。古代稱人格品德崇高、學識才能有極高成就的人為"聖"，如聖賢、詩聖、書聖等。在君主時代，聖字則多用為對帝王的尊稱，如聖上、聖旨、聖恩等。

【聖明】封建時代稱頌君主的套詞，言英明無所不知。
【聖哲】超凡的道德才智。又指聖哲的人。

　　　　　　聖

甲骨文　　　　　金文　　　　　小篆

In the Oracle-Bone Inscriptions and Bronze Inscriptions, the character 聖 looks like a man listening to someone talking. The part 口 represents the man talking, and the big ear on top of the man listening suggests that he has an acute hearing. So the character 聖 originally meant an acute sense of hearing, but it could also mean to be bright and intelligent and to have profound wisdom. In ancient times, people of noble character and great learning were known as 聖, e.g. 聖賢 (sage), 詩聖 (poet sage), 書聖 (calligrapher sage). Under the feudal system, however, 聖 was more usually used as an honorific title of the emperor, e.g. 聖上 (the emperor), 聖旨 (imperial edict) and 聖恩 (the grace of the emperor).

【聖明】 the wise emperor
【聖哲】 (1) extraordinary wisdom (2) wise man

tīng

甲骨文的聽字，從耳從口，表示用耳來接受別人的言談。聽的本義指用耳朵來感受聲音，引申為聽從、接受，又引申為決斷、治理之義。

【聽命】接受命令。

【聽政】處理政務。引申為執政。

【聽其自然】任憑人或事物自然發展變化，不去干涉。

【聽天由命】指聽從天意和命運的安排而不作主觀努力。

甲骨文

金 文

小 篆

In the Oracle-Bone Inscriptions, the character 聽 consists of 耳 (ear) and 口 (mouth), signalling an ear is receiving speech from a mouth. The primary meaning of 聽 is to perceive sound by the ear, but it has also taken on the meanings of listening to or accepting (others' advice), making decisions and administering.

【聽命】to be at sb's command

【聽政】to administer government affairs; to be in
power

【聽其自然】to let things take their own course

【聽天由命】to submit to the will of destiny; to resign
oneself to one's fate

niè

聶字是個會意字，從三耳，表示眾人口耳相傳之意。《說文解字》："聶，附耳私小語也。"故聶的本義為附耳私語。現在則多用作姓氏名。

小篆

聶 is an ideograph. In its original complicated form, it is made up of three ear parts (耳), signalling that many people are passing some news by word of mouth. Xu Shen says in his *Origin of Chinese Characters,* " 聶 means to have a word in sb.'s ear", and that was its original meaning. Nowadays, however, it is more usually used as a surname.

shēng

甲骨文的聲字，像一個人手持小槌敲打懸掛的石磬，從耳表示用耳可以聽到石磬發出來的聲音。聲的本義指聲音、聲響，又指音樂、言語、音信，引申為聲勢、名譽之義。

【聲色】說話的聲調和臉色。又指音樂歌舞和女色。

【聲援】聲勢相通，互相援助。

【聲東擊西】指戰鬥中設計造成對方錯覺，而突襲其所不備之處。

甲骨文

小篆

In the Oracle-Bone Inscriptions, the character 聲 looks like a man striking a chime stone with a small mallet in hand. It has 耳 (ear) as a component, signalling that through ear one can hear the sound coming from the chime stone. It primarily means "sound", "noise", but it can also mean "music", "speech" and "message"; from which have derived the senses of "momentum" and "reputation".

【聲色】(1) voice and countenance (2) woman and song

【聲援】to express support for

【聲東擊西】to make a feint to the east and attack in the west

qǔ

古代兩軍作戰，戰勝一方的將士是以割取敵人的首級或俘虜的耳朵來記功的。甲骨文的取字，像一隻手拿着一隻被割下來的耳朵，表示割取耳朵的意思，引申為捕獲、索取、收受、採用等義。

甲骨文　　　　金文　　　　小篆

In ancient wars, the army authority would judge a soldier's contribution by the number of the enemies'heads or the captives'ears he brought back. In the Oracle-Bone Inscriptions, the character 取 looks like an ear in a hand, signalling the cutting off of an ear. From this meaning have derived its senses of "capture", "take", "accept" and "adopt".

zì

甲骨文的自字，像人的鼻形，是"鼻"字的初形，其本義即指鼻子。後來自字多用作第一人稱代詞，指自己；而在"自"下增加一個"畀"字作為聲符，另造了一個"鼻"字來表示鼻子的意思。

【自由】指能按自己的意願行動，不受他人限制。

【自然】天然，非人為的；又指不造作，非勉強的。

【自相矛盾】比喻言行不一致或互相抵觸。

| 甲骨文 | 金文 | 小篆 |

Being the original form of 鼻 (nose), the character 自 in the Oracle-Bone Inscriptions has the shape of a human nose. But it has come to be used in the sense of oneself, so a new character 鼻, made up of 自 and a phonetic 畀 has been created for the sense of nose.

【自由】freedom

【自然】(1) natural world (2) natural

【自相矛盾】self-contradictory

sì

四，是一個數目字。甲骨文、金文的四字，是用四條橫畫來表示“四”這個數目。它和一、二、三等數目字一樣，都屬於指事字的範疇。而小篆的四字則是一個會意字，像人口中發出來的聲氣，當是“呬”的本字。因此，四字作為數目字，乃是借用了“呬”的本字。

【四平八穩】形容說話、做事、寫文章十分穩重，有時也指做事只求不出差錯，缺乏創新精神。

【四面八方】指各個方面。

甲骨文

金 文

小 篆

The character 四 is a numeral, meaning "four". In the Oracle-Bone Inscriptions and Bronze Inscriptions, it is made up of four horizontal lines. Like 一 (one), 二 (two) and 三 (three), it is also indicative. But in the Later Seal Character, the character 四 is an ideograph, looking like a mouth producing sounds. Hence 四 was the original form of 呬. In this sense, the numeral 四 is a phonetic loan.

【四平八穩】(1) very steady; well organized (2) lacking in initiative and overcautious

【四面八方】all directions

kǒu

口字的形狀，正像人或動物的嘴，其本義就是嘴巴。嘴巴是人或動物飲食、發聲的器官，所以以口為偏旁的字多與吃喝和言語有關；而口字也可用作言語的代名詞，如口舌、口角等。口形中空，故凡形狀像口的物象都可以口為喻，如山口、海口、洞口、關口、瓶口、碗口、瘡口、決口等。

【口實】口中的食物，又指話柄，即可供別人批評或談論的資料。

【口若懸河】比喻人健談，説話如河水傾瀉，滔滔不絕。

【口誅筆伐】指用言語或文字譴責他人的罪狀或錯誤言行。

甲骨文　　　　　　小篆

The character 口 has the shape of an open mouth of a man or an animal, hence the primary meaning "mouth". As the mouth is an organ for a man or an animal to eat, drink and produce sounds, characters with 口 as a component are often related to eating, drinking and speaking. And it may even be used as a substitute for speech, e.g. 口舌 (exchange of words), 口角 (quarrel). Devoid of any stroke in the centre, 口 may also refer to anything with an opening, e.g. 山口 (mountain pass), 海口 (seaport), 洞口 (mouth of a cave), 關口 (strategic pass), 瓶口 (mouth of a bottle), 碗口 (top of a bowl), 瘡口 (open part of a sore) and 決口 (breach; break).

【口實】a cause for gossip

【口若懸河】to talk volubly

【口誅筆伐】to condemn both in speech and in writing

qiàn

甲骨文的欠字，像一個跪着的人，昂首張嘴，大打呵欠的樣子，它的本義就是“張口出氣”，也即打呵欠。以欠為偏旁的字，如吹、歌、歇等，大都與“張口出氣”有關。至於欠債、虧欠的“欠”，則用的是假借義，與本義無關。

甲骨文

小篆

In the Oracle-Bone Inscriptions, the character 欠 looks like a man on his knees, yawning with the mouth wide open. Hence the original meaning "to open one's mouth and exhale", i.e. "to yawn". Characters with 欠 as a component, e.g. 吹 (to blow), 歌 (to sing), 歇 (to have a rest), usually have to do with the opening of the mouth and exhaling. The character 欠 in words like 欠債 (to be in debt) and 虧欠 (to have a deficit), different from the original in meaning, is a phonetic loan.

chuī

吹字由口和欠組成，欠字本來像一個人張口出氣的樣子，再加上一個口，強調用嘴巴呼氣，所以吹的本義為"合攏嘴唇用力呼氣。"自然界空氣的流動也可稱為吹，如"風吹雨打"。而一個人信口開河，胡說八道則叫做"吹牛"或"吹牛皮"。

甲骨文

金 文

小 篆

The character 吹 is made up of 口 (mouth) and 欠 (a man opening his mouth and exhaling). By conjoining these two parts it is brought out that the exhalation is done through the mouth. Hence its primary meaning is to round one's lips and exhale with great strength. It may also be used to describe the natural movement of air, e.g. 風吹雨打 (the wind blowing and the rain beating). And to boast or talk big is 吹牛/吹牛皮 (literally "to blow the ox") in Chinese.

xián

【次】

甲骨文　　　　　　小篆

涎字的本義指口水、唾液。甲骨文、金文的涎是個會意字，像一個人張着口，口裡流出幾點口水的樣子；小篆涎字從水從欠，仍是會意字；楷書涎字從水延聲，則變成了形聲字。

【涎皮賴臉】厚着臉皮跟人糾纏，惹人厭煩。

The character 涎 means "salive". In the Oracle-Bone Inscriptions and Bronze Inscriptions, this character is an ideograph, in the shape of a man opening his mouth, with water dropping from it. In the Later Seal Character, it is still an ideograph, but made up of 水 (water) and 欠 (a man with an open mouth). In the Regular Script, however, it becomes a phonetic compound, with 水 (water) as the radical and 延 as the phonetic.

【涎皮賴臉】shameless and loathsome; cheeky

yǐn

斯文人飲酒，是先把酒斟入酒杯，然後再慢飲細品。而甲骨文的飲字，則像一個人彎腰低頭，伸着舌頭抱壜痛飲的樣子，可見古人飲酒也是豪興過人。飲的本義指喝酒，後來才引申為指一般的喝，如飲水、飲茶等。

【飲水思源】北周庾信《微調曲》："落其實者思其樹，飲其流者懷其源。"後人取其意，用以喻指不忘本源。又作"飲水知源"。

【飲鴆止渴】飲毒酒解渴。比喻不顧後患而用有害的辦法解決眼前困難。

甲骨文

金文

小篆

Nowadays when a man drinks, he usually pours the wine into a glass and tastes it slowly. However, in the Oracle-Bone Inscriptions, the character 飲 looks like a man bending over an enormous jar, hanging out his tongue and drinking deeply, which suggests people tended to drink in quantities in ancient times. Originally 飲 meant to take in alcoholic drink only, later its meaning has been extended to the taking of any liquid, e.g. 飲水 (to drink water), 飲茶 (to drink tea).

【飲水思源】(also 飲水知源) When drinking water, one should think of its source; Never forget where one's happiness comes from.

【飲鴆止渴】to drink poison to quench thirst; to seek temporary relief regardless of the consequences

gān

古文字的甘字，從口從一，一為指事符號，表示口中所含食物，它的本文指食物味美，特指味甜。引申為指甘心、樂意、情願等義。

【甘旨】指美味。

【甘言】即甜言蜜語，指諂媚奉承的話。

【甘拜下風】與人比較，自認不如，願居下列。

甲骨文　　　　　小篆

In ancient writing systems, the character 甘 is composed of 口 (mouth) and 一 (an indicating sign for the food in the mouth here). It primarily refers to the delicious, especially sweet, taste of some food, from which has derived its sense of (doing sth.) willingly and readily, such as 甘心.

【甘旨】delicious food

【甘言】honeyed words

【甘拜下風】to willingly admit defeat

tián

甜和"甘"的本義完全相同。甜字從甘從舌,甘指味道甜美,而舌則是辨味的器官。所以甜的本義指味道甘美,引申為美好之義;又指醋適,形容覺睡得踏實。

【甜美】甘甜可口。又指愉快、舒服。

【甜頭】微甜的味道,泛指好吃的味道。又指好處、利益。

【甜言蜜語】為了討人喜歡或哄騙人而說的好聽的話。

小 篆

The primary meaning of 甜 is the same as 甘. The character 甜 is composed of 甘 (sweet taste) and 舌 (tongue, an organ for tasting), hence its use for something which tastes sweet. From this meaning has derived its reference to anything that is pleasant, even a sound sleep, as in (睡得真)甜.

【甜美】 sweet and pleasant

【甜頭】 sweet taste; benefit

【甜言蜜語】 sweet words and honeyed phrases

yuē

古文字的曰字，像口中加一橫或一曲畫之形，表示從口裡發出聲音，即說話的意思。曰的本義為說、道，引申為叫、叫做，又引申為"為、是"，含有判斷之意。

甲骨文　　　　　　金 文　　　　　　小 篆

In ancient writing systems, the character 曰 looks like a mouth, to which is added a horizontal stroke indicating the sound coming from the mouth. Hence the primary meaning "speaking", from which have derived its extended meanings "to be known as", "to act as", or simply "to be".

shé

舌的本義就是舌頭。甲骨文的舌字，下面的口是嘴的象形，從嘴中伸出來並帶有口液的東西，就是人的舌頭。《說文解字》："舌，在口所以言也，別味也。"人的舌頭有兩大功能：發音說話和辨味，所以與說話和食味有關的字多從舌，如舐、舔、甜等。

【舌耕】古代把教書授徒稱為"舌耕"，意即以口舌為謀生工具。

【舌人】古代指通他國語言、擔任翻譯職務的官員。

【舌劍唇槍】比喻一個人言辭犀利，能說會道。

甲骨文

金文

小篆

Its primary meaning is "tongue". In the Oracle-Bone Inscriptions, the character 舌 looks like something coming out of the mouth with drops of saliva dripping, i.e. tongue. The *Origin of Chinese Characters* says, "The tongue is an organ which enables a man to speak and taste". The tongue of a human being has two important functions: to produce speech and to taste. That is why characters relating to speech and taste mostly have a component of 舌, e.g. 舐 ((fml) to lick), 舔 (to lick), and 甜 (sweet).

【舌耕】(arch.) to teach

【舌人】(arch.) interpreter

【舌劍唇槍】to cross verbal swords; to argue heatedly

yán

甲骨文、金文的言字，下面部份是口舌的象形，而在舌頭之上加一短橫作為指示符號，表示人張口搖舌正在説話的意思，因此言字的本義為説話，如"直言不諱"（有話直説，毫無顧忌）。引申為名詞，指説話的內容，即言論、言語，如"言簡意賅"（言語簡練而意思完備，形容説話，寫文章簡明扼要）。

甲骨文

金 文

小 篆

In the Oracle-Bone Inscriptions and Bronze Inscriptions, the character 言 looks like a tongue at the top of which is added a short stroke, signalling that a man is waving his tongue, i.e. speaking. Therefore the primary meaning of 言 is "to speak", e.g. 直言不諱 (to call a spade a spade), from which has derived its use for what is talked or written about, e.g. 言論 (speech); 言語 (talk); 言簡意賅 (〔of speech or article〕concise and comprehensive).

yīn

音和言都是指從口中發出聲音，最初本無區別，所以金文音、言可以互用。後來二字的用法發生分別，言字專指人說話的動作或說話的內容，而音字則泛指從口中發出來的任何聲響，所以音字就在言字的基礎上附加一小橫，以示區別。音的本義指聲音，又指樂聲，引申為指消息、信息等。

【音信】往來的信件和消息。

【音容】指人的聲音和容貌。

【音樂】用有組織的樂聲來表達人們思想感情、反映現實生活的一種藝術。

金文

小篆

音 and 言 both referred to the sound made in the mouth and meant the same at the beginning. They were interchangeable in the Bronze Inscriptions. Gradually, however, differences appeared in the usage of these two characters. 言 began to denote exclusively the activity of speaking or what is said while 音 kept its original sense, i.e. sound made in the mouth. To show the difference in writing there was an extra stroke inserted in the mouth part for 音. Nowadays 音 primarily refers to sounds, including musical sounds, and its extended meanings include "information", "message", etc.

【音信】 mail; message

【音容】 one's voice and countenance

【音樂】 music

yá

牙，即牙齒。小篆的牙字，像人的牙齒上下交錯之形；古文的牙字從齒，其意更為顯著。在古代，牙多指象牙，如牙尺、牙板、牙管等；又用作牙旗的簡稱。

【牙口】指牲口的年齡。又指老年人牙齒的咀嚼力。

【牙爪】即爪牙，指官吏的隨從差役。

【牙雕】在象牙上雕刻形象、花紋的藝術，也指用像牙雕刻成的工藝品。

金文

小篆

牙 means "tooth". In the Later Seal Character, the character 牙 has the shape of an upper tooth interlocked with a lower tooth. In the Ancient Script, 牙 has a component 齒, which brings out its meaning more noticeably. In former times, 牙 was usually used to refer to the tooth of an elephant, e.g. 牙尺 (ivory ruler), 牙板 (ivory tablet) and 牙管 (ivory penholder). And 牙 was used as an abbreviation of the general's banner (牙旗).

【牙口】 the age of a draught animal; the condition of an old person's teeth

【牙爪】 (also 爪牙) talons and fangs; lackeys; underlings

【牙雕】 ivory carving

chǐ

齒就是牙齒。甲骨文的齒是一個象形字，像人口中上下兩排牙齒之形。金文、小篆的齒字增加了一個止字符號表示讀音，齒字於是由原來的象形字變成了形聲字。

【齒舌】猶言口舌，指人的議論。

【齒髮】牙齒與頭髮，借指人的年齡。

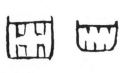

甲骨文　　　　　　金文　　　　　　小篆

齒, the same as 牙, also means "tooth". In the Oracle-Bone Inscrioptions, the character 齒, a pictograph, looks like the two rows of teeth in a mouth. In the Bronze Inscriptions and Later Seal Character, there is a phonetic 止 added on the top, resulting in a phonetic compound.

【齒舌】(also 口舌) exchange of words

【齒髮】(lit.) teeth and hair; age

xiāo

囂字由"頁"和四個"口"組成，頁指人頭（參見"頁"字條），一個人四面都是口，表示說話的人很多，聲音嘈雜，有"吵鬧"、"喧嘩"之義，如成語"甚囂塵上"（指人聲喧鬧，塵土飛揚，後來用於形容議論紛紛，多含貶義）。

【囂塵】指喧鬧和塵埃。（見"甚囂塵上"）
【囂張】指為人跋扈，放肆張揚之義，如"氣焰囂張"。
【囂浮】指為人心浮氣躁，做事不沉着。

金 文

小 篆

The character 囂 consists of a head part (頁) and four mouth parts (口), i.e. a man with four mouths at the corners. It signals that many people are speaking at the same time, hence the meaning "noisy". For example, it is used in the idiom 甚囂塵上 (noisy and dusty) to describe a situation, usually pejoratively, in which many people are talking about something at the same time.

【囂塵】noisy and dusty
【囂張】arrogant and aggressive
【囂浮】impetuous; flashy

xùn

甲骨文、金文的訊字是個會意字，像一個人雙手被繩索反縛在背後之形，被縛之人即為戰俘或罪犯，左邊的"口"表示審問之意。因此，訊字的本義為"審問戰俘或罪犯"，又特指戰俘，如"折首執訊"（砍敵人的頭和抓到俘虜）。小篆以後，訊字變為形聲字，原來的本義就罕為人知了。於是訊字就被用為一般的"詢問"、"查問"之義；引申為名詞，指信息、音訊，如唐儲光羲詩："有客山中至，言傳故人訊。"

甲骨文　　　　　金文　　　　　小篆

In the Oracle-Bone Inscriptions and Bronze Inscriptions, the character 訊, and ideograph, looks like a man with his two hands bound at the back, plus a mouth part on the left. The man bound signifies a prisoner of war or a criminal, and the mouth stands for interrogation. Hence 訊 originally meant "to interrogate a prisoner of war or a criminal". It may also denote the prisoner of war in particular, as is used in 折首執訊 (to chop off the heads of enemies or capture them). In the Later Seal Character, it becomes a phonetic compound and the original meaning is lost. It has come to be used in the sense of "enquiry", from which derive the meaning of "message" or "information". For example, Chu Guangxi of the Tang Dynasty has the lines: 有客山中至, 言傳故人訊 (a guest coming to the mount, brings news of an old friend).

shǒu

手是人體上肢的總稱，一般指腕以下能夠持物的部份。古文字的手字，正像一隻人手的形狀，上面的分支代表五個手指，下面是手臂。在漢字中，凡從手的字都與手或手旁（扌）的動作有關，如打、拍、扶、拿等。

【手下】指所屬的人，猶部下。

【手冊】記事小本。今也稱各種專業資料或一般知識性小冊子。

【手忙腳亂】形容遇事慌張，不知如何是好。

金文

小篆

The character 手 is a cover term for the upper limb of a human being, but it generally refers to the moveable part below the wrist, i.e. hand. In ancient writing systems, 手 has the shape of a man's upper limb: the upper branches denoting the five fingers and the lower part the arm. Characters with 手 as a component all indicate activities related to hand, e.g. 打 (to hit), 拍 (to pat), 扶 (to support with the hand) and 拿 (to take).

【手下】 (also 部下) subordinate

【手冊】 handbook

【手忙腳亂】 in a frantic rush

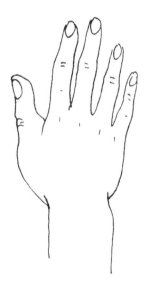

zhǎo

爪字的本義為覆手持取，其實也就是"抓"的本字。甲骨文爪字，像一隻向下伸出的手而特別突出手指的部份；金文的爪字則更在指端添上指甲，所以爪字的本義也指人的手指，又是指甲和趾甲的通稱，後來引申為指動物的腳——爪子。

【爪牙】爪和牙，是鳥獸用於攻擊和防衛的主要工具。引申為指武臣；又比喻為得力的助手、親信、黨羽等。

甲骨文　　　　金　文　　　　小　篆

As the original form of 抓 (grasp), the character 爪 meant to grasp something with the palm downward at the beginning. In the Oracle-Bone Inscriptions, it looks like a hand reaching downward with the fingers branching out. In the Bronze Inscriptions, there are finger nails added at the fingertips, so 爪 has come to mean primarily fingers, or fingernails and toenails. Later, its meaning has been further extended to cover the claws of animals.

【爪牙】(also 牙爪) talons and fangs; lackeys; underlings

gōng

肱是指人的胳膊從肩到肘的部份，也泛指胳膊。甲骨文的肱字，是在手形（又）的臂肘部位加一個隆起的指示符號，以表示臂肘所在的位置。此字形為《說文》小篆所本。而小篆肱字的異體在原字形上增加肉旁（月），又為楷書肱字所本。

甲骨文

小篆

肱 refers to the upper arm, or sometimes the whole arm. In the Oracle-Bone Inscriptions, the character 肱 looks like an arm, with a raised sign indicating the position of elbow. This is the origin of the character 肱 in the Later Seal Character, as is recorded in the *Origin of Chinese Characters*. Its variant in the Later Seal Character is the result of an addition of 月 to the original form, which in turn becomes the basis of 肱 in the Regular Script.

ZUǑ

左和右一樣，最初本是一個象形字。甲骨文就是一隻向左伸出的手形，後來才在手形下加"工"，成為左字的定形。所以左字的本義指左手，引申為方位名詞，凡在左手一邊的都叫"左"，與"右"相對。

【左右】左和右兩方面，又指旁側，引申為指身邊跟隨或侍候的人；用作動詞，則有輔助、支配、影響等義。

甲骨文　　　　金文　　　　　小篆

The character 左, like 右, was a pictograph at the beginning. In the Oracle-Bone Inscriptions, it looks like a hand stretching towards the left. The final form was established after the part 工 was added to it later. Hence it has the primary meaning of left hand, from which has derived its locative use to refer to anything which is on the left-hand side, opposite to 右 (right).

【左右】 (1) the left and right hands; attendants (2) to assist; to influence; to control

yòu

右字本是一個象形字。甲骨文的右字，就像是一隻向右邊伸出的手形。此字又可隸定為"又"，是右的本字。後來由於"又"多借用為副詞，所以金文就在"又"下增加一個"口"，作為表示右手或左右的右的專字。因此，右的本義指右手，引申為方位名詞，凡在右手一邊的皆稱"右"，與"左"相對。

| 甲骨文 | 金 文 | 小 篆 |

The character 右 was a pictograph at the beginning. In the Oracle-Bone Inscriptions, it looks like a hand stretching toward the right. This character could be regularized as 又, which was the original form of 右. As 又 was more usually used in the function of an adverb, a component 口 was added to it at the time of the Bronze Inscriptions to make it a separate character. So the character 右 means "right hand", or as a locative, "right-hand side", opposite to 左 (left).

cùn

寸字是個指事字。小篆的寸字，從又從一，"又"是手形，"一"為指示符號，在手下之左側，指的是手掌以下約一寸的地方，即中醫診脈的部位，又稱"寸口"。所以，寸的本義是指寸口，為經脈部位名稱。寸又用作長度單位名稱，十分為一寸，十寸為一尺。又形容極短或極小，如寸土、寸步、寸陰等。

【寸心】(1) 即心。心位於胸中方寸之地，故稱"寸心"。

(2) 微小的心意。

【寸進】微小的進步。

【寸隙】短暫的空閒。

【寸步難移】形容走路困難。

小篆

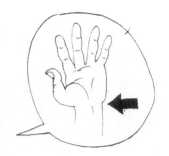

The character 寸 is an indicative. In the Later Seal Character, it consists of 又 and 一; the former means "the right hand" and the latter is a sign marking the position on the lower arm about a little longer than an inch away from the wrist. This is the place where a traditional Chinese doctor feels the pulse of a patient. This shows that 寸 was originally the name of a point on the network of channels through which, according to the traditional Chinese medicine, vital energy circulates. But 寸 is also a measure of length, equal to ten 分 or one tenth of 尺 in the Chinese System, and one third or a decimetre in the Metric System. Consequently it may also be used to describe things which are short or small, as is shown in expressions like 寸土 (an inch of land), 寸步 (a tiny step) and 寸陰 (an extremely short time).

【寸心】(1) heart (2) (a small token of) feelings

【寸進】a little progress

【寸隙】a short moment of leisure

【寸步難移】unable to move a single step

yǒu

古文字的友字，像兩隻同時伸出來的右手，兩手相交表示握手，所以甲骨文的友字還特意用橫畫把兩隻手連在一起。握手是為了表示友好，就像現在常見的老友重逢，大家都伸出右手緊緊相握，以表達親密友好之情。因此，友字的本義就是我們現在所說的"朋友"。不過在古代，"朋"和"友"的含義是有區別的："同門為朋"，即跟從同一個老師學習的人稱為"朋"；"同志為友"，即是說志同道合的人才能稱為"友"。

甲骨文

金 文

小 篆

In ancient writing systems, 友 looks like two stretching-out right hands, signalling two people are shaking hands. In the Oracle-Bone Inscriptions, there are sometimes even two horizontal strokes linking the two hands to emphasize the point. The purpose of shaking hands with someone is to show one's friendship with him, just like what happens when old friends meet nowadays. So the primary meaning of 友 is what is now known as 朋友 (friend). In ancient times, however, 朋 and 友 had different meanings: 同門為朋 (those who learn under the same teacher are 朋); 同志為友 (those who follow the same ideal are 友).

pān

小篆的攀字本是個會意字，突出強調一雙向兩邊伸出的手，以表示用雙手抓住東西引身向上攀援的意思。後來的攀變成為從手樊聲的形聲字。攀的本義為攀援，即用手抓住東西向上爬的意思，引申為牽挽、抓牢，又引申為依附、拉攏之義。此外，攀還有拗、折的意思。

【攀折】拉折，折取。

【攀龍附鳳】比喻依附有聲望的人而立名。後來特指依附帝王以建立功業。

小篆

In the Later Seal Character, the character 攀 was originally an ideograph, using a pair of hands stretching out in opposite directions to indicate that a man is grasping at things in order to climb up. At a later stage, it changed into a phonetic compound with 手 as the radical and 樊 as the phonetic. The primary meaning of 攀, therefore, is "to climb", from which have derived its extended meanings "to take hold of", "to attach oneself to" and "to seek connections with". In addition, it may mean "to pull down and break off (twigs)" and "to pick (flowers)."

【攀折】 to pull down and break off (twigs); to pick (flowers)

【攀龍附鳳】 to play up to people of power and influence, esp., the emperor and his ministers

fǎn

反即"扳"字的初文。古文字的反字,像一個人在懸崖峭壁下用手向上攀援之狀,本義即為扳、攀,引申為翻轉、反覆之義,又引申為方向正反的反。隨着引申義的進一步擴大,反字的本義漸漸隱晦,於是只好在原字上又增加一個手旁,另造了一個"扳"字來表示攀援之義。

| 甲骨文 | 金文 | 小篆 |

反 was the original form of 扳 (pān, meaning the same as 攀). In ancient writing systems, 反 looks like a man climbing a steep cliff with hands, hence the original meaning "to climb", from which have derived its meanings of "turn over" and "the opposite", As it is more and more used in its extended meanings, and its original meaning is falling into disuse, a new character 扳, with a component 手 added to 反, has been created to express the meaning "to climb".

zhēng

古文字的爭字，像上下兩隻手在同時搶奪一件物體的形狀。爭的本義為搶奪，引申為爭鬥、競爭、爭辯、爭取等義。

【爭端】爭訟的依據。後多指引起雙方爭的事由。

【爭執】爭論中各執己見，互不相讓。

【爭風吃醋】因追求同一異性而嫉妒、爭吵。

甲骨文

小篆

In ancient writing systems, the character 爭 looks like two hands, one up and the other down, fighting to get an object. The primary meaning of 爭 is "to fight for", from which have derived its extended meanings "to fight", "to compete", "to argue", "to strive", etc.

【爭端】controversial issue

【爭執】to disagree; to dispute

【爭風吃醋】to fight for a man's (woman's) favour; to quarrel from jealousy

shòu

甲骨文、金文的受字，上面一隻手，下面又是一隻手，中間為"舟"，表示一方給予、一方接受的意思。所以受字的本義，既有給予的意思，又有接受的意思。在古書中兩種用法並存。後來在受字旁再加手旁，另造一個"授"字來表示用手給予的意思。這樣，受字後來就專作"接受"的意思來使用了。

【受用】接受財物以供官府開支，又指得到好處、利益。

【受命】古帝王統治者託神權以鞏固統治，自稱受命於天。今又指接受任務和命令。

【受寵若驚】受人寵愛而感到意外的驚喜和不安。

甲骨文　　　金文　　　小篆

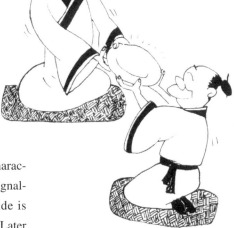

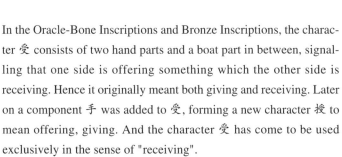

In the Oracle-Bone Inscriptions and Bronze Inscriptions, the character 受 consists of two hand parts and a boat part in between, signalling that one side is offering something which the other side is receiving. Hence it originally meant both giving and receiving. Later on a component 手 was added to 受, forming a new character 授 to mean offering, giving. And the character 受 has come to be used exclusively in the sense of "receiving".

【受用】 to benefit from; to enjoy

【受命】 to receive instructions

【受寵若驚】 to be overwhelmed by an unexpected favour

yuán

爰為"援"的本字。甲骨文爰字，像人一隻手抓住棍棒的一端而將另一端遞到另一個人的手中，以表示援引之意。所以《說文解字》稱："爰，引也。"爰字後來多引申為付與、更換等文，又用作語首助詞。其本義則為"援"字所代替。

【爰居】遷居。

【爰田】指輪休耕種的田地。

甲骨文　　　　　金文　　　　　小篆

爰 was the original form of 援. In the Oracle-Bone Inscriptions, the character 爰 looks like a man holding one end of a stick in hand and giving the other end to another man, signalling "to lead (the way)". Thus Xu Shen says in his *Origin of Chinese Characters*, " 爰 means to lead (the way)". Nowadays, however, 爰 is mainly used in the senses "to hand over", "to replace", or as a sentence initial particle. And its original meaning is expressed by 援.

【爰居】to change residence

【爰田】fields used rotationally

dòu

鬥

甲骨文的鬥字，像兩個人在打架，你抓住我的頭髮，我給你一拳，扭成一團的樣子。它的本義是廝打、搏鬥，引申為爭鬥、戰鬥之義。

甲骨文　　　　　　　　小篆

In the Oracle-Bone Inscriptions, the character 鬥 looks like two men in a fight, grasping each other's hair and grappling together. Its primary meaning is to exchange blows, to wrestle, but it is also used in the general sense of fight.

nào

鬧字是個會意字。小篆的鬧字從市從鬥，表示有人在市集上相爭打鬥之意。鬧的本義為喧嘩、不安靜，引申為吵鬧、擾亂等義。

【鬧哄】吵鬧。

【鬧事】煩擾之事。又指聚眾搗亂，破壞社會秩序。

小篆

The character 鬧 is an ideograph. In the Later Seal Character, it consists of 市 (market) and 鬥 (fight), signalling people are fighting in the market. The primary meaning of 鬧 is "noisy", "unquiet", from which have derived the senses of "quarrel", "make trouble", etc.

【鬧哄】 to quarrel; to wrangle

【鬧事】 to make trouble; to create disturbance

ruò

甲骨文若字，像人用雙手梳理自己頭髮之形。梳理頭髮，可以使其通順，所以若字有順的意思，引申為指順從、順應，在甲骨文中則用為順利、吉利之義。此字後來多借用為如、像、似等義，其本來的意義卻漸漸消失。

【若即若離】好像接近，又好像隔離。形容對人保持一定距離，態度模棱。

【若無其事】像沒有那回事一樣。形容遇事鎮定或不把事放在心上。

甲骨文　　　金文　　　小篆

In the Oracle-Bone Inscriptions, the character 若 looks like a man combing his hair with his two hands. Through combing the hair may become smooth, hence 若 originally meant "smooth", and "obedient", "conformable" were its extended meanings. In the Oracle-Bone Inscriptions, it is used in the sense "(to accomplish something) smoothly and successfully". Nowadays, however, it means "like", "the same as", and its original meaning has fallen into disuse.

【若即若離】to be neither close nor far apart; to maintain a lukewarm relationship

【若無其事】to appear as if nothing had happened; calm

fú

甲骨文、金文的俘字，從爪從子，像以手逮人之形；或從
彳，表示驅人行走之意。俘的本義為擄獲，即在戰爭中擄掠人
口；又指俘虜，即在戰爭中被擄掠的人口。

甲骨文　　　　　金　文　　　　　小　篆

In the Oracle-Bone Inscriptions and Bronze
Inscriptions, the character 俘, consisting of
爪 (to grasp) and 子 (man), looks like a hand
capturing a man. Sometimes, it has 彳 (to
walk) as its component, signalling to drive
someone along the road. The primary meaning of 俘 is to capture people in the war, but
it is also used to refer to those captured, i.e.
captives.

fù

金文的付字，從人從又，像人用手把一件東西遞交給另外一個人的樣子。字或從寸，與從"又"同義。所以，付的本義為交付、給與。

【付託】交給別人辦理。

【付賬】交錢結賬。

【付諸東流】把東西扔在水中沖走。多用來比喻希望落空，前功盡棄。

　金 文　　　　小 篆

In the Bronze Inscriptions, the character 付, consisting of 人 (man) and 又 (the right hand), looks like a man handing over something to another. Sometimes it has 寸 instead of 又, but means the same. Hence the primary meaning of 付 is to hand over, to give.

【付託】to entrust

【付賬】to pay a bill

【付諸東流】(lit.) to throw into the eastward flowing stream; to have one's previous efforts all wasted

jí

　　一個人在前面奔跑，另外一個人從後面追上來用手把他抓住，這就是及字所表達出來的意思。及的本義為追上、趕上，引申為到或至，又用作連詞，相當於"和"、"與"的作用。

甲骨文　　　　　　金 文　　　　　　小 篆

What the character 及 expresses is: a man catches up from behind and seizes the man who was previously running in the front. The original meaning of 及, therefore, was to catch up with, from which have derived the meanings "reach" or "come up to". But it can also be used as a conjunction, similar to 和 or 與 (and).

fú

金文扶字從夫從又，像用手攙扶一個人的形狀，小篆扶字從手夫聲，則變為形聲字。扶的本義為攙扶，引申為扶持、扶植、扶助、支持等義，又引申為倚持、倚仗之義。

【扶病】支持病體。現指帶病工作或行動。

【扶掖】攙扶，扶助。

【扶搏】乘風盤旋而上，比喻得意。

金文　　　　　小篆

In the Bronze Inscriptions, the character 扶, consisting of 夫 (man) and 又 (the right hand), looks like a man supporting another with his hand. In the Later Seal Character, it changes to a phonetic compound, with 手 as its radical and 夫 as its phonetic. The primary meaning of 扶 is to support, from which have derived its extended meanings "to help sustain", "to foster", "to prop up" and "to depend".

【扶病】 (to work) in spite of illness

【扶掖】 to support; to help

【扶搏】 fly up by the cyclone; to rise steeply in rank

chéng

甲骨文、金文的承字，像雙手托着一個跪着的人的形狀。承的本義為捧着，引申為接受、承擔，又引申為繼續、繼承之義。

【承乏】謙辭，表示所任職位一時無適當人選，暫由自己充任。

【承襲】沿襲。又指繼承封爵。

【承上啟下】承接前者，引出後者，多指文章內容的轉折。

甲骨文

金文

小篆

In the Oracle-Bone Inscriptions and Bronze Inscriptions, the character 承 looks like two hands holding a man on his knees. The primary meaning of 承 is to hold, from which have derived its extended meanings "to accept", "to undertake", "to continue" and "to succeed (to something)".

【承乏】 self-depreciatory, used by sb. who is about to accept a new position to mean though he is unqualified for it, he will take it up temporarily for lack of a better choice

【承襲】 (1) to follow (a tradition, etc.) (2) to inherit

【承上啟下】 to form a connecting link between the preceding and the following (as in a piece of writing, etc.)

chéng

甲骨文的丞字，像一個人陷落坑中，有人以雙手將他援救出來；金文的丞字省去坑形，但以手援救之義不變。所以丞字的本義為援救，其實也就是拯救的"拯"的本字；又引申為"輔佐"、"協助"之義。又古代中央和地方長官的副職或助手多稱"丞"，如大理寺丞、府丞、縣丞等。

【丞相】古代中央政府的最高行政長官，職責為協助皇帝處理國家政務。

甲骨文

金 文

小 篆

In the Oracle-Bone Inscriptions, the character 丞 looks like a man in a pitfall, and there are two hands on top in an attempt to save him. In the Bronze Inscriptions, the part representing the pitfall is omitted, but the meaning "to save someone with the hands" is not changed. Hence the original meaning of 丞 was to save. In other words, it was the original form of 拯 (rescue). And to assist and help is one of its extended meanings. In the past 丞 was also used as a noun to refer to the assistant officers in the central or local governments, e.g. 大理寺丞 (assistant director of Dalisi Bureau), 府丞 (vice-mayor) and 縣丞 (county magistrate's assistant).

【丞相】prime minister

yìn

甲骨文、金文的印字，像用手按着一個人的頭，其本來的意思就是按壓，也就是壓抑的"抑"的本字。印字後來由按壓之義引申為專指需要按壓才能留下印跡的圖章印信。先秦時候的印稱為"璽"；秦始皇統一中國後，規定只有皇帝的印才能稱璽，其他人的一律叫做"印"。而凡是由按壓留下的痕跡都可以稱為印，如手印、腳印、印刷等。

甲骨文　　　　　金文　　　　　小篆

In the Oracle-Bone Inscriptions and Bronze Inscriptions, the character 印 looks like a hand pressing the head of a man. Hence its original meaning "to depress." In other words, 印 was the original form of 抑 (repress). But it was later on used with reference to a seal or stamp, which had to be depressed in order to leave any mark. Before the Qin Dynasty, seals were generally known as 璽. However, after the unification of China by the First Emperor of Qin, it was stipulated that only the seal of the emperor could be called 璽, and all the others would have to be called 印. And the character 印 is also used for other marks which result from the act of depressing, e.g. 手印 (finger print), 腳印 (foot print) and 印刷 (printing).

tuǒ

古文字的妥字，像一個女子被人用手按頭，跪在地上俯首帖耳的樣子。妥字的本文指服帖、屈服，引申為安穩、穩當之義。

【妥帖】穩當、牢靠。
【妥善】妥當完善。
【妥協】用讓步的方法避免衝突或爭執。

甲骨文　　　　金　文　　　　小　篆

In ancient writing systems, the character 妥 looks like a woman on her knees obediently, whose head is pressed by a hand. The primary meaning of 妥 is "obedient", "submissive", from which have derived its extended meanings of "steady" and "reliable".

【妥帖】steady; reliable
【妥善】well arranged
【妥協】to compromise

XĪ

古文字的奚字，像一個人被人用繩索拴住脖子，繩的一端則被抓在另一個人的手裡。用繩索把人拴住，牽着他去幹活以免逃脫，這是奴隸社會常見的現象，而被拴住的人就是那些沒有自由的奴隸。因此，奚的本義是指奴隸。古代自由民犯了罪，被拘入官府為奴的，也稱做"奚"。現在用作姓氏的奚氏，其來源大概也與古代的奴隸有關。

【奚奴】本指女奴，後通稱男女奴僕為"奚奴"。

甲骨文

金 文

小 篆

In ancient writing systems, the character 奚 looks like a man around whose neck is a rope and the other end of the rope is in the hand of another man. It was a commonplace in the slave society to bind a man with a rope and to lead him to work so that he could not run away. And those who were bound were slaves, who had no freedom whatsoever. So the original meaning of 奚 was slave. But it could also be used with reference to any freeman who had committed a crime and become a servant to an officer. The character 奚, now used as a surname, perhaps also originated from the slave system.

【奚奴】(1) female slave (2) servant

ZÚ

足字是個象形字。甲骨文的足，像一腳趾、腳掌、腳脛俱全的人腳之形；金文字形略有簡化，除仍保留趾形（止）外，掌、脛部份則以一圓圈代替。足的本義為腳，後借用為充實、充足、足夠等義。漢字中凡從"足"之字都與腳及其動作有關，如跟、蹈、路、跳、踐等。

【足下】古代下稱上或同輩相稱的敬詞。

【足色】指金銀的成色十足。

【足夠】達到應有的或能滿足需要的程度。

【足智多謀】智慧高，善於謀劃。

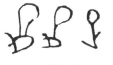

甲骨文

金文

小篆

足 is a pictograph. In the Oracle-Bone Inscriptions, the character 足 has the shape of a complete human foot: from toe to heel, even including the ankle. In the Bronze Inscriptions, the character is simplified: only the toe is retained, the other parts being reduced to a circle. The primary meaning of 足 is foot, but it is also used in the senses of "substantial", "sufficient" and "enough". Characters with 足 as a component all have to do with foot and activities connected with it, e.g. 跟 (to follow), 蹈 (to dance), 路 (road), 跳 (to jump) and 踐 (to trample).

【足下】 honorific, used in a letter to address a friend

【足色】 (of gold or silver) of standard purity

【足夠】 enough; sufficient

【足智多謀】 wise and full of stratagems; resourceful

zhǐ

甲骨文止字，是人的腳趾形，其本義為腳趾，又泛指人的
腳。"腳不前行"為止，所以止字又有停止、靜止、棲息等
義。而在漢字中，凡由"止"字所組成的字，大都與腳的行為
動作有關，如步、此、陟、涉等。

甲骨文	金 文	小 篆

In the Oracle-Bone Inscriptions, the character 止 has the
shape of a human toe. Hence it primarily refers to the toe,
but it is also used in a general sense to refer to the foot. As
止 means the foot which stays in place, it also takes on the
meanings "to stop", "to be at a standstill" and "to rest".
Characters with 止 as a component all have to do with
activities connected with the foot, e.g. 步 (step), 此 (here),
陟 (to ascend a height) and 涉 (to wade).

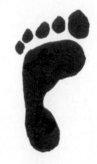

bù

甲骨文、金文的步字，像一前一後兩個腳趾的形狀，表示一左一右兩足交替前行的意思，所以步的本義為行走、步行。步又是一種長度單位。古代以一舉足為跬（**kuǐ**），舉足兩次為一步。如《荀子·勸學》："不積跬步，無以致千里。"又周代以八尺為一步，秦代以六尺為一步，三百步為一里。

甲骨文　　　　　金文　　　　　小篆

In the Oracle-Bone Inscriptions and Bronze Inscriptions, the character 步 looks like two toes, one in front of the other, signalling the two feet are moving forward alternatively. Hence its primary meaning "to walk". 步 may also be used as a noun referring to the distance covered in walking. But how long this distance is varies with the system used. According to an informal system, 步 is equal to two steps while one step is known as 跬. Thus *Xun Zi* (Hsun-Tzu) says, "不積跬步, 無以致千里. Without the accumulation of single steps, one cannot travel the distance of a thousand miles", In the formal system of the Zhou Dynasty, 步 is equal to eight 尺 whereas in that of the Qin Dynasty, it is six 尺 long and three hundred 步 constitute 里 (equal to 500 hundred metres in the Metric System.).

ZǑU

　　金文的走字，上面是一個甩開兩臂向前奔跑的人形，下面的"止"代表腳，表示行動之意。因此，走的本義為跑、奔跑，又指逃跑。古代跑步叫做"走"，走路則稱為"行"。近古時代，走字才漸漸由跑步之義轉變成行走之義。漢字中凡從"走"的字，大多與跑的動作有關，如趨、赴、趕、超、趣等。

| 金 文 | 石 鼓 文 | 小 篆 |

In the Bronze Inscriptions, the upper part of the character 走 looks like a man running forward with his arms swinging, and the lower part 止 stands for the foot. Hence the original meaning of 走 was to run, or to run away. In Classical Chinese, 走 meant "to run" while "to walk" (the present-day meaning of 走) was expressed by the character 行. It was not until the Song Dynasty that the meaning of 走 was gradually shifted from "run" to "walk". Characters with 走 as a component most have to do with running, e.g. 趨 (to hurry), 赴 (to go), 趕 (to rush), 超 (to overtake) and 趣 (〔arch.〕to hurry).

qǐ

甲骨文的企字，像一個獨體的人形而特別突出了人形的足部，以表示踮腳站立的意思。有的企字的形體，足部與人體分離，於是成為一個從人從止的合體字。這種變體，為小篆企字所本。企的本義為舉踵，即踮起腳跟的意思，今用為盼望之義。

【企佇】踮起腳跟，翹首而望。

【企求】希望得到。

【企羨】仰慕。

【企圖】圖謀、打算。多含貶義。

甲骨文

小篆

In the Oracle-Bone Inscriptions, the character 企 looks like a man with his foot especially prominent, signalling that the man is standing on tiptoe. Sometimes, the foot is separated from the body, resulting in a two part character consisting of 人 (man) and 止 (foot). This is the origin of the form in the Later Seal Character. The original meaning of 企 was "to stand on tiptoe". But it is now more usually used in the sense "to expect".

【企佇】to stand on tiptoe and look into the distance

【企求】to desire to gain

【企羨】to admire; to look up to

【企圖】to attempt

bēn

金文奔字由一個"夭"字和三個"止"組成。夭是一個甩臂奔跑的人形，下面加上三個止（腳趾）表示很多人一起奔跑。石鼓文奔字由三個夭和三個止組成，正是眾人奔走的真實寫照。所以，奔的本義是眾人奔走，引申為快跑、急走、逃亡等義。後來由於形近訛誤，小篆奔字夭下面的三隻腳（止）變成三叢草（卉）。這樣，眾人奔走的奔就變成一個人在草上飛走了。

金 文

石鼓文

小 篆

In the Bronze Inscriptions, the character 奔 is made up of a part like a man running with his arms swinging (夭) and three toe parts (止), signalling that many people are running together. In the Stone-Drum Inscriptions, it is made up of three 夭 and three 止, and the meaning of many people on the run is brought out more clearly. Hence the original meaning of 奔 is many people on the run, from which have derived its extended meanings "to run fast", "to hurry" and "to flee from home". However, the three toes were mistakenly changed into three clusters of grass in the Later Seal Character, resulting in a change of image from many people on the run to one man running on grass.

xiān

古文字的先字,從止(即腳趾)在人上,一隻腳走在人家的前頭,這就是先。所以先字的本義為前,與"後"相對;又指時間上的在前,即"早"的意思。

【先生】年長有學問的人,又特指老師。現在則多用為對成年男士的尊稱。

【先河】河是海的本源,故祭祀時先祭河後祭海。後用來指事物或學術的創始人和倡導者。

【先鋒】作戰時率領先頭部隊在前迎敵的將領。

【先導】在前引導。又指以身作則,為人之先。

甲骨文

金文

小篆

In ancient writing systems, the character 先 has a toe part on top of a man part, signalling that a man has taken a step ahead of another. Hence the primary meaning of 先 is "before in position", as against 後 (back). But it can also mean "before in time", i.e. "earlier".

【先生】(1) teacher (2) mister

【先河】the originator of a new theory

【先鋒】vanguard

【先導】guide

zhī

甲骨文的之字，上面的"止"代表向外邁出的腳，下面一
橫代表出發的地方，表示離開此地，去到彼處的意思。因此，
之字的本義為往、至、去到。此字後來多借用為虛詞，有代
詞、連詞、介詞、副詞、助詞等多種用途，其本義反而少有人
使用了。

【之子】這個人。

【之死靡它】至死不變。

【之乎者也】四字都是古漢語的語助字。常用以諷刺舊式文人的
咬文嚼字、食古不化。

甲骨文

金 文

小 篆

In the Oracle-Bone Inscriptions, the chatacter 之
has a foot part on top of a horizontal line. The former
signifies the action to take a step forward and the
latter denotes the starting point. Hence the original
meaning of 之 was "to go to (a place)". However it
is more usually used as a particle in the functions of
pronoun, conjunction, preposition, adverb, etc.,
rather than in its original sense.

【之子】this man

【之死靡它】to remain the same until death

【之乎者也】pedantic terms; archaisms

cǐ

此

古文字的此字，從止從人，止即趾，代表腳，又含有停步的意思。甲骨文的此字，像一個人站立不動的樣子，而主要是強調人站立的地方。因此，此的本義是指人站立的地方（即此地），引申為指示代詞"這"，與"彼"、"那"相對。又引申為指這樣、這般。

【此起彼伏】這裡起來，那裡落下，表示連續不斷。

甲骨文　　　　金文　　　　小篆

In ancient writing systems, the character 此 consists of 止 and 人. 止 means "toe" or "foot", but it may also mean "to stop". In the Oracle-Bone Inscriptions, this character was used to refer to a man standing still, and, perhaps more so, the place where a man stood. But that was its original meaning. Nowadays it is used as a demonstrative, meaning "this", opposite to 彼 or 那 (that), or an adverb, meaning "in this way".

【此起彼伏】as one falls, another rises

zhèng

正為"征"的本字。甲骨文正字，上部的方框代表四面圍牆的城邑，下從止，表示舉趾向城邑進發征行的意思。金文正字，上面的方框或填實為方塊，或簡化成一橫，漸失形象意味。正的本義為征行、行伐；引申為中正、平直之義，與"偏"、"斜"相對；又指正面，與"反"相對。

【正大光明】正直無私，光明磊落。

【正襟危坐】理好衣襟端正地坐着，表示嚴肅或尊敬。

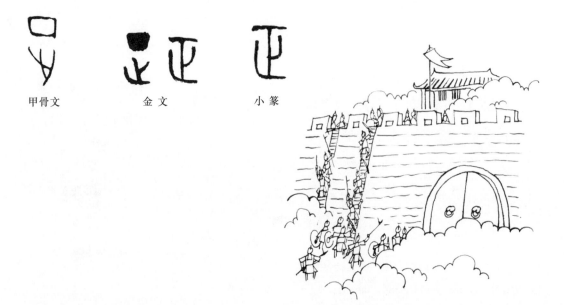

甲骨文　　　　金 文　　　　小 篆

正 was the original form of 征. In the Oracle-Bone Inscriptions, the upper part of the character 正, the square, stands for a town with walls on its four sides, and the lower part 止 means to take steps towards the town and attack it. In the Bronze Inscriptions, its upper part is either replaced by a solid square or simplified into a horizontal line, gradually losing its pictorial sense. The original meaning of 正 was to go on an expedition, especially a punitive one. But it is now usually used in the sense of "upright", "straight", as against 偏 (slanting), 斜 (tilted). It can also be used to refer to the right side, opposite to 反 (the reverse side).

【正大光明】open and aboveboard

【正襟危坐】to straighten one's clothes and sit properly; to be all seriousness

nì

甲骨文逆字，上面像一個迎面而來的人形，而下面的止形則是相迎而往，所以逆字的本義為迎，如《國語‧晉語》二："呂甥逆君於秦。"由於二人逆向而行，所以逆字又有倒向、不順、違背等義。

【逆流】指水倒流，又指迎着水流的方向而向上行。

【逆境】指不順利的境遇。

【逆旅】客舍，指迎止賓客之處。

【逆取順守】以武力奪取天下曰逆取，修文教以治天下曰順守。

甲骨文　　　　金文　　　　小篆

In the Oracle-Bone Inscriptions, the upper part of the character 逆 looks like a man coming towards here, while the lower part 止 suggests going towards there. Hence the original meaning of 逆 was to go to meet. For example, there is a line "呂甥逆君於秦 (Lü Sheng went to meet the King in Qin)" in *Guo Yu*. When one goes to meet another, the two of them go in opposite directions. So 逆 takes on the meanings of "opposite" and "contrary".

【逆流】adverse current

【逆境】adverse circumstances

【逆旅】(arch.) guesthouse

【逆取順守】to seize power by force and rule by civil means

dá

甲骨文達字，像一個人（大）沿着大路（彳）向前行走，有的達字加"止"形表示行走之意。因此達字的本義是指在大路上行走，含通達、到、至等義，如四通八達、抵達等；引申為指對事理認識得透徹，如達觀、達識等；又有以物相送、表達之義，如轉達、傳達、詞不達意等。

甲骨文

金文

小篆

In the Oracle-Bone Inscriptions, the character 達 consists of a man part (大) and a road part (彳), signalling a man is walking on a road. To emphasize the point, sometimes a component 止 is added. So the original meaning of 達 was "to walk on a road", with the implication "to reach", "to arrive", e.g. 四通八達 (to extend in all directions) and 抵達 (to arrive). But it is also used in the sence "to understand thoroughly", e.g. 達觀 (to take things philosophically), 達識 (insightful); and in the sense "to convey", e.g. 轉達 (to pass on), 傳達 (to relay) and 詞不達意 (The words fail to convey the idea.)

yí

甲骨文的疑字，像一個人扶杖站立，左右旁顧之形；或從彳，表示出行迷路、猶豫不定的意思。疑的本義指迷惑、猶豫不定，引申為疑問、懷疑之義。

【疑似】是非難辨。

【疑義】指難於理解的文義或問題。

【疑神疑鬼】指神經過敏，無中生有。

甲骨文

金文

小篆

In the Oracle-Bone Inscriptions, the character 疑 looks like a man standing with the support of a walking stick and looking at the sides, signalling that he is not decided where to go. Sometimes it has a component 彳 to emphasize the point that the man has lost his way. The primary meaning of 疑 is "confusion" and "undecided", from which has derived its sense of "doubt".

【疑似】suspected to be

【疑義】doubtful point

【疑神疑鬼】to be terribly suspecious

zhì

古文字的陟字，像一左一右兩隻腳沿着陡坡向上登爬之形。其本義指登高，引申為升進、提高之義。

【陟降】升降，上下。又指日晷影的長短變化。

甲骨文

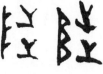

金 文

小 篆

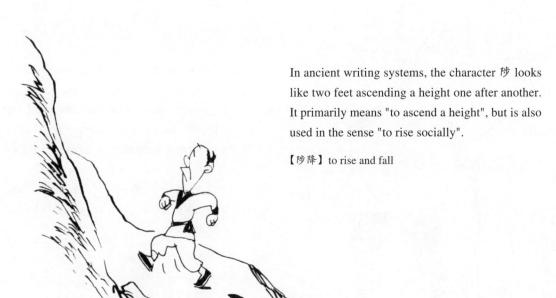

In ancient writing systems, the character 陟 looks like two feet ascending a height one after another. It primarily means "to ascend a height", but is also used in the sense "to rise socially".

【陟降】to rise and fall

jiàng

甲骨文、金文的降字，像一前一後兩隻腳從高坡上往下走的樣子。降的本義指從高處向下走，與"陟"相對，引申指降落、降低、下降，又引申為貶抑之義。同時，降字還可以讀 **xiáng**，用作動詞，有降伏、投降之義。

【降臨】來到。

【降水】下雨。

【降心相從】抑己而從人。

【降（xiáng）龍伏虎】使龍虎降伏，形容本領之大，法力之高。

甲骨文

金文

小篆

In the Oracle-Bone Inscriptions and Bronze Inscriptions, the character 降 looks like two feet descending from a height one after another. The primary meaning of 降, opposite to 陟, is to descend, from which have derived its extended meanings "to fall", "to lower" and "to belittle". In addition, 降, pronounced as xiáng, may mean "to subdue", "to surrender", etc.

【降臨】to befall

【降水】to rain

【降心相從】to suppress one's unwillingness to follow others

【降龍伏虎】to subdue the dragon and tame the tiger; to overcome powerful adversaries

shè

甲骨文、金文的涉字，中間是彎彎的一道水流，兩邊是兩隻足形，一左一右、一前一後，表示正在蹚水過河。小篆涉字左右都是水、中間一個步字（上下兩隻足形），也表示徒步渡水之意。涉的本義為步行渡水，引申為遊歷、到、面臨、進入等義，再引申為關連之義，如干涉、牽涉等。

【涉世】經歷世事。

【涉獵】廣泛涉及，指讀書多而不專精。

甲骨文

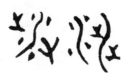

金文

小篆

In the Oracle-Bone Inscriptions and Bronze Inscriptions, the character 涉 has a part like a meandering flow of water on each side of which is a foot part, signalling that a man is wading through it. In the Later Seal Character, the character 涉 has 步 (to walk) in between two 水 (water), also signalling "to wade through water". But its meaning has been extended to cover the senses "to travel", "to reach", "to face", "to enter" and "to connect".

【涉世】to experience

【涉獵】to do desultory reading; to read cursorily

wèi

胃，指胃臟，屬消化器官，為人體五臟之一。胃是一個象形兼會意的字。古文字的胃字，上部是一個胃囊的形象，其中的四個小點代表胃中待消化的食物；下部從月（肉），則表示胃是人的肉體器官。

　金 文　　　　　小 篆

胃 refers to the stomach. the organ in which food is digested. The character 胃 is both a pictograph and ideograph. In ancient writing systems, its upper part looks like a bag containing food to be digested represented by the four dots in it; its lower part 月 (a variant of 肉, flesh), suggesting that the stomach is a fleshy organ.

lǚ

呂

古文字的呂字，像兩塊人（或動物）的脊骨，脊骨一塊接一塊連成一串，便是脊椎，所以小篆呂字中間加一豎表示連接之意。呂的本義指脊骨。這個意義後來為新造的"脊"字所取代。而呂字則借用來指古代音樂十二律中的陰律，總稱"六呂"；又用作姓氏名。

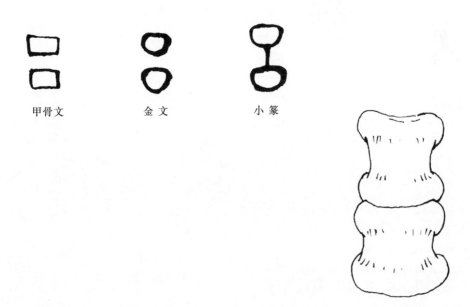

甲骨文　　　　　金 文　　　　　小 篆

In ancient writing systems, the character 呂 looks like two backbones of a man. The backbones linked together constitute a spine, that is why in the Later Seal Character, there is a vertical line linking the two bones. However, this original meaning, i.e. spine, is now expressed by a later creation脊. And the character 呂 is used as a cover term for six of the twelve tones recognized in traditional Chinese musical theory, known as 六呂. Besides, it is also used as a surname.

jǐ

脊，即脊骨，指人背部中間的椎骨。小篆的脊字，上部背肌和脊骨之形，下部從肉（月），表示骨肉相連之意。脊的本義指脊骨，引申為指物體中間高起的部份，如山脊、屋脊等。

【脊樑】脊骨為全身骨骼的主幹，如屋之有樑，故名。

【脊椎動物】有脊椎骨的動物，包括魚類、兩棲動物、爬行動物、鳥類和哺乳動物等。

小篆

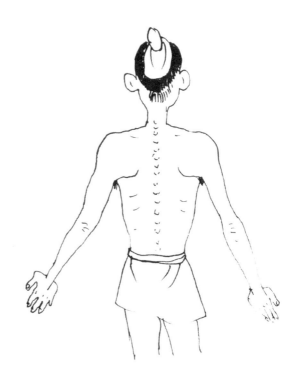

脊 refers to the spine, the row of bones in the centre of the back of a man. In the Later Seal Character, the upper part of the character 脊 has the shape of a spine in between back muscles, and the lower part is 肉 (flesh), suggesting that the spine is part of a human body. The primary meaning of 脊 is spine, but it is also used metaphorically for anything that has a rising middle part, e.g. 山脊 (mountain ridge), 屋脊 (the ridge of a roof).

【脊樑】spine

【脊椎動物】vertebrate

xìn

囟，即囟門，也叫囟腦門兒，是指嬰兒頭頂骨未合縫的地方。小篆的囟字，像人頭頂骨之形，中間交叉的地方即為囟門。

甲骨文

金 文

小 篆

囟 refers to the fontanelle, the membranous space in an infant's skull at angles of parietal bones. In the Later Seal Character, the character 囟 looks like a human skull seen from above, the cross in it represents the fontanelles.

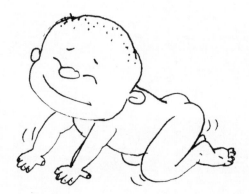

SĪ

在古代，人們誤認心為人的思維器官，故有關思想、意會和情感方面的字都從"心"。後來隨着科學水平的提高，人們慢慢意識到腦在人的思維中的重要作用。小篆的思字從囟從心，囟即腦門，表示人的思維是心腦並用的結果。楷書思字從田從心，則屬於訛變。思的本義為思考、想，引申為想念、懷念之義，又指思路、思緒。

【思想】思考，又指念頭、想法。作為一個哲學概念，思想是指客觀存在反映在人的意識中經過思維活動而產生的結果。

璽文

小篆

In ancient times, people mistakenly thought that the heart was the organ for thinking, and characters which had something to do with thinking, ideas and feelings all had 心 as a component. It is only in modern times that people realize it is the brain that does the thinking. In the Later Seal Character, the character 思 consists of 囟 and 心, the former referring to the brain here and the latter the heart. In other words, thinking is seen as a process performed by the brain and heart together. In the Regular Script, 思 consists of 田 and 心, resulting from an erroneous derivation. The primary meaning of 思 is "to think", from which have derived the senses: "to think of", "to cherish the memory of" and "train of thought".

【思想】(1) to think (2) ideas

xīn

心的本義指心臟，古文字的心字即像一個心臟器官的形狀。心是人體器官的主宰，古人誤認為它是思維的器官，所以心又是思想、意念、感情的通稱。心臟在人體的中央位置，故心還有中央、中心之義。凡從心和它的偏旁（忄，小）的字，大都與人的思想、意念和感情有關，如志、忠、性、怕、恭、忝等。

【心匠】指獨特的構思、設計。

【心法】佛教稱佛經經典文字以外，以心相傳授的佛法為心法。又指修心養性的方法。

【心得】內心有所體會。

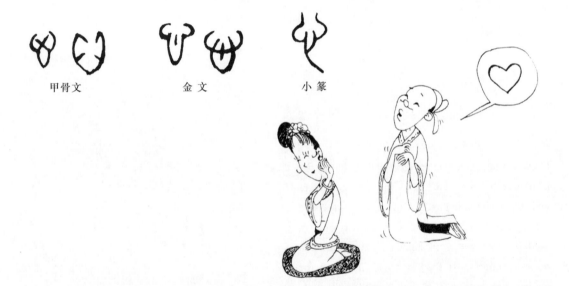

甲骨文　　　　　金文　　　　　小篆

心 refers to the heart. In ancient writing systems, the character 心 has the shape of a heart. The heart is the most important organ of a human body. And people in ancient times mistook it for an organ for thinking, so the character 心 is also a cover term for thinking, ideas and feelings. The heart is situated in the centre of a human chest, hence 心 also means "centre" and "central". Characters with 心 as a component most have to do with human thinking, ideas and feelings, e.g. 志 (aspiration), 忠 (loyalty), 性 (temperament), 怕 (afraid), 恭 (respectful), 忝 (regretfully), etc.

【心匠】 ingenuity

【心法】 (Buddhism) Buddhist ideas which are passed on through the meeting of minds rather than the use of words

【心得】 what one has learned from work, study, etc.

yōu

金文的憂字，像人以手掩面之形，表示愁悶形於顏面的意思；或從心，表示心中鬱悶之意。所以，憂的本義即指憂愁、煩悶，又指令人擔憂之事。

【憂愁】因遭遇困難或不如意的事而苦悶。
【憂患】困苦患難。
【憂慮】憂愁擔心。

金文

小篆

In the Bronze Inscriptions, the character 憂 looks like a man covering his face with a hand, signalling there are worried expressions on the face. Sometimes, it has 心 (heart) as a component, signalling that the man is in a gloomy mood. Hence 憂 means "worried", "depressed", but it can also refer to things which make one worried.

【憂愁】 to worry
【憂患】 suffering; misery
【憂慮】 worried; concerned

mèng

夢是指人們在睡眠中的一種幻象。古代醫術落後，不明疾病的原因，因此常把疾病歸咎於夢魘作祟。夢魘就是作噩夢，古人認為是疾病或災難的先兆。甲骨文夢字，像一人依床而睡，而瞠目披髮、手舞足蹈的樣子，正是表示睡中做夢的意思。

【夢幻】夢中幻想，比喻空妄。

【夢想】夢寐懷想，形容思念深切。又指空想，妄想。

【夢囈】睡夢中説的話，即夢話。後多用以比喻胡言亂語。

【夢筆生花】相傳唐代大詩人李白夢見所用的筆，頭上生花，從此才情橫溢，文思豐富。後用來比喻文人的才思大進。

甲骨文

小篆

夢 means "dream", the things one experiences during sleep. In ancient times, when medical science was at a low stage of development, people did not know much about the causes of illness, and they often linked illness with nightmare. They thought terrible dreams were omens of coming illness of disaster. In the Oracle-Bone Inscriptions, the character 夢 looks like a man on a bed, with open eyes and loose hair, and moving his hands and legs in confusion, signalling that the man is in a dream.

【夢幻】illusion

【夢想】to dream of

【夢囈】(1) somniloquy (2) rigmarole

【夢筆生花】(lit.) seeing one's writing brush in blossom in a dream; of superb literary talent

guǐ

古人認為人死之後變而為鬼。甲骨文的鬼字,下部是人形,説明鬼是人死後變成的;頭部特大而且怪異,這就是我們今天所説的"大頭鬼"。鬼的本義是指人死後的魂靈。它慣居幽冥,出沒無形。所以鬼字又有隱祕不測的意思,引申為機智、狡詐之義。漢字中凡從鬼的字,大都與鬼神魂靈有關,如魂、魄、魔、魅等。

【鬼才】才氣怪譎。

【鬼斧】比喻技術精巧,非人工所能為。

【鬼使神差】鬼神派遣、驅使。指被不可知的力量所支配,形容不由自主。

甲骨文　　　　　金　文　　　　　小　篆

People in the past believed that men would become ghosts after death. In the Oracle-Bone Inscriptions, the lower part of the character 鬼 has the shape of a man, but its upper part, the head, is monstrous and disproportionately big, signalling that it is a big-headed ghost changed from a dead man. The primary meaning of 鬼 is the soul of a man after death. As the soul lives in the nether world and has no fixed form, the character 鬼 can also mean "mysterious", "cunning" and "resourceful". Characters with 鬼 as a component most have to do with ghost and soul, e.g. 魂 (soul), 魄 (spirit), 魔 (devil), and 魅 (demon).

【鬼才】uncanny talent

【鬼斧】superlative workmanship

【鬼使神差】as if done by ghosts and gods

wèi

甲骨文、金文的畏字，像一手持魔杖，頭形怪異的鬼怪形，表示特別威風的意思。因此，畏字的本義指威風、威嚴，通"威"，引申為恐嚇、嚇唬，再引申為恐懼、害怕、擔心、敬服等義。

【畏友】指自己敬畏的朋友。

【畏途】艱險可怕的道路，比喻不敢做的事情。

【畏首畏尾】怕這怕那，比喻顧忌太多。

| 甲骨文 | 金文 | 小篆 |

In the Oracle-Bone Inscriptions and Bronze Inscriptions, the character 畏 looks like a monstrous, big headed ghost with a stick in hand, suggesting an awe-inspiring appearance. Hence 畏 originally meant, the same as 威, "awe-inspiring". But in the present-day usage, it has taken on the meanings of "frightening", "fearsome", "worried" and even "respect".

【畏友】 a respectable friend

【畏途】 a dangerous road; a perilous undertaking

【畏首畏尾】 to be full of misgivings; to be overcautious

yì

上古時代，巫風盛行。在舉行巫術活動的時候，要讓人頭戴一些兇惡猙獰的面具跳舞，以驅除鬼怪病魔。甲骨文的異字，正像一個人頭戴奇特的大面具而手舞足蹈的樣子。因面具表情兇惡猙獰，不同於常人，所以異字就有了奇特、怪異之義，引申為不同的、特別的等義。

甲骨文

金 文

小 篆

In ancient times, witchcraft was a commonplace. When a wizard performed magic, he would wear a fierce looking mask and dance, in order to drive away evil demons. In the Oracle-Bone Inscriptions, the character 異 looks like a man dancing with a big, fierce-looking mask. As the mask looks ferocious, different from the normal face, the character 異 takes on the meanings of "strange", "unusual", "different" and "special", too.

器 具 類

Appliance

gē

戈是古代的一種兵器，長柄，上端有橫刃，可以用來橫擊、鈎殺，主要盛行於商周時代。甲骨文和早期金文的戈字，正像這種兵器之形。它是古代常用的幾種主要武器之一。如《荀子》："古之兵，戈、矛、弓、矢而已矣。"因此，在漢字中凡從"戈"的字大都與武器和戰爭、格殺有關，如戟、武、戎、戒、戍、伐等。

| 甲骨文 | 金 文 | 小 篆 |

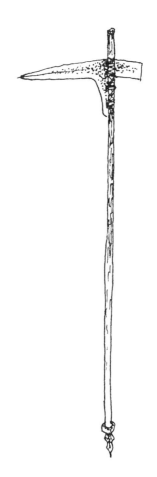

戈 is a type of ancient weapon, widely used in the Shang Dynasty and Zhou Dynasty. With a long handle and a horizontal blade at the head, it may be used to strike or hook. In the Oracle-Bone Inscriptions and early Bronze Inscriptions, the character 戈 has the shape of this weapon. It is one of the main weapons in ancient China. For example, *Xun Zi* (Hsün-Tzu) says, "There is no weapon other than 戈, 矛, 弓 and 矢 in ancient times". Characters with 戈 as a component most have to do with weapon, war and fight, e.g. 戟 (a spearlike weapon), 武 (military), 戎 (army), 戒 (to guard against), 戍 (to defend) and 伐 (to attack).

jiè

　　古文字的戒字，像一個人兩手拿着武器——戈。它的本義為持戈警戒，引申為防備、警告；又引申為禁止、戒除等義，如戒煙、戒酒等。

甲骨文

金文

小篆

In ancient writing systems, the character 戒 looks like a man holding a weapon in his hands. Its primary meaning is "to guard against", from which has derived its extended meaning "to warn". But it can also be used in the senses "to prohibit" and "to give up", e.g. 戒煙 (to give up smoking), 戒酒 (to give up drinking).

xián

咸字從戌從口。從甲骨文、金文看,戌是一種長柄大斧,口為人口,在這裡表示人頭。大斧砍人頭,所以咸的本義是殺戮。《說文解字》:"咸,皆也,悉也。"把咸字釋作皆、都、悉、盡之義,這其實也是咸字本義"殺盡"的引申。

甲骨文　　　　　金文　　　　　小篆

The character 咸 consists of 戌 and 口. Judging from the Oracle-Bone Inscriptions and Bronze Inscriptions, 戌 is a big axe with a long handle, and 口 denotes the head of a man here. Hence 咸 meant originally to use an axe to chop off a head, i.g. to kill. Xu Shen says in his *Origin of Chinese Characters,* "咸 means all, the whole lot". This gloss of 咸 in the sense of "all", "the whole lot", is in fact a derivative from its original meaning "to kill everyone".

fá

伐字從人從戈,是個會意字。甲骨文、金文的伐字,像人執戈砍擊敵人頭頸之形。伐的本義為砍斫,引申為指擊刺、攻殺,又引申為征討、進攻之義。此外,伐字還含有勝利有功的意思,所以誇耀自己的功勞、才能也叫"伐"。

【伐交】破壞敵人和它盟國的邦交。

【伐智】誇耀自己的才智。

【伐罪】征討有罪者。

甲骨文　　　　　金文　　　　　小篆

伐 is an ideograph, consisting of 人 and 戈. In the Oracle-Bone Inscriptions and Bronze Inscriptions, the character 伐 looks like a man chopping the head of an enemy with 戈. The primary meaning of 伐 is "to chop", from which have derived its extended meanings "to strike" and "to attack". In addition, 伐 can also mean "victory", "achievement" and "to boast of (one's achievements)".

【伐交】to destroy the enemy's friendly relationship with its neighbouring countries

【伐智】to boast of one's ability and wisdom

【伐罪】to attack the punishable

shù

　　古文字的戍字，從人從戈，像人扛（或執）戈之形，表示武裝守衛的意思，其本義指保衛、防守、守衛邊疆。

【戍卒】指駐守邊疆的士兵。

【戍邊】駐守邊疆。

甲骨文　　　　　金文　　　　　小篆

In ancient writing systems, the character 戍, consisting of 人 and 戈, looks like a man carrying 戈, signalling he is defending his land. Hence the primary meaning of 戍 is "to defend", "to guard the frontiers".

【戍卒】soldiers in garrison

【戍邊】to garrison the frontiers

róng

戎字在早期金文中是一個圖形化的文字，像一個人一手持戈一手執盾的樣子。此字後來省去人形，在甲骨文中戎像一戈一盾相併在一起之形，而金文戎字的盾形則省訛為"十"，與甲字的古體寫法相近，故小篆的戎字訛變為從甲從戈。戎是兵器的總稱，又可代指戰爭、軍隊和士兵。此外，戎又是古代對西北少數民族的泛稱。

【戎士】將士。

【戎馬】戰馬。又借指戰爭、軍事。

【戎裝】軍裝。

甲骨文

金文

小篆

In the early Bronze Inscriptions, the character 戎 is a pictograph, looking like a man holding 戈 (an affensive weapon) in one hand and 盾 (a shield) in the other. In the Oracle-Bone Inscriptions, the man part is omitted, leaving only a combination of 戈 and 盾. In the late Bronze Inscriptions, the shield part is reduced to a cross (十), similar to the original form of 甲. That is why the character 戎 in the Later Seal Character consists of 甲 and 戈 by mistake. 戎 is a general term for arms, but it can also be used to refer to war and army. Besides, 戎 was also a cover term for the national minorities in the northwest in the past.

【戎士】generals and soldiers

【戎馬】(1) army horse (2) army life

【戎裝】martial attire

wǔ

武與"文"相對。古文字的武字，從戈從止，戈是武器的代表，止本是足趾的象形，表示行進。所以武字的本義乃是指有關軍事的活動，是有關軍旅和技擊、強力之事的通稱，又引申為勇猛、剛健之義。

【武力】兵力。又指強暴的力量。
【武功】戰功，指軍事方面的功績。
【武烈】威猛剛烈。
【武裝】軍事裝備。又指用武器來裝備，用作動詞。
【武藝】武術上的本領。

甲骨文

金文

小篆

武 is the opposite of 文 (civil). In ancient writing systems, the character 武 consists of 戈 and 止. 戈 is a cover term for weapon, and 止 (foot) here means "to go forward". So the primary meaning of 武 is military operation. It is a general term for activities connected with army and fighting. It can also be used in the sense of "valiant" and "vigorous".

【武力】force
【武功】battle achievement
【武烈】powerful and strong
【武裝】(1) military equipment (2) to equip with arms
【武藝】military arts

zhàn

戰字從單從戈，單本是一種捕獵工具，也可用作殺敵武器，而戈則是一種常用的兵器。"單"與"戈"結合，表示干戈相向、兵戎相見，所以戰的本義指兩軍交戰，即戰爭、戰鬥之義，泛指比優劣、爭勝負。

【戰士】士兵，戰鬥者。
【戰爭】國家或集團之間的武裝衝突。
【戰戰兢兢】恐懼戒慎貌，又指顫抖。

金文

小篆

The character 戰 consists of 單 and 戈. The former, 單, an instrument for catching animals, may also be used as a weapon, and the latter, 戈, is a common weapon. The combination of 單 and 戈 means to use weapons against each other, so the primary meaning of 戰 is two armies engaged in a battle, i.e. fight, or war. It may also refer to any activity in which different sides are competing for a prize.

【戰士】soldiers
【戰爭】war
【戰戰兢兢】trembling with fear

WǑ

"我"是什麼東西？由甲骨文我字形體可知，"我"原來是一種兵器的形象。這是一種長柄而帶齒形刃口的兵器，是用來行刑殺人或支解牲口的。這種兵器後世罕見，所以我字本義也不常用，後來就借用為第一人稱代詞，指自己、自己的。

【我們】代詞，稱包括自己在內的若干人或很多人。

【我行我素】自行其是。不以環境為轉移，也不受別人的影響。

甲骨文

金文　　　　小篆

What is 我? From the shape of the character 我 in the Oracle-Bone Inscriptions, we know that it is a type of weapon. It has a long handle and a blade like the teeth of a saw, used for the execution of criminals or the dismemberment of animals in ancient times. This weapon is rarely seen in later ages, so the original meaning of 我 is rarely used. It is more usually used as a pronoun to refer to the first person, the speaker himself.

【我們】we

【我行我素】to persist in one's old ways

yuè

　　戉是"鉞"的本字。鉞是古代的一種兵器，以青銅或鐵製成，形狀像板斧而較大。古代斧形兵器種類較多，形狀和用途各異。甲骨文和金文中的戉字，像一長柄環刃的兵器之形，指的當是斧形兵器中的一種。

| 甲骨文 | 金 文 | 小 篆 |

戉, the original form of 鉞, is an ancient weapon, made of bronze or iron, looking like a big broad axe. There were various types of axe in ancient times, of different shapes and uses. The character 戉 in the Oracle-Bone Inscriptions and Bronze Inscriptions looks like a weapon with a long handle and round blade, a member of the axe family.

suì

甲骨文和早期金文中的歲字，像一把長柄斧鉞之形，其上下兩點即表示斧刃上下尾端迴曲中之透空處。歲的本義是一種斧鉞，借用為年歲之歲，泛指時間、光陰，所以金文歲字增加兩個止形（即步字），表示日月變更、時光流逝的意思。

【歲入】指一年的收入，後用以指國家一年的財政收入。
【歲月】指年月、時序，泛指時間。
【歲朝】一歲之始，即農曆元旦。

甲骨文　　　　　　　金文　　　　　　小篆

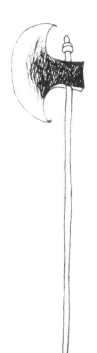

In the Oracle-Bone Inscriptions and early Bronze Inscriptions, the character 歲 looks like an axe-type weapon with a long handle. The two dots in the blade position indicate that the blade bends at the two ends and the dotted positions are devoid of anything. Though originally referring to a type of axe, 歲 is more usually used in the sense of "age", "year" and more generally "time". In the late Bronze Inscriptions, there are two foot parts (止) added, suggesting that time passes like a man walking from one place to another.

【歲入】annual income
【歲月】years; time
【歲朝】the New Year's day of Chinese lunar calendar

wáng

王，是古代君主的稱號。甲骨文與金文中的王字，是一種斧狀的兵器——鉞的形象。鉞是用於殺戮的兵器，後來成為一種執法的刑具。古代的軍事首領用它來指揮、監督士兵作戰，所以鉞就成為一種權力的象徵物；而手執大鉞的人就被稱為"王"。在原始社會軍事民主制時代，軍事首領——王就是至高無上的君主。夏商周時代，只有天子才能稱王，到戰國時各諸侯國的國君也紛紛自封為王。秦始皇統一中國，改君主的稱號為"皇帝"。秦漢以後，王就不再是君主的稱號，而成為皇室和有功大臣的最高封號。

甲骨文　　　　金 文　　　　小 篆

王 was the title of the monarch in ancient times. In the Oracle-Bone Inscriptions and Bronze Inscriptions, the character 王 looks like an axe-type weapon —鉞, an instrument for the execution of criminals. As military commanders used it to direct the army and urge the soldiers to charge forward, 鉞 became a symbol of power, and the one who had 鉞 in his hand was known as 王. In the primitive society, the military commander, i.e. 王 was the highest ruler of a land. By the time of the dynasties of Xia, Shang and Zhou, only the monarch of a country could be referred to as 王. In the Warring States period, however, the rulers of the states all called themselves 王. Then the First Emperor of Qin unified China, and he changed the title from 王 to 皇帝 (emperor). After that 王 became the highest title granted to princes or ministers of great achievements, no longer the title of the monarch.

shì

早期金文中的士字，和"王"一樣，是斧鉞的象形。不過，"王"是一種具有權力象徵意義的執法刑具——黃金大鉞，而"士"則是指一般的斧狀兵器或刑具。士字的本義指手執兵器（或刑具）的武士或刑官，如士卒（指戰士）、士師（指獄官）等；引申為指成年的男子，如士女（指成年的男女）。士還代表一種社會階層，其地位在庶民之上，如士族（指在政治上、經濟上享有特權的世家大族）、士子（多指士大夫，即做官的人，也是舊時讀書應考的學子的通稱）等。

金 文

小 篆

In the early Bronze Inscriptions, the character 士, like 王, is in the shape of an axe. While 王 refers to a big broad axe, a symbol of power, however, 士 refers to ordinary axe-type weapons. The primary meanings of 士 is the warrior or law executor, who holds a weapon in hand, e.g. 士卒 (soldiers), 士師 (jailer). But it is also used in the general sense of adult man, e.g. 士女 (men and women). In addition, 士 may also refer to a social stratum, e.g. 士族 (gentry) and 士子 (scholar or scholar-bureaucrat).

bīng

甲骨文的兵字，像一個人雙手擎着一把非常鋒利的武器——斤（即斧頭），其本義即指作戰用的武器（又稱兵器），如"兵不血刃"、"短兵相接"等。引申為手持兵器作戰的人——戰士（又稱士兵），如"兵強馬壯"。進一步引申為指軍隊、軍事、戰爭等義，如"兵不厭詐"、"兵荒馬亂"等。

甲骨文

金文

小篆

In the Oracle-Bone Inscriptions, the character 兵 looks like two hands holding up a sharp axe (斤). Hence its original meaning "weapon", e.g. 兵不血刃 (the edges of the swords not being stained with blood), 短兵相接 (to fight at close quarters). But its meaning has been extended to cover the person who holds the weapon-soldier, e.g. 兵強馬壯 (strong soldiers and sturdy horses). It can also be used to refer to army, military affairs, or war, e.g. 兵不厭詐 (There can never be too much deception in war.) and 兵荒馬亂 (the turmoil and chaos of war).

Xī

甲骨文析字，左邊是一棵樹（木），右邊是一把曲柄大斧（斤），是用斧劈木的意思，其本義為劈開。由劈開這個本義，析字可引申出分開、離散之義，如成語"分崩離析"；又有分辨、剖解之義，如"分析"、"剖析"，又陶淵明《移居》詩："奇文共欣賞，疑義相與析。"

甲骨文

金 文

小 篆

In the Oracle-Bone Inscriptions, the character 析 has a tree part (木) on the left and an axe with a crooked handle (斤) on the right, signalling the splitting of a tree with an axe. From the original meaning of splitting have derived the extended meaning of separation and segmentation, e.g. 分崩離析 (to fall to pieces). And it may also be used in the sense "to analyse". Thus *Tao Yuanming* writes in his poem *House-moving*, " 奇文共欣賞, 疑義相與析 (A remarkable work should be shared and its subtleties discussed.)"

zhé

甲骨文的折字，像用斧頭（斤）把一棵小樹攔腰斬斷，其本義為斬斷。引申為把東西弄斷。把東西弄斷，可以用斧頭砍，也可以直接用手折，而用手折斷一件東西，須先使之彎曲，因此折字又有彎曲之義，如曲折、轉折等；進一步引申為"使人從心裡屈服"之義。折字由折斷之義，還可引申為夭折（指人早死）、損失、挫折、虧損等義。

【折腰】彎腰。晉代文豪陶淵明曾任彭澤令，有一次上司派人來巡視，下面的人告訴他要立即束帶迎謁，陶淵明歎道："吾不能為五斗米折腰向鄉里小兒。"於是辭職歸田。後因稱屈身事人為折腰。而在古代詩文中，則稱地方低級官員為折腰吏。

甲骨文

金文

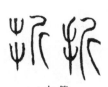

小篆

In the Oracle-Bone Inscriptions, the character 折 looks like a small tree being cut down with an axe. From this original meaning derives its meaning "to break". To break something one may use an axe, or simply use one's hand. And to break something with one's hand, one will first have to bend it. So the character 折 has also taken on the meaning "to bend", e.g. 曲折 (winding), 轉折 (to turn). It can also be used metaphorically in the sense of "convinced". From the meaning to break have also derived the meanings "to die young (夭折)", "setback (挫折)", etc.

【折腰】 to stoop, from *Tao Yuanming* of the Jin Dynasty, who said, "I wouldn't stoop to welcome a rustic fellow for five dǒu of millet (the amount of his salary)" and resigned thereupon from his post of the county magistrate in Pengze (in present-day Jiangxi Province), when a supervisor from a higher authority came and his assistants told him that he should go and welcome the official.

xīn

新為"薪"的本字。甲骨文、金文的新字，右邊的"斤"代表斧頭，左邊是一段木柴的形狀，表示用斧頭劈柴的意思。新的本義指木柴，俗稱"柴火"。此字後來多借用為"新舊"之"新"，故另造"薪"字來代替它的本義。

【新奇】新鮮而奇特。

【新穎】新鮮而別致。

【新聞】新近聽説的事，泛指社會上最近發生的新事情。又指新知識。

【新仇舊恨】指對往事和現狀的煩惱、怨恨情緒。

甲骨文

金文

小篆

新 was the original form of 薪. In the Oracle-Bone Inscriptions and Bronze Inscriptions, the character 薪 has an axe part (斤) on the right, and a part representing a piece of wood on the left, signalling the splitting of wood with an axe. The original meaning of 新 was wood split up, i.e. fire-wood. But 新 is often used in the sense of "new", opposite to 舊 (old), so a new character 薪 has been created to express its original meanings.

【新奇】novel

【新穎】new and original

【新聞】news

【新仇舊恨】new anxiety piled on old

jiàng

匠字從匚從斤，"匚"是一種可以用來裝木工用具的敞口木箱，"斤"是木工用的斧頭，所以匠字的本義當指木工，又稱"木匠"。古代只有木工才稱"匠"；後來凡具有專門技術或在某方面有突出成就的人都可以叫做"匠"，如鐵匠、能工巧匠、巨匠等。

【匠心】巧妙的心思，謂精思巧構，如工匠的精心刻造，別出心裁。多指文學藝術創造性的構思。

小篆

The character 匠 consists of 匚 and 斤; the former stands for the open toolbox of a carpenter and the latter one of his tools-axe. So the primary meaning of 匠 is "carpenter". Gradually, however, anyone with a special skill or of great achievement in one field may be referred to as 匠, e.g. 鐵匠 (blacksmith), 能工巧匠 (skillful craftsman) and 巨匠 (great master).

【匠心】ingenuity; craftsmanship

jīn

甲骨文的斤字,像一把曲柄的斧頭之形,斧頭上加箭頭表示它的鋒利。斤的本義即指斧頭,是古代的一種兵器。現在的斤字,則多用作重量單位名稱。但在漢字中,凡從"斤"的字卻都與斧頭及其作用有關,如斧、新、斷、析、折、斫等。

【斤斧】即斧頭。引申為指以作品請人改正。

【斤斤】聰明鑑察。引申為指拘謹或過份計較細事,如"斤斤計較"。

| 甲骨文 | 金 文 | 小 篆 |

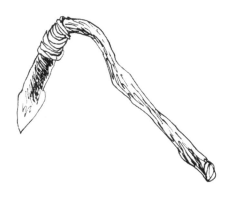

In the Oracle-Bone Inscriptions, the character 斤 looks like an axe with a crooked handle, and the arrow on it signals that it is very sharp. The original meaning of 斤 was axe, used as a weapon in ancient times. Characters with 斤 as a component most have to do with the axe and its uses, e.g. 斧 (axe), 新 (firewood), 斷 (to break), 析 (to split), 折 (to bend) and 斫 (to cut). Nowadays, however, 斤 is more usually used as a measure of weight.

【斤斧】(1) axe (2) (to ask others to help) prune one's writing

【斤斤】to fuss about

fù

父

父，本是"斧"字的初文。金文的父字，像一隻手抓住一柄石斧的樣子。在原始社會父系時代，石斧是一種主要的武器和生產工具。而手持石斧與敵人作戰或從事艱苦的野外勞動，是成年男子的責任，所以父就引申為對成年男子的一種尊稱，後來又成為對親生父親及其同輩男子的稱呼。

| 甲骨文 | 金文 | 小篆 |

父 was the original form of 斧. In the Bronze Inscriptions, the character 父 looks like a hand holding a stone axe. In the primitive society, the stone axe was one of the most important weapons and tools. And it was the responsibility of the adult man to fight with the enemy and to work in the fields with the stone axe, hence 父 became a term of address for the adult man. Gradually, it has taken on the present-day meaning of "father".

xīn

從早期金文的字形來看，辛像一把形似圓鑿而末尾尖銳的刀具之形，是一種用來黥面的刑具。此字後來多用為干支名，是天干的第八位。此外，辛還有辛辣之義，也指辛味的蔬菜。又引申為悲痛、酸楚、勞苦等義。漢字中凡從"辛"之字，大多與刑罰及辛味有關，如辜、辟、辣等。

【辛苦】辛，辣味；苦，苦味。比喻艱勞。

【辛酸】辣味和酸味。引喻為悲痛苦楚。

甲骨文

金 文

小 篆

Judging from the early Bronze Inscriptions, the character 辛 looks like something with a round end and a pointed head, referring to an instrument of torture for tattooing the face of a criminal. But this character is now mainly used as a name of the eighth Heavenly Stem, part of a traditional Chinese system of sequense. In addition, 辛 also has the meaning of "hot in taste", and can refer to vegetables which taste hot. Its meaning can be further extended to cover "sad", "bitter" and "hard". Character with 辛 as a component most have to do with torture and hot taste, e.g. 辜 (guilt), 辟 (to cut) and 辣 (hot taste).

【辛苦】hard; laborious

【辛酸】sad; bitter

pì

辟為"劈"的本字。甲骨文、金文的辟字,左邊是一跪着的人形,右邊是一把刑刀(辛),下面的小方框或小圓圈則代表人頭,表示用行刑大刀把犯人的頭砍下來的意思。這就是古代"大辟"之刑的形象描繪。辟的本義為砍、劈;又用作刑罰名,如"劓辟"(割鼻子)、"墨辟"(臉上刺字)等;引申指法律、法度,又指最高執法人、君主。現在"復辟(bì)"一詞,是指恢復君主統治的意思。此外,辟還有徵召之義,如"辟(bì)召"(因推薦而徵召入仕)。

甲骨文　　　　　　　金 文　　　　　　小 篆

辟 was the orignial form of 劈. In the Oracle-Bone Inscriptions and Bronze Inscriptions, the character 辟 has a man on his knees on the left and a knife for the execution of death penalty on the right. Sometimes, at the lower part in between the man and the knife there is a little square or circle, which stands for the head cut off. Therefore the character 辟 is a vivid description of the execution of a criminal, and it originally meant "to cut", "to chop". But it may also refer to other forms of punishment, e.g. 劓辟 (to cut off the nose), 墨辟 (to tattoo the face with insulting words); from which have derived its meanings of "law", "legal system" and its use to refer to the highest law-executor, the monarch. That is why the present-day term 復辟 (bì) means the restoration of a dethroned monarch. In addition, 辟 can also mean "to call up", e.g. 辟 (bì) 召 (to draft).

máo

矛是古代的一種兵器，在長桿的一端裝有青銅或鐵製成的槍頭，主要用於刺擊。金文的矛字，像一件上有鋒利矛頭、下有長柄的兵器形狀。漢字中凡從"矛"之字，都與矛這種兵器及其作用有關，如矜、稍等。

【矛盾】矛和盾，比喻事物互相抵觸的兩個方面。

金 文

小 篆

矛 is a type of ancient weapon, which has a long handle at the end of which is a spearhead made of bronze or iron. In the Bronze Inscriptions, the character 矛 looks like a picture of this weapon. Characters with 矛 as a component all have to do with this weapon and its uses, e.g. 矜 (the handle of a spear), 稍 (lance).

【矛盾】 spear and shield; contradictions

shū

殳是古代的一種兵器，多用竹木製成，也有用銅等金屬製成的，一般頂端有稜，主要用於撞擊。金文的殳字，像人手持兵器狀。在漢字中，凡從"殳"的字往往與打、殺、撞擊等義有關，如毆、毀、殺、段等。

【殳仗】儀仗的一種。

【殳書】古代書體之一。因此種書體多用在兵器上，故名。

金文　　　　　小篆

殳 is a type of ancient weapon with a hooked edge at the head. It is usually made of bamboo, but sometimes made of bronze or other metal as well. In the Bronze Inscriptions, the character 殳 looks like a man holding this weapon in hand. Characters with 殳 as a component usually have to do with hitting, killing and striking, e.g. 毆 (to hit), 毀 (to destroy), 殺 (to kill) and 段 (to segment).

【殳仗】a weapon carried by a guard of honour

【殳書】a type of ancient writing, mainly seen on weapons

dāo

刀，本是一種兵器，又泛指一種可以用來斬、削、切、割物體的工具。古文字的刀字，正是一把短柄弧刃的砍刀形象。在漢字中，凡從"刀"（刂）的字大都與刀及其作用有關，如刃、刑、剎、利、剖、剝等。

【刀兵】指武器。又指戰爭。

【刀耕火種】原始的耕種方法，把地上的草木燒成灰作肥料，就地挖坑下種。

【刀光劍影】形容激烈的廝殺、搏鬥或殺氣騰騰的氣勢。

【刀山火海】比喻非常危險和困難的地方。

甲骨文

小 篆

刀, originally the name of a type of sword, is a general term for any tool which functions as a knife, i.e. to cut or chop. In ancient writing systems, the character 刀 looks like a chopper with a short handle and an arching edge. Characters with 刀 (刂) as a component most have to do with the knife and its uses, e.g. 刃 (edge), 刑 (to kill), 剁 (to chop up), 利 (sharp), 剖 (to cut open), 剝 (to peel), etc.

【刀兵】(1) weapon (2) war

【刀耕火種】slash-and-burn cultivation

【刀光劍影】the glint and flash of cold steel

【刀山火海】(lit.) a mountain of swords and a sea of flames; most dangerous places; most severe trials

rèn

　　刃字是一個指事字。此字為刀上加一點作為指示符號,以指明刀口所在的位置。因此,刃的本義指刀鋒、刀口;又泛指刀,如利刃、白刃等;用作動詞,則是用力殺死的意思。

【刃具】指刀一類的工具。

甲骨文

小篆

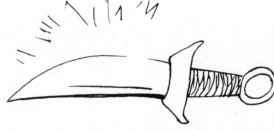

The character 刃 is an indicative. It is composed of a knife part and a sign indicating the position of edge. Hence the primary meaning of 刃 is the point or edge of a knife. But it can also refer the knife as a whole, e.g. 利刃 (a sharp knife), 白刃 (naked sword). And it can be used as a verb, meaning to kill with a knife.

【刃具】cutting tool

fēn

分字從八從刀，八本身就有分別之意，表示用刀把一件物體剖開。分的本義為分別、別離，即把一個整體變成幾部份或使相聯的事物分開，與"合"相對。由此引申，則分字還有辨別、分配等義。

【分崩離析】形容集團、國家等分裂瓦解。

【分道揚鑣】比喻因目標不同而各奔各的前程或各幹各的事情。

【分庭抗禮】原指賓主相見，站在庭院的兩邊，相對行禮。現在用來比喻平起平坐，互相對立。

甲骨文	金文	小篆

The character 分 consists of 八 (to separate) and 刀 (knife), signalling to divide something into two parts with a knife. The primary meaning of 分, opposite to 合 (to combine), is to segment something into several parts or to separate things which are otherwise connected. From this meaning have derived its extended meanings "to distinguish" and "to distribute".

【分崩離析】to disintegrate; to fall into pieces

【分道揚鑣】to separate and go different ways

【分庭抗禮】to stand up to sb. as an equal; to make rival claims as an equal

古文字的利字，從禾從刀，表示用刀割禾之意。用刀割禾，說明刀的鋒利。因此，利字的本義為鋒利、銳利，引申為指利益、功用，又有順利、吉利等義。

【利用】物盡其用。又指藉助外物以達到某種目的。

【利令智昏】一心貪圖私利，使頭腦發昏，忘掉一切。

甲骨文　　　　　金文　　　　　小篆

In ancient writing systems, the character 利 consists of 禾 (standing grain) and 刀 (knife), signalling to cut the grain with a knife. To cut down the grain, the knife must be sharp enough. So the character 利 means "sharp" and "acute" primarily. But it can also be used in the senses of "benefit (利益)", "favourable (順利)" and "lucky (吉利)".

【利用】to make use of

【利令智昏】to be blinded by lust for gain

bié

甲骨文的別字，右邊像一堆骨頭的形狀，左邊是一把刀，表示用刀把骨頭從肉中剔除出來的意思。因此，別的本義為剔骨，引申為分開、區別，進一步引申為分離、分支、差別、類別等義。

【別致】特別、新奇，跟尋常不同。

【別出心裁】獨創一格，與眾不同。

【別有天地】另有一種境界，形容風景等引人入勝。

【別具隻眼】比喻有獨到的見解。

甲骨文

小篆

In the Oracle-Bone Inscriptions, the right part of the character 別 looks like a heap of bones and the left a knife, signalling to separate bone from flesh with a knife. Hence the original meanings of 別 was to pick bone, from which have derived the extended meanings: "to separate", "to distinguish", "branches", "differences" and "types".

【別致】unique; unconventional

【別出心裁】to try to be different

【別有天地】a place of unique beauty

【別具隻眼】to have a special insight

yuè

刖，是古代一種砍腳的酷刑。甲骨文的刖字，像用一把鋸子把人的一條腿鋸斷的樣子，是刖刑的一種形象描繪。小篆刖字從肉從刀，同樣是個會意字，但已經沒有了象形的意味。刖字的本義是指把腳砍斷，是古代一種酷刑的名稱；引申為砍斷、截斷之義。

【刖跪】指斷足之人。跪，即足。

【刖趾適履】又作"削足適履"。比喻不顧實際，勉強遷就，生搬硬套。

甲骨文

小篆

刖 refers to an ancient form of punishment: to cut away a leg. In the Oracle-Bone Inscriptions, the character 刖 looks like a man's leg being severed with a saw, a vivid description of the cruel punishment. In the Later Seal Character, the character 刖 consists of 肉 (flesh) and 刀 (knife); though still an ideograph, there is no longer any trace of picture-like image. From the main use of 刖 as a name of punishment has derived the more general sense of the cutting off of anything.

【刖跪】 man with a leg cut off

【刖趾適履】 (also 削足適履)(lit.) to cut the feet to fit the shoes; to act in a Procrustean manner

yì

甲骨文劓字，從刀從自（鼻的初文），表示用刀割取鼻子的意思。以刀割鼻為劓，是古代五種常用刑罰中的一種。按古代法律，凡不服從命令、擅改制度，或盜竊、打傷他人者，都要處以劓刑。

甲骨文　　　　金文　　　　小篆

In the Oracle-Bone Inscriptions, the character 劓 consists of 刀 (knife) and 自 (the original form of 鼻, nose), signalling to cut off a nose with a knife. It was one of the five common punishments in ancient times to cut off the nose of a man. According to the law at that time, anyone who disobeyed orders, changed regulations without permission, stole things or wounded others would have his nose cut off as a punishment.

qì

　　古文字的契字，右邊是一把刀形，左邊的一豎三橫表示是用刀在一塊小木條上刻下的三個記號。它形象地反映了上古時代結繩記事之外的另一種主要記事方法——契刻記事。楷書的契字增加"木"旁，則表示這種契刻記事是以木條為材料的。後來"木"誤寫成"大"，就成了今天的"契"字。契的本義為刻，引申為符契，又引申為契約、文卷；用作動詞，則有符合、投合之義。

【契合】融洽、相符、投合。
【契約】雙方或多方同意訂立的條款、文書。

甲骨文

小篆

In ancient writing systems, the character 契 has a knife part on the right and a vertical stroke with three horizontal strokes on the left, depicting vividly one of the ways of recording events beside tying knots in a rope, i.e. marking with a knife. In the Regular Script, 契 has an additional component 木 (wood), signalling the marks are made on wood. Later on, the component 木 was mistakenly written as 大, hence the present form of 契. From its original meaning of marking with a knife, 契 has evolved to refer to things which have marks on, especially those recording agreements between different sides, i.e. contracts. It can also be used as a verb, meaning "to agree".

【契合】 to agree with
【契約】 contract

shǐ

矢就是箭。不過在古代，矢和箭的含義稍有區別：木箭為矢，竹箭為箭；現在則基本通稱為箭。矢箭是用來射傷敵人或野獸的武器。甲骨文、金文的矢字，正像弓箭之形，箭頭、箭桿、箭尾俱全，其本義即指弓箭，如“有的放矢”（放箭要對準靶子，比喻說話做事要有針對性）。由於矢與誓在古代同音，所以矢字有時也可借用為誓，如“矢志不移”（誓死永不變心）。

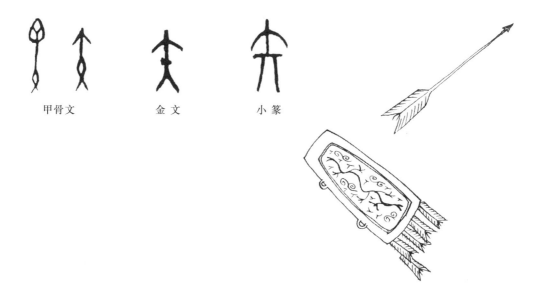

甲骨文　　　　金　文　　　　小　篆

矢 refers, the same as 箭, to a very important weapon: arrow. In ancient times, however, there was a little difference between 矢 and 箭: the former is made of wood and the latter bamboo. In the Oracle-Bone Inscriptions and Bronze Inscriptions, the character 矢 looks like an arrow, with its head, shaft and tail all present. And "arrow" is its main meaning, e.g. 有的放矢 (to shoot the arrow at the target; to have a definite object in view). As 矢 and 誓 (to vow) sounded the same in ancient times, 矢 is sometimes used in the sense of 誓, e.g. 矢志不移 (to vow to adhere to one's chosen course).

zhì

甲骨文、金文的至字，上面是一倒矢之形，下面一橫代表地面，像一枝箭射落到地面之形。因此，至字的本義為到、到達，又引申為極、最之義。

【至於】表示達到某種程度。又用在一句話的前面，表示另提一事。

【至交】關係最為密切的朋友。

【至高無上】最高；沒有更高的。

【至理名言】最正確、最有價值的話。

甲骨文

金 文

小 篆

In the Oracle-Bone Inscriptions and Bronze Inscriptions, the character 至 looks like an upside-down arrow on a horizontal line standing for the ground, signalling an arrow has reached the ground. Therefore, the primary meaning of 至 is "to reach", from which have derived its meanings of "the extreme point" and "the most".

【至於】(1) to go so far as (2) as for

【至交】most intimate friend

【至高無上】most lofty; supreme

【至理名言】famous dictum; maxim

shè

唐代的武則天是一個喜歡別出心裁的人，特別喜歡亂造字、亂改字。有一次她對大臣們說：「射字由身字和寸字組成，一個人的身高只有一寸，應該是指矮小的意思；而矮字由矢和委組成，委有發放之意，把箭（矢）發放出去，應該是射箭的意思。所以這兩個字應該掉換過來使用才是。」其實射字的本義就是射箭。古文字的射字就是一個人用手拉弓發箭的形象，只是到了小篆，弓箭之形訛變成身字，右邊的手變成了寸，原來的形象完全消失，無從會意，才讓武則天鬧了這麼個大笑話。

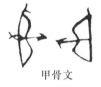

甲骨文

金 文

小 篆

Wu Zetian (Wu Tse-t'ien), Empress of the Tang Dynasty, fond of coining new characters and altering existing ones, once said to her ministers, "The characters 射 and 矮 should exchange their meanings. 射 should mean 矮 (short), since its components are 身 (body) and 寸 (a measure of length, a little longer than an inch), and a man of about an inch is short. On the other hand, 矮 should mean 射 (to shoot), since its components are 矢 (arrow) and 委 (to let go), and to let go an arrow means to shoot." In most of the ancient writing systems, however, the character 射 looks like a man drawing a bow. It is only in the Later Seal Character that the part signalling bow and arrow, by mistake, becomes bodylike and the part signalling hand becomes 寸. The original picturelike image has disappeared all together. And it is no longer possible to judge its meaning from its shape. That is why Wu Zetian made herself a laughing stock by her suggestion.

jí

疾原本是個會意字。甲骨文、金文的疾字，均像一個人腋下中箭之形，表示受了箭傷，其本義是指外傷。但從小篆開始，疾字變成了從疒矢聲的形聲字，其意義也發生了變化，即由原來專指外傷變成泛指小病（比較輕的病）。所以，古代疾、病有別，一般來說，重病為"病"，輕病為"疾"。另外，疾的本義為以矢射人，矢飛急速，所以疾字又有快、急促的意思。

【疾言厲色】言語急促，神色嚴厲，常形容對人發怒時說話的神情。

【疾惡如仇】憎恨壞人壞事如同仇敵。

甲骨文　　　　　　金　文　　　　　　小　篆

疾 was originally an ideograpb. In both the Oracle-Bone Inscriptions and Bronze Inscriptions, the character 疾 looks like a man hit by an arrow under the armpit, signalling to be wounded by an arrow. It can also refer to wound in general. In the Later Seal Character, however, the character 疾 becomes a phonetic compound, with 疒 (illness) as the radical and 矢 as the phonetic, and its meaning is also changed from "wound" to "ailment". Though at the beginning 疾 meant some what differently from 病, which referred to serious illness. As the original meaning of 疾 was to shoot someone with an arrow and arrows fly fast, 疾 can also mean "fast" and "quick".

【疾言厲色】harsh words and stern looks

【疾惡如仇】to hate evil as much as one hates an enemy

hóu

甲骨文、金文的侯字，像一支箭（矢）正向箭靶子射去之形，其本義即指箭靶。上古時代，人們以弓矢為常用武器，他們中力強善射的人常常被大家推為首領。射箭中侯（靶）就是善射，故稱善射者為"侯"。後來侯成為爵位名稱，為五等爵中的第二等，又可作為對達官貴人或士大夫之間的尊稱。

【侯服玉食】穿王侯的衣服，吃珍貴的食物，形容生活窮奢極侈。

甲骨文　　　　　金　文　　　　　小　篆

In the Oracle-Bone Inscriptions and Bronze Inscriptions, the character 侯 looks like an arrow flying to the target, hence the original meaning "target for archery". In ancient times, bow and arrow was a very important weapon, and those who were good at shooting were usually selected as leaders. As 侯 meant target, those who were good at hitting the target were also known as 侯. In the Chinese system of nobility, 侯 ranks the second, equivalent to marquis. But it can also be used as a general term for high officers and noble lords.

【侯服玉食】luxurious clothing and sumptuous food

hán

甲骨文、金文的函字，像一隻裝着箭矢的箭囊之形，囊的一邊有鼻扣，可以把它懸掛在人的腰間。函的本義指箭囊，即裝箭的袋子，俗稱"箭壺"。函是用來盛放箭矢的，故有容納、包含之義，又泛指匣子、盒子、封套、信封等，引申為指書信、信件。

甲骨文

金 文

小 篆

In the Oracle-Bone Inscriptions and Bronze Inscriptions, the character 函 looks like a bag containing an arrow, i.e. a quiver. The quiver has an eyelet on its side so that it may be attached to the belt of a man. From this original meaning of "quiver" have derived its more general meanings: "to contain", and "container", especially "envelope". Nowadays it is more usually used in the sense of "letter" — the contained in an envelope.

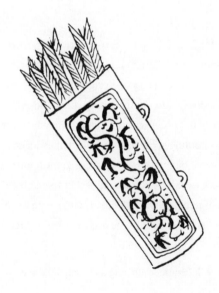

fú

甲骨文、金文的箙本是一個會意字，像一個插箭的架子，上面倒插着箭矢的形狀。它的本義即指盛箭的用具。小篆的箙字變成從竹服聲的形聲字。之所以從竹，是因為箭架多用竹木做成。

甲骨文

金文

小篆

In the Oracle-Bone Inscriptions and Bronze Inscriptions, the character 箙, an ideograph, looks like a rack for holding arrows. And that is its primary meaning. In the Later Seal Character, it becomes a phonetic compound, with 竹 (bamboo) as its radical as it is usually made of bamboo, and 服 as its phonetic.

gōng

弓是一種用來射箭的武器。以堅韌之木為幹，以絲為弦，搭箭弓上，可以引弦而發之。甲骨文的弓字，正像一把這樣的弓形；金文的弓字，則有弓背而省略弓弦，變成了無弦之弓。由於弓背的形狀是彎曲的，所以弓字又有彎曲之義。凡從"弓"之字，都與弓及其作用有關，如弦、彈、張、弛、弩等。

【弓腰】即彎腰。

【弓月】指半月。形狀似弓，故稱。

甲骨文

金文

小篆

弓 refers to the weapon used for shooting an arrow, i.e. bow. In the Oracle-Bone Inscriptions, the character 弓 is in the shape of a complete bow with its string and back. In the Bronze Inscriptions, the character 弓 looks like a bow with its back only, a stringless bow. As the bow back is curved, the character 弓 has also taken on the meaning of "curve". Characters with 弓 as a component all have to do with the bow and its uses, e.g. 弦 (string), 彈 (to shoot a pellet), 張 (to stretch), 弛 (to relax), 弩 (volley-bow), etc.

【弓腰】to bend forward

【弓月】half-moon

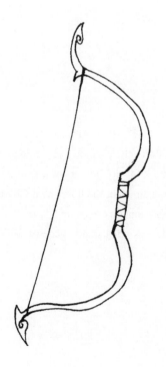

yǐn

甲骨文和早期金文中的引字，像一個人挽弓拉弦之形。後來的金文引字則省去人形，僅在弓形上保留一短畫以表示拉弓之意。引的本義為開弓，引申為拉、牽挽之義，又含有延長、拉長及帶領、勸導等義。

【引導】帶領。

【引誘】誘導，多指引人做壞事。

【引而不發】射箭時拉開弓卻不把箭放出去。比喻善於引導或控制。

【引狼入室】比喻把敵人或壞人引入內部。

甲骨文　　　　　金　文　　　　　小　篆

In the Oracle-Bone Inscriptions and early Bronze Inscriptions, the character 引 looks like a man drawing a bow. In the late Bronze Inscriptions, the man part is left out, but a short stroke is added to the bow part to signal the drawing of it. The primary meaning of 引 is to draw a bow, but it is also used in the more general sense of pulling. Other extended meanings of 引 include "to lengthen", "to elongate", "to lead" and "to persuade".

【引導】to guide

【引誘】to lure

【引而不發】to draw the bow but not discharge the arrow; to adopt a heuristic approach

【引狼入室】to invite a wolf into the house; to open the door to a dangerous foe

xián

弦，是指繃在弓背兩端之間的繩狀物，多用牛筋或絲麻製成，用來彈射箭矢。小篆的弦字，從弓從玄，玄即絲繩，表示以絲繩作為弓弦的意思。弦除了用作弓弦之意外，還可以用來指繃在樂器上用來彈撥發聲的線；泛指繃直的線狀物。

【弦外之音】比喻言外之意。

小篆

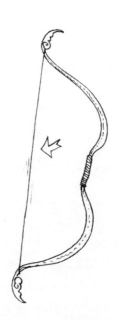

弦 refers to the stringlike material, made of ox sinew or silk, stretched between the two ends of a bow back for shooting an arrow. In the Later Seal Character, the character 弦 consists of 弓 (bow) and 玄 (silk cord), signalling a string made of silk. Apart from this use, the character 弦 may also refer to the strings stretched across a musical instrument to give sound, or any other stringlike things.

【弦外之音】overtones

dàn

甲骨文的彈字，像在弓弦上加一顆圓形丸粒的形狀，用以表示可以發射的彈丸。小篆彈字從弓單聲，則變成形聲字。彈的本義指彈丸，又指彈弓。該字還讀為**tán**，用作動詞，表示用彈弓發射彈丸之義，引申為用手指撥弦或敲擊之義。

【彈丸】供彈弓射擊用的丸。又比喻狹小。

【彈(tán)劾】檢舉、抨擊官吏的過失、罪狀。

【彈(tán)弦】彈奏弦樂器。

【彈(tán)冠】用手指彈去冠上灰塵。又"彈冠相慶"，比喻因即將作官而互相慶賀。多用於貶義。

甲骨文

小篆

In the Oracle-Bone Inscriptions, the character 彈 looks like a pellet on a bow-string, ready to be shot. In the Later Seal Character, it becomes a phonetic compound with 弓 as the radical and 單 as the phonetic. The character 彈 primarily refers to the pellet, or the catapult, the instrument for shooting a pellet. But it may also be used as a verb, pronounced as tán, meaning "to shoot a pellet", from which have derived its senses of "plucking (a stringed musical instrument)" and "playing (a keyboard musical instrument)".

【彈丸】(1) pellet (2) a tiny area

【彈(tán)劾】to impeach

【彈(tán)弦】to pluck a stringed musical instrument

【彈(tán)冠】(lit.) to dust off the hat; (also 彈冠相慶)(derog.) to congratulate each other on the prospect of getting good appointments

dùn

盾，即盾牌，是古代一種用來防護身體、遮擋刀箭的武器。金文的盾字，或從十豚聲，其中的"十"即盾的象形。

【盾威】指兵力士氣。

【盾鼻】盾牌的把手。

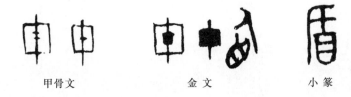

甲骨文　　　　金文　　　　小篆

盾 refers to the shield, an instrument for protecting one self from arrows, blows, etc. In the Bronze Inscriptions, the character 盾 sometimes has " 十 " as the radical and 豚 as the phonetic, and "十" is a sign for shield.

【盾威】strength and morale of troops

【盾鼻】shield handle

jiǎ

甲是古代軍人作戰時穿的革製護身服，上面綴滿金屬硬片，以防止刀兵的傷害。甲骨文、金文的甲字，像甲塊片片相連的形狀。有的則簡化為十字形。它的本義即指鎧甲，引申指動物身上起保護作用的硬殼，如龜甲、甲殼、指甲等。甲字又用作天干名，是十個天干中的第一位，故引申指居第一位之義。

【甲兵】鎧甲和兵器，泛指武備、軍事。又指披堅執銳的士兵。

【甲子】用干支紀年或算歲數時，六十組干支輪一周叫一個甲子。又代指歲月、年歲。

【甲第】舊時豪門貴族的宅第。又指科舉考試的第一等。

甲骨文　　　　　金　文　　　　　小　篆

甲 means "armour", the protective covering made of leather and metal, worn in former times by soldiers in fighting to prevent themselves from getting wounded. In the Oracle-Bone Inscriptions and Bronze Inscriptions, the character 甲 looks like plates of armour linked together; and sometimes it is simply represented by a cross. 甲 primarily refers to armour, from which has derived its use for the hard shells of animals, e.g. 龜甲 (tortoise-shell), 甲殼 (crust), 指甲 (nail). The character 甲 is also the name of one of the ten Heavenly Stems, a traditional Chinese system of sequence. As it ranks first there, 甲 has taken on the meaning of first as well.

【甲兵】(1) armour and arms (2) soldiers well armed and protected

【甲子】a traditional Chinese way of counting years, consisting of sixty years in a cycle

【甲第】(1) residence of nobility in former age (2) the first place in an imperial examination of feudal China

jiè

古文字的介字，像一個側立的人形，人身前後的兩點代表護身的鎧甲，表示人身上穿着鎧甲的意思。介的本義指人穿的鎧甲。介為人身裏甲，引申為指處於兩者之間，如介居。此外，介還有剛硬、耿直、孤傲等義。

【介士】披甲的武士。又指耿直的人。

【介居】處於二者之間。又指獨處、獨居。

【介特】單身孤獨的人。又指孤高，不隨流俗。

【介紹】使雙方相識或發生關係，用作聯繫、接洽、舉薦的意思。

【介入】插進兩者之間干預其事。

【介意】在意，把不愉快的事記在心裡。

【介蟲】有硬殼的蟲類。

甲骨文

石鼓文

小篆

In ancient writing systems, the character 介 looks like the side view of a man in between two dots standing for armour. The original meaning of 介 was the armour worn by men. As the armour covers the man, in other words, the man is in between the front and back parts of armour, 介 has also taken on the meaning of "in between", e.g. 介居 (to be situated between). In addition, 介 can also mean "upright and outspoken" and "proud and aloof".

【介士】(1) armour-clad soldier (2) upright person

【介居】(1) to be situated between (2) in solitude

【介特】(1) person in isolation (2) proud and aloof

【介紹】to introduce

【介入】to intervene

【介意】to take offence; to mind

【介蟲】scale insect

xìng

幸本指手銬，是古代鎖執犯人的一種刑具。甲骨文幸字，正像一副中空而兩端有轄的手銬形狀。幸的本義是手銬，是專用來拘鎖犯人的。可以説它是不幸的象徵。但它卻又有逢凶化吉、幸運、慶幸等意義。因此，帝王親臨也稱"幸"，如巡幸（巡行考察）、寵幸等。

【幸災樂禍】對他人遭災罹禍不同情反而高興慶幸。

甲骨文

金 文

小 篆

幸 originally meant handcuffs. In the Oracle-Bone Inscriptions, the character has the shape of a pair of ancient handcuffs: there are fasteners on the two ends while the middle part is empty. As handcuffs are used to fasten the wrists of a criminal, they become the symbol of misfortune. However, the character 幸 has also mysteriously taken on the opposite meaning: "good fortune", "luck" and "blessing". Thus the visit to a place by the emperor is known as 幸, e.g. 巡幸 (fortunate visit), 寵幸 ([to gain] favour with the emperor).

【幸災樂禍】to take pleasure in other's misfortune

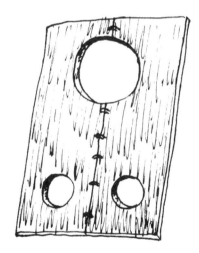

zhí

甲骨文的執字，像一個人雙手被手銬枷鎖扣住的形狀，其本義為拘捕。由拘捕的意思，執字又引申出持、拿、掌握、掌管、施行、堅持等義。

【執法】執行法令。又指執法的官吏。
【執政】掌握政權、主持政務。又指主管某一事務的人。
【執意】堅持己意。
【執照】證明身份的憑據、證件。

甲骨文

金文

小篆

In the Oracle-Bone Inscriptions, the character 執 looks like a man with his two hands in handcuffs. The original meaning of 執 was "to arrest", from which have derived its extended meanings of "hold", "grasp", "master", "administer", "execute", "stick to", etc.

【執法】(1) to enforce the law (2) law-executor
【執政】(1) in power; in office (2) person in charge
【執意】to insist on
【執照】testimonial; identification

xíng

刑，即刑罰，特指對犯人的體罰。甲骨文的刑字，像人被鎖拘在一個木製的籠框中的樣子。把犯人關在囚籠中遊街示眾，是古代對犯人常用的一種體罰方式。金文刑字的人形訛變為刀形，又移出籠外；而囚籠之形又與"井"字形相近，故小篆刑字就訛變成為從刀井聲的形聲字。

【刑法】懲罰罪犯的法律。

【刑罰】古代刑與罰有區別：刑指肉刑、死刑；罰指以金錢贖罪。後來泛指對罪犯實行懲罰的強制方法。

【刑訊】用刑具逼供的審訊。

金 文　　　　小 篆

刑 means punishment, especially corporal punishment. In the Oracle-Bone Inscriptions, the character 刑 looks like a man in a cagelike framework made of wood. It was a common punishment in the old days to parade a criminal in a cage through the streets. In the Bronze Inscriptions, the man part of 刑 becomes knifelike and is moved to the outside of the cage. As the shape of a cage is very close to that of a well (井), in the Later Seal Character, 刑 becomes, by mistake, a phonetic compound with 刀 (knife) as the radical and 井 (well) as the phonetic.

【刑法】criminal law

【刑罰】punishment

【刑訊】inquisition by torture

yǔ

圉字從口從幸，口像牢籠，幸為手銬枷鎖，故其本義為監牢。甲骨文的圉字，像一人帶銬蹲坐牢籠之中。正是牢獄的形象描繪。所以古代的牢獄又稱"囹圉"或"圄圉"。此外，圉字還有養馬之義。

甲骨文　　　　　　金 文　　　　　小 篆

The character 圉 consists of 口 and 幸. The former stands for prison and the latter handcuffs. Hence the primary meaning "prison". In the Oracle-Bone Inscriptions, the character 圉 looks like a man with handcuffs in a prison cell. That is why prison in former times is also known as 囹圉 or 圄圉. In addition, 圉 can also mean "to breed horses".

bào

甲骨文的報字，像一個被鐐銬鎖着雙手的罪人跪地聽候判決的樣子，後面還有人用手按着他的頭，使之服罪。它的本來意思為判決犯人，或按罪判刑。判刑需要向上報告和向下公佈，由此報字又引申出"報告"、"傳達"、"通知"等義。

甲骨文

金 文

小 篆

In the Oracle-Bone Inscriptions, the character 報 looks like a handcuffed offender on his knees, who is about to be sentenced, and there is a man pressing his head from behind so as to make him obedient. The original meaning of 報 was to sentence an offender according to his crime. To sentence an offender, one must report it to the higher authorities and publicly declare it. Hence the character 報 has taken on the meanings of "report" and "inform" as well.

biān

鞭是一種用來驅趕牲畜的用具，古代也用作刑具，俗稱"鞭子"。金文的鞭是個會意字，像人手持鞭子之形，又像以鞭抽打人身之形，故鞭字又可用作動詞，有鞭打的意思。

【鞭策】鞭打，用策趕馬。比喻嚴格督促以激勵上進。

【鞭長莫及】鞭子雖長，難及馬腹。比喻力量達不到。

【鞭辟入裡】形容能透徹說明問題，深中要害。

金文　　　　　　　　　小篆

鞭 refers to the whip, an instrument for driving cattle along or hitting people. In the Bronze Inscriptions, the character 鞭, an ideograph, looks like a man with a whip in hand, or a man beating another with a whip. So 鞭 may also be used as a verb, meaning to beat with a whip.

【鞭策】 to spur on

【鞭長莫及】 beyond the reach of one's power

【鞭辟入裡】 penetrating

gān

古文字的干字，像一桿頭上分叉的長柄工具，古代用作武器。這種叉形武器，既可用於進攻，又可抵擋敵人的兵器，類似盾的作用，後代專指防禦性武器，成為盾的代名詞。"干"是一種武器，引申為動詞，含有觸犯的意思，如干犯、干涉、干預等。

【干戈】指用於防禦的盾和用於進攻的戈戟。干戈是古代戰爭的常用兵器，故也用為兵器的通稱，後代多用來代指戰爭，如"化干戈為玉帛"（變戰爭為和平。玉帛是和親的禮物，代指和平）。

甲骨文　　　　金文　　　　小篆

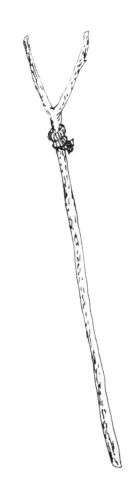

In ancient writing systems, the character 干 looks like a two-tined fork with a long handle. This forklike weapon may be used both to attack the enemy and to protect oneself. But its meaning has evolved over the years and it has come to refer to defensive weapons only, a substitute for 盾 (shield), in other words. Nevertheless, 干 is a weapon; and used as a verb it means to violate, e.g. 干犯 (to offend), 干涉 (to interfere) and 干預 (intervene).

【干戈】(lit.) shield and spear; weapons; war

dān

單，本是古代的一種打獵工具，也可用作殺敵的武器。甲骨文、金文的單字，像一件長柄兩角的杈桿之形。這種杈桿，可以用來刺擊或抵擋野獸；它的上端叉角上還縛有石塊，可以甩出去擊傷獵物。這種打獵工具盛行於原始社會時代，後世罕見。而單字則多借用為單獨、單一、單薄等義，其本義已漸消失，罕為人知。

【單純】簡單純一，不複雜。

【單刀直入】比喻說話直截了當，不繞彎子。

【單槍匹馬】比喻單獨行動，沒有別人幫助。

甲骨文

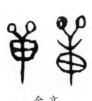

金文

小篆

單 was an instrument for hunting or fighting in ancient times. In the Oracle-Bone Inscriptions and Bronze Inscriptions, the character 單 looks like a two-tined fork with a long handle. One may stab animals or people with its forks or hit them by throwing the stone fastened to its head. This type of weapon was very common in the primitive society, but rarely seen in later ages. So its original meaning has died out, and 單 is nowadays more usually used in the senses of "alone", "single", "thin", etc.

【單純】simple; pure

【單刀直入】to come straight to the point

【單槍匹馬】single-handed

wǎng

網是捕魚鱉鳥獸的工具。甲骨文網字,左右兩邊是木棍,中間網繩交錯、網眼密佈,正是一張網的真實形狀。金文的網字略有簡化,而楷書的網則增加絲旁表示類屬,增加聲符亡表示讀音,屬於繁化。在漢字中凡由網字和它的變形(罒)所組成的字大都與網及其作用有關,如羅、罟、罾等。

【網羅】搜羅、徵集。

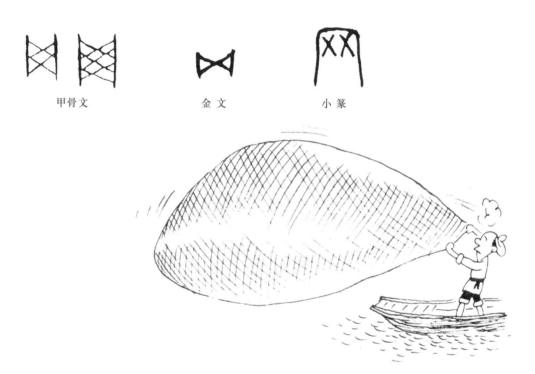

甲骨文　　　　　金文　　　　　小篆

網 means "net", an instrument for catching fish or birds. In the Oracle-Bone Inscriptions, the character 網 looks exactly like a net, strings woven together between two sticks with regular spaces. In the Bronze Inscriptions, its structure is simplified, while in the Regular Script it undergoes an opposite process, added with a thread part (糹) as its radical, and a phonetic part 亡. Characters with 網 and it's anamorphosis (罒) as a component most have to do with the net and its uses, e.g. 羅 (a net for catching birds), 罟 (fishing net) and 罾 (a fishing net with wood or bamboo sticks as framework).

【網羅】(lit.) to catch with a net; to enlist the services of

luó

甲骨文羅字，上面是一張網，下面是一隻鳥的形象，表示鳥在網中的意思。羅的本義為以網捕鳥，如"門可羅雀"等；引申為搜羅、收集等義，如"網羅人才"等。此外，羅字還可用作名詞，指羅網，如"天羅地網"等。

甲骨文

小 篆

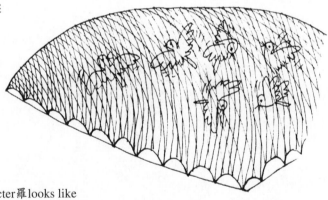

In the Oracle-Bone Inscriptions, the character 羅 looks like a net on a brid, signalling to catch a bird with a net. And that is its primary meaning, e.g. 門可羅雀 ((lit.) One can catch sparrows on the doorstep; Visitos are few and far between.), 網羅人才 (to enlist able men). 羅 may also be used as a noun, e.g. 天羅地網 (nets above and snares below).

bì

畢是古代用來捕捉鳥獸的一種帶柄的小網。甲骨文的畢字，正像這種長柄網形。或從又，表示以手把持之意。金文畢字從田，則表示畢是用來田獵的工具。所以《説文解字》稱："畢，田網也。" 此字後來多用為結束、終止、完成之義，又引申為皆、全、完全之義。其本義則逐漸消失。

【畢生】一生；終生。

【畢命】結束生命（多指橫死）。

【畢業】完成學業，指學習期滿並達到規定的要求。

甲骨文

金文

小篆

畢was a small net with a handle for catching birds in former times. In the Oracle-Bone Inscriptions, the character 畢 looks like a picture of this type of net; sometimes it has the part 又, signalling it is to be held by a hand. In the Bronze Inscriptions, it has a component 田 (field), indicating it is an instrument for hunting in the fields. Thus, *Xu Shen* says in his *Origin of Chinese Characters,* " 畢 is a net for field hunting". However, this character is nowadays more usually used in the sense of "end", "completion" and "all", whereas its original meaning is lost.

【畢生】all one's life

【畢命】to get killed

【畢業】to graduate

qín

甲骨文的禽字，像一張帶柄的網形，是一種用來捕捉鳥雀的工具。禽的本義指捕鳥的網，又通"擒"，有捕捉的意思。禽又是鳥類的通稱，同時也泛指鳥獸。

【禽獸】飛禽走獸的統稱，也單指獸類。又罵人之語，猶言"畜牲"。

【禽獸行】指違背人倫的行為。後稱亂倫為禽獸行。

金文

小篆

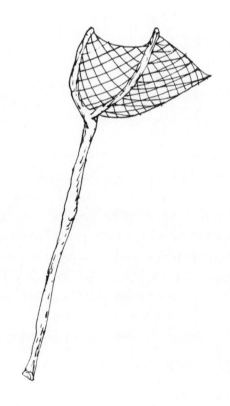

In the Oracle-Bone Inscriptions, the character 禽 looks like a net with a handle, an instrument for catching birds. The original meaning of禽was "net for catching birds", but it can also be used as a verb, meaning the same as 擒, "to catch". 禽 is also a general term for birds, sometimes it may even cover the meaning of beasts as well.

【禽獸】birds and beasts
【禽獸行】bestial acts, esp. incestuous acts

gāng

甲骨文剛字，像用刀斷網之形，表示堅硬鋒利之意；金文增加"山"形，故又含有穩固、堅強之義。

【剛強】性格堅強，不怕困難或不屈服於惡勢力。

【剛勁】（指姿態、風格等的）挺拔有力。

【剛正不阿】剛強正直，不迎合，不偏私。

【剛愎(bì)自用】傲慢而固執，不接受別人的意見而一意孤行。

甲骨文

金文

小篆

In the Oracle-Bone Inscriptions, the character 剛 looks like a net beside a knife, signalling hard and sharp. In the Bronze Inscriptions, a mountain part (山) is added to reinforce its sense of firmness.

【剛強】firm; unyielding

【剛勁】bold; vigorous

【剛正不阿】upright and never stooping to flattery

【剛愎(bì)自用】self-willed; headstrong

wǔ

午為"杵"的本字。甲骨文和金文的午字，像一個兩頭粗圓中間腰細的棒槌之形，本義即指杵。杵是用來春米的，用作動詞暗含有抵觸之義，故從"午"的字多含有觸犯、違背之義，如忤、迕等。午字後來多借用為干支名，是十二地支的第七位。它的本義則為杵字所代替。

【午時】舊式計時法指上午十一點到下午一點的時間。又泛指日中的時候。

【午夜】半夜；夜裡十二點前後。

甲骨文

金文

小篆

午 was the original form of 杵, referring to the pestle. In the Oracle-Bone Inscriptions and Bronze Inscriptions, the character 午 looks like a pestle, whose two ends are rounded and bigger than the middle. As a pestle is used for husking rice, characters with 午 as a component most have a sense of "offending" and "violating", e.g. 忤 (disobedient), 迕 (to go against). But 午 is now mainly used as a name of the seventh Earthly Branch, a traditional Chinese system of sequence, and its original meaning is expressed by 杵.

【午時】from 11 a.m. to 1 p.m.; midday

【午夜】midnight

chōng

古代沒有碾米的機器，為穀物脫殼全靠手工操作。這種手工勞動就叫做"舂"。古文字的舂字，像人雙手握杵搗碎臼中糧食的樣子，其本義就是"舂米"，即用杵在臼中搗去穀物的皮殼。

甲骨文

金文

小篆

舂 means to husk rice. This was done by hand before the invention of husking machines. In ancient writing systems, the character 舂 looks like a picture of this activity: two hands holding a pestle on top of a mortar, signalling to remove the husks of grain by striking with a pestle in a mortar.

jiù

臼是古代的舂米器具，多用石頭鑿成，中間凹下以盛穀物。甲骨文、金文的臼字，像一個舂米用的石臼形。它的本義就指舂米用的石臼，又指形狀似臼之物。漢字中凡從"臼"之字，大都與臼類或坑類有關，如舀、舂、臽等。

【臼科】指坑坎。又比喻陳舊的格調，又稱"窠臼"。

陶 文

小 篆

臼 means "mortar", a vessel made from stone, for containing grain to be husked. In the Oracle-Bone Inscriptions and Bronze Inscriptions, the character 臼 has the shape of a mortar. It refers to mortar and mortarlike things at that. Characters with 臼 as a component most have to do with mortarlike things, e.g. 舀 (to ladle), 舂 (to husk) and 臽 (pitfall).

【臼科】(lit.) pit; (also 窠臼) set pattern

yǎo

舀字從爪從臼，是個會意字。小篆的舀字，像用手到臼中取稻米之形。舀的本義為探取、抱取；引申為專指用瓢、勺等取東西（多指液體）。

【舀子】舀水、油等液體用的器具。

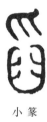

小 篆

The character 舀, an ideograph, consists of 爪 (hand) and 臼 (mortar). In the Later Seal Character, the character 舀 looks like the grasping of rice from a mortar with a hand. Its original meaning was to lift things from a mortar. But its meaning has been shifted and it now means to get something, especially liquid, with a ladle or spoon.

【舀子】ladle

甲骨文的力字，是古代一種耕地的農具——耒的象形：上端為長柄，下端彎曲的部份是用來鏟土的耒頭，中間加一豎橫是用來踏腳的。所以，力字的本義是指一種農具，即耒。用耒來耕地是要使勁用力的，故力字引申為指力量、力氣，又引申為指能力、威力、權力等。

【力不從心】想作某事而力量達不到，即心有餘而力不足。

【力爭上游】努力爭取先進。上游，江河的上流，比喻先進。

甲骨文

金文

小篆

In the Oracle-Bone Inscriptions, the character 力 looks like a farm implement for ploughing: the upper part is the handle, the lower part is the ploughshare, and the vertical stroke suggests the place to step on. In other words, the original meaning of 力 was 耒 (plough). As it takes a great deal of strength to turn over land with a plough, the character 力 has taken on the meaning of "strength", from which derive the meanings of "ability", "power", etc.

【力不從心】ability falling short of one's wishes

【力爭上游】to strive for the best

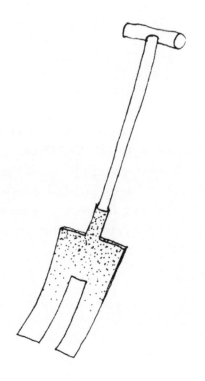

nán

男字由"田"、"力"兩部份組成，其中"力"就是古代農具"耒"。古代男耕女織，用耒在田裡耕作是成年男子的專職，所以男字的本義即指成年男子，泛指男性，與"女"相對，又專指兒子。

【男婚女嫁】指兒女婚嫁成家。

甲骨文

金文

小篆

The character 男 consists of 田 (field) and 力 (plough). It was a tradition for men to till the fields and women to weave cloth in former times. So the character 力, to plough the fields, has come to refer to the people who do the ploughing i.e. adult men. Later its meaning has been broadened to cover the whole male sex, opposite to 女 (female). But it may also refer to son in particular.

【男婚女嫁】A man should take a wife and a woman should take a husband.

lěi

耒是古代一種鬆土的農具,形狀似錘而頂端分叉作齒形。早期金文的耒字,從又從力(力即耒),像一隻手持着一把耒的樣子。小篆的耒字,手形的"又"省變為三撇,下面的耒形(力)則訛為"木"。這種訛化後的結構,為楷書耒字所本。漢字中凡從"耒"之字,都與農具或農作有關,如耜、耕、耤、耦等。

【耒耜】古代一種像犁的農具,也用作農具的統稱。

金文

小篆

耒was a spadelike tool with a forked head for breaking land in ancient times. In the early Bronze Inscriptions, the character 耒 looks like a hand holding a forked plough. In the Later Seal Character, the hand part is simplified into three left-falling strokes and the plough part becomes wood (木) by mistake. This mistaken structure is the origin of the character 耒 in the Regular Script. Characters with 耒 as a component all have to do with farming tools or crops, e.g. 耜 (a spade-like tool), 耕 (to plough), 耤 (cultivation), 耦 (two men ploughing side by side).

【耒耜】forked plough; farming tool

jí

甲骨文耤是一個會意字，像一個人手持農具耒在用力鏟土之形，其本義即為耕種。金文耤字增加"昔"旁表示讀音，小篆以後更加以簡化，成為一個從耒昔聲的形聲字。耤在古籍中多寫作藉，如藉田，又作籍田。

甲骨文

金 文

小 篆

In the Oracle-Bone Inscriptions, the character 耤, an ideograph, looks like a farmer turning over land strenously with a plough, hence its meaning "to cultivate the ground". In the Bronze Inscritpions, the part 昔 is added to indicate its pronunciation. In the Later Seal Character, its structure is simplified, resulting in a phonetic compound with 耒 as the radical and 昔 as the phonetic. But in ancient books, the character 耤 was usually written as 藉 e.g. 藉田 (also 籍田, field cultivated by the emperor in name).

chén

辰為"蜃"的本字。金文的辰字，即像蜃形。蜃屬蛤蚌類，有大而堅硬的扁殼，上古時代的人們用它磨製成除草的工具。如《淮南子》一書記載："古者剡（音 yǎn，削尖）耜（音 sì，古農具）而耕，摩（磨）蜃而耨（音 nòu，鋤草）。"辰字後來多借用為干支名，是十二地支的第五位。辰又是日、月、星的通稱，也泛指時辰、時光、日子等。

【辰光】時間。
【辰時】舊式計時法指上午七點到九點的時間。

甲骨文

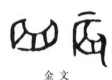

金文

小篆

辰 was the original form of 蜃 (giant clam). Thus the character 辰 in the Bronze Inscriptions is in the shape of a clam. Giant clams have big and hard shells, which can be used as tools for weeding. For example, *Huai Nan Zi* records, "In the past people sharpened ploughs to turn over land and whetted clams to remove weeds". However, the character 辰 is now mainly used as a name of the fifth Earthly Branch, a traditional Chinese system of sequence. It is also a general term for the celestial bodies like the sun, moon and stars, and may refer to time or days.

【辰光】time
【辰時】from 7:00 to 9:00 in the morning

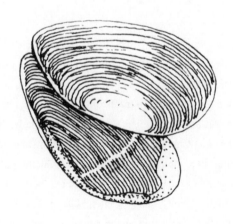

nóng

甲骨文的農字，像以蜃耨苗之形，以會耕作之意。金文農字從田，以表示農田耕種之事，其意更加明顯。所以農字的本義為耕種，又特指耕種之人，即農民。

【農夫】從事耕作的人。

【農事】耕種的活動。

【農時】指春耕、夏耘、秋收，農事的三時。

甲骨文

金文　　　　　　小篆

In the Oracle-Bone Inscriptions, the character 農 looks like the removal of weeds between crops with a clam, signalling cultivation. In the Bronze Inscriptions, it has 田 (field) as a component, and the meaning "to cultivate land" is expressed more clearly. Apart from this primary meaning, 農 may also refer to the people who do the cultivation, i.e. farmers.

【農夫】farmer

【農事】farm work

【農時】farming season

qí

甲骨文其字，很像一隻簸箕的形狀，所以其就是箕的本字，本義即指簸箕，是一種揚米去糠的器具。因簸箕係用竹編製，故加竹頭成為"箕"。而其字則被借用為代詞，復指上文的人或事；又借用為連詞，表示假設或轉折；還可用作副詞，表示猜測或祈求的意思。

甲骨文	金文	小篆

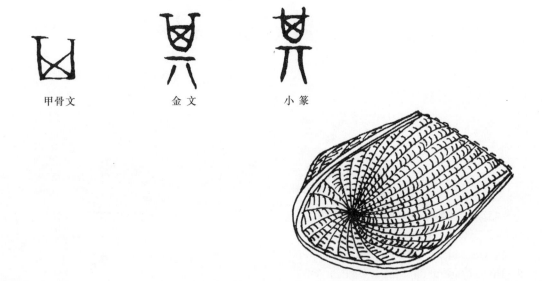

In the Oracle-Bone Inscriptions, the character 其 looks like a pan, an instrument for winnowing. In other words, 其 was the original form of 箕 (winnowing pan). As it is made of bamboo, a bamboo part is added to 其 to form箕. And the character其is now mainly used as a third person pronoun, especially in the possessive case; a conjunction, expressing presupposition or contrast; or an adverb, expressing assumption or wish.

kuài

塊字本來是個會意字。小篆的塊字，像把土塊盛於筐內之形，它的本義即指土塊。此字後來變為形聲字，如小篆的異體作從土鬼聲，而簡化字則變為從土夬聲。塊字由土塊之義，引申為泛指塊狀之物，如鐵塊、煤塊、石塊等；又引申為孤高、磊落不平之義。

【塊阜】土丘，小山。

【塊然】孤傲不拘的樣子。又指孤獨無聊。

【塊壘】心中鬱結不平。

小篆

The character 塊 was originally an ideograph. In the Later Seal Character, it looks like a basket containing lumps of soil. And lumps of soil is its primary meaning. But it has changed into a phonetic compound later. For example, the variant in the Later Seal Character has 土 (soil) as its radical and 鬼 as its phonetic; and its simplified form has 土 as the radical and 夬 as the phonetic. 塊 is also used generally for anything which is in the shape of a lump, e.g. 鐵塊 (lumps of iron), 煤塊 (lump coal), 石塊 (stone). In addition, it can mean "proud and aloof" and "open and upright".

【塊阜】hill

【塊然】proud and aloof

【塊壘】gloomy; depressed

kāng

康是"糠"的本字。甲骨文的康字,主體像一簸箕形狀,下面的四點代表穀糠,表示用簸箕把碾碎的穀皮和細屑簸揚出來。這些簸揚出來的穀皮和細屑,就是我們所說的糠。所以康字的本義是指穀糠。康字後來多借用為安樂、安寧之義,又引申為豐盛、廣大等義,故又專門造了一個"糠"字來代表它的本義。

【康莊】四通八達的大道。《爾雅 • 釋宮》:"五達謂之康,六達謂之莊。"

【康寧】平安,無疾病患難。

甲骨文　　　金文

康 was the original form of 糠. In the Oracle-Bone Inscriptions, the character 康 looks like a winnowing pan with four dots standing for husks below it, signalling to blow off the husks with a winnowing pan. These husks, or bran, are known as 糠, hence 康 originally referred to husks. The character 康, however, is now mainly used in the senses of "peace and happiness", "plentiful" and "broad". Its original meaning is expressed by 糠。

【康莊】broad road
【康寧】healthy and peaceful

fèn

甲骨文的糞字，像人一手持帚一手持箕，正在掃除塵土之形，它的本義為掃除，掃除塵土。因掃除的是髒物，所以糞字可引申為指糞便、污穢；又引申為施肥、施糞的意思。

【糞土】糞便和泥土，比喻令人厭惡的事物或不值錢的東西。引申為鄙視。

【糞除】掃除。

小篆

In the Oracle-Bone Inscriptions, the character 糞 looks like a man sweeping away the dirt with a broom and a dustpan. Hence its orignal meaning "to clean" and "to sweep away the dirt". As what is swept away is dirty, the character 糞 is also used to refer to excrement and urine; or as a verb, meaning "to apply manure".

【糞土】dung and dirt; detestable and worthless things; to despise

【糞除】to clean

qì

甲骨文的棄字，下邊是兩隻手，中間為"其"（簸箕）。上部為"子"（嬰兒），"子"的周圍幾點代表初生嬰兒身上殘留的胎液，整個字像人雙手捧箕把初生而死的嬰兒拋棄掉的樣子。因此，棄的本義指拋棄、丟掉，引申為廢棄、違背之義。

【棄井】廢井。

【棄市】古代在鬧市執行死刑，陳屍街頭示眾，稱為棄市。

【棄暗投明】比喻背棄邪惡勢力，投向正義一方。

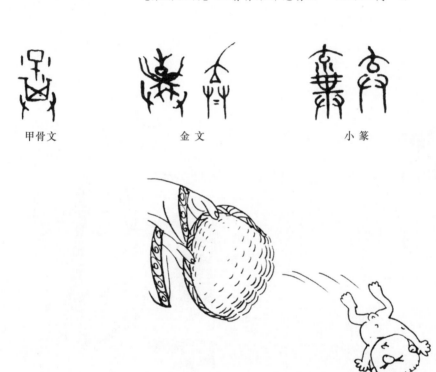

甲骨文　　　　　　金 文　　　　　　小 篆

In the Oracle-Bone Inscriptions, the character 棄 looks like two hands holding a dustpan in which is a dead newborn, and the dots around it stand for birth water, signalling to throw away a dead baby. Hence the primary meaning of 棄 is "to throw away", from which have derived the meanings "to discard", and "to go against".

【棄井】 a disused well

【棄市】 to leave a dead body in the streets

【棄暗投明】 to forsake darkness for light; to leave the evil and join the righteous cause

zhǒu

帚即掃帚，又稱掃把。甲骨文、金文中的帚是個象形字，像一把倒立着的掃帚的形狀：上部是帚棕，下部為把柄；有的在掃帚中間還用繩子加以綑紮。到了小篆以後，帚字形體發生較大變化，就不再像掃帚的形狀了。在古代，掃地做家務是婦女們幹的事情，所以婦女的"婦"字，即由女和帚組成，以表示其職責之所在。

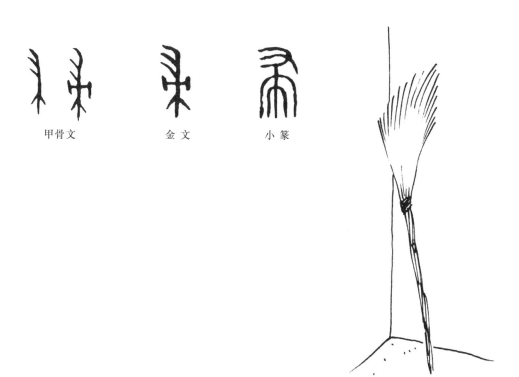

甲骨文　　　　　金　文　　　　　小　篆

帚 means "broom". In the Oracle-Bone Inscriptions and Bronze Inscriptions, the character 帚, a pictograph, looks like an upside-down broom: the upper part is the head and the lower part is the stick; sometimes there is an additional horizontal stroke signalling the binding string. In the Later Seal Character, it has undergone some change in its shape, loosing its picturelike image. As it was the responsibility of the housewife to clean the room in former times, 帚 (broom) was used together with 女 (female) to form the character 婦 (woman).

fù

古代社會，男女分工明確。男主外，女主內。男子在外耕田、種地、打獵，女子則在家織布、掃地、做飯。甲骨文、金文的婦字，正像一個女子手持掃帚之形。手持掃帚在家掃地做家務，這是已婚女子的日常工作。所以婦字的本義指已婚的女子，有時也指妻子。

【婦女】即"婦人"，指已婚女子。現在則多用作成年女性的通稱。

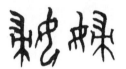

甲骨文

金文　　　　　　小篆

It was an old tradition for the man to work in the fields and the woman to work at home. While the man tills the land or goes hunting outside, the woman weaves cloth, sweeps the floor and does the cooking at home. That is why in the Oracle-Bone Inscriptions and Bronze Inscriptions, the character 婦 looks like a woman holding a broom. It is the housewife's responsibility to do the domestic chores, so 婦 primarily means "married woman" or "wife".

【婦女】women, esp. married ones

qīn

甲骨文的侵字，像人手持掃把驅趕牛群之形，表示侵奪他人財產之意。侵的本義為侵佔、掠奪，引申為指進犯、攻佔，進一步引申為欺凌、迫害之義。

【侵佔】以不法手段強將他人之物擄為己有。

【侵略】侵犯掠奪。

【侵吞】暗中佔有。又指用武力吞併別國或佔有其部份領土。

甲骨文

金文

小篆

In the Oracle-Bone Inscriptions, the character 侵 looks like a man driving cattle with a broom, signalling the annexation of others' property. Its primary meaning is "occupy" and "seize", from which have derived the extended meanings of "invade", "attack", "bully" and "persecute".

【侵佔】to invade and occupy

【侵略】aggression

【侵吞】(1) to embezzle (2) to annex

xīng

甲骨文、金文的興字，像眾手共舉一副築版（一種築土牆的工具）之形。這是眾人夯土築牆勞動場面的形象描繪。有的興字加上口形，表示一邊舉夯築土，一邊呼喊號子以協同動作。因此，興的本義為抬、舉，引申為起、起來、興起、建立，進一步引申為興旺、興盛之義。

甲骨文

金文

小篆

In the Oracle-Bone Inscriptions and Bronze Inscriptions, the character 興 looks like many hands lifting a tamping plate together. This is a vivid description of many people building together an earth wall by tamping. Sometimes there is a mouth part (口) in the character to signal that they are chanting while tamping. Hence the original meaning of 興 was "to lift", from which have derived the extended meanings of "rise", "set up", "flourish" and "thrive".

dīng

丁是個再簡單不過的字，一橫一豎鉤，好寫又易認，似乎只有文盲才不識，所以過去常用"目不識丁"這樣一個成語來挖苦那些不學無知的人。那麼丁字到底是個什麼東西呢？不說出來你可能還真不知道哩！甲骨文、金文中的丁字，原來只是一顆釘子的形象：從上面俯視，是圓形（或方形）的釘帽；從側面看，則好似一個楔子，所以丁字的本義就是釘子。丁是"釘"的本字。

【丁是丁，卯是卯】丁指凸出的榫頭，卯即卯眼。口語"丁是丁，卯是卯"，表示做起事來認真嚴肅，不肯隨便通融之義。

| 甲骨文 | 金文 | 小篆 |

丁 is a most simple Chinese character, consisting of a horizontal stroke and a vertical hook. It is so easy to write and recognize that almost everybody should be able to know it, hence the idiom 目不識丁 (ignorant of even the character 丁; utterly ignorant) is often used to mock those illiteracy. However, you may not know what 丁 meant originally if I do not tell you. In the Oracle-Bone Inscriptions and Bronze Inscriptions, the character 丁 has the shape of a nail: seen from the top, it is round (or square); and seen from the side, it is like a wedge. Therefore 丁 was the original form of 釘 and meant "nail" at the beginning.

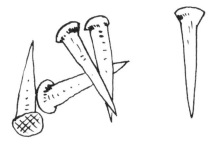

【丁是丁，卯是卯】(lit.) The tenon is a true tenon and the mortise is a true mortise; to be conscientious and meticulous.

zhuān

甲骨文專字，像一隻手在轉動紡錘的樣子，表示用紡錘盤線的意思。專的本義指紡錘，又可用作動詞，音 **tuán**，通"團"或"摶"，有盤旋、轉動的意思。此字後來多借用為單獨、單純、獨一等義。

【專心】一心一意，不分心。

【專斷】獨自決斷。

【專家】指專門從事某種事業或學問而有成就的人。

【專精】集中精力，專心一志。

甲骨文　　　　　小篆

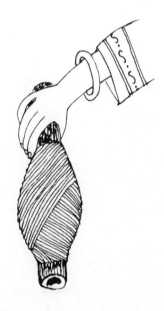

In the Oracle-Bone Inscriptions, the character 專 looks like a hand turning round a spindle, signalling to twist the thread in spinning with a spindle. The original meaning of 專 was "spindle", and it could also be used as a verb, pronounced as tuán, meaning the same as 團 or 摶, "to turn round", "to circle". Nowadays, however, it is more usually used in the senses of "alone", "pure" and "single".

【專心】with undivided attention

【專斷】to make an arbitrary decision

【專家】expert; specialist

【專精】to concentrate one's attention

　　甲骨文和早期金文的工字，像是一把帶柄的利斧形狀。斧是匠人勞動的用具，故工字的本義指用具、工具；引申為指從事手工勞動的人，即工匠。工匠作工要細緻而精巧，故工字又引申出細密、精巧之義。

【工夫】工程和勞動人力，又指素養、造詣。或作功夫。

【工巧】精緻、巧妙。又指善於取巧。

【工藝】手工技藝。

| 甲骨文 | 金　文 | 小　篆 |

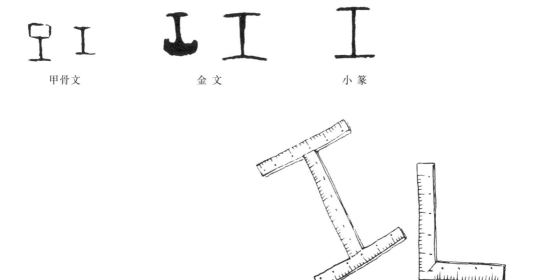

In the Oracle-Bone Inscriptions and early Bronze Inscriptions, the character 工 looks like an axe with a handle. The axe is a very important tool of a carpenter, so from its primary meaning of "tool" has derived the sense of "craftsman", the man who uses this tool. The craftsman must work with great care and skill, and the character 工 has further taken on the meanings of "careful" and "skillful".

【工夫】 (also 功夫) (1) work; effort (2) workmanship

【工巧】 exquisite

【工藝】 craft

qū

曲

甲骨文、金文的曲字，像一把曲尺之形，其本義指彎曲。與"直"相對；引申為曲折、隱祕、婉轉等義。曲字還可以讀 **qǔ**，指音樂的曲調。

【曲意】委曲己意而奉承別人。

【曲筆】封建時代史官不據實直書，有意掩蓋真相的記載。

【曲解】錯誤地解釋客觀事實或別人的原意（多指故意）。

【曲直】有理和無理。又作"是非曲直"。

【曲房】深邃幽隱的密室。

【曲學】偏頗狹隘的言論。也指孤陋寡聞的人。

【曲高和寡】曲調高深，能跟着唱的人很少。比喻人品、言行、作品高超，難得知音。

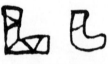
甲骨文

小 篆

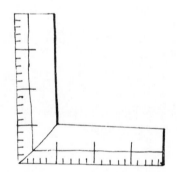

In the Oracle-Bone Inscriptions and Bronze Inscriptions, the character 曲 looks like a carpenter's square. Its primary meaning is "bent", opposite to 直 (straight), from which have derived its senses of "winding", "hidden" and "indirect". Pronounced as qǔ, 曲 can also refer to the tune of a song.

【曲意】to go out of one's way (to curry favour)

【曲筆】to misrepresent (in order to cover up the truth)

【曲解】to misunderstand

【曲直】right and wrong

【曲房】a hidden and secret room

【曲學】(1) biased opinion (2) ill-informed

【曲高和寡】(lit.) melodies of superior taste find few to join in chorus; caviar to the general

jù

巨為“矩”的本字。矩是一種畫角量方的曲尺。如《荀子》：“圓者中規，方者中矩。”其中規指圓規，矩為曲尺。金文的巨字，像一個人手持一把曲尺的形狀，其本義即指曲尺。此字後來多借用為大、最、極等義，故另造“矩”代替它的本義。

【巨室】大廈、大屋。又指有世襲特權的豪門貴族。

【巨眼】指善於鑑別是非真偽的眼力、見識。

金文　　　　小篆

巨 was the original form of 矩, referring to the carpenter's square. Thus *Xun Zi* (Hsün-Tzu) says, "The circles are as perfect as drawn with a pair of compasses, and the squares with a carpenter's square." In the Bronze Inscriptions the character 巨 looks like a man holding a carpenter's square in hand. However the character 巨 is now mainly used in the sense of "huge" and "gigantic", and its original meaning is expressed by 矩.

【巨室】(1) huge house (2) aristocratic family

【巨眼】of excellent judgment

zhàng

小篆的丈字，從十從又，像人手（又）持量尺（十）測量長度之形。丈的本義為丈量，又是長度單位的名稱。十尺為一丈，十丈為一引。此外，丈字還用作對成年或老年男子的尊稱。

【丈量】用步弓、皮尺等量土地面積。

【丈人】古時對老年男子的尊稱。今又指岳父。

【丈夫】成年男子。又特指妻子對其配偶的稱呼。

小篆

In the Later Seal Character, the character 丈 consists of 十 (ruler) and 又 (hand), signalling to measure length with a ruler in hand. The primary meaning of 丈 is to measure, but it is also used as a measure of length, equal to ten 尺 or one tenth of 引 in the Chinese System, and three metres and one third in the Metric System. In addition, 丈 can also be used as an honorific term for the adult man, especially the aged.

【丈量】to measure (land)

【丈人】(1) aged man (2) father-in-law

【丈夫】(1) adult man (2) husband

zhōng

古代的旌旗由多條叫做"斿"（音 yóu）的飄帶組成。飄帶有多有少，其中以王的旗飄帶最多，有十二"斿"。甲骨文、金文的中字，像一杆多斿的旗，旗杆中段束紮木塊，以加強旗杆的抗折強度。這個木塊就叫"中"。由於它位處旗杆中段，把斿中分為上斿下斿，所以中的本義為當中、中間，引申為指裡面、內中。為人處世中正平和，不偏不倚，無過不及，也叫做"中"，如中行、中庸等。

甲骨文　　　　　　金　文　　　　　　小　篆

In ancient China, a banner may consist of several streamers known as 斿. The number of streamers in a banner is determined by the rank of the owner, and the banner of a king may have as many as twelve streamers. In the Oracle-Bone Inscriptions and Bronze Inscriptions, the character 中 looks like a banner with several streamers, and there is a piece of wood bound to the middle of the mast to make it stronger. This wood is known as 中, but as it is situated in the middle part of the mast, the character 中 takes on the meaning of "middle", "central", from which derive its meanings of "inside" and "amidst". To adopt a moderate approach in politics, not adhering to any extreme views is also known as 中, e.g. 中行 (the middle course), 中庸 (〔the doctrine of〕the mean).

lǚ

古人出征作戰，先要召集將士於大旗之下，發佈訓誥，整裝待發。甲骨文和金文的旅字，像聚眾人於旗下之形，其本義即為師旅，泛指軍隊，又特指軍隊的編制單位（古代以五百人為一旅）。此外，旅字還有"眾人成群"和"在外客居"的意思。

【旅行】眾人成群而行，結伴而行。現在用為離家出行之義。

【旅店】即客寓，旅客停留住宿之所。又稱旅舍、旅館。

【旅進旅退】與眾人共進退。也可用作貶義詞，形容隨波逐流。

甲骨文

金文

小篆

In former times, when soldiers were about to go to battle, they would assemble under a banner and listen to the orders first. In the Oracle-Bone Inscriptions and Bronze Inscriptions, the character 旅 looks like a group of people assembling under a banner. So the primary meaning of 旅 is a group of soldiers, expecially a brigade of 500 soldiers. But it may refer to troops in general as well. In addition, 旅 may also mean "a crowd of people" or "travel".

【旅行】to travel

【旅店】inn; hotel

【旅進旅退】to always follow the steps of others, forward or backward; to have no definite views of one's own

xuán

甲骨文、金文的旋字，像旗下有趾（止）之形，表示用旗幟引領眾人行進之意，"止"上的"口"形則表示行進的目標。旋的本義是指軍隊出征返回，即凱旋歸來的意思，泛指返回、歸來，引申為盤旋、旋轉之意。

【旋復】回還，歸來。

【旋踵】把腳後跟轉過來，比喻時間極短。

【旋律】聲音經過藝術構思而形成的有組織、有節奏的和諧運動。

甲骨文

金文

小篆

In the Oracle-Bone Inscriptions and Bronze Inscriptions, the character 旋 looks like a foot under a banner, signalling people are marching forward with a banner in the lead; and sometimes there is a square part standing for the destination above the foot part. The primary meaning of 旋 is the returning of army in triumph, but it can also mean returning in general. An extended meaning of it is "to revolve".

【旋復】 to return

【旋踵】 (lit.) to face about; in an instant

【旋律】 melody

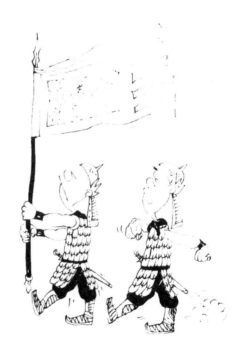

yóu

【游】

古代重大的戶外活動或軍事行動，都要大張旗鼓以壯聲威。甲骨文和早期金文的遊字，像一人手持大旗在行走，大旗上方旗幅飄揚的樣子。它的本義為執旗行進，又特指旗幅上的飄帶飾物，"斿"是其本字。金文的遊字或加"止"形，表示行動之意，有遨遊、行走的意思。至於小篆中從水斿聲的游字，則是表示在水中浮行的意思。

甲骨文

金 文

小 篆

In ancient times, whenever there was an outdoor activity or military operation, banners and drums would be used to add to its grandness. In the Oracle-Bone Inscriptions and early Bronze Inscriptions, the character 遊 looks like a man marching forward with a banner in hand, and the streamers are fluttering in the wind. The original meaning of 遊 was to march with a banner, but it could also refer to streamers in particular, though strictly speaking the true character for this sense is 斿. In the Bronze Inscriptions, sometimes there is a foot part (止) in the character, the modern derivative being 遊, signalling movement on foot. In the Later Seal Character, the character may have 水 (water) as its radical, signalling movement in water.

ZÚ

古代同一氏族或宗族的人，不但有血緣關係，同時也是一個戰鬥單位或武裝集團。甲骨文、金文的族字，從矢在旗下，樹旗所以聚眾，箭矢則代表武器。所以，族字的本義即指氏族、宗族和家族而言，用為動詞，則有聚結、集中之義。

【族姓】指同族和異姓。又指大族、望族。

【族黨】聚居的同族親屬，也指聚族而居的村落。

甲骨文

金文

小篆

In ancient times, a tribe or a clan was not only a group of people of the same blood, but also a military organization. In the Oracle-Bone Inscriptions and Bronze Inscriptions, the character 族 looks like arrows under a banner; arrows stand for arms and the banner represents a place where people assemble. The primary meaning of 族 is "tribe", "clan" or "family". When it is used as a verb, it means "to gather" and "to assemble".

【族姓】 (1) all the people, including those of different family names (2) distinguished family

【族黨】 blood relatives living together

chē

車指的是陸地上有輪子的運輸工具。甲骨文、金文的車字，像一輛輿、輪、軸、轅、衡、軛俱全的馬車之形。小篆的車字，則僅有車輿、輪、軸，是簡化的車字。凡從"車"的字，大都與車及其功用有關，如軌、輪、轉、載、軍等。

【車水馬龍】形容車馬眾多，來往不絕。

【車載斗量】形容數量很多，表示不足為奇。

甲骨文

金文

小篆

車 refers to the means of transportation which has wheels and runs along roads. In the Oracle-Bone Inscriptions and Bronze Inscriptions, the character 車 looks like a cart with all its components such as carriage, wheels, axle, shaft and yoke. In the Later Seal Character, it is reduced to something with carriage, wheels and axle only. Characters with 車 as a component most have to do with 車 and its uses, e.g. 軌 (track), 輪(wheel), 轉(to turn), 載(to carry) and 軍 (army).

【車水馬龍】 incessant stream of horses and carriages

【車載斗量】 enough to fill carts and be measured by the dǒu (a measure vessel); common and numerous

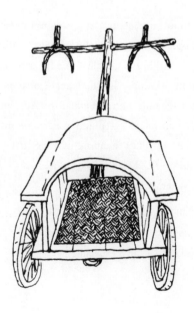

liǎng

　　兩為"輛"的本字。古代的一駕馬車多用兩匹馬來拉，故馬車的衡上多配有雙軶。金文的兩字，像馬車前部的衡上有雙軶之形。所以兩字的本義可以用來代指車輛。又用作數詞，指一對，一雙，專用於馬匹等成雙配對之物。兩字還可用為量詞，車一駕為"一兩"，布一疋也可稱為"一兩"。此外，兩又是常用的重量單位名稱，按現在的用法，十錢為一兩，十兩為一斤。

【兩全】對兩方面都有利無損。

【兩兩】成雙相對。

金　文

小　篆

兩 was the original form of 輛. In former times, a cart was usually drawn by two horses, so there was usually a yoke for two horses in a cart. And the character 兩 looks like such a yoke in the Bronze Inscriptions. Hence 兩 originally could be used as a substitute for cart. But it is more usually used as a numeral, meaning "two". In the past, it could also be used as a classifier for vehicles, a function assumed nowadays by 輛. In addition 兩 is a measure of weight, equal to ten 錢 or one tenth of 斤 in the Chinese System, and 50 grams in the Metric System.

【兩全】 to be satisfactory to both parties

【兩兩】 in pairs

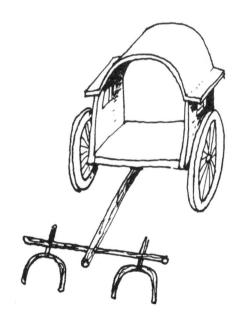

niǎn

金文的輦字，像二人拉車的樣子，其本義指人拉的車，秦漢以後特指帝王或皇后乘坐的車，如帝輦、鳳輦等。

【輦下】指京師，猶言在皇帝車駕之下。

【輦轂】天子的車輿，代指天子。又指京師。

金 文

小 篆

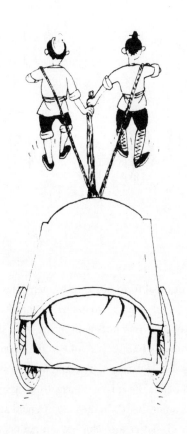

In the Bronze Inscriptions, the character 輦 looks like a cart drawn by two men, hence its original meaning "cart drawn by men". Since the Qin and Han dynasties, however, the character 輦 has come to be used specially for the carriage of the emperor or empress, e.g. 帝輦 (emperor's carriage), 鳳輦 (empress's carriage).

【輦下】in front of the emperor's carriage; capital

【輦轂】emperor's carriage; emperor; capital

yú

古文字的輿字，像四隻手共持一副坐轎之形。其本義為抬轎，引申為抬、負荷之義；又指轎（也稱"肩輿"或"步輦"），引申為指車箱。古代把人的身份分為十等，輿為第六等，屬於地位平凡低微的一等，因此引申為指一般的眾人。

【輿士】抬轎或推車的人。

【輿論】公眾的言論。

甲骨文

小篆

In ancient writing systems, the character 輿 looks like four hands carrying a sedan. Its original meaning was to carry a sedan, and it could be used in the general sense of carrying. But it could also refer to the sedan or carriage. In addition 輿 was a name of the sixth rank in an old ten-rank system of people, referring to people of low social status, in other words, common people.

【輿士】(1) sedan carrier (2) cart driver

【輿論】public opinion

hōng

轟字由三個車字組成，表示群車奔馳、轟然作響的意思。轟用作象聲詞，本義指群車轟鳴之聲，泛指巨大的響聲。它又可用作動詞，有轟鳴、轟炸、轟擊、轟趕等義。

【轟動】驚動。指同時驚動很多人。

【轟隆】像聲詞，形容雷聲、爆炸聲、機器聲等。

【轟轟烈烈】形容氣魄雄偉，聲勢浩大。

小篆

The character 轟 in its original complicated form is made up of three cart parts, signalling that many carts are running together, making a great noise. Used as an onomatopoeic word, it refers to the noise made by the carts running at the same time, or any similar noise. When used as a verb, it can mean "to thunder", "to bomb", "to shell", "to drive", etc.

【轟動】 to cause a sensation

【轟隆】 to rumble

【轟轟烈烈】 on a grand and spectacular scale

zhōu

甲骨文、金文的舟字，像一隻小木船的簡單形象，其本義即為船。舟又用作器物名，古人稱擱茶碗的小托盤為"茶舟"，今人也叫"茶船"。漢字中凡以舟為義符的字大都與船及其作用有關，如航、舫、艦、艇、艘等。

【舟樑】浮橋，即連船為橋。又稱"舟航"。

甲骨文　　　金文　　　小篆

In the Oracle-Bone Inscriptions and Bronze Inscriptions, the character 舟 looks like a simple boat, hence its primary meaning "boat". It can also refer to the saucer, known as茶舟in former times and also茶船nowadays. Characters with舟as a component most have to do with the boat and its uses, e.g. 航 (to sail), 舫 ((fml.) boat), 艦 (warship), 艇 (light boat) and 艘 (a classifier for boats).

【舟樑】pontoon bridge

yú

　　金文的俞字,左邊為舟,右邊像一把尖銳的木鑿,像人用鑿把一棵大木挖空而成舟形,旁邊的一點表示挖鑿的木屑。所以俞字的本義為鑿木造船,又指挖鑿而成的獨木舟。此字後世多用為歎詞,又用作姓氏,其本義則罕為人知。

金 文

小 篆

In the Bronze Inscriptions, the character 俞 has a boat part on the left and a chisellike part on the right, with a dot beside standing for bits of wood cut off. The original meaning of 俞 was to make a boat by cutting a deep hollow in a log, and it could also refer to the dugout canoe. However, it is more usually used as an exclamation in classical Chinese, and as a surname in modern Chinese, while its original meaning is lost.

qián

前字是個會意字。古文字的前，從止從舟，從止表示行進之意，從舟表示乘船而行。《說文解字》："不行而進謂之前。"前的本義為向前行進，引申為指方位和時間，與"後"相對。

【前途】前面的路。也指未來的境況。又作"前程"。

【前車之鑑】比喻以往失敗的經驗，可引為後來的教訓。

甲骨文

小篆

前 is an ideograph. In ancient writing systems, the character 前 consists of 止 (foot) and 舟 (boat); the former means to move forward and the latter to go by boat. Thus Xu Shen says in his *Origin of Chinese Characters,* "To go forward without moving one's legs is known as前." The primary meaning of前 is to move forward, but it can also mean before in position or time, opposite to 後 (after).

【前途】 (also前程) future; prospect

【前車之鑑】 warning taken from the overturned cart ahead; a lesson from the failure of one's predecessor

háng

甲骨文航字，像人手持長篙撐船之形。它的本義當指渡船、航行，又指船，特指方舟（即兩船相併）。小篆的航變為形聲字。《說文解字》："航，方舟也，從方亢聲。"方，即指方舟。此外，空中飛行也稱為"航"。

【航海】海上行船。

【航空】指飛機在空中飛行。

【航海梯山】渡海登山。指跋涉山川。

甲骨文

小篆

In the Oracle-Bone Inscriptions, the character航 looks like a man punting a boat with a long pole. Its primary meaning is "to punt a boat", "to sail". But it may also mean "boat", especially "twin-boat" (方舟). In the Later Seal Character, the character 航 becomes a phonetic compound. That is why Xu Shen says in his *Origin of Chinese Characters,* " 航, or 方舟, has 方 as its radical and 亢 as its phonetic." In addition 航 can also mean "to travel in the air".

【航海】navigation

【航空】aviation

【航海梯山】to travel across rivers and mountains

yù

甲骨文的玉字，像用繩子聯貫在一起的一串玉璧的形狀，本義當指玉器，泛指玉石。玉石是一種礦石，質地細膩溫潤而光澤透明，可用來製造裝飾品或作雕刻的材料。古人往往把美好、珍貴的東西加上個"玉"字作為修飾詞，如玉顏、玉體、玉女等。漢字中凡從"玉"的字大都與玉石或玉器有關，如環、珍、琳、瓊、球等。

【玉帛】瑞玉和縑帛，是古代祭祀、會盟時用的珍貴禮品，又泛指財物。

【玉成】成全。敬辭。

【玉潔冰清】比喻高尚純潔。

甲骨文

金文

小篆

In the Oracle-Bone Inscriptions, the character 玉 looks like a number of jade articles strung together with a thread, hence its primary meaning "jade article," or simply "jade". As a precious stone, jade is often made into ornaments or sculptures. Thus people often use 玉 as a modifier for beautiful or precious objects, e.g. 玉顏 (good looks), 玉體 (fair body), 玉女 (beautiful girl). Characters with 玉 as a component most have to do with jade, e.g. 環 (ring; hoop), 珍 (treasure), 琳 (beautiful jade), 瓊 (fine jade) and 球 (ball).

【玉帛】jade objects and silk fabrics; precious gifts; property

【玉成】to help make a success

【玉潔冰清】as pure as jade and as clean as ice; pure and noble

guī

圭，是古代帝王諸侯舉行禮儀時握在手中的一種玉器，上尖下平，形狀略似"土"字形。圭字從重土，指的就是這種土字形的玉器。小篆圭字或加玉旁，表明圭的玉質屬性。

【圭臬】指圭表（臬就是測日影的表），比喻準則或法度。

金 文

小 篆

圭 is a tablet of jade held in hand by ancient rulers on ceremonial occasions. With its pointed head and broad base, it looks like the character 土. That is why the character 圭 has two 土, one upon the other. In the Later Seal Character, the character 圭 sometimes has 玉 as a component, emphasizing that it is made of jade.

【圭臬】 sundial; criterion; standard

gòng

共是"拱"或"供"的本字。早期金文的共字,像一個人雙手捧着一塊玉璧。玉璧是貴重之物,常用來作為宗廟祭祀的供奉之物。因此,共字有拱手捧璧,供奉於前的意思,引申為環抱、拱衛和供給等義。因兩手同捧一物,故又引申為共同、在一起、一齊等義,如"同舟共濟"。

甲骨文

金文

小篆

共 was the original form of 拱 or 供. In the early Bronze Inscriptions, the character 共 looks like a man holding a piece of jade in two hands. Jade is of great value, and is often used as one of the offerings to ancestors at memorial ceremonies. Hence 共 originally meant to hold a jade object as an offering, from which derived its extended meanings "to encircle" and "to surround and protect" now written as 拱, and "to supply" now written as 供. When holding something, both hands are used at the same time, so 共 has also taken on the meaning of "being together", e.g. 同舟共濟 (to cross a river in the same boat; people in the same situation help each other).

nòng

古文字的弄字，像雙手捧玉玩賞的樣子，其本義為玩玉，引申為"玩弄"、"遊戲"之義。在古代，真正有玉可玩或有資格弄玉者，大抵不外帝王將相、公卿大夫以及妃嬪姬妾、公主千金之輩，所以弄玉是一種十分高雅的文化生活，現在的弄字則多帶貶義，如弄權（玩弄權勢）、愚弄、戲弄、弄巧成拙（指本欲取巧反而敗事）等。

【弄臣】指為帝王所親近狎玩之人。

【弄璋弄瓦】古代稱生男為弄璋，生女為弄瓦。語出《詩經·小雅》："乃生男子，……載弄之璋"；"乃生女子，……載弄之瓦。"

甲骨文

金文

小篆

In ancient writing systems, the character 弄 looks like two hands playing with a piece of jade, hence its original meaning to play with jade, or to play in general. In the past those who had jade objects to play with must be very rich, such as kings, ministers, generals, and their family members, so to play with jade was a highbrow cultural activity. Nowadays, however, the character 弄 often has pejorative sense, e.g. 弄權 (to manipulate power for personal ends), 愚弄 (to make a fool of), 戲弄 (to play tricks on), 弄巧成拙 (to try to be clever only to end up with a blunder).

【弄臣】 ministers who only know how to flatter the king

【弄璋弄瓦】 (lit.) to play with jade or tile; to give birth to a boy or a girl

bǎo

在古代，玉器是一種非常罕見而寶貴的東西，而海貝殼用來作為交換的貨幣使用，代表一個人的財富，更是彌足珍貴。甲骨文的寶字，像是在屋子裡放着的一顆貝和一塊大玉琮，表示一個人所佔有的珍貴之物或財富，所以寶字的本義是指珍貴之物。金文的寶字，增加缶旁表示讀音。這種寫法一直沿用到楷書時代，使寶字由原來的會意字變成形聲字。

甲骨文

金 文

小 篆

In the Oracle-Bone Inscriptions, the character 寶 looks like a shell and a piece of jade in a house. Used as a medium for exchanging goods in ancient times, the seashell was a symbol of wealth, and jade objects were rare and precious. So the form of 寶 suggests that the owner of the house has great treasure and wealth. In the Bronze Inscriptions, there is a part 缶 added to indicate its pronunciation, resulting in a phonetic compound. The character 寶 in the Regular Script also has this structure.

bān

古文字的班字，像刀在兩玉之間，表示把玉石分開的意思。班的本義為分玉，引申為分發、分佈、排列等義。班字也可用作名詞，表示位次、等級之義；又用作軍隊或集體單位名稱。

【班次】班列的次序。指學校班級的次序，又指定時往來的車船開行的次數。

【班師】指軍隊出征回來。

【班門弄斧】在大匠門前擺弄斧頭，比喻不自量力。班，即魯班，古代有名的巧匠。

甲骨文　　　　小篆

In ancient writing systems, the character 班 looks like two pieces of jade with a knife in the middle, signalling to divide a jade stone with a knife. The original meaning of 班 was to divide a jade stone, from which have derived the senses of "distribution", "dispersal" and "arrangement". 班 may also be used as a noun, meaning "rank", "grade", or referring to a unit of the army- squad.

【班次】(1) (school) classes (2) (of bus, ship, plane, etc.) number of runs

【班師】to withdraw troops from the front; to return after victory

【班門弄斧】to display one's skill in using an axe before the master carpenter Lu Ban; to display one's slight skill before an expert

bèi

貝是有介殼的軟體動物的總稱，但在古代主要是指海貝。甲骨文、金文的貝字，正像海貝貝殼的形狀。在古代中原地區，海貝是一種珍貴的裝飾品。這大概是因為離海太遠，得來不易，故人們都視為珍寶，串起來掛在頸上，懸於胸前，以示富有。後來貝又成為最早的一種貨幣，代表一定的財富，所以凡由"貝"所組成的字，大都與錢財或貴重之義有關，如財、貨、貫、貿、貴、賃、貸等。

【貝書】即貝葉書，又稱貝編，佛經的泛稱。古代印度用貝葉寫佛經，故名。

【貝聯珠貫】形容聯貫整齊美好的樣子。

甲骨文

金文

小篆

貝 means "shellfish", though it mainly referred to those types living in the sea in ancient China. In the Oracle-Bone Inscriptions and Bronze Inscriptions, the character 貝 looks like a seashell. Far away from the sea, it was not easy for people of central China in ancient times to obtain a seashell. And seashells were seen as valuable ornaments to be made into necklaces and worn by rich people. The seashell was also one of the oldest currencies and a symbol of wealth. Characters with 貝 as a component most have to do with money or treasure, e.g. 財 (property), 貨 (goods), 貫 (a string of a thousand coins), 貿 (trade), 貴 (expensive), 賃 (to rent) and 貸 (loan).

【貝書】 books written on shells; Buddhist Scripture (the Sanskrit Patter)

【貝聯珠貫】 in beautiful order

péng

　　古代以貝五枚為一掛，兩掛為一朋。甲骨文、金文中的朋字，正像兩掛貝的形狀，其本義即指貝兩掛。後用作貨幣計量單位，如《詩經》："既見君子，錫（賜）我百朋。"後世朋字，多用為朋友之義，又指黨與、同類，引申為比附、勾結之義。

【朋友】古代指同師同志的人，"同門曰朋，同志曰友。"今指彼此有來往、有交情的人。

【朋黨】為私利目的而勾結同類，又指那些排斥異己的宗派集團。

【朋比】依附勾結。多用為貶義。

甲骨文

金 文

小 篆

In former times, five shells formed a string, and two strings of shells were known as 朋. In the Oracle-Bone Inscriptions and Bronze Inscriptions, the character 朋 looks like two strings of shells, which was what it originally meant. Later it was used as a monetary unit, as is shown in the *Classic of Poetry,* "When encountering a friend, a hundred péng I was offered". Nowadays, however, 朋 is more usually used in the senses of "friend", "comrade", or as a verb, meaning "to associate".

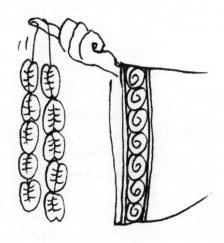

【朋友】friend

【朋黨】clique

【朋比】(derog.) to associate with

dé

　　貝在上古時代是一種珍貴難得之物，後來用作貨幣。甲骨文得字像一隻手抓住一隻海貝的樣子，表示有所獲得的意思，其本義為取得、獲得、得到。金文得字或加彳旁，表示行為動作之意。

【得失】得到的和失去的。事之成敗、利弊、損益或優劣等都可
　　　　稱為得失。

【得寸進尺】比喻貪得無厭。

【得不償失】得到的抵不上失去的。

甲骨文

金　文

小　篆

The seashell, used as a currency in ancient times, was precious, and difficult to obtain. In the Oracle-Bone Inscriptions, the character 得 looks like a hand grasping a seashell, signalling success in obtaining something, hence its primary meaning "obtaining". In the Bronze Inscriptions, it sometimes has a part 彳 added, indicating it refers to an action.

【得失】gain and loss

【得寸進尺】Give him an inch and he'll take an ell;
　　　　　acquisitively

【得不償失】The loss outweighs the gain.

yīng

貝在古代是一種非常難得的珍貴之物，除用作貨幣外，婦女們還把它們串起來掛在脖子上作為裝飾。嬰字從二貝在女上，其本義即指戴在女人脖子上的串貝頸飾。所以《説文解字》稱："嬰，頸飾也。"此字後來多用來指初生的女孩，又泛指幼童。

【嬰孩】指不滿一歲的小孩兒。

金文

小篆

The seashell was precious, and difficult to come by in ancient times. It was used as an ornament, strung together and worn on the neck by women, as well as a currency. The character 嬰 consists of two shell parts (貝) and a woman part (女), signalling the necklace of shells worn by women. Thus the *Origin of Chinese Characters* says, " 嬰 means necklace." Nowadays, however, it refers to the newborn baby, and the female baby in particular.

【嬰孩】baby

zhù

貯是個會意字。甲骨文的貯字,像藏貝於箱櫃之中,其本義為儲存、收藏。金文貯字形體發生訛變,變成貝在宁下,小篆以後則貝在宁左,於是貯就由原來的會意字變成了從貝宁聲的形聲字。

甲骨文

金 文

小 篆

In the Oracle-Bone Inscriptions, the character 貯, an ideograph, looks like a shell in a chest, hence its primary meaning "to store". In the Bronze Inscriptions, it has undergone some change in the form, the shell part (貝) is put under the chest part (宁). In the Later Seal Character, the chest part (宁) is moved to the right of the shell part (貝), resulting in a phonetic compound, with 貝 as the radical and 宁 as the phonetic.

mǎi

古文字的買字，從網從貝，是用網取貝的意思。"貝"是古代的貨幣，可以用它來換取貨物。買即指收購，是一種拿錢換取貨物的行為，與"賣"相對。

【買辦】官府中掌管採購和其他雜務的差役。

【買櫝還珠】典出《韓非子·外儲説左上》。楚國人到鄭國去賣珍珠，把珍珠裝在極其華貴的匣子裡。結果鄭國人出錢買走匣子，卻把珍珠退還。比喻沒有眼光，取捨不當。

甲骨文

金 文

小 篆

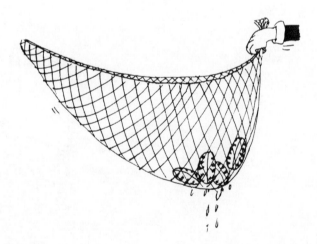

In ancient writing systems, the character 買 consists of a net part (網) and a shell part (貝), signalling to obtain something with a net in exchange for a shell. The shell was used as a currency, a medium for exchanging goods in former times. So 買 means to buy, to obtain something in exchange for money, opposite to 賣 (to sell).

【買辦】 purchasing agent; comprador

【買櫝還珠】 to keep the glittering casket and give back the pearl to the seller; of poor judgment

fù

小篆的負字，從人從貝，貝是財富的象徵，人有財富則心有所恃，故《說文解字》稱："負，恃也。從人守貝，有所恃也。"負的本義為倚恃、依仗，引申為賠償、虧欠、辜負之義，又因為以背載物及擔負、負擔等意思。

小篆

In the Later Seal Character, the character 負 consists of 人 (man) and 貝 (shell). As the shell is a symbol of wealth, a man in possession of it will feel backed up in a way. Thus the *Origin of Chinese Characters* says, "負，consisting of 人 and 貝, means to have a backing." The original meaning of 負 was "to rely on", from which have derived the extended meanings "to compensate", "to be in arrears" and "to fail to live up to". In addition, 負 can also mean "to carry".

shí

《説文解字》："實，富也。"金文實字從宀從田從貝，家中有田有貝，表示富有。小篆實字從宀從貫，貫指錢幣，故也有富足之意。所以，實的本義為富足、殷實；又指財富、財物；引申為指充滿，與"空虛"相對；又指真實，與"虛假"相對。

【實際】指客觀存在的現實。

【實踐】實地履行。

【實惠】實在的利益、好處。

【實事求是】從實際出發，求得正確的結論。

金文　　　　　小篆

Xu Shen says in his *Origin of Chinese Characters,* "實 means rich". In the Bronze Inscriptions, the character 實 consists of 宀 (house), 田 (field) and 貝 (shell), signalling the family has fields and money. In the Later Seal Character, the character consists of 宀 (house) and 貫 (a string of a thousand coins), also signalling rich. Thus the original meaning of 實 was "rich", "substantial", or "wealth", "property". Its extended meanings include "full", opposite to 空 (empty); and "real", opposite to 假 (false).

【實際】reality

【實踐】practice

【實惠】material benefit

【實事求是】to seek truth from facts

jī

几

【幾】

古代無桌椅，人們習慣席地而坐，而常於座側或身前置一小几，用於倚靠。這種几，實際上就是後來桌子的一種雛形。其形長而窄，較矮。小篆的几字，略似其形，其本義即指案几之几。現在的几字，則多用來作為"幾"字的簡體，讀為jǐ。

【几杖】几案與手杖，以供老人平時靠身和走路時扶持之用，故古代以賜几杖為敬老之禮。

【几案】泛指桌子。

小篆

In ancient times, there were no chairs or tables. People would sit on the ground, and there was something beside to support one's back or arm. This object is thin and long, and has short legs, something like a tea table. The character 几 in the Later Seal Character looks like such a small table. Nowadays, however, the character 几 is mainly used as the simplified form of 幾, pronounced as jǐ and meaning "a few".

【几杖】small table and walking stick

【几案】table

chǔ

金文的處字，像一個人坐在櫈上之形；或從虎頭作為聲符，表示這個字的讀音。處的本義為坐，引申為居停、居住之義，又指跟別人一起生活、交往。現在的處字，則多用為處置、辦理之義。

【處分】處理。又指對犯罪或錯誤的人按情節輕重做出處罰決定。

【處境】所處的境地。

【處世】在社會上活動，跟人往來。

【處事】處理事務。

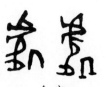

金文　　　　　　小篆

In the Bronze Inscriptions, the character 處 looks like a man sitting on a stool, sometimes with 虎 as its phonetic. The original meaning of 處 was to sit, from which have derived its extended meanings of "situate", "reside" and "get along with". But it is mainly used in the senses of "manage" and "deal with" nowadays.

【處分】 punishment

【處境】 (unfavourable) situation

【處世】 to conduct oneself in society

【處事】 to attend to business

chuáng

【床】

　　古代的牀，是一種可供人坐臥的器具。甲骨文的牀字，是一豎立的牀形，牀腳牀面俱全，為牀字的初文。小篆牀字加"木"，表示牀是用木材做成的。楷書牀字俗體又作"床"，為今簡化字所本。

【牀席】牀上的墊席。

【牀上施牀】比喻重疊。

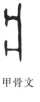

甲骨文　　　　　　小　篆

In former times 牀 referred to an article of furniture for both sitting and sleeping. In the Oracle-Bone Inscriptions, the character 牀 looks like a bed on end, with both its board and posts. In the Later Seal Character, a wood part (木) is added to it, signalling that it is made of wood. The vulgarism in the Regular Script is written as 床.

【牀席】mattress

【牀上施牀】(lit.) to pile one bed upon another; needless duplication

xí

席是一種供坐臥鋪墊的用具，多用葦篾、竹篾或草等編織而成。《說文解字》所載"古文"的席字，像屋宇下一張草席的形狀。所以席的本義指墊席，引申為指席位、坐次、筵席等義。

【席地】古人鋪席於地以為座。以稱坐在地上為席地。

【席捲】像捲席子一樣把東西全部包捲進去。比喻全部佔有。

【席不暇暖】形容事務極忙，或迫不及待，連坐定的時間都沒有。

【席地幕天】以地為席，以天為幕。形容胸襟曠達。

古文

小篆

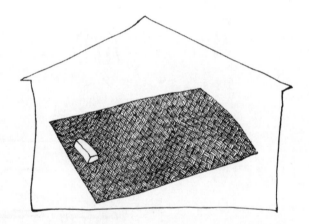

席 refers to a matlike cushion, made of reed, bamboo or straw, on which people can sit or lie. The character 席 in the Ancient Script as is recorded in the *Origin of Chinese Characters* looks like a straw mat under the roof of a house. The primary meaning of 席 is matlike cushion, from which have derived the meanings of "seat", "order of seats" and "feast".

【席地】(1) to sit on the cushion (2) to sit on the ground

【席捲】to roll up all the things like a mat

【席不暇暖】too busy to sit on a cushion to warm it

【席地幕天】(lit.) to take the earth as the seat and the sky as the roof; broad-minded

yīn

因是"茵"的本字。古文字的因字，像一個人仰面臥於席墊之上，它的本義是指草席。由於因有席、墊之義，故可引申為依靠、根據、憑藉、沿襲等義，進一步引申，又有原因、因緣之義。

【因果】即因果報應。根據佛教輪迴的説法，善因得善果，惡因得惡果，即做善事得善報，做惡事得惡報。

【因循】沿襲舊法而不加變更。

【因人成事】依賴他人之力而成事。

【因地制宜】根據各地情況而制定適宜的辦法。

【因勢利導】順應着事物發展的趨勢加以引導。

甲骨文　　　　　　金文　　　　小篆

因 was the original form of 茵. In ancient writing systems, the character 因 looks like a man lying on a matlike cushion. Its original meaning was "straw mat". As a mat is something supporting a man, the character 因 has taken on the senses "to rely on", "on the basis of", "to depend", "to follow", and even the senses of "cause" and "reason".

【因果】(1) cause and effect (2) (Buddhism) karma

【因循】to follow the old rules

【因人成事】to rely on others for the success in work

【因地制宜】to suit measures to local conditions

【因勢利導】to adroitly guide action according to circumstances

gǔ

鼓是一種圓柱形、中空、兩端蒙皮的打擊樂器。古代兩軍作戰，以擊鼓鳴金來指揮進退（金指銅鐘，擊鼓表示進攻，鳴金表示收兵）。古文字的鼓字，像人手持鼓槌敲擊鼓面的形狀，其本義為擊鼓；引申為指敲擊、拍打、彈奏，如鼓掌（拍手掌）、鼓瑟（彈奏琴瑟）；再引申為振動、振作、激勵等義，如鼓動、鼓勵、鼓舞、鼓足幹勁等。此外，鼓形外凸，所以鼓字又有隆起、凸出之義，如鼓腹（腆起肚子）。

| 甲骨文 | 金 文 | 小 篆 |

鼓 means "drum", a percussion instrument consisting of a skin stretched tight over the two sides of a hollow circular frame. In former times, the army general used the drum to signal the beginning of attack against the enemy and the bell to withdraw the troops. In ancient writing systems, the character 鼓 looks like a man beating a drum with a drumstick. From its primary meaning of "beating a drum" have derived the extended meanings "to beat", "to strike" and "to play (a musical instrument)", e.g. 鼓掌 (to clap one's hands), 鼓瑟 (to pluck the stringed instrument se).It can also mean "to agitate (鼓動)", "to encourage (鼓勵)"and "to inspire (鼓舞)". As the drum has a rounded body, the character 鼓 is also used in the sense of "bulging out", e.g. 鼓腹 (to bulge the stomach).

péng

甲骨文、金文的彭字，左邊是一豎立鼓形，右邊幾點像鼓聲聲浪之形，所以彭是一個象聲字，表示擊鼓之聲。由這個本義，彭字又可引申為水流湍急的意思，如"洶湧彭湃"。其中彭又作"澎"，音 pēng。

甲骨文

金文

小篆

In the Oracle-Bone Inscriptions and Bronze Inscriptions, the character 彭 has a drum part on the left and some dots on the right, signalling the sound produced by beating the drum. So 彭 is an onomatopoeic word for the sound of a drum. From this meaning has derived its use for the sound produced by rushing water, e.g. 洶湧彭湃 (surging and turbulent 〔water〕) in which 彭 may also be written as 澎, pronounced as pēng.

XǏ

甲骨文的喜字，像一門安放在口形支架上的大鼓的形狀，鼓兩側的點表示擊鼓所發出的聲音，說明有喜慶的事而擊鼓慶賀。喜的本義指喜慶、吉慶，引申指快樂、喜悅，又引申為喜歡、愛好之義。

【喜出望外】遇到出乎意外的喜事而特別高興。

【喜形於色】抑制不住的高興流露在臉色上。

甲骨文　　　　　金文　　　　　小篆

In the Oracle-Bone Inscriptions, the character 喜 looks like a drum on a square frame, with some dots on the two sides standing for the sound produced, signalling the beating of a drum on an occasion of celebration. From this primary meaning of celebration have derived its extended meanings: "happy", "joyous" and "to like".

【喜出望外】 to be pleasantly surprised

【喜形於色】 to be visibly pleased

hé

【龢】

古文字的和字，左邊像一多條竹管合併而成的笙簫之形，代表一種吹奏樂器，右邊的"禾"則是聲符表示讀音。因此，和字的本義應該是指樂聲的調和、和諧，引申為溫和、柔和等義。

【和平】指戰亂平息，秩序安定。

【和戎】戎，指少數民族。古代漢族和少數民族結盟友好，稱為"和戎"。

【和親】和睦相親。又指與敵方議和，結為姻親。

【和光同塵】把光榮和塵濁同樣看待，指不露鋒芒、與世無爭而隨波逐流的處世態度。

甲骨文

金文

小篆

In ancient writing systems, the character 和 has a wind instrument made of bamboo pipes on the left, and the phonetic 禾 on the right. The primary meaning of 和 is , therefore, "harmonious tune", from which have derived the meanings of "mild" and "gentle".

【和平】peace

【和戎】to be on friendly terms with minority nationalities

【和親】(1)in harmony (2) to become in-laws with the enemy

【和光同塵】of the same hidden virtue and the same commonplace; to drift with the current

yuè

上古時代的弦樂器（如琴瑟）想必是比較簡單的。相傳
"舜作五弦之琴，以歌南風"，周文王、周武王各加一弦，才
成了今天的七弦琴。甲骨文、金文的樂字，像絲弦繃附在木上
之形，指的正是這種絲弦樂器，又是所有樂器的總稱，後來又
引申為泛指音樂。樂聲悅耳，能使人感到快樂，所以樂字又可
用作動詞，有喜悅、快樂、歡喜等義。而用作動詞的樂字不讀
yuè，而讀 **lè**。

甲骨文　　　　　金文　　　　　小篆

It is understandable that the ancient stringed instruments were very simple. According to legend, "Shun invented a five-stringed plucked instrument for the tunes of the South." And King Wen and King Wu of the Zhou Dynasty each added a string to it, resulting in a seven-stringed plucked instrument of today. In the Oracle-Bone Inscriptions and Bronze Inscriptions, the character 樂 looks like a musical instrument consisting of strings stretched over a piece of wood. This character not only referred to the seven-stringed instrument but all types of musical instrument. And nowadays it means "music". As music is pleasing to the ear and gives people satisfaction, the character 樂 used as a verb, pronounced as lè, can mean to be happy, cheerful or joyful.

qín

琴是古代的一種弦樂器。小篆的琴字，是這種樂器一端的側視圖形：字形下部的弧曲部份表示琴身，上面的兩個 "王" 字形則是用來繃弦的琴柱。此外，琴還是某些樂器的總稱，如鋼琴、提琴、胡琴、口琴等。

小篆

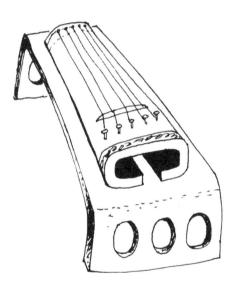

琴 is an ancient stringed instrument. In the Later Seal character, the character 琴 looks like a diagram of this musical instrument seen from one end: the circular part at the bottom stands for its body and the two 王 parts at the top for the string holders. But it can also be used as a general term for some musical instruments, e.g. 鋼琴 (piano), 提琴 (violin), 胡琴 (Chinese fiddle) and 口琴 (mouth organ).

gēng

庚

從早期甲骨文和早期金文的庚字形體來看，庚是一種兩邊有吊錘，可以用來搖動的樂器，類似現在所見的“撥浪鼓”。此字後世多用為干支名，是天干的第七位，其本義則鮮為人知。

甲骨文

金 文

小 篆

Judging from the early Oracle-Bone Inscriptions and early Bronze Inscriptions, the character 庚 refers to a musical instrument like a rattle-drum. There is a threaded bead on each side, which will hit the body and rattle when the instrument is rocked. However, this character is now mainly used as a name of the seventh Heavenly Stem, a traditional Chinese system of sequence, and its original meaning is lost.

qìng

磬是古代一種打擊樂器，以玉、石或金屬為材，形狀如矩。甲骨文的磬字，像人手持槌棒敲打懸掛着的磬器之形。小篆磬字加"石"旁，表示磬器多由玉石製成。由於磬形如矩曲折，所以磬又有彎腰、屈身之義。

【磬折】指屈身彎腰以示恭敬。又指敬服。

甲骨文　　　　　小篆

磬, in the shape of a carpenter's square, is an ancient percussion instrument, made of jade, stone or metal. In the Oracle-Bone Inscriptions, the character 磬 looks like a man striking the hanging chime stone with a mallet. In the Later Seal Character, it has a stone part (石) added, signalling that it is usually made of stone. As this instrument has a bent like the carpenter's square, the character 磬 can also mean to bend over.

【磬折】to bow to show one's reverence

yè

業是古代樂器架上裝飾用的大版，刻如鋸齒狀，用來懸掛鐘、鼓、磬等，下面的支柱則往往做成雙手托樑的人形。金文的業字，就是這樣一個樂器架的簡單構形圖。只是後來支柱的人形訛變成"木"，到小篆時就已經失去它原來的形象了。業字後來多用為事務、職業、產業、學業等義，其本義則逐漸消失。

【業務】職業上的事務。

【業主】產業的所有人。

【業師】受業的老師。

【業精於勤】學業的精純在於勤奮。

金文　　　小篆

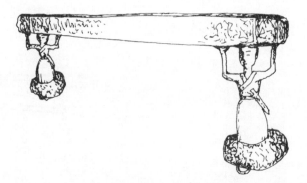

業 refers to a frame which has teeth on the top for holding musical instruments such as bells, drums and chime stones, and whose posts are in the shape of a man supporting a beam with his two hands. In the Bronze Inscriptions, the character 業 looks like a sketch of this instrument frame. In the Later Seal Character, however, its manlike posts are changed into a wood part (木) by mistake, losing its original image. Its meaning is also changed, and is nowadays more usually used in the senses of "business", "profession"， "industry" and "course of study".

【業務】professional work

【業主】owner of a business

【業師】teacher

【業精於勤】Proficiency comes from hard work

yǐn

尹字是個會意字。古文字的尹字，像人手持杖之形。手杖是一種權力的象徵。手握權杖即表明有權力處理大小事務，故尹字有治理之義。後來尹字多用作官名，如京兆尹、縣尹等。而作為姓氏的尹，則是從"尹氏"這種官職名稱演變而來的。

甲骨文　　　　　　金　文　　　　　　小　篆

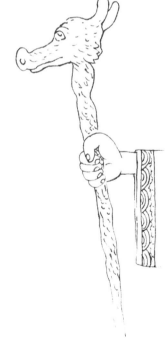

尹 is an ideograph. In ancient writing systems, the character 尹 looks like a man holding a sceptre in hand. The sceptre is a symbol of power. A man who has a sceptre in hand is a man in charge, so 尹 has the meaning of "governing". The character 尹 is often used as an official title, e.g. 京兆尹 (head of the capital city), 縣尹 (county magistrate). And the use of 尹 as a surname comes from the official title.

jūn

君字從尹從口。甲骨文的尹字,表示一人手持指揮棒指揮別人做事;尹下加口,表示能對官吏發號施令。以此會意,君即指統治人民的一國之主,後來又引申為對人的尊稱,如嚴君、家君、夫君等。君還可用作動詞,有統治、主宰的意思。

【君子】對統治者和貴族男子的通稱,常與被統治的所謂小人或野人對舉。又泛指有才德的人。

甲骨文　　　　　金文　　　　　小篆

The character 君 consists of 尹 and 口, the former signalling to direct people to do something with a baton in hand and the latter to issue orders. Hence 君 refers to people who are in a position to order others, especially the highest ruler of a country. But it may also be used as an honorific term, e.g. 嚴君 (my father), 家君 (my father), 夫君 (my husband). When it is used as a verb, it means "to rule" and "to dominate".

【君子】gentleman

bǐ

筆是用於書寫的工具。毛筆的使用，在中國有非常久遠的歷史。從考古發掘出來的實物看，最早的毛筆出於戰國時代；但從種種跡象推測，毛筆的實際使用可以上推到原始社會末期。甲骨文、金文的筆字，像用手抓着一支毛筆的樣子。這種筆有較粗的筆桿，桿頭上的分叉代表筆毛。早期的毛筆多用木桿，秦代蒙恬造筆，改用竹管，故小篆的筆字增加竹旁。

【筆札】相當於現在所說的紙、筆。古代無紙，書於札（木簡）。這裡代指公文、書信，又指書法。

【筆墨】本指筆和墨，借指詩文及寫作之事。

甲骨文

金文

小篆

筆 refers to the instrument for writing, i.e. pen. In China the first type of pen is known as 毛筆 (writing brush). Judging from the archaeological excavations, the writing brush was first used in the period of Warring States. But we may well assume from other sources that the use of writing brush might date as far back as the end of the primitive society. In the Oracle-Bone Inscriptions and Bronze Inscriptions, the character 筆 looks like a hand with a writing brush in its grasp; the three-tined part at the head standing for its hair part. Early writing brushes had wooden shafts. Starting with Meng Tian in the Qin Dynasty, however, bamboo shafts took the place of wooden ones. That is why in the Later Seal Character a bamboo part (竹) is added to the character.

【筆札】 (lit.) writing brush and wooden slip; pen and paper; writing

【筆墨】 pen and ink; writing

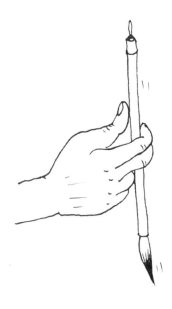

huà

甲骨文和早期金文的畫字，像人用手執筆在紙上畫交叉線條、作圖畫之形。這就是畫字的本義——作圖、繪畫。畫字又有劃分之義，相當於後來的“劃”字，所以金文和小篆的畫字又增加一個“田”字，表示劃分田界的意思。

【畫卯】簽到的意思。因為舊時官署在卯時（清晨五時到七時）開始辦公，吏役都必須按時到衙門簽到，這就叫做“畫卯”。

甲骨文

金文

小篆

In the Oracle-Bone Inscriptions and Bronze Inscriptions, the character 畫 looks like a man drawing crosses with a writing brush, hence the primary meaning "drawing". As the character 畫 also means "to delimit", which is now usually expressed by 劃, in the late Bronze Inscriptions and Later Seal Character there is a field part (田) added, signalling the delimitation of boundaries between fields.

【畫卯】to sign in at the period from 5:00 to 7:00 in the morning known as 卯

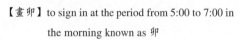

cè

在古代紙還沒有發明和大量製造以前，人們用於書寫的主要材料是竹簡（一種經過加工修整的窄長竹片）。通常一條竹簡只能寫一行字，而把許多條竹簡用繩子聯結起來，就成為冊。古文字的冊字，正是這種編簡成冊的形象描繪。後來的冊字，就被用為書本、書籍之義。

【冊府】指藏書的地方。

甲骨文

金 文

小 篆

Before the invention of paper, one of the main materials used for writing in China was bamboo slips. And the slips bound together make a book. In ancient writing systems, the character 冊 has the shape of many bamboo slips bound together, hence its meaning "book" and "volume".

【冊府】 library

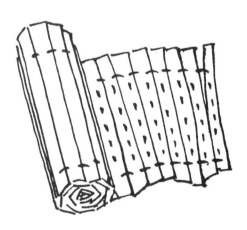

diǎn

甲骨文典字，像雙手捧冊狀；金文、小篆的典，則是將簡冊供放案上之形。所謂典即典冊，是指那些記載法律、典章制度的重要書籍；引申為指法則、制度和一般的常道、準則；典還可用作動詞，有掌管、從事、抵押等義。

【典籍】指法典圖籍等重要文獻。

【典式】範例、模範。

【典故】指常例、典制和掌故，又指詩文中引用的古代故事和有來歷出處的詞語。

【典客】官名，秦代始置，掌管接待少數民族和諸侯來朝等事務。

甲骨文　　　　　金 文　　　　　小 篆

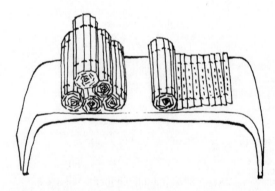

In the Oracle-Bone Inscriptions, the character 典 looks like two hands holding a book. In the Bronze Inscriptions and Later Seal Character, the structure of the character is changed: the book is on a table, instead of two hands. But the meaning is not changed. That is 典 refers to books recording codes of laws and regulations. And it is also used to refer to the provisions and regulations in these books, or general codes of behaviour. Used as a verb, it means "to be in charge of", "to be engaged in" or "to mortgage something".

【典籍】ancient codes and records

【典式】model

【典故】classical allusion; literary quotation

【典客】officer in charge of foreign relations in the Qin Dynasty

shān

古代用毛筆蘸墨在竹簡上寫字，遇有錯字，就用小刀把墨跡刮掉重寫。刪字從冊從刀，冊即簡冊，表示用刀把簡冊上的錯字或多餘的字刮掉的意思。因此，刪的本義為削除、去掉，引申為減少、削減之義。

【刪改】去掉或改動文辭中某些字句或某些部份。

【刪汰】刪削淘汰。

小篆

When people wrote on bamboo slips with a writing brush, they used a knife to scrape the wrong characters. And that is what is meant by the character 刪, consisting of 冊 (book) and 刀 (knife). From its primary meaning of "deleting" have derived the meanings "to abridge" and "to abbreviate".

【刪改】to delete and change; to revise

【刪汰】to cut off

bǔ

古人迷信鬼神，凡事必先占卜，以斷吉凶。所謂卜，是用火艾灼燒龜殼使之出現裂紋，然後根據這些裂紋（又稱兆紋）的方向和特點來預測吉凶。古文字的卜字，正像這種兆紋的形狀，所以卜是個象形字。又卜字的讀音bǔ，是模仿龜甲爆裂的聲音，故它又是一個象聲字。卜由占卜之義，可以引申為預測、估量、選擇等義。

【卜筮】古時占卜，用龜甲稱卜，用著草稱筮，合稱卜筮。
【卜居】用占卜的方法選擇定居之地。後泛指擇地定居。

甲骨文

金文

小篆

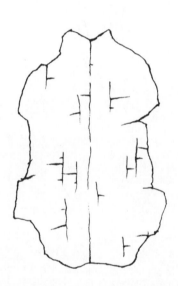

In former times people were superstitious and would try to have the result foretold before doing anything. In China, one of the ways to foretell the future is to bake a tortoise-shell gently until it cracks. And the direction, length and other features of the cracks would be seen as omens of the future event: whether it would result in success or failure. In ancient writing systems, the character 卜 looks like the cracks on a baked tortoise-shell. In this sense it is a pictograph. But the pronunciation of 卜 is like the sound produced when a tortoise-shell cracks, and in this sense, it may be seen as an onomatopoeia. From its meaning of future-telling have derived its senses of "predict", "estimate" and "select".

【卜筮】divination
【卜居】to select a place for one's home

zhān

【佔】

占字從卜從口，表示占卜時要用語言來解釋兆紋以斷吉凶的意思。因此，占的本義是指視兆以斷吉凶，引申為泛指占卜活動。凡用龜、蓍、銅錢、牙牌等來推斷吉凶禍福的迷信活動，都可稱為"占"，如占卦、占課等。此外，占又讀為 **zhàn**，是據有、佔據的意思，寫作"佔"。

【占兆】占卜時以火灼龜甲，龜甲上的裂紋叫占兆。

【占夢】圓夢，即根據夢中所見附會預測人事的吉凶。

甲骨文　　　　　小篆

The character 占 consists of 卜 and 口, signalling that in the act of future-telling, one needs to express the omen through speech organs. Hence 占 primarily means "to express omen in words". But it may refer to the activity of future-telling in general. All forms of future-telling, whether using tortoise-shell, yarrow stem, copper cash or elephant-tooth tablet, may be referred to as 占, e.g. 占卦 (divination), 占課 (to divine by tossing coins). In addition 占 may be pronounced as zhàn, meaning "to occupy", "to possess", the original complicated form being 佔·

【占兆】cracks on a baked tortoise-shell

【占夢】to divine by interpreting dreams

qiě

且

且是"祖"的本字，原讀 zǔ。古文字的且字，是一塊牌位板子的象形，它是在宗廟祭祀時用來代表祖先的靈位的，所以且字的本義即指祖宗、祖先。作為祖宗的且，因為與宗廟祭祀有關，於是增加"示"旁為意符而變成祖。而原來的且字現在則讀為 qiě，借用為連詞，如並且、況且、尚且、而且等；又表示暫且、姑且之義。

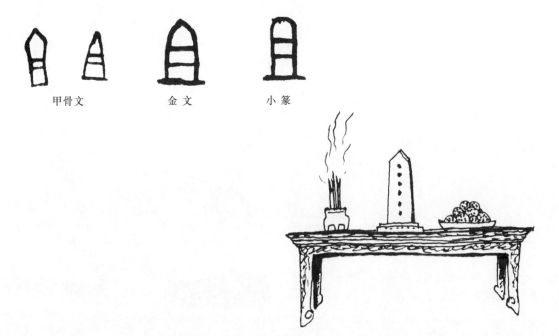

甲骨文　　　　　金文　　　　　小篆

且 was the original form of 祖. In ancient writing systems, the character 且 looks like a memorial tablet, which was used to represent the soul of an ancestor in a memorial ceremony, hence its original meaning "ancestor". As it is related to gods and spirits, a spirit part (示) is added to show its meaning more clearly, resulting in a new character 祖. The original 且, instead, is used now as a conjunction, e.g. 並且 (and...as well), 況且 (moreover), 尚且 (even) and 而且 (but also); or used in the senses of "for the time being (暫且)", "tentatively (姑且)". Its pronunciation is also changed from zǔ to qiě.

shì

古人迷信鬼神，凡事都要請求神靈的指導和保祐，所以有關祭祀鬼神的活動特別多。甲骨文的示字，像一橫一豎兩石塊搭成的石桌，石桌上可以供放祭品，用以拜祭祖先或鬼神，其本義指供放祭品的石桌，也即所謂的"靈石"。因此，凡以"示"為偏旁的字，如福、祭、祝等，均與祭祀神、祖有關。拜祭祖先神靈，一般是有事相告以求庇祐，所以示字又有"以事相告"之義，引申為顯示、表示，即給人看的意思，如示威（顯示威風或尊嚴）、示弱（表示比別人力量小）、指示等。

甲骨文

小篆

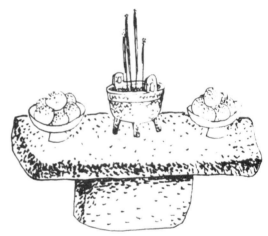

People in former times were superstitious and would call on gods and spirits for guidance and protection in anything they were going to do, so there were often sacrifice-offering ceremonies. In the Oracle-Bone Inscriptions, the character 示 looks like a stone table made of a stone plate on top of a stone stand. This is a type of altar used in sacrifice-offering ceremonies for presenting offerings, hence the original meaning of 示 "stone table", or "spirit stone (靈石)". Characters with 示 as a component most have to do with offering sacrifices to gods and ancestors, e.g. 福 (blessing), 祭 (to offer a sacrifice) and 祝 (to pray). People usually offer sacrifices to gods and ancestors in order to tell them their difficulties so that gods and ancestors would help them overcome the difficulties. As a result, the character 示 has taken on the sense of "show", "present", e.g. 示威 (to display one's strength), 示弱 (to give the impression of being weak) and 指示 (to direct).

zhù

古文字的祝字，像人跪在祭桌前有所禱告的樣子，表示祈禱、求神降福的意思，引申為祝頌、祝賀、慶祝等義。此外，祠廟中專司祭祀祝告的人（即男巫）一般也叫做"祝"。後代有作為姓氏的祝氏，其來源大概也與其祖先的祭司巫祝職業有關。

甲骨文　　　　　　金文　　　　　　小篆

In ancient writing systems, the character 祝 looks like a man on his knees saying his prayers before the altar. Hence the primary meaning of 祝 is "to pray" and "to plead with gods for blessing", from which have derived the extended meanings "to express good wishes", "to congratulate" and "to celebrate". In addition the person who is in charge of a sacrifice-offering is also known as 祝. And this may be the origin of the surname 祝, i.e. they adopted their family name from their occupation.

fú

甲骨文的福字，像雙手捧酒樽往祭桌上進奉酒食之狀，表示以酒祭神以求降福，引申為指神靈所降賜的"福氣"。古代稱富貴壽考等為"福"，如《尚書·洪範》："五福：一曰壽，二曰富，三曰康寧，四曰攸好德，五曰考終命。"又引申為指一般的幸福、好運氣，與"禍"的意義相對，如《老子》："禍兮福所倚，福兮禍所伏。"（災禍中蘊含着好運，幸福裡隱藏着災禍。）

甲骨文

金文

小篆

In the Oracle-Bone Inscriptions, the character 福 looks like two hands placing a jar of wine onto an altar, signalling to offer wine to gods in the hope of obtaining blessing, hence the meaning "blessing". In ancient times, there were five types of blessing as is recorded in *Shang Shu* (the Book of History), "The five types of blessing are: longevity, wealth, peace, virtue and to die a natural death." But it can also be used for happiness or good fortune in general, opposite to 禍 (misfortune). Thus *Lao Zi* (Lao-Tzu) says, "Good fortune lieth within bad, bad fortune lurketh with good".

jì

　　祭是一個會意字，像人手持肉塊供放到祭桌上，表示以酒肉祭祀和供奉神、祖的意思。祭在後代成為一種對死者表示追悼、敬意的儀式，如祭奠、公祭等。此外，祭字還可用作姓氏。不過用作姓氏的祭字不讀 jì，而應該讀作 zhài。

【祭酒】醊酒祭神。古代舉行祭祀活動，一般要推舉一個職位尊貴或年長者來主持祭禮。這個人就叫做"祭酒"。後來祭酒演變成一種官職的稱號，主管宗廟禮儀和文化教育。如國子監祭酒，就是當時最高學府國子監的主管官。

甲骨文

金文

小篆

祭, an ideograph, looks like a man placing a piece of meat onto an altar, signalling to offer meat and wine to gods and ancestors. But it also refers to the memorial ceremony for the dead, e.g. 祭奠 (to hold a memorial ceremony for), 公祭 (a public memorial meeting). In addition, 祭 is a surname, but it is pronounced as zhài, instead of jì.

【祭酒】 (lit.) to offer wine to gods; person in charge of the sacrifice-offering ceremony; minister in charge of culture and education

diàn

甲骨文、金文的奠字,像置酒樽於祭壇之上,表示以酒食相祭的意思,如祭奠。由此引申為進獻,如奠雁,又引申為安置、安定、建立等義,如奠基(打下建築物的基礎,比喻一種大事業的創始)、奠都(確定首都的地址)等。

【奠雁】即獻雁。古婚禮,新郎到新娘家迎親,先進雁為禮。

甲骨文

金文

小篆

In the Oracle-Bone Inscriptions and Bronze Inscriptions, the character 奠 looks like a jar of wine on an altar, signalling to offer wine and meat to gods and ancestors. From this primary meaning have derived the extended meanings "to present", e.g. 奠雁 (to present a wild goose); "to set up" and "to establish", e.g. 奠基 (to lay a foundation), 奠都 (to establish a capital).

【奠雁】 to present a wild goose (According to the old tradition, when a bridegroom goes to the bride's family to invite her to the wedding ceremony, he should first offer a wild goose as a gift.)

...

zūn

尊為“樽”或“罇”的本字，是古代的一種酒器。古文字的尊字，像一個人雙手捧樽的樣子，表示向人敬酒的意思。楷書的尊字，下面的雙手形則變成了一隻手（寸）。尊的本義是雙手敬酒，表示敬重、推崇的意思，引申為尊貴、高貴之義，又引申為指尊長、長輩。

【尊彝】古代酒器。也泛指祭祀用的禮器。

【尊俎】古代盛酒肉的器皿。尊為酒器，俎為載肉之具。後常用為宴席或外交場合的代稱。

甲骨文　　　金文　　　小篆

尊, as the original form of 樽 or 罇, referred to a jarlike wine container. In ancient writing systems, the character 尊 looks like a man holding a big jar with his two hands, signalling to offer wine to others. In the Regular Script, the twin-hand part becomes a single-hand part (寸). The original meaning of 尊 was to offer wine with both hands, suggesting respect for the other. From this meaning have derived the senses of "respected", "noble", and its use for elders and betters.

【尊彝】ancient wine container; utensil for the sacrifice-offering ceremony

【尊俎】wine and meat containers; feast

yǒu

甲骨文、金文的酉字，像一個酒罈子的形狀，它的本義當指酒罈或酒壺。此字後來借用為干支名，為地支中的第十位。在漢字中凡從"酉"的字大都與酒有關，如酖、醉、釀、酌、配等。

【酉時】舊式計時法指下午五點鐘到七點鐘的時間。

甲骨文

金文

小篆

In the Oracle-Bone Inscriptions and Bronze Inscriptions, the character 酉 looks like a wine jar, hence its original meaning "wine jar" or "wine pot". However, this character is now mainly used as a name of the tenth Earthly Branch, a traditional Chinese system of sequence. Characters with 酉 as a component most have to do with wine, e.g. 酖 (to drink to one's heart's content), 醉 (drunk), 釀 (wine-making), 酌 (to drink) and 配 (to mix a drink).

【酉時】from 5 p.m. to 7 p.m.

jiǔ

酒是一種用穀類或果類發酵製成的飲料,如米酒、葡萄酒等。酒字從水從酉,酉是裝酒的罈子,水代表液體,因此酒的本義是指作為飲料的酒水、酒液。

【酒池肉林】聚酒成池,懸肉成林。形容窮奢極欲。

【酒酣耳熱】形容酒興正濃。

【酒囊飯袋】只會喝酒吃飯而不幹實事,用於諷刺無用之人。

甲骨文

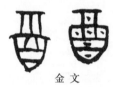

金 文

小 篆

酒 is a general term for alcoholic drink made from grains or fruits, e. g. 米酒 (rice wine), 葡萄酒 (wine). The character 酒 consists of 水 and 酉, the former standing for water and the latter the jar for containing wine, hence its primary meaning "alcoholic drink".

【酒池肉林】(lit.) to have a pond of wine and a forest of hanging meat; extremely extravagant and luxurious

【酒酣耳熱】warmed with wine

【酒囊飯袋】(lit.) wineskin and rice bag; a good-for-nothing

zhuó

酌字從酉從勺，酉是盛酒的罈子，勺則是專門用來舀酒的工具。所以酌的本義為挹取，又指斟酒、飲酒，引申為酒的代稱。同時，酌還引申為斟酌、估量之義。

【酌量】本指計量酒米而言，也泛指估量。

【酌斷】酌情裁斷。

【酌金饌玉】極言貴族豪門飲食的窮奢極欲。

金 文

小 篆

The character 酌 consists of 酉 and 勺, the former standing for a wine jar and the latter a ladle for lifting wine, hence the original meaning to fetch wine. But it is now used in the senses of "pouring out wine", "drinking wine", and even as a substitute for the character 酒 (wine). In addition, 酌 is also used in the senses "to consider" and "to estimate".

【酌量】to consider; to use one's judgment

【酌斷】to settle a matter as one sees fit

【酌金饌玉】(lit.) to drink gold and eat jade; to go to the extremes of extravagance

pèi

金文的配字，像一個人蹲在酒罈邊上，表示向酒中兌水或添加香料的意思。其本義當指調酒。配即調配，指把不同的東西調和或湊在一起。因此，配字還有湊合、匹對的意思。如男女兩性結合，就叫做婚配。

【配角】原指戲劇、電影等藝術表演中的次要角色，又比喻做輔助工作或次要工作的人。

【配偶】婚配。又指夫妻中的一方。

甲骨文

金文

小篆

In the Bronze Inscriptions, the character 配 looks like a man squatting beside a wine jar, signalling to prepare a drink by adding water or other ingredients to spirit, hence the primary meaning "to mix an alcoholic drink". As to mix a drink, one needs to put different things together, the character 配 has taken on the meaning of "combining", "pairing", e. g. 婚配 (to join in marriage).

【配角】 supporting role

【配偶】 (1) to marry (2) spouse

fù

　　金文的富字，像房屋中一隻酒罈子的形狀，屋中有酒表示富有。所以富字的本義為富有，即財物豐饒的意思，與"貧"相對；又指財物、財富；引申為充裕、豐饒之義。

【富貴】指有錢又有地位。

【富庶】特產豐富，人口眾多。

【富國強兵】使國家富有，兵力強大。

金文

小篆

In the Bronze Inscriptions, the character 富 looks like a wine jar inside a house. It is a sign of wealth to have wine in the family, hence the primary meaning of 富 is "rich" and "in possession of wealth", opposite to 貧 (poor). It may also mean "wealth", "possessions", "abundant" and "plentiful".

【富貴】 (to have) wealth and rank

【富庶】 rich and populous

【富國強兵】 to make one's country rich and build up its
　　　　　　 military power

jué

　　爵是古代的一種飲酒器具。這種酒器，三足兩柱，有流有
鋬，並仿雀形。它盛行於商周時代，是天子分封諸侯時賜給受
封者的一種賞賜物。所以"爵"後來就成了"爵位"的簡稱，
如《禮記》："王者之制祿爵，公、侯、伯、子、男，凡五
等。"

【爵祿】爵位和俸祿。

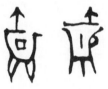

　　甲骨文　　　　　　　　金 文　　　　　　　小 篆

爵 refers to an ancient utensil for drinking, which
has a v-shaped lip, a handle, and three legs in the
bottom and two ornamental posts at the top. It was
very popular in the Shang Dynasty and used as a
gift form the king to the lords when they were given
their titles. That is why the character 爵 has come
to mean "title of nobility". For example, the *Book
of Rites* says, "The king has made five ranks of
nobility: duke, marquis, earl, viscount and baron".

【爵祿】 rank and salary

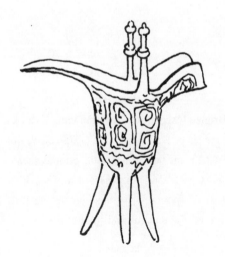

jiǎ

斝，是古代的一種酒器，圓口、平底，有三足，兩柱、一鋬。甲骨文、金文的斝字，即像其形；而小篆斝字從斗，則是後起的寫法。

甲骨文

金 文

小 篆

斝 refers to an ancient utensil for drinking, which has a round mouth, a flat bottom, three legs, two posts, and a handle. In the Oracle-Bone Inscriptions and Bronze Inscriptions, the character 斝 is in the shape of this utensil. In the Later Seal Character, however, it has a new form, with 斗 as a component.

hú

壺是一種由陶瓷或金屬等製成的容器，主要用來盛裝液體，如茶壺、酒壺等。古文字的壺字，頸窄腹圓，有耳有蓋有底座，是一把酒壺的形象。

甲骨文

金文

小篆

壺 refers to a vessel for liquids, made of baked clay or metal, e.g. 茶壺 (teapot), 酒壺 (wine pot). In ancient writing systems, the character 壺 is in the shape of a wine pot, with a narrow neck, a round belly, two ears, and a lid on the top and a stand at the bottom.

fǒu

甲骨文的缶字，像一件帶蓋的容器形狀：下面的口代表器皿，上面則是器蓋。缶是一種用以汲水或盛裝液體的容器，圓腹小口有蓋。缶多屬陶器，後來也有銅製的缶。漢字中凡從"缶"的字大都指陶器或與陶器有關，如罇、罐、缸、缺、磬等。

甲骨文　　　　　　　金 文　　　　　　　小 篆

In the Oracle-Bone Inscriptions, the character 缶 looks like a vessel with a round belly and small mouth: the lower part is the belly and the upper part the ild. It is a vessel for containing liquids, usually made of baked clay, though sometimes also made of bronze. Characters with 缶 as a component most have to do with earthenware, e.g. 罇 (ancient wine container), 罐 (jar), 缸 (earthen vat), 缺 (a broken earthen utensil), 磬 (chime stone).

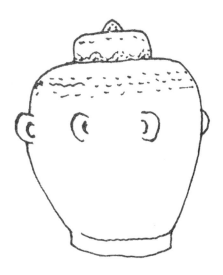

dǐng

鼎是古代的一種烹飪容器，常見者為三足兩耳大腹。甲骨文和早期金文的鼎字，正像鼎之有耳有足大腹的形狀，是鼎器的形象寫照。在古代，鼎不但是烹煮食物的容器，也是宗廟祭祀用的一種禮器。同時作為一種重要的宗廟禮器，它又是國家政權的象徵。所以鼎的形象，有較為豐富深邃的文化含義。

【鼎立】鼎有三足，比喻三方勢力並峙抗衡，如鼎足分立。

【鼎臣】指三公重臣。因鼎是宗廟重器，所以用來比喻職位重要的三公大臣。

【鼎沸】形容水勢洶湧，如鼎中沸騰的開水。也用來形容局勢的不安定。

【鼎盛】指昌盛或正當昌盛之時。

【鼎新】即更新。鼎為烹煮之物，生者使熟，堅者使柔，故有更新之義。又有鼎革或革故鼎新之說。

甲骨文

金文

小篆

鼎 refers to an ancient cooking-vessel, usually with three legs, two loop handles and a big belly. In the Oracle-Bone Inscriptions and early Bronze Inscriptions, the character 鼎 looks like a vivid picture of this vessel. In ancient times, this vessel was an important utensil at ancestral temples for offering sacrifices, as well as a daily cooking vessel. As such it was further seen as a symbol of state power. That is why the image of 鼎 has profound cultural implications in Chinese history.

【鼎立】 to stand like the three legs of a tripod; tripartite confrontation

【鼎臣】 important ministers

【鼎沸】 like a seething cauldron

【鼎盛】 at the height of power and splendors

【鼎新】 to replace the old with the new

yuán

員為“圓”的本字。甲骨文、金文的員字，下面是個鼎形，在鼎口的上方畫一個圓圈以表示鼎口是圓形的。小篆的員字從貝，乃是由“鼎”訛變而來。所以，員的本義當指圓鼎，泛指圓形或圓形之物。後來員字多用來指人員，指定數的人或物。於是另造“圓”字來代替它的本義。

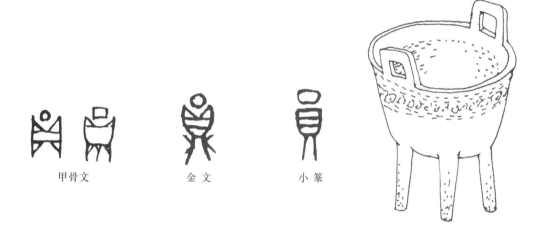

甲骨文　　　　　　金 文　　　　　　小 篆

員 was the original form of 圓. In the Oracle-Bone Inscriptions and Bronze Inscriptions, the character 員 looks like a cooking-vessel with a circle above it, indicating that the mouth of the vessel is round. In the Later Seal Character, the character 員, resulting from a wrong development, has 貝 as a component. As the original meaning of 員 was "round vessel", it might also refer to a circle or other circular things. But the character 員 is now more usually used in the senses of "person engaged in some activity" and "specified number of people or things". Its original meaning is expresssed by another character 圓.

bài

甲骨文的敗字，像手持棍棒敲擊鼎或貝的樣子。銅鼎是飲食和祭祀的重器，貝則為當時通行的貨貝，都是珍貴之物。以棒擊鼎或貝，是敗字的本義，表示擊毀、毀壞的意思，引申為指破壞、敗壞。敗字的用義非常廣泛，食物腐爛或變質變味可以說是"腐敗"或"敗味"；草木凋殘衰落也可稱為敗，如"殘枝敗葉"；軍隊被人擊潰，叫做"戰敗"；事業不成功或遭到挫折和損失，則稱為"失敗"。

甲骨文

金 文

小 篆

In the Oracle-Bone Inscriptions, the character 敗 looks like a man striking a cooking-vessel (or seashell) with a stick. The bronze cooking-vessel (an important utensil in daily life and sacrifice-offering ceremonies) and seashell (the currency at that time) were both valuable objects. To strike them with a stick signals to destroy, and that is the primary meaning of 敗. But 敗 is a character of many senses, e.g. food becoming unfit to eat may be referred to as 腐敗 or 敗味; dead twigs and withered leaves are known as 殘枝敗葉; an army suffering a defeat is 戰敗; and to encounter a failure in work is 失敗.

zé

上古無紙，人們常常把一些重要的文書或法律條文刻鑄在鍾鼎一類的青銅器上。甲骨文則字從鼎從刀，表示用刀把文字刻在銅器身上的意思。小篆則字的鼎形簡化訛變成貝，從貝從刀，則無從會意。由於銅器上刻的文字多為法律條文，故則字含有法則、規則的意思；引申為指法典、規章、模範、榜樣等。則字還可用作動詞，有效法的意思。

金 文

小 篆

Before the invention of paper, people used to inscribe important documents and legal provisions on bronze objects like bells and cooking-vessels. In the Oracle-Bone Inscriptions, the character 則 consists of a cooking-vessel part and a knife part, signalling to inscribe characters on the bronze object. In the Later Seal Character, the cooking-vessel part becomes a seashell part by mistake, making it incapable of revealing meaning through form. As the writing inscribed on bronze objects are usually legal documents, the character 則 has taken on the senses of "rule" and "regulation". It is also used in the senses of "standard" and "norm". Used as a verb, it means "to follow the example of".

jù

具是古代的一種主要炊具和食具,凡宴享賓朋或宗廟祭祀都離不開它。甲骨文的具字,像雙手舉(或搬)鼎之形,其本義為搬弄器具,引申為供置、供設、備辦和完備等義。同時,具也指食器,泛指一般的器具或工具。金文中的具字,或誤鼎為貝,又變貝為目,原來的字形和會意就變得面目全非了。

【具食】備辦酒食。

【具體而微】指某事(或物)內容大體具備而規模較小。

甲骨文　　　　金文　　　　小篆

As an important cooking utensil, 鼎 was used extensively in feasts and sacrifice-offering ceremonies. In the Oracle-Bone Inscriptions, the character 具 looks like two hands lifting a cooking-vessel, hence its original meaning "to carry utensils", from which have derived the senses "to provide", "to supply", "to prepare" and "to complete". Meanwhile it may refer to table-ware, or implements in general. In the Bronze Inscriptions, however, the cooking-vessel part (鼎) by mistake becomes a seashell part (貝), which in turn becomes an eye part (目), destroying the original association between form and meaning completely.

【具食】 to prepare food and wine
【具體而微】 small but complete

huò

甲骨文的鑊字，像人用手把鳥雀放入鼎、鬲一類的炊具中烹煮之形。金文以後的鑊字則由原來的會意變成為形聲。鑊的本義為烹煮，又指烹煮肉食的大鍋。

【鑊亨】古代酷刑名，指把人置於鑊中而烹之。亨，通"烹"。

甲骨文

金文　　　　　　　　　　小篆

In the Oracle-Bone Inscriptions, the character 鑊 looks like a hand putting a bird into a utensil to be cooked. But in the Bronze Inscriptions, it changes from an ideograph into a phonetic compound. Its original meaning was "to cook", and it is also used in the sense of a big cooking utensil, i.e. cauldron.

【鑊亨】(a form of torture, 亨 means the same as 烹) to place a criminal in a cauldron and cook him

lì

鬲是古代的一種炊具，有陶製和銅製兩種，其形狀與鼎相近：大腹、兩耳、三足。只不過鼎的三足為實心足，較細；而鬲的三足中空，足粗呈袋狀，俗稱"袋足鼎"。甲骨文、金文的鬲字，正是這種巨腹袋足的器物形像。漢字中凡從"鬲"的字大都與炊具或炊事有關，如融、鬵、鬻、鬺等。

甲骨文

金 文

小 篆

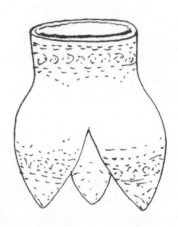

鬲 refers to an ancient cooking utensil, made of baked clay or bronze, similar to 鼎 in shape: with three legs, two loop handles and a big belly. It differs from 鼎 in that its legs are thick and hollow inside, like bags, hence the name bag-legged vessel. In the Oracle-Bone Inscriptions and Bronze Inscriptions, the character 鬲 looks like a picture of this vessel. Characters with 鬲 as a component most have to do with cooking, e.g. 融 (to melt), 鬻 (rice gruel), 鬵 (cauldron), 鬺 (to boil; to cook).

chè

徹與"撤"古本一字。甲骨文、金文的徹字，從鬲從又，像人用手（又）撤去食具（鬲）之形。徹字的本義為撤除，後來則多用為通、透之義。

【徹夜】通宵。

【徹底】通透到底，自始至終。

【徹骨】深透入骨，極言深刻。

甲骨文

金文

小篆

徹 was originally a variant form of 撤. In the Oracle-Bone Inscriptions and Bronze Inscriptions, the character 徹 consists of 鬲 (a cooking utensil) and 又 (hand), signalling to take away the utensil with hand. The original meaning of 徹 was "to take away", but it is now mainly used in the sense of "thorough" and "penetrating".

【徹夜】all night

【徹底】thorough

【徹骨】to the bone; to the utmost limits

yǎn

甗是古代的一種炊器，分上下兩層，上層形狀似甑，下層為鬲，中間為穿孔的箅，其用途相當於現代的蒸鍋。甲骨文和早期金文的甗是個象形字，像這種器物之形；後來甗字變成為形聲字，字形也越變越繁複。

甲骨文

金 文

小 篆

甗 refers to an ancient steaming utensil, which consists of two layers: the upper layer is 甑 with a perforated bottom and the lower layer is 鬲. In the Oracle-Bone Inscriptions and early Bronze Inscriptions, the character 甗 is a pictograph in the shape of this utensil. Later, however, it became a phonetic compound, resulting in a more complex form.

zēng

曾為"甑"的本字。甑是古代一種用來蒸食物的炊具。甲骨文曾字，下面的"田"字形代表甑底的箅，上面逸出的兩筆像蒸氣，表示用甑蒸食物的意思。所以曾的本義為甑，引申為指中間隔兩代的親屬關係，如曾祖、曾孫。曾還讀為cénɡ，用作副詞，表示從前有過的某種行為或情況，如"曾經滄海"等。

甲骨文

小篆

曾 was the original form of 甑, referring to an ancient steaming utensil. In the Oracle-Bone Inscriptions, the character 曾 has a part 田 standing for its perforated bottom, and the two strokes atop represent steam, hence its original meaning "to steam food". But it also refers to family relations three stages away, e.g. 曾祖 (great-grandfather), 曾孫 (great-grandson). 曾 may also be pronounced as céng, used as an adverb, meaning "having had the experience of", e.g. 曾經滄海 (to have sailed the seven seas; to have experienced great things).

dòu

豆是古代的一種食器，形似高足盤，後多用於祭祀。甲骨文、金文的豆字，像一上有盤下有高圈足的容器，盤中一橫是指事符號，表示盤中所盛之物。豆作為一種容器，又可用作一種容量單位，如《左傳》："齊舊四量：豆、區（ōu）、釜、鍾；四升為豆。"現在的豆字，多用為指豆類植物，即"豆菽"之豆。

甲骨文

金文

小篆

豆 referred to an ancient high-legged dinner plate, which was often used in sacrifice-offering ceremonies as well. In the Oracle-Bone Inscriptions and Bronze Inscriptions, the character 豆 looks like a vessel consisting of a deep plate on the top and a ringlike stand at the bottom, and the stroke inside the plate stands for food. The character 豆 was also an ancient measure of volume, for example, *Zuo Zhuan* (Spring and Autumn with Commentary by Tsu Chiu-ming) says, "There were originally four measures of volume: 豆, 區, 釜 and 鍾; and four shēng make a dòu (豆)". Nowadays, however, 豆 mainly refers to the plant of bean family.

dēng

甲骨文、金文中的登字，像人兩手捧豆(古代用以盛放食器的一種高腳盤)向上供奉的樣子，"豆"上兩個"止"形，表示向前進獻的動作。所以登字本義為向上進奉，引申為上升、登高、前進等義。

【登科】古代稱參加科舉考試被錄取為"登科"，又稱"登第"。

【登龍門】古代傳説，黃河的鯉魚能跳過龍門就會變化成龍。比喻得到有權力或名望的人的引薦提拔而提高地位和身價。

【登堂入室】古代宮室，前為堂，後為室。"登堂入室"在這裡喻指一個人學藝造詣精絕，深得師傳。

【登峰造極】升上山峰絕頂，比喻一個人學藝高深精絕，勝過眾人。

甲骨文

金文　　　　　小篆

In the Oracle-Bone Inscriptions and Bronze Inscriptions, the character 登 consists of three parts: two feet part, a high-legged plate part and two hands part; signalling to go forward and present the offering in the plate. The original meaning of 登 was to present offerings upwards, from which have derived its extended meanings "to go upwards", "to ascend" and "to advance".

【登科】(also 登第) to have passed the imperial examination

【登龍門】(lit.) (of a carp) to jump over a high gate to become a dragon; to have arisen to high positions

【登堂入室】to pass through the hall into the inner chamber; to become extremely proficient in one's profession

【登峰造極】to reach the peak of perfection

《説文解字》："豐,行禮之器也。"古文字的豐字,像一個高足的器皿(豆)中盛滿玉器之形。豆中盛玉是用來敬奉神祇的,所以豐的本義是指祭祀時的行禮之器。漢字中凡從"豐"之字都與祭祀行禮有關,如祭祀時行禮用的酒稱為"醴",而有關祭祀之事則稱為"禮"。

甲骨文

金文

小篆

Xu Shen says in his *Origin of Chinese Characters*. "豐 is a utensil used in ceremonies". In ancient writing systems, the character 豐 looks like a high-legged plate (豆) full of jade objects. These jade objects were meant to be offered to gods and spirits, so the character 豐 referred to utensils used in sacrifice-offering ceremonies. Characters with 豐 as a component most have to do with sacrifice-offering ceremonies, for example, the wine used in these ceremonies is known as 醴, and the ritual acts in these ceremonies are known as 禮.

fēng

古文字的豐字，像一高足器皿（豆）中盛滿稻穗或麥穗一類的穀物之形，以表示莊稼豐收之意。所以豐的本義指豐收，引申為茂盛、充實、富饒之義。

【豐年】農作物豐收的年頭。

【豐滿】充足。又指人體胖得勻稱好看。

【豐美】多而好。

【豐衣足食】形容生活富裕足實。

甲骨文　　　　　　金　文　　　　　　小　篆

In ancient writing systems, the character 豐 looks like a high-legged plate (豆) full of rice ears or wheat ears, signalling there is a bumper harvest of crops. The primary meaning of 豐 is "bumper harvest", and its extended meanings include "luxuriant", "substantial" and "rich".

【豐年】bumper harvest year

【豐滿】(1) plentiful (2) well-developed

【豐美】lush

【豐衣足食】to have ample food and clothing

guǐ

【殷】

篹是古代祭祀宴享時盛黍稷等食物的器皿，圓腹、侈口、圈足，多為銅製。甲骨文、金文的篹字，像人手持匕柶向一盛滿食物的圈足篹中舀取食物之形。而小篆的篹字從竹從皿，這大概是因為後世的篹多改用竹製的緣故吧。

甲骨文

金文

小篆

篹 refers to an ancient vessel, with a round belly, big mouth and ringlike stand, usually made of bronze, and used to contain food in feasts or sacrifice-offering ceremonies. In the Oracle-Bone Inscriptions and Bronze Inscriptions, the character 篹 looks like a man taking food with a spoon from such a vessel. In the Later Seal Character, it consists of 竹 (bamboo) and 皿 (vessel), perhaps reflecting the fact that at that time 篹 was made of bamboo.

jí

甲骨文、金文的即字，左邊是一隻高腳的豆（一種食器），上面盛滿了食物，右邊是一個跪坐的人形，像一個人準備進食的樣子。它的本義是"就食"。要就食必須走近食物，所以即字又有"走近"、"靠近"之義，如成語"若即若離"、"可望不可即"等；後來又借用為副詞，有"馬上"、"立刻"之義。

甲骨文　　　　　　金文　　　　　　小篆

In the Oracle-Bone Inscriptions and Bronze Inscriptions, the character 即 has a high-legged plate (豆) full of food on the left and a man on his knees on the right, signalling the man is about to eat. Hence its original meaning was "to dine". In order to eat food, one must get close to it, so 即 has taken on the meanings of "approaching", "close to", e.g. 若即若離 (to appear to be neither close nor far apart), 可望不可即 (within sight but beyond reach). It may also be used as an adverb, meaning "immediately" and "at once".

jì

既字左邊為一食器，右邊一個跪坐的人，頭向背後扭轉，不再看擺在面前的食物，表示已經吃飽了，準備離開，所以它的本義為食盡、吃完了。引申為完、盡、結束等義，又引申為時間副詞，表示"已經"的意思，如"既然"、"既往不咎"等。

甲骨文

金 文

小 篆

The character 既 has a plate part on the left and a man part on the right. The high-legged plate is covered by a lid and the man on his knees is turning away his head, not looking at it any more. This signals that the man has finished eating and is ready to leave. So the primary meaning of 既 was "to eat up". And its extended meanings include "to finish", "to complete" and "to be over". It may also be used as an adverb, meaning "already", e.g. 既然 (since; such being the case), 既往不咎 (to let bygones be bygones).

xiǎng

甲骨文、金文的饗字，像兩人圍着盛有食物的食器相對而食之形。饗字本義為兩人對食，後來引申為指用酒食款待人。小篆的饗字，是一個上鄉下形（食）的形聲字。

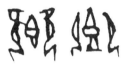

甲骨文　　　　　　金　文　　　　　　小　篆

In the Oracle-Bone Inscriptions and Bronze Inscriptions, the character 饗 looks like two men sitting around a food container and eating. Hence its original meaning "two men eating together", from which has derived the meaning "to treat somebody to food and wine". In the Later Seal Character, the character 饗 is a phonetic compound, with the phonetic on top of the radical.

shí

甲骨文食字，下邊像一豆形容器，裡面裝滿食物，上邊是器蓋，連起來看，像盛在容器中的食物形。所以食字本義是指可以吃的食物，引申為動詞表示吃。在漢字中，凡以食為偏旁的字，都與食品或吃有關，如飯、飲、餅、飽、饗、餐等。

【食客】舊時指寄食於富貴之家並為之所用的門客，現在也指飲食店、餐廳的顧客。

【食言】背棄諾言，謂言而不行，如食之消盡。

【食古不化】指學古人，讀古書，而不知運用，如食物之不消化。

甲骨文

金文

小篆

In the Oracle-Bone Inscriptions, the character 食 looks like a high-legged plate full of food with its angled lid lifted above it. Hence its primary meaning "food to be eaten", from which has derived the meaning "to eat". Characters with 食 as a component all have to do with food and eating, e.g. 飯 (cooked rice), 飲 (to drink), 餅 (a round flat cake), 飽 (to have eaten one's fill), 饗 (to treat someone to dinner) and 餐 (to eat).

【食客】(1) a person sponging on an aristocrat (2) a customer to a restaurant

【食言】to go back on one's word

【食古不化】to swallow ancient learning without digesting it

hui

甲骨文、金文的會字,下面的口代表容器,上面是器蓋,中間是裝在容器中的東西,表示器、蓋相合的意思。所以會字的本義為匯合、聚合,引申為指相逢、見面,同時又指有目的集會或某些團體,如晚會、報告會、工會等。此外,會字還有理解、懂得、通曉、擅長等義、如體會、能説會道等。

金文　　　　　　小篆

In the Oracle-Bone Inscriptions and Bronze Inscriptions, the character 會 consists of three parts: the lid of a container, the thing contained and the belly of a container, signalling that the different parts match well. So the character 會 means "to get together", "to assemble" and "to meet". It may also refer to some activities or organizations in which people get together, e.g. 晚會 (evening party), 報告會 (public lecture), 工會 (trade union). In addition, 會 may also mean "to understand", "to be able to", e.g. 體會 (to realize), 能説會道 (to have the gift of the gab).

hé

古文字的合字，下面的口代表裝東西的容器，上面是蓋子，表示器、蓋合攏在一起的意思。所以合的本義為相合、關閉、收攏，引申為聚會、聯結等義。

【合同】會合齊同，和睦。又指契約文書。

【合作】指為了共同的目的一起工作或共同完成某項任務。

【合璧】指把不同的東西放在一起而配合得宜。

甲骨文

金文

小篆

In ancient writing systems, the character 合 looks like the lid and belly of a container put together. Its primary meaning is "to combine", "to close", and its extended meanings include "to get together" and "to join".

【合同】(1) to get along well (2) contract

【合作】 to cooperate

【合璧】 to match well

níng

甲骨文寧字，像室內桌上安放器皿，表示安定、安靜之意；金文加"心"，心安就是寧。因此，寧的本義就是安寧。寧字又可讀作nìng, 用作副詞，表示寧願、寧可、難道、竟、乃等義。

【寧靜】安定清靜。

【寧缺毋濫】指選拔人才或挑選事物，寧可少一些，也不要不顧質量貪多湊數。

【寧為玉碎，不為瓦全】比喻寧願為正義事業犧牲，不願喪失氣節，苟且偷生。

金文

小篆

In the Oracle-Bone Inscriptions, the character 寧 looks like a house in which there is an object on a table, signalling that it is a peaceful and quiet place. In the Bronze Inscriptions, a heart part (心) is added to emphasize the point that it is "the heart" — the inside of a man that is quiet. Hence the primary meaning of 寧 "quiet". 寧 may also be used as an adverb, pronounced as nìng, meaning "rather", "would rather".

【寧靜】peaceful; quiet

【寧缺毋濫】rather go without than have something shoddy

【寧為玉碎，不為瓦全】rather be a shattered vessel of jade than an unbroken piece of potery; better to die in glory than live in dishonour

fán

　　"凡"是"盤"字的初文。盤是一種侈口淺腹圈足的器具，甲骨文、金文的凡字即像其形。所以，凡的本義即指盤子。此字後來多用為大概、要括等義，又用為世俗、凡庸之義，其本義則為盤字所取代。

【凡人】平庸的人。又指俗世之人，與"仙人"相對。

【凡要】簿書的綱要、總目。

【凡庸】平常，一般。

甲骨文　　　　金文　　　　小篆

凡 was the original form of 盤, referring to a shallow plate with a ringlike stand. In the Oracle-Bone Inscriptions and Bronze Inscriptions, the character 凡 is in the shape of such a plate. Nowadays, however, it is more usually used in the senses of "in general", "ordinary", and its original sense is expressed by 盤.

【凡人】(1) ordinary people (2) mortal

【凡要】outline; essentials

【凡庸】commonplace

pán

盤是古代盛水或食物的淺底器皿，多為圓形。甲骨文的盤字，像人手持匕向一圈足的器皿中舀取食物之形。金文盤字的器形訛變成"舟"，字變為"般"；或加"皿"表示它是器皿；或加"金"，表示它是由金屬銅製成。小篆的盤字從"木"，則表示它是用木製成。盤字除作為器名，還可用作旋轉、纏繞、盤問、盤算等義。

【盤旋】環繞着飛或走。又指徘徊、逗留。

【盤根錯節】樹根盤繞，枝節交錯。比喻事情繁難複雜，不易解決。

甲骨文

金文

小篆

盤 refers to an ancient shallow plate with a ringlike stand. In the Oracle-Bone Inscriptions, the character 盤 looks like a man taking food from such a plate with a spoon. In the Bronze Inscriptions, the plate part by mistake becomes a boat part; sometimes there is a vessel part (皿) added to indicate its use, or a metal part (金) to indicate its material. In the Later Seal Character, the character has 木 as a component, signalling that it is made of wood. In addition, 盤 may also mean "to rotate", "to twine", "to interrogate" and "to calculate".

【盤旋】(1) to circle (2) to linger

【盤根錯節】with twisted roots and gnarled branches; complicated and difficult to deal with

yí

匜，是古代洗手盛水的用具。洗手時，把匜中的水倒在手上，下面用盤承接。金文的匜字，像一有流、有柄的匜形；字或從皿，表示其為器皿；又從金，表示它是由金屬銅製成。

金 文

小 篆

匜 refers to an ancient utensil for washing hands. It is in the shape of a gourd-shaped ladle, with a lip and handle. When washing, one pours out water from it, which runs through one's hands to a basin below. In the Bronze Inscriptions, the character 匜 looks like such a ladle; sometimes there is a vessel part (皿) indicating its use, or a metal part (金) indicating its material.

mǐn

甲骨文皿字，像一帶圈足的容器；金文皿字或加金旁，表明器皿是由金屬銅所製。皿字的本義就是裝東西的器具，是碗盤一類飲食用器的總稱。在漢字中，凡由皿字組成的字大都與器皿及其用途有關，如盂、盆、盛、盥、溢、盈等。

甲骨文

金文

小篆

In the Oracle-Bone Inscriptions, the character 皿 looks like a vessel with a ringlike stand. In the Bronze Inscriptions, there is sometimes a metal part (金) added to indicate that it is made of metal such as bronze. So the character 皿 is a general term for vessels such as bowls and plates. Characters with 皿 as a component most have to do with vessels and their uses, e.g. 盂 (broad-mouthed jar), 盆 (basin), 盛 (to fill 〔a vessel〕), 盥 (to wash 〔one's hands and face〕), 溢 (to overflow) and 盈 (to be filled with).

yì

益為"溢"的本字。古文字的益字，像皿中之水滿而外溢之形，本義為水溢出器皿，引申為水漲。因水滿而外溢，所以益字又有富足、富饒之意，引申為增加，再從增加的東西引申為利益、好處等。

【益友】指於己有益之友。

【益智】增益智慧。

甲骨文

金文

小篆

益 was the original form of 溢. In ancient writing systems, the character 益 looks like a vessel overflowing with water. Hence the original meaning "the overflow of water" or "the rise of water level". As water overflows only when there is too much of it, the character 益 has also taken on the meanings of "rich", "abundant", "to increase", "benefit" and "profit".

【益友】 good friend

【益智】 helpful to intelligence

guàn

　　金文盥字，像有水從上倒下，兩手接水沖洗，下面的皿是接水的容器，本義為洗手，即以手承水沖洗。如《禮記》："盥者，手受之而下流於盤。"盥本來僅指洗手而言，可是到了後世，洗臉洗手均稱為"盥"，如盥櫛（指梳洗）。現代所用的"盥洗室"，是既可洗手也可洗臉的。

甲骨文

金文

小篆

In the Bronze Inscriptions, the character 盥 looks like water running down through two hands and there is a basin below, hence the primary meaning "washing one's hands". For example, *the Book of Rites* says, " 盥 means washing one's hands with running water, which ends in a basin below". Nowadays, however, the character 盥 may also refer to the washing of one's face, e.g. 盥櫛 (washing one's face and combing one's hair). And the room known as 盥洗室 (washroom) is a place where one washes one's face as well as hands.

xuè

甲骨文血字，像血滴滴入皿中之形，本義是指人或其他動物的血液。

【血色】指深紅色。如白居易《琵琶行》：“血色羅裙翻酒污。”

【血性】指剛強正直的性格。

【血親】指有血統關係的親屬。

【血肉】血液和肌肉，比喻關係極其密切。

【血案】兇殺案件。

【血戰】激烈拚搏的戰鬥。

甲骨文

金 文

小 篆

In the Oracle-Bone Inscriptions, the character 血 looks like drops of blood dripping into a vessel, hence its meaning "blood".

【血色】deep red

【血性】courage and uprightness

【血親】consanguinity

【血肉】flesh and blood

【血案】murder case

【血戰】bloody battle

jìn

甲骨文的盡字，像人手持竹枝刷洗器皿之形，表示器中空淨之意。《說文解字》稱："盡，器中空也。"盡由器中空淨的本義引申出完、竭盡之義，又引申為終止、完全、達到極限等意思。

【盡力】竭盡材力。

【盡忠報國】竭盡忠貞以報效國家。

【盡善盡美】指完美至極。

甲骨文

金文

小篆

In the Oracle-Bone Inscriptions, the character 盡 looks like a man brushing a vessel with bamboo branches in hand, signalling the vessel is empty. Thus the *Origin of Chinese Characters* says, " 盡 means a vessel is empty". From this primary meaning have derived its extended senses of "exhausted", "end", "complete" and "to the limit".

【盡力】 to try one's best

【盡忠報國】 to be loyal and patriotic

【盡善盡美】 perfect

yì

易

甲骨文的易字，像用手把一個器皿中的水注入另一個器皿中之形。這個字形後來經過不斷簡損，只截取保留器皿中帶耳的一片和水滴三點，故到小篆時就訛變得面目全非了。易的本義為給與，在金文中常用作賞賜之"賜"，又有交換、更換、改變之意。後世的易字，則多用作容易（與"難"相對）、平易之義。

【易轍】改變行車的軌道，比喻更改行事的方法。

【易與】輕鄙之詞，指容易對付。

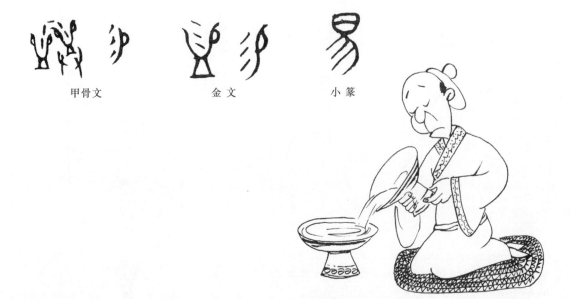

甲骨文　　　　　金 文　　　　　小 篆

In the Oracle-Bone Inscriptions, the character 易 looks like water being poured from one vessel to another. However this character has undergone a series of changes in its form. At the end there is left only the part with a loop handle and three dots standing for drops of water. That is why the character 易 in the Later Seal Character has assumed a completely different form from that in the Oracle-Bone Inscriptions. The original meaning of 易 was "to give", but it is also used in the senses of "change" and "exchange". The more usual sense of it, however, is "easy", opposite to 難 (difficult).

【易轍】 to run on a different track; to do things in a different way

【易與】 easy to deal with

gài

金文的蓋字，像一個器皿上面有物覆蓋的樣子，本義即指器物上部的覆蓋物，即蓋子。小篆蓋字從草頭，本義是指用茅草編成的覆蓋物，即苫子。又泛指車蓋、傘蓋等。蓋字用作動詞，有覆蓋、覆壓之義，引申為壓倒、勝過之義。

【蓋世】壓倒當世。多指本領高強，無人能敵。

【蓋棺論定】指人死後，一生的是非功過才有公平的結論。

金　文　　　　　小　篆

In the Bronze Inscriptions, the character 蓋 looks like a vessel with something above it, hence its primary meaning: the thing on top of a vessel, i.e. cover. In the Later Seal Character, it has a grass part, referring to a type of cover made of cogongrass. It may also refer to covers in general, such as 車蓋 (canopy), 傘蓋 (umbrella). When it is used as a verb, it means "to cover", "to top" and "to surpass".

【蓋世】unparalleled anywhere in the world

【蓋棺論定】The final judgment can be passed on a person only when the lid is laid on his coffin.

dǒu

甲骨文、金文的斗字，像一把有長柄勺子形。斗是古代盛酒的器具，又是量糧食的器具，引申為容量單位：十升為一斗，十斗為一石。因斗字像一把大勺形，所以天上由七顆星組成的像一把大勺子的星群也稱為斗，即北斗星。凡從"斗"的字，大都與量器有關，如斛、料、斟等。

【斗室】一斗見方的屋子。形容非常狹小。

【斗膽】像斗一樣大的膽子。形容大膽。多作謙辭。

| 甲骨文 | 金文 | 小篆 |

In the Oracle-Bone Inscriptions and Bronze Inscriptions, the character 斗 looks like a dipper with a long handle. In ancient times this type of dipper was not only used to lift wine but also to measure the amount of grain. So 斗 is also a measure of capacity, equal to ten 升 or one tenth of 石 in the Chinese System, and a decalitre in the Metric System. As the group of seven stars seen only from the northern part of the world are in the shape of a dipper, they are known as 北斗星 (the Big Dipper). Characters with 斗 as a component most have to do with the measuring dipper, e.g. 斛 (a square-mouthed vessel, used as a measure of capacity equal to five 斗), 料 (to measure the amount of rice grain with 斗), 斟 (to lift wine with a ladle).

【斗室】 (lit.) a room with a capacity of dǒu; a small room

【斗膽】 (lit.) to have a gall bladder with a capacity of dǒu; to make bold

liào

料字從米從斗，是個會意字，表示用斗量米的意思。料的本義為量米，引申為泛指計量、計算、統計，又引申為估量、預料、猜度之義。此外，料還有照料、整理的意思；用作名詞，則指可供使用的原料、物料。

【料民】古代稱調查統計人口數量為"料民"。

【料事】猜度事情，又指處理事情。

【料想】猜測，預料。

【料持】料理，安排。

金文

小篆

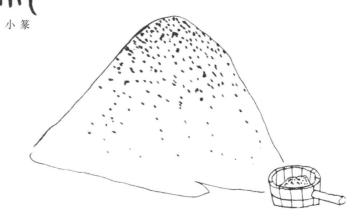

The character 料, an ideograph, consists of 米 (rice) and 斗 (measuring dipper), signalling to measure the amount of rice grain with a dipper. But 斗 may also be used in the sense of measuring in general and has taken on the senses "to calculate", "to estimate", "to predict" and "to speculate". In addition, it may mean "to take care of" and "to put in order". As a noun, it may refer to the material to make something.

【料民】 (arch.) popluation census

【料事】 (1) to make predictions (2) to attend to business

【料想】 to presume

【料持】 to take care of

sháo

小 篆

勺，是一種舀東西的用具，略作半球形，有柄。甲骨文的勺字，即是這種有長柄的勺子形狀，勺中的一點代表所舀取的食物。勺的本義指勺子，用作動詞，有舀取之義。

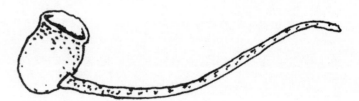

勺 means "ladle", a tool for lifting things, consisting of a small bowl with a handle. In the Oracle-Bone Inscriptions, the character 勺 looks like a picture of such a tool, the dot in it standing for the food it holds. It may also be used as a verb, meaning to lift something out of a container with a ladle.

bǐ

　　匕即匕柶，是古代用來舀取食物的器具，曲柄淺斗，相當於現在的羹匙。甲骨文、金文的匕字，像匕匙之形。此字形體與"比"字所從的人形十分近似，互相混淆，故小篆的匕字即訛變為反人之形。

【匕首】短劍，柄頭如匕，故名。

【匕箸】匙和筷。

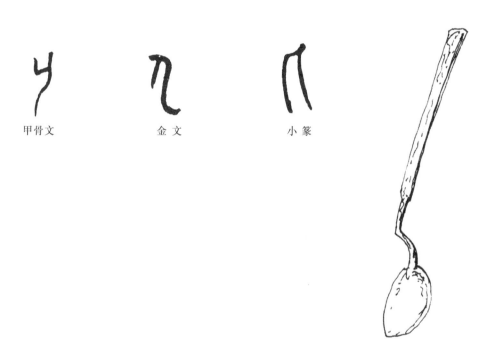

甲骨文　　　　金文　　　　小篆

匕 refers to an ancient spoonlike tool, with a shallow bowl and a bent handle. In the Oracle-Bone Inscriptions and Bronze Inscriptions, the character 匕 is in the shape of such a spoon. As it looks very similar to the man part in 比, the character 匕 in the Later Seal Character mistakenly changes to an otherway-round man part.

【匕首】dagger

【匕箸】spoon and chopsticks

zhǐ

甲骨文、金文的旨字，從匕從口，匕是取食的工具，像用匕臿取食物放入口中之形；旨又或從甘，表示食物味道甘美之意。所以旨的本義指味道甘美，又指美味。此字後來則多用為意圖、用意、目的、意義等義。

【旨酒】美酒。

【旨要】要旨，主要的意思。

【旨趣】宗旨、意義。

甲骨文

金文

小篆

In the Oracle-Bone Inscriptions and Bronze Inscriptions, the character 旨 consists of 匕 (spoon) and 口 (mouth), signalling to eat with a spoon. Sometimes the character 旨 has 甘 (sweet taste) as a component, signalling that the food is delicious. The original meaning of 旨 was "sweet taste" or "delicacy", but it is now more usually used in the senses of "intention", "purpose", "aim" and "purport".

【旨酒】excellent wine

【旨要】main purpose

【旨趣】purport

ZŬ

俎是古代祭祀時陳置牛羊祭品的案几。金文的俎字就是這種案几的象形：右邊的"且"代表案面，左邊則是兩個倒丁字形的腳座。作為宗廟用器，俎在古代也是一種祀器，後世則用作切肉的砧板。

【俎豆】俎是置牲的案几，豆是盛祭品的器皿，是祭祀時兩種常用的祀器，故用俎豆代指祀器。又代指祭祀。

【俎上肉】指砧板上的肉，比喻任人宰割。

甲骨文

金 文

小 篆

俎 refers to an ancient table for presenting sacrifices such as beef and mutton at offering ceremonies. In the Bronze Inscriptions, the character 俎 looks like such a table on end: the right is the surface board and the left legs. As a utensil for sacrifice-offering, this table is also seen as a ritual object. In daily life, however, it is more usually used as a chopping block.

【俎豆】 (lit.) table and plate; ritual objects; sacrifice-offering ceremony

【俎上肉】 (lit.) meat on a chopping block; to be partitioned by others at will

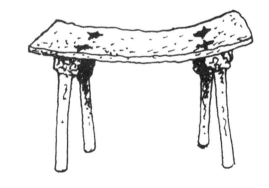

yòng

用即"桶"的本字。甲骨文、金文和小篆的用字,均像日常用器的桶形,因而引申為施用之用,分別有使用、功用(作用)、費用等義。

【用武】使用武力,用兵,或比喻施展才能。

【用命】服從命令,效勞出力。

【用度】各種費用開支的總稱。

【用途】指某一事物應用的方面或範圍。

甲骨文	金文	小篆

用 was the original form of 桶. In the Oracle-Bone Inscriptions, Bronze Inscriptions and Later Seal Character, the character 用 looks like a tub in each case. As the tub is a common object for daily use, the character 用 has taken on the meanings "to use", "to employ", "function" and "expenses".

【用武】to use force; to dispaly one's abilities or talents

【用命】to obey orders

【用度】expenditure

【用途】use

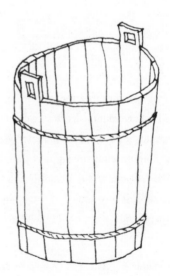

qū

甲骨文的區字，像櫥架中藏置眾多器物之形。它的本義為藏匿，又指藏匿東西的地方，引申為指區域，即有一定界限的地域。區字用作動詞，則有區分、區別之意。此外，區又讀 **ōu**，是古代一種量器的名稱。

【區中】人世間。

【區宇】疆土境域。區，指疆域；宇，指上下四方。

【區處】分別處置，安排。又指居住的地方。

甲骨文

金　文

小　篆

In the Oracle-Bone Inscriptions, the character 區 looks like a cupboard for storing things. Its original meaning was "to store" or "the place to store things", from which have derived the meanings of "region" and "district". Used as a verb, it means "to distinguish" and "to differentiate". In addition, 區 pronounced as ōu refers to an ancient measure of capacity.

【區中】 the world

【區宇】 territory

【區處】 (1) to deal with different cases in different ways,
(2) residence

zhù

甲骨文、金文鑄字，像雙手持坩鍋向下面的一個器皿模子中澆灌銷鎔的銅水之義，表示澆鑄。小篆鑄字從金壽聲，變成為形聲字。鑄的本義為鎔煉金屬以成器，引申為陶冶、製造、培育等義。

【鑄錯】造成重大錯誤。

甲骨文

金 文

小 篆

In the Oracle-Bone Inscriptions and Bronze Inscriptions, the character 鑄 looks like a man pouring a crucible of melted bronze into a mould below with the hands, hence the primary meaning "casting". In the Later Seal Character, the character 鑄 becomes a phonetic compound, with 金 (metal) as the radical and 壽 as the phonetic. Apart from its primary meaning, 鑄 is also used in the general sense of making things out of a mould, have derived the meanings of "fabrication", "incubation" and "mould".

【鑄錯】 to make a gross error

qì

器字由"犬"和四個"口"組成。這裡的口指的是可以裝東西的器皿,表示許多器皿集中堆放在一起,有狗(犬)在中間看守。器字最初的本義可能指陶器,如《老子》:"埏埴以為器。"(攪和泥土做成陶器)後泛指一般的器具、工具,如《論語》:"工欲善其事,必先利其器。"(工匠要做好他的工作,一定要先磨利他的工具。)引申為指有形的具體事物,與抽象的"道"相對,如《易經‧繫辭上》:"形而上者謂之道,形而下者謂之器。"

【器度】指一個人的肚量和氣魄。

金文　　　　小篆

The character 器 is made up of a 犬 and four 口, the former referring to the dog and the latter standing for vessels, signalling a number of vessels guarded by a dog. At the beginning, it might refer to pottery only. For example *Lao Zi* (Lao-Tzu) says, "埏埴以為器 (One mixes clay with water to make a pot)". Later, its meaning was broadened and it could refer to any utensil or instrument. Thus the *Analects of Confucius* says, "工欲善其事, 必先利其器 (A workman must first sharpen his tools if he is to do his work well)". But it is also used in a more general sense, referring to anything tangible and concrete, opposite to the abstract notion 一道 (way; reason). So the *Book of Changes* says, "形而上者謂之道, 形而下者謂之器 (The formless, intangible is known as dào, and the formal, tangible is known as qì)".

【器度】tolerance and breadth of mind

guàn

小篆的冠字，上面是一頂帽子之形，下面從人從寸，像人用手把帽子戴在頭上之形。冠的本義為戴帽。因冠在人頭之上，所以冠字又可引申為超出眾人、位居第一之義，如冠軍。此外，冠又是帽子的總稱。

【冠冕】冠、冕都是戴在頭上的帽子，比喻受人擁戴或出人頭地。又用作仕宦的代稱。

【冠軍】列於諸軍首位，即勇冠三軍的意思。後稱在比賽中得第一名的為"冠軍"。

小篆

In the Later Seal Character, the character 冠 is made up of three parts: a hat part (冖) on the top, a man part (元) on the left and a hand part (寸) on the right; signalling a man is putting on a hat. Hence its primary meaning "to put on a hat". Apart from this verbal sense, it may also refer to head-gear in general. As a hat is put on the head, the character 冠 has also taken on the sense of "the first" and "the best".

【冠冕】hat; leader; officer
【冠軍】champion

miǎn

免為"冕"的本字。甲骨文、金文的免字,像一個人頭戴一頂大帽子的形狀,甲骨文免字在帽子的上面還有羊角的裝飾。免字的本義為冠冕,即帽子。免字後來多用作除去、脫掉之義,又引申為避免、罷免、赦免等義,其本義逐漸消失,故另造"冕"字代替之。

【免冠】脫帽,表示謝罪。

【免俗】行為禮儀不同於世俗。

金文

小篆

免 was the original form of 冕. In the Oracle-Bone Inscriptions and Bronze Inscriptions, the character 免 looks like a man with a top hat on; sometimes there are even sheep horns on the top as ornaments. Hence its original meaning "top hat". Nowadays, however, the character 免 is mainly used in the senses "to remove", "to take off", "to avoid", "to dismiss" and "to exempt". Its original meaning is expressed by 冕.

【免冠】to take off one's hat

【免俗】without vulgar tastes

mào

冒為"帽"的本字。金文冒字,下邊的"目"代表眼睛,眼睛上面是一頂帽子的形象。冒的本義指帽子。由於帽子是戴在頭上的,所以冒字就有覆蓋之意。又因為帽子是由人頭頂着的,故冒又有頂着之意,引申為頂撞、觸犯、突出、頂起以及假冒、頂替等義。此外,冒字還有冒失、冒昧之義,以及不顧環境惡劣而行動之義(如冒雨,冒險)。

【冒犯】言語或行動衝撞了對方。
【冒充】假的頂替真的。
【冒失】魯莽、輕率。

金文

小篆

冒 was the original form of 帽. In the Bronze Inscriptions, the character 冒 has an eye below a covering, signalling that it is a headgear. As the headgear is put on the head, the character 冒 also means "to cover". On the other hand, from the sense of "atop the head" have derived the senses "to contradict", "to offend", "to stand out", "to pretend to be", etc. In addition, it may also mean "to make bold to ", "to act with out due consideration", and "to act in spite of difficulties" (e.g. 冒雨 "to brave the storm", 冒險 "to take a risk 〔 to do sth 〕").

【冒犯】to offend
【冒充】to pretend to be
【冒失】rash

zhòu

金文的冑字，像人頭上戴着頭盔，眼睛露在外面的形狀。冑的本義指頭盔，又稱"兜鍪（móu）"，是古代作戰時戴的帽子。後來冑字又引申為指帝王或貴族的後裔，如帝冑、貴冑等。

金 文

小 篆

In the Bronze Inscriptions, the character 冑 looks like a head with a helmet on, and the eye is not covered by it. Hence its primary meaning "helmet", also known as 兜鍪, a headgear worn by soldiers in fighting. But 冑 may also refer to the descendants of kings and lords, e.g. 帝冑 (a scion of royalty), 貴冑 (a scion of nobility).

huáng

金文的皇字，下面是一個"王"，上面是一頂裝飾華麗的帽子的形狀，所以皇是古代帝王所戴的一種冠帽。如《禮記·王制》："有虞氏皇而祭。"（有虞氏頭戴皇冠主持祭禮。）引申為指帝王、君主，如三皇五帝、皇帝等。皇字由皇冠之義引申為輝煌、華美之義，如冠冕堂皇。由帝王、君主之義引申為大、至尊等義，如皇天、皇考等。

金文　　　　　　　小篆

In the Bronze Inscriptions, the character 皇 has a king part (王) below a hat with ornaments, signalling it is a hat worn by kings, i.e. crown. For example, the *Book of Rites* records, "有虞氏皇而祭 (You Yu, also known as Shun, put on the crown and presided over the ceremony)". From this original meaning has derived its use to refer to rulers such as emperors and kings, e.g. 三皇五帝 (the earliest eight rulers in Chinese recorded history) and 皇帝 (emperor). As the crown is magnificent with ornaments, the character 皇 has also taken on the meanings of "splendid" and "magnificent", e.g. 冠冕堂皇 (〔lit.〕 magnificent crowns). It is also used in the senses of "great" and "reverend", e.g. 皇天 (Heaven) and 皇考 (forefather).

SĪ

絲的本義是指蠶絲。甲骨文的絲字，像用兩小把蠶絲扭結成繩線的樣子。又指纖細如絲之物，如柳絲、蛛絲等。絲還用作長度或重量的計量單位名稱：十忽為一絲，十絲為一毫。

【絲綢】用蠶絲或人造絲織成的紡織品的總稱。

【絲毫】形容極小或很少。

【絲竹】古代樂器的總稱：絲，指弦樂器，如琴、瑟；竹，指管樂器，如簫、笛。又代指音樂。

甲骨文

金文

小篆

絲 means "silk". In the Oracle-Bone Inscriptions, the character 絲 looks like two strings made of silk. It may also refer to things which are thin and long, e.g. 柳絲 (fine willow branches), 蛛絲 (spider thread). 絲 is also a measure of weight, equal to ten 忽 or one tenth of 毫 in the Chinese System, and half a milligramme in the Metric System.

【絲綢】 silk cloth

【絲毫】 the slightest amount

【絲竹】 (1) traditional stringed and wind instruments (2) music

jīng

金文的經字本是個象形字，像繃撐在織布機上的三根"經線"之形；後來增加絲旁（糸），於是經字變成左形右聲的形聲字。經的本義是指織物的縱線，與"緯"相對。南北為經、東西為緯。經緯是道路主幹的方向，引申為指大道，又引申為指常行的道理、規則、法制、原則等。此外，經字還可用作動詞，有經歷、量度、治理等義。

【經典】舊時指作為思想典範的書籍。又指宗教典籍，如佛經。

【經脈】人體內的縱行脈管。

【經濟】經國濟民。

金文

小篆

In the Bronze Inscriptions, the character 經, a pictograph, originally looked like three warp threads fixed on a loom. Later, a silk part (糸) was added to it, resulting in a phonetic compound. The primary meaning of 經 is the thread running along the length of cloth, as against 緯, the thread running across the cloth. The two characters 經 and 緯 are also used metaphorically for roads. Those going northwards or southwards are known as 經 and those going eastwards or westwards 緯. From this meaning have derived its senses of "main road", "common practice", "rule", "regulation" and "principle". Besides it may also be used as a verb, meaning "to experience", "to measure" and "to manage".

【經典】(1) chassics (2) scriptures

【經脈】(traditional Chinese medicine) channels through which vital energy circulates, regulating bodily functions

【經濟】economy

suǒ

甲骨文索字，像一條扭結而成的繩子，又像有人用雙手在搓製繩子；金文索字增加屋形，則像人在室內搓製繩索之形。古代"大者謂之索，小者謂之繩"，所以索的本義是指粗繩子。因繩索有所繫聯，可以尋繹，故索字有尋求、探尋之義，如按圖索驥(照圖上畫的樣子去尋找好馬，比喻根據線索去尋找或追究)；又有討取之義。

【索隱】尋求事物隱僻之理。

【索居】指散居，或離群獨居。

金 文

小 篆

In the Oracle-Bone Inscriptions, the character 索 looks like a rope made by twisting, or two hands twisting a rope. In the Bronze Inscriptions, a house part is added at the top to signal that people twist ropes inside a house. In the past 索 and 繩 meant differently, the former referred to thick ones and the latter thin ones. As ropes may be used to link things and lead one thing to another, the character 索 has also taken on the senses "to search", e.g. 按圖索驥 (to look for a steed with the aid of its picture; to try to locate something by following up a clue); and "to ask for".

【索隱】 to seek the hidden truth

【索居】 to live alone

xì

系

甲骨文、金文的系字，像人用手把兩縷（或三縷）絲線連接在一起。系字的本義為連接、聯屬。自上而連屬於下稱為系，所以系字又有相繼、繼承的意思，引申為世系、譜系、系統之義。

【系孫】遠世子孫。

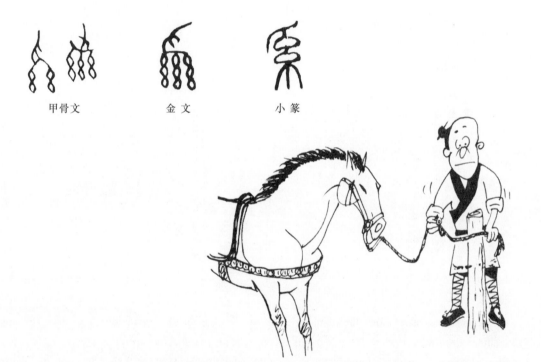

甲骨文　　　　金 文　　　　小 篆

In the Oracle-Bone Inscriptions and Bronze Inscriptions, the character 系 looks like a hand linking two or three silk threads together. Hence its primary meaning "to link". As things linked together will be in an order of precedence, the character 系 has taken on the senses of "succession", "system", "hierarchy" and "family tree".

【系孫】remote descendants

jué

金文的絕是個會意字，像用一把刀把兩條絲繩從中割斷的樣子。小篆絕字從系色聲，則變為形聲字。絕的本義為斷，引申為隔絕、杜絕、窮盡、超絕等義，又有最、極、獨特等義。

【絕甘分少】比喻和眾人同甘苦。

【絕無僅有】極其少有。

【絕聖棄智】先秦老莊學派主張，摒棄聖賢才智，清靜無為，而後始能實現太平至治。

金文

小篆

In the Bronze Inscriptions, the character絕is an ideograph, looking like a knife cutting short two silk strings. In the Later Seal Character, 絕 becomes a phonetic compound, with 糸 as the radical and 色 as the phonetic. The primary meaning of 絕 is "to cut off", from which have derived the senses: "to separate", "to exhaust", "unique" and "extremely".

【絕甘分少】to share comforts and hardships

【絕無僅有】unique

【絕聖棄智】(from *Lao Zi* 〔Lao-Tzu〕) to rid of wisdom and learning

jīn

巾是一個象形字。古文字的巾字，就像是掛着的一幅布或一條手巾。它的本義是指擦抹用的布，類似現在的手巾；後又引申為指頭巾、領巾。漢字中凡從"巾"的字皆與布疋有關，如布、市、幅、常、帷、幕、幡等。

【巾子】頭巾，如幞（fú）頭、巾幘之類。

【巾幗】幗是古代婦女戴的頭巾，巾幗代指婦女。

甲骨文

金文

小篆

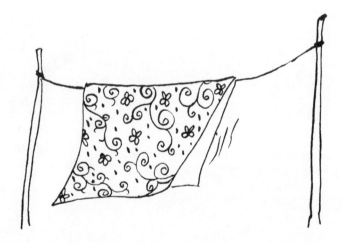

巾 is a pictograph. In ancient writing systems, it looks like a piece of cloth hanging there. It primarily refers to a piece of cloth for washing one's face, i.e. a towel, but it may also refer to a scarf or kerchief. Characters with 巾 as a component all have to do with cloth, e.g. 布 (cloth), 市 (towel-shaped clothing), 幅 (classifier for cloth), 常 ([裳 a variant of] lower garment), 帷 (curtain), 幕 (tent) and 幡 (long narrow flag).

【巾子】scarf

【巾幗】(1) kerchief (2) woman

fú

市為"韍"的本字，指蔽膝，即古代祭服前面遮蓋膝部的部份。市字從一從巾，一像博帶，故市是指衣袍前面博帶以下的部份。

金　文　　　　小　篆

市 was the original form of 韍, referring to the front lower part of a traditional Chinese gown, worn at sacrifice-offering ceremonies. The character 市 is made up of a stroke standing for the belt and a towel part (巾)，signalling it refers to the front part of a gown below the belt.

dài

帶是一種用皮、布等做成的扁平狀物。小篆的帶字，上部像一條束縛東西的帶子，下部從巾，表示是用布做成。所以帶字的本義是指束衣用的布帶，又泛指腰帶或類似的東西。帶字還可用作動詞，有佩帶、攜帶、帶領等義。

【帶累】連帶受累。

【帶鈎】束腰皮帶上的金屬鈎。

【帶甲】披甲的將士。

楚　簡　　　　　小　篆

帶 means "belt". In the Later Seal Character, the character 帶 is made up of two parts: the upper part looks like a belt binding things together and the lower part mainly consists of a towel part (巾), signalling that it is a belt made of cloth. Nowadays, however, it may refer to belts of other material or anything in the shape of a belt as well. Used as a verb, it may mean "to bear", "to carry" and "to lead".

【帶累】 to implicate

【帶鈎】 belt buckle

【帶甲】 soldiers in armour

yī

古文字的衣字，是一件古代上衣的輪廓圖形：上為衣領，左右為衣袖，中間是交衽的衣襟。所以衣字的本義指上衣。古代衣服，上為衣，下為裳。衣又泛指衣服、服裝。衣還可以讀為 yì，用作動詞，表示穿衣的意思。凡從"衣"的字，大多與衣服和布疋有關，如初、襯、衫、裘、表、袂等。

【衣缽】原指佛教中師父傳給徒弟的袈裟和飯缽，後泛指傳授下來的思想、學術、技能等。

【衣冠禽獸】穿戴着衣帽的禽獸，指外表斯文卻行為卑劣如同禽獸的人。

【衣錦還鄉】穿着錦繡服裝返回家鄉，表示富貴得意。

甲骨文

金文

小篆

In ancient writing systems, the character 衣 looks like a sketch of a traditional Chinese upper garment: the upper part is the collar, the lower left and right parts the sleeves, and the middle part the front of the garment where the two pieces meet. Hence its primary meaning "upper garment", whereas the lower garment was known as 裳 in former times. However, the character 衣 may also be used as a general term for clothing. Pronounced as yì, it is used as a verb, meaning "to wear clothes". Characters with 衣 as a component most have to do with cloth and clothing, e.g. 初 (to cut out garments), 襯 (lining), 衫 (unlined upper garment), 裘 (fur coat), 表 (outer garment) and 袂 (sleeve).

【衣缽】a Buddhist monk's mantle and alms bowl which he hands down to his favourite disciple; legacy

【衣冠禽獸】a beast in human clothing

【衣錦還鄉】to return to one's hometown in silken robes so as to show off one's riches

cháng

常與裳古本一字。小篆的常 (裳) 字是個形聲字,從巾尚聲,或從衣尚聲,本義指人穿在下身的裙裝 (上身稱"衣")。後世常、裳二字的用法發生分歧,其中裳字仍保留着它的本義,指下身的裙;而常字則多借用為恆久、經常之義,又用來指法典、倫常等。

【常式】固定的法制。又指一定的格式或制度。

【常典】常例、正常的法度。又指經典。

【常談】平常的言談。

金文

小篆

常 was originally a variant form of 裳. In the Later Seal Character, the character 常 (裳) is a phonetic compound, with 巾 or 衣 as the radical and 尚 as the phonetic, signalling the traditional Chinese lower garment. Nowadays, the two characters 常 and 裳 are different in meaning. 常 is mainly used in the senses of "permanent", "constant", "regulations" and "feudal order of importance", while 裳 retains its original use.

【常式】regular format

【常典】common practice

【常談】platitude

chū

初字從衣從刀，表示用刀一類工具裁剪衣物之意。初字的本義為裁衣，引申為指事情的開始，又有原來、當初等含義。

【初心】起初的心願。

【初文】文字學上指同一個字的初期寫法，與“後起字”相對。

【初春】即早春、孟春，多指春季的第一個月。

甲骨文

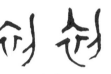
金文

小篆

The character 初 consists of a garment part (衣) and a knife part (刀), signalling to cut out garments with scissors. As the cutting up of cloth is the beginning of sewing, the character 初 has taken on the meanings of "beginning" and "original".

【初心】the original intention

【初文】the original form of a character

【初春】the first month of the spring season

biǎo

上古時代，人們以野獸的皮毛為衣。這種衣服一般是皮在裡而毛在外。小篆的表字，從衣從毛，指的就是裘皮衣露在外面的毛。所以表字的本義是指外表、外面；用作動詞，有顯露、表彰之義；又引申為指標記、標幟。

【表白】對人解釋，說明自己的意思。

【表情】表達情感。今指表現在外貌上的情態。

【表象】顯露在外的徵象。

【表裡如一】比喻思想和言行完全一致。

小篆

In ancient times, people used to wear animal skin. As this type of clothing usually has fur in the outside, the character 表 in the Later Seal Character consists of a garment part (衣) and a fur part (毛), referring to the fur on the outside of the clothing. Hence the primary meaning "outside" and "surface". As a verb, it may mean "to show" and "to express", from which has derived its use to refer to signs and marks.

【表白】 to make clear one's intention

【表情】 (1) to express one's feelings (2) facial expressions

【表象】 outside signal

【表裡如一】 to think and act in the same way

qiú

甲骨文的裘字，像一件上衣的形狀，衣的外邊有茸茸的毛，表示是用皮毛作的衣服。金文裘字在衣形中間增添一個"又"字表示讀音，到小篆就完全變成了一個從衣求聲的形聲字。所以，裘的本義是指皮衣，即皮毛服裝。裘又可用作姓氏，這大概是與裘氏祖先的出身於製皮工匠有關吧。

【裘馬】車馬衣裘，比喻生活豪華。

【裘葛】裘為冬衣，葛為夏服，泛指四季衣服。又指寒暑的變化，指一年。

甲骨文

金　文

小　篆

In the Oracle-Bone Inscriptions, the character 裘 looks like an upper garment made of fur, the extra strokes in the middle part standing for fur. In the Bronze Inscriptions, the part 又 is added to indicate its pronunciation. In the Later Seal Character, it becomes a complete phonetic compound, with 衣 as its radical and 求 as its phonetic. Hence its primary meaning "fur coat". 裘 is also a surname, perhaps reflecting the fact that their forefathers were fur coat makers.

【裘馬】(lit.) fur coat and horse; to live in luxury

【裘葛】fur coat and ko-hemp clothing; clothing for the four seasons; a year

zú

古文字的卒字，是在衣襟下加一短畫作為指示符號，表示衣上有題識（zhì）的意思。這種有題識的衣服一般用作士兵或差役的制服。所以，卒的本義指士兵或差役的制服，引申為指士兵、差役。卒字用作動詞，有完畢、結束之義，又指人死。

【卒伍】周代軍隊的編制名稱，後來泛指軍隊。

【卒章】詩、詞、文章的結尾。

【卒業】完成未竟的事業。又指修習完全部的課程。

金 文

小 篆

In ancient writing systems, the character 卒 looks like a garment with a short stroke in the front, signalling that it is a garment with a label attached. This type of clothing was used as a uniform for the rank and file in the army or the government service. Hence its original meaning "the uniform for the rank and file", but it may also refer to the person who wears it, such as soldier and corvee. Used as a verb, it means "to complete", "to end" and "to die".

【卒伍】army

【卒章】the ending part of a poem or article

【卒業】(1) to complete a course of action (2) to graduate

yì

古文字的裔字，上從衣，下部像衣袍的下襬之形，指的就是衣裾。所以裔的本義為衣裾，即衣袍的下襬，又泛指衣服的邊緣，引申為指邊遠地區，也指邊遠地區的民族。裔由衣袍下襬意，還可引申為指下代、後代之義。

【裔土】荒遠的邊地。

【裔夷】邊遠的少數民族。

【裔冑】後代。

甲骨文

小篆

In ancient writing systems, the character 裔 is made up of a garment part (衣) and a part standing for the lower part of a gown, hence its original meaning "the lower part of a gown". But it may also refer to the hem of a gown, or more generally the fringe of a garment, from which has derived its use to refer to border areas and the nationalities living there. From its reference to the lower part of a gown has also derived its meaning of descendants.

【裔土】 remote area

【裔夷】 minorities in the outlying areas

【裔冑】 descendants

yī

甲骨文的依字，從人從衣，像人在衣中之形，表示穿衣的意思。所以，依的本義為着（zhuó）衣，引申為倚靠、憑藉之義，又有附從、按照的意思。

【依附】依賴，附屬。

【依阿】胸無定見，曲意逢迎，隨聲附和。

【依傍】倚靠。

【依據】憑藉、靠托。又指根據。

甲骨文

小篆

In the Oracle-Bone Inscriptions, the character 依 consists of a man part (人) and a garment part (衣), and the former is inside the latter, signalling to put on clothes. From this original meaning have derived its extended meanings: "to rely on", "to attach to" and "in accordance with".

【依附】to depend on; to attach oneself to

【依阿】to echo what others say in order to curry favour with them or for want of one's own judgment

【依傍】to rely on

【依據】(1) according to (2) basis

shuāi

衰為"蓑"的本字。蓑即蓑衣,是一種用草或棕製成的防雨用具。小篆的衰字,從衣從冉,其中的冉像蓑衣草絲(或棕絲)冉冉披垂的樣子,表現了蓑衣最基本的形象特徵。此字後來多用為衰弱之義,指事物由強盛漸趨微弱,與"盛"相對。於是另造"蓑"字代替它的本義。

【衰亡】衰落滅亡。

【衰朽】老邁無能。

【衰紅】凋謝的花。

小 篆

衰 was the original form of 蓑, which refers to a rain cape made of straw or plam-bark. In the Later Seal Character, the character 衰 consists of a garment part (衣) and a part signalling the hanging straw (or palm-bark) threads (冉). Nowadays, however, this character is mainly used in the sense of "declining", opposite to 盛 (thriving), and its original meaning is expressed by 蓑.

【衰亡】 to decline

【衰朽】 feeble and decaying

【衰紅】 withered flower

bì

敝是一個會意字。甲骨文的敝字,右邊是手持木棍之形,左邊的"巾"是一塊布,巾上的四點表示破碎的布屑。所以,敝字的本義指破舊、破爛,引申為疲敗、衰敗之義。

【敝人】德薄之人。後用為自謙之辭。

【敝屣】破舊的鞋,比喻沒有價值的東西。

【敝帚自珍】破舊的掃帚,自己卻當寶貝一樣愛惜。比喻自己的東西雖不好,可是自己珍視。又作"敝帚千金"。

甲骨文　　　　　小篆

敝 is an ideograph. In the Oracle-Bone Inscriptions, the character 敝 has a hand with a stick on the right and a cloth part (巾) with four dots standing for holes on the left. Hence its original meaning "shabby" and "worn-out", from which have derived the senses of "tired out" and "on the decline".

【敝人】 (1) a person lacking in virtue (2) (self-depreciatory) me

【敝屣】 worn-out shoes; a worthless thing

【敝帚自珍】 (also 敝帚千金) to value one's own old broom; to cherish sth. of little value simply because it is one's own

dōng

甲骨文、金文的東字，像一個兩頭束紮的大口袋。它的本義當指的是口袋中所裝之物，也就是我們今天所說的"東西"。此字後來多借用為方位名詞，作"東方"講。所謂東方，即指日出的方向，與西方相對。

【東西】東邊和西邊；又用於泛指各種具體或抽象的事物。

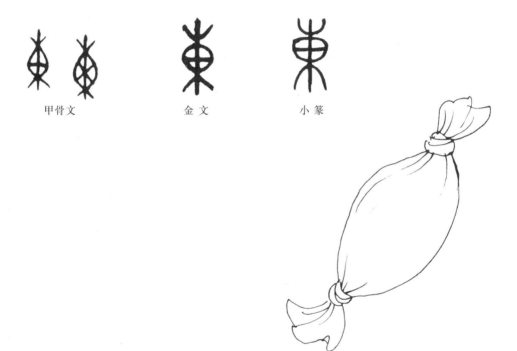

甲骨文　　　　金文　　　　小篆

In the Oracle-Bone Inscriptions and Bronze Inscriptions, the character 東 looks like a bag with its two ends tied up. It originally referred to the thing inside the bag, namely, what we now call 東西 — thing. But this character is more usually used as a locative, meaning "east", where the sun rises, as against 西 (west).

【東西】(1) east and west (2) thing

lù

　　录為"渌"或"漉"的本字。金文的录字，像木架上吊着的一個布袋，袋中裝有濕物，下邊的幾點是從袋中濾出來的水滴。所以，录的本義為濾，即液體往下滲的意思。在簡化字中，录字被用來代替從金录聲的"錄"字，它又有記載、抄寫、採取、任用的意思。

甲骨文

金文

小篆

录 was the original form of 渌 or 漉. In the Bronze Inscriptions, the character 录 looks like a bag of wet things hung on a wooden rack dripping water. Hence its original meaning "to let water go through", i.e. "to filter". However, in the modern simplified form, 录 is used in the senses of the original 錄 with 金 as the radical and 录 as the phonetic, such as "recording", "copying", "adopting" and "employing".

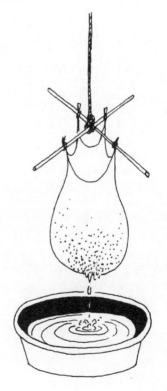

gōu

句為"鈎"或"勾"的本字。甲骨文、金文的句字，像兩把彎鈎勾住一個扣環之形。它的本義為勾住，又指彎鈎，引申為彎曲之義。句又讀為 jù ，指一句話，或一句中停頓的地方。

【句兵】戈戟之類的兵器。

【句枉】彎曲。

【句（jù）讀（dòu）】句和逗，指文章中休止和停頓之處。

甲骨文

金文

小篆

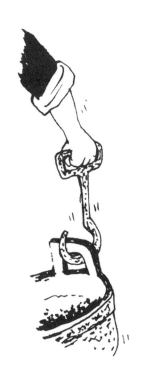

句 was the original form of 鈎 or 勾. In the Oracle-Bone Inscriptions and Bronze Inscriptions, the character 句 looks like two hooks around an eye. Hence it originally meant "to hook", "hook" and "bent". 句 pronounced as jù, means "sentence" or "sense group".

【句兵】weapons such as spears

【句枉】bent

【句讀】 (lit.) full stop and comma; places in writing where the reader may pause

sǎn

　　傘是一種擋雨或遮太陽的用具，用布、油紙、塑料等製成，中間有柄，可以張合。傘這種用具產生的時代較晚，故傘字出現的時代也比較晚。在小篆和稍後的隸書中無傘字。楷書的傘字，是一把張開的傘的形象：上面是傘蓋，傘蓋下面是傘骨和傘柄。可以說，傘是楷書構造中的象形字。

傘means "umbrella", a circular screen of cloth, oil cloth, plastics, etc., in collapsible form raised on radial ribs attatched to a central stick used for protection against rain or sunshine. This implement was not invented until very late, and there was no character referring to it in early writing systems. In the Regular Script, the character 傘 looks like an open umbrella, with its cover, frame and handle. Hence it is a pictograph.

建 築 類
Architecture

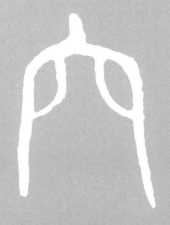

xué

人類最早的居住建築是一種半地下式的土室,即在平地上先挖出一個大土坑,然後以坑壁為牆,再用茅草在坑頂上搭成斜的屋頂。古文字的穴字,正是這種原始土堡的象形。因此,穴的本義就是指的這種半地下式的土室,引申為指坑穴、洞穴,又泛指孔洞。凡從"穴"的字,大都與坑穴或孔洞有關,如窟、窖、窩、竇、窗等。

小篆

The earliest human building was perhaps semi-underground, that is, they would dig a big hole in the ground and build a slant covering of straw or grass on the top, and live in it. In ancient writing systems, the character 穴 looks like a picture of this type of earth house. From this original meaning has derived its use to refer to a hole, cave or anything with an opening. Characters with 穴 as a component most have to do with holes or openings, e.g. 窟 (cave), 窖 (cellar), 窩 (nest; den), 竇 (hole) and 窗 (window).

chuān

小篆

穿字從牙在穴中，表示（老鼠等）用牙齒穿孔打洞的意思。穿的本義為穿孔，打洞，又指洞孔，引申為鑿通、破、透之義，又指穿過、通過、貫通，又引申為指穿戴。

【穿窬】穿壁翻牆。指偷竊行為。

【穿鑿】鑿通，又指牽強附會，於理不可通者，強求其通。

【穿雲裂石】形容聲音高揚激昂。

The character 穿 has a tooth part (牙) under a hole part (穴), signalling that animals like mice make holes with their teeth. Hence its primary meaning "to make a hole" or "hole", from which have derived the extended meanings "to penetrate", "to break through", "to pass through" and "to wear".

【穿窬】(lit.) to go through a wall; to steal

【穿鑿】 (1) to pierce through (2) to give a farfetched interpretation

【穿雲裂石】(lit.) to pierce clouds and break stones; (of sound) loud and excited

gè

各是一個會意字。甲骨文、金文的各字，下面的口代表原始人居住的穴居，上面的倒"止"表示有人從外而入的意思。各字的本義為至、來、到，後來借用為指示代詞，表示不止一個、每一個的意思，如各自、各種等。

【各行其是】各自按照自己以為對的去做。

【各得其所】每一個人或事物都得到合適的安置。

甲骨文　　　　　　金　文　　　　　　小　篆

各 is an ideograph. In the Oracle-Bone Inscriptions and Bronze Inscriptions, the character 各 has a house part (口) under an upside-down foot part (止), signalling to arrive at a house. Hence its original meaning "to reach", "to arrive at". But it is now used as a pronoun, meaning "every" and "each", e.g. 各自 (each side), 各種 (every type).

【各行其是】Each does what he thinks is right.

【各得其所】Each is in his proper place.

chū

遠在上古時代，人們就開始學會了建造房屋。最初的房屋是一種半地穴式的簡單建築，即在地上挖一淺坑，以坑壁為牆，然後再在坑頂搭上草棚。整個房子一半在地下，一半在地上。而屋子的出入通道有的是斜坡，有的是土階。甲骨文、金文的出字，正像一隻腳從土坑中向外邁出之形，表示人從屋中向外走出的意思。因此，出字的本義是指外出，引申為發出、產生、出現、顯露等義。

| 甲骨文 | 金 文 | 小 篆 |

People began to build houses early in ancient times. But that type of house was very simple, made by digging a hole in the ground and covering the top. As the house was semi-under ground, the entrance formed a slope. In the Oracle-Bone Inscriptions and Bronze Inscriptions, the character 出 looks like a foot stepping out of the hole, signalling to go out of the house. Hence its primary meaning "to go out", from which have derived the extended meanings "to send out", "to produce" and "to appear".

qù

甲骨文、金文的去字,從大從口,大像背面遠去的人形,口是原始人居住的穴居。去表示人離開居穴,其本義為離開、離去,如去國(指離開本國、遠走他鄉);引申為指去掉、棄除之義,如去偽存真(去除虛偽的、表面的,保存真實的、本質的)。現在的去字,與古代去字用法正好相反。如"我去北京",是我到北京去的意思,而不是離開北京。

【去處】可去的地方,又指場所、地方。

【去就】指去留,進退。

甲骨文

金文

小篆

In the Oracle-Bone Inscriptions and Bronze Inscriptions, the character 去 consists of 大 and 口, the former standing for a man seen from the back and the latter the semi-underground house. Hence its primary meaning "to leave", e.g. 去國 (to leave one's motherland). It is also used in the sense "to get rid of", e.g. 去偽存真 (to eliminate the false and retain the true). But it is used in a different way nowadays. For example, 去北京 now means "to go to Beijing" rather than "to leave Beijing".

【去處】 place to go; place; site

【去就】 to leave or to stay

liù

六為"廬"的本字。從甲骨文和金文的字形看,六像是一間結構簡陋的房屋形。所以,六的本義是指草廬,是一種建於田間或郊野作為臨時居所的房子。由於讀音相近的關係,六借用為數詞,故另造一個從广廬聲的"廬"字來代替它的本義。

【六合】指上下和東西南北四方,代指天下或宇宙。

【六親】指父、母、兄、弟、妻、子。又泛指親屬。

【六神無主】形容驚慌或着急而沒有主意。六神:指心、肺、肝、腎、脾、膽六臟之神。

甲骨文　　　　　　金文　　　　　　小篆

六 was the original form of 廬. In the Oracle-Bone Inscriptions, the character 六 looks like a house of simple structure, hence its original meaning "nut". Nowadays, however, 六 is used as a numeral, meaning "six", and its original meaning is expressed by a later creation 廬, which has 广 as its radical and 盧 as its phonetic.

【六合】 the six directions of above, below, east, west, north and south; the world

【六親】 father, mother, elder brother, younger brother, wife and children; relatives

【六神無主】 (lit.) all six vital organs (heart, lungs, liver, kidneys, spleen and gall bladder) failing to function; in a state of utter stupefaction

yú

甲骨文余字，上部為屋頂，下面為樑架和支柱，整個字形像一側面的房屋架構圖。因此，余字的本義是指房舍，後借用於第一人稱代詞。

甲骨文

金 文

小 篆

In the Oracle-Bone Inscriptions, the character 余 looks like the framework of a house seen from the side, with its roof, beam and pillar, Hence its original sense "house". But it is used as a first person pronoun now.

jiā

干欄建築是古代民族的一種居住形式。這種居室的最大特點是上層住人,屋下可以圈養牲口。家字從宀從豕,是屋中有豕(豬)的意思。人畜雜居,正是干欄居室的特點。而有室有豕,是一個家庭的基本像徵。所以家的本義是指家室、家庭,又指家族。

【家常】日常家居。又指居家常見的事物。

【家喻戶曉】家家戶戶都知道。

甲骨文

金 文

小 篆

There was a type of housing in ancient times, in which people themselves lived upstairs, and kept domestic animals downstairs. Reflecting this type of housing, the character 家 consists of a house part (宀) and a pig part (豕), signalling there is a pig in the house. A house with a pig is a symbol of family, hence its primary meaning "household" and "family".

【家常】(1) the daily life of a family (2) ordinary
【家喻戶曉】known to every family

qǐn

古文字的寢字，均像有人手持掃帚在室內打掃房屋的形狀；楷書的寢字則在室內還安放有牀（爿）的樣子，用以表示這是人睡覺的房子。因此，寢的本義指臥室、寢室，即人睡覺的地方；引申為指躺臥、睡覺、休息；進一步引申為停止、停息之義。此外，寢由臥室之義，引申為指君王的宮室，又指帝王的陵墓。

【寢具】臥具。

【寢兵】停息干戈。

【寢殿】帝王陵墓的正殿。

甲骨文

金文

小篆

In all ancient writing systems without exception, the character 寢 looks like a hand with a broom under a roof. In the Regular Script, it even has a bed part (爿), signalling it is a room for sleeping. Hence its primary meaning "bedroom". But it is also used in the senses "to lie down", "to sleep" and "to rest". It may even mean "to stop". In addition, from its sense of bedroom has derived its reference to a palace or mausoleum.

【寢具】bedding

【寢兵】to stop fighting

【寢殿】coffin chamber in the mausoleum

sù

甲骨文的宿字，像一個人跪坐草席之上，或躺在室中的一條席子上，表示歇息、睡眠的意思。宿的本義為歇息、住宿、過夜。因住宿都在夜晚，所以又把一夜稱為"一宿"。宿還有隔夜的意思，如宿雨（昨夜之雨）、宿醒（酒後困疲如病）等；引申為早先、平素之義，如宿債（舊債）、宿願（平素的心願）等。

【宿世】佛教指過去的一世，即前生。

【宿舍】住所。

【宿將】老將，指老成持重、久於其事的戰將。

甲骨文

金文

小篆

In the Oracle-Bone Inscriptions, the character 宿 looks like a man kneeling on a straw cushion, or lying on a cushion under a roof, signalling to rest or sleep. Hence its primary meaning "to rest", "to sleep" and "to stay overnight". As one sleeps at night, the character 宿 also refers to night. And it may also refer the night before, e.g. 宿雨 (the rain last night), 宿醒 (hangover from drinking too much). From this meaning has derived its sense of "long-standing", e.g. 宿債 (old debt), 宿願 (long-cherished wish).

【宿世】previous life

【宿舍】dormitory

【宿將】veteran general

ān

古文字的安字，像一個女子安然坐於室中之形。古人用女子靜坐家中操持家務，表示沒有戰爭、沒有災禍，生活過得很平安、很舒適。所以安字的本義為安定、安全、安逸，引申為習慣、滿足。此外，安字還可用作動詞，有安置、安放的意思。

【安土重遷】安於本土，不願輕易遷移。

【安身立命】指精神和生活有寄託。

【安居樂業】安於所居，樂於本業。也作安家樂業、安土樂業。

甲骨文　　　　　　金文　　　　　　小篆

In ancient writing systems, the character 安 looks like a woman sitting peacefully in a house, signalling there is no war or other disaster and life is quiet and comfortable. Hence its meanings "peaceful", "safe", "easy and comfortable" and "satisfied". Used as a verb, it means "to put" and "to find a place for".

【安土重遷】 to be attached to one's native land and unwilling to leave it

【安身立命】 to settle down and get on with one's pursuit

【安居樂業】 (also 安家樂業 and 安土樂業) to live and work in peace and contentment

dìng

定字從宀從正，宀代表房子，而"正"在古文字中多用為征伐之征，表示足所到的地方。甲骨文、金文的定字，足跡邁向室內，表示人回到家中，回到家中即是平安無事，所以定字的本義為安定、平安，又有停留、停止之義。定字後來還引申為決定、確定等義。

【定局】已成的局面。局，本指棋盤，引申為局面、大局。

【定奪】裁決可否。

【定論】確定不移的原則或論斷。

甲骨文

金文

小篆

In ancient writing systems, the character定consists of 宀 and 正, the former standing for a house, and the latter, a destination plus a foot part, signifying the place one has arrived at. In the Oracle-Bone Inscriptions and Bronze Inscriptions, the foot heads toward the house, signalling the man has come back home safely. Hence its primary meaning "peaceful", "safe" and "to stop". But it may also mean "to decide" and "to fix".

【定局】inevitable outcome

【定奪】to make a final decision

【定論】final conclusion

kè

客字的結構為寶蓋頭下面一個各，寶蓋頭是房屋的形象，而各則是有人自外而來的意思（"各"兼表聲）。所以，客字的本義是指來賓、客人，又指旅居他鄉的人。此外，客還特指專門從事某種活動的人，如俠客、劍客、墨客等。

【客子】旅居異地的人。

【客官】指在別的諸侯國作官。又指對顧客的敬稱。

【客思】懷念家鄉的心情。

【客氣】言行虛矯。不是出自真誠，這是貶義的客氣。也有用為褒義的，指謙恭而彬彬有禮的樣子。

金 文

小 篆

The character 客 consists of 宀 and 各, the former standing for a house and the latter meaning "to arrive at" and indicating its pronunciation at the same time. Hence its primary meaning "somebody from another place", i.e. "guest". In addition, it may refer to a person engaged in some particular pursuit, e.g. 俠客 (chivalrous master of martial arts), 劍客 (swordsman) and 墨客 (man of letters).

【客子】emigrant

【客官】(1) official in a foreign land (2) customer

【客思】homesick

【客氣】polite

bīn

　　甲骨文的賓字，像家中有人或有人從外面走進屋內之形，表示有客人來到的意思。金文賓字增加貝字，表示賓客往來必有財物相贈之事。賓字的本義指外來的客人，如來賓、外賓；用作動詞，引申為歸順、服從之義。

【賓從】指賓客及其僕從，又有歸順、服從之義。

【賓館】賓客居住的館舍。

【賓至如歸】形容主人招待周到，客人來到這裡就像回到家裡一樣舒服方便。

甲骨文

金文

小篆

In the Oracle-Bone Inscriptions, the character賓 looks like a man coming into a room from outside, signalling the coming of a visitor. In the Bronze Inscriptions, a seashell part (貝) is added to signal the visitor has come with some presents. Hence the primary meaning of 賓 is "visitor", e.g. 來賓 (visitor), 外賓 (foreign visitor). Used as a verb, it means "to submit oneself to".

【賓從】(1) a visitor and his followers (2) to submit oneself to

【賓館】guesthouse

【賓至如歸】to make guests feel at home

guǎ

金文的寡字，從宀從頁，頁為人形，表示房子裡面只有一個人的意思。所以寡的本義指單獨、孤獨。古代婦人喪夫，男子無妻或喪偶，都叫做"寡"。寡還有少、缺少的意思，與"多"相對。

【寡人】寡德之人。古代王侯或士大夫自謙之詞。

【寡合】少有合得來的人。

【寡居】指婦人夫死後獨居。

【寡斷】辦事不果斷。

【寡不敵眾】人少難以抵擋眾敵。

金文　　　　小篆

In the Bronze Inscriptions, the character 寡 consists of 宀 and 頁, the former standing for a house and the latter a person, signalling there is only one person in the house. Hence its primary meaning "alone". In former times, a woman who lost her husband, and a man who had no wife or lost his wife, were both referred to as 寡. But 寡 also means "few" and "short of", opposite to 多 (many).

【寡人】(lit.) one who is lacking in virtue; (self-depreciatory) (used esp. by a ruler) me

【寡合】to lack friends

【寡居】widowed

【寡斷】indecisive

【寡不敵眾】to be hopelessly outnumbered

kòu

　　甲骨文的寇字，像一個人手持棍棒在室內擊打另一個人的樣子，表示有人入室為盜。所以，寇字的本義為劫掠、侵犯，引申為指盜匪或入侵者。

甲骨文　　　　　　　小篆

In the Oracle-Bone Inscriptions, the character 寇 looks like a man hitting someone with a stick inside a house, signalling someone has broken in. Hence its primary meaning "to rob" and "to invade", and it may also refer to one who robs or invades, i.e. robber or invader.

qiú

囚字從口從人，像一個人被關在土牢中的形狀。它的本義為拘禁、囚禁，又指囚犯、犯人，引申為指戰俘。

【囚拘】像犯人一樣受拘束。

【囚首喪面】髮不梳如囚犯，面不洗如居喪。形容蓬頭垢面的樣子。

甲骨文

小篆

The character 囚 consists of 口 and 人, signalling a man is in a jail. Its primary meaning is "to imprison", "prisoner" and "prisoner of war".

【囚拘】with no freedom as if a prisoner

【囚首喪面】with unkempt hair like a prisoner and dirty face as if in mourning; unkempt

lìng

　　古文字的令字，像一人跪坐屋中之形，表示在室中接受命令的意思。令的本義為發令、號令、指使，又指命令、指令，引申為善，美好之義。

【令愛】尊稱對方的女兒。又作"令嬡"。

【令箭】古代軍隊中發佈命令時用作憑據的東西，形狀像箭。

【令行禁止】有令必行，有禁必止。形容法制森嚴。

甲骨文

金 文

小 篆

In ancient writing systems, the character 令 looks like a man sitting in a room, signalling to accept orders in a room. The primary meaning of 令 is "to order", "to command", or as a noun "order", from which has derived its extended meaning of "good".

【令愛】(also 令嬡) (honorific) your daughter

【令箭】an arrow used as a token of authority

【令行禁止】strict execution of orders and prohibitions

mìng

甲骨文命字，像一人在屋宇之下發號施令的樣子；金文增加口形，表示從口中發出命令。因此，命字的本義為差使、命令。在上古時代，奴隸主的一聲命令，就決定了奴隸的命運甚至生命，所以命字又有生命、命運之義。

金 文

小 篆

In the Oracle-Bone Inscriptions, the character 命 looks like a man issuing orders under a roof. In the Bronze Inscriptions, a mouth part (口) is added to signal that the order comes from a mouth. Hence its primary meaning "order". In the old days, a slave's fate, including his life, would be decided by an order from the slave owner, so the character 命 has taken on the senses of "life" and "fate".

xiǎng

甲骨文、金文的享字，像一座簡單的廟宇建築的形狀。廟宇是供奉祭品、舉行祭祀活動的地方，故享有供獻之義，即把祭品獻給祖先神靈；又通"饗"，指鬼神享用祭品；引申為享受、享用以及宴饗等義。

【享年】享有的年歲，對人而言。

【享國】帝王在位年數。

【享樂】享受生活的安樂。多用作貶義。

甲骨文

金 文

小 篆

In the Oracle-Bone Inscriptions and Bronze Inscriptions, the character 享 looks like a simple temple. The temple is a place for sacrifice-offering ceremonies, hence 享 means to offer sacrifiecs to gods and the spirits of ancestors. It may also be used in the same sense as 饗, i.e. to entreat gods and spirits to dinner; from which has derived its more general sense "to enjoy".

【享年】 to die at the age of

【享國】 the length of the reign of an emperor

【享樂】 to lead a life of pleasure

zōng

宗字從宀從示，"宀"是屋宇之形，"示"則代表祭祀之事。因此，宗的本義是指供奉祖先、舉行祭祀活動的祠堂、宗廟，引申為指祖宗、宗主、宗族，又引申為派別之義。宗字用作動詞，則有尊崇之義。

【宗祠】同一宗族用來祭祀共同祖先的祠堂、家廟。

【宗派】宗族的支派。又指學術、政治、藝術、宗教等的派別。

【宗教】佛教以佛所説為教，以佛弟子所説為宗，合稱宗教，指佛教的教義。現泛指對神道的信仰為宗教。

甲骨文

金文

小篆

The character 宗 consists of 宀 and 示, the former standing for a house and the latter the stone table used in sacrifice-offering ceremonies. Hence it primarily refers to the place where sacrifice-offering ceremonies are held, i.e. the ancestral temple. From this use have derived its extended meanings of "ancestor", "the head god", "patriarchal clan" and "sect". As a verb, it means "to worship".

【宗祠】 ancestral temple

【宗派】 sect; faction

【宗教】 religion

gōng

　　宮字從宀從呂，"宀"是屋宇之形，從"呂"則表示房屋眾多、宮室相連的意思。因此，宮的本義當指比較大的房屋建築或建築群。後世的宮，專指帝王所居住的房屋或地方；又稱宗廟、佛寺、道觀等大型建築或建築群為"宮"。此外，宮也可泛指一般的房屋。

【宮室】古時對房屋的通稱。

【宮殿】泛指帝王居住的高大華麗的房屋。

【宮廷】帝王居住的地方。又指朝堂，即皇帝接受大臣參拜並與大臣一起議政的地方。

甲骨文　　　　金文　　　　小篆

The character 宮 consists of 宀 and 呂, the former standing for a house and the latter rooms one after another. Hence its primary meaning "a complex of buildings", from which has derived its reference to the palace, ancestral temple, Buddhist temple, and Taoist temple. 宮 may of course refer to ordinary houses as well.

【宮室】(arch.) house

【宮殿】palace

【宮廷】imperial court

gāo

甲骨文、金文的高字，像樓閣層疊的形狀：其上部是斜頂的屋宇，下部為樓台，中間的口則表示進入樓台的門。以樓閣的高聳來表示崇高之意而與低、卑相對，這就是高字的本義。引申為高大、高遠、高深以及加高、提高等義；又指年老，如高齡；再進一步引申為抽象的高尚、高明、高潔等義。

【高門】高大之門，指富貴之家。

【高手】指技藝詩文書畫造詣高深的人。

【高堂】高大的殿堂，又指父母。

【高屋建瓴】從高的屋層向下倒水。建，傾倒；瓴，水瓶。比喻居高臨下，勢不可擋。

甲骨文　　　　金文　　　　小篆

In the Oracle-Bone Inscriptions and Bronze Inscriptions, the character 高 looks like a traditional Chinese two-storeyed building with its pitched roof, upstairs and downstairs, and the part 口 standing for the gate. As storeyed buildings are higher than bungalows, the character 高 means "high", opposite to 低 (low). From this primary meaning have derived its senses of "tall and big", "high and far away", "profound", and as a verb, "to heighten" and "to raise". It may also refer to age, e.g. 高齡 (advanced age); or other abstract qualities, e.g. 高尚 (lofty), 高明 (brilliant) and 高潔 (noble and unsullied).

【高門】(lit.) tall gate; wealthy family

【高手】master-hand

【高堂】(1) tall hall (2) parents

【高屋建瓴】(lit.) to pour water off a steep roof; to sweep down irresistibly from a commanding height; operate from a strategically advantageous position

jīng

甲骨文、金文的京字，像建築在高土台上的宮室形象，其本義指高岡，即人為的高大土丘，並含有高、大之義。因為古代都城和君王的宮室大都建在高處，所以又把首都和王室所在稱為"京"，如京城、京輦（皇帝坐的車子叫輦，所以京城也叫"京輦"）、京畿（國都和國都附近的地方）、京室等。

甲骨文　　　　　金 文　　　　　小 篆

In the Oracle-Bone Inscriptions and Bronze Inscriptions, the character京looks like a house built on a terrace. Hence its original meaning "mound", suggesting "high" and "big". As capitals in ancient times were usually built on high places, the character 京 has taken on the meaning of "capital", e.g. 京城 (capital city), 京輦 (capital city), 京畿 (capital and its environs) and 京室 (imperial court).

liáng

良是"廊"的本字。甲骨文的良字，像屋有廊廡之形：中間的"口"代表屋室，上下兩頭的曲折通道則是連接屋與屋之間的迴廊。所以，良字的本義是指迴廊，又稱走廊。此字後來多用為良好、善良等義，其本義則由"廊"字來代替。

【良玉不瑑 (zhuàn)】指美玉不待雕刻而成紋。

【良辰美景】美好的時光，宜人的景色。

【良金美玉】喻指美好的事物。

甲骨文

金 文

小 篆

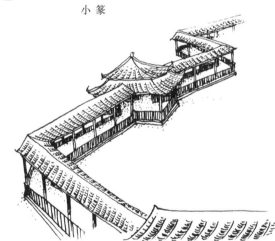

良 was the original form of 廊. In the Oracle-Bone Inscriptions, the character 良 looks like a house with verandas: the square part in the middle standing for a house and the bent lines on the two sides verandas linking this house to others. Hence its original meaning "veranda". Nowadays, however, it is used in the senses of "good and kindhearted", and its original meaning is expressed by 廊.

【良玉不瑑】 Jade of excellent quality has beautiful natural veins.

【良辰美景】 beautiful scene on a bright day

【良金美玉】 (lit.) good gold and beautiful jade; fine things

cāng

古文字的倉字，是一房屋建築的形象：上面是屋頂，中間的戶代表門窗，下面的口是指台基。倉的本義指倉房，是貯藏穀物的所在。古代糧倉，圓的叫"囷"，方的叫"倉"。現在則籠統稱之為倉庫。然而在古代，倉和庫是有嚴格區別的，裝糧食的叫"倉"，裝其他物品的才稱為"庫"，絕不相混。

【倉皇】匆忙、慌張。又作倉惶。

甲骨文　　　金文　　　小篆

In ancient writing systems, the character 倉 looks like a house with its pitched roof, door and window, and terrace. The primary meaning of 倉 is "barn", the building in which one stores grain, though in former times, 倉 only referred to square barns while the circular ones were known as 囷. What is more, the character 倉 now may refer to any type of store-house, expressed by the two characters 倉庫, which again were strictly distinguished in the past. 倉 referred to places where one stored grain, only buildings for storing other things were called 庫.

【倉皇】in a panic

kù

庫字從广從車，像車在屋內之形，它的本義，是指儲藏兵甲戰車的屋舍。後泛指儲藏財物的屋舍，如書庫、金庫等。

【庫藏】庫中所儲藏。

【庫存】指庫中現存的現金或物資。

金文

小篆

The character 庫 consists of 广 and 車, the former standing for a house and the latter a vehicle. Hence its original meaning — a building to keep vehicles, especially war vehicles. Nowadays, however, it may refer to buildings for storing anything, e.g. 書庫 (stack room), 金庫 (treasury).

【庫藏】to have in storage

【庫存】goods in stock; cash in hand

lǐn

古代的糧倉為了防潮，常常在倉底用大石塊把它和地面架空。甲骨文的廩字，像在兩塊大石之間架木搭成的倉囷之形；金文廩字則像一座有窗戶的房屋形；而小篆廩字加"广"加"禾"，表示它是儲藏禾穀的屋宇。所以，廩字的本義是指糧倉，引申為指糧食，又有儲藏、儲積之義。

【廩粟】倉中的糧食。

甲骨文

金 文

小 篆

In order to protect the grain against damp, there were usually stones underneath in a barn. In the Oracle-Bone Inscriptions, the character 廩 looks like a grain bin on top of two big stones. In the Bronze Inscriptions, the character looks like a house with a window. And in the Later Seal Character, a house part (广) and a grain part (禾) are added to signal that it is a building for storing grain. Hence its primary meaning is "barn", but it may refer to grain as well. And as a verb, it means "to store".

【廩粟】grain in store

yì

甲骨文、金文的邑字，上部的方框代表四面圍牆的城池，下面一個席地而坐的人形，表示居住。所以邑字的本義是指人們聚居的地方，後來泛指一般的城市。古代大城稱"都"，小城叫"邑"。邑又指大夫的封地。漢字中凡從"邑"（阝）的字大多與城邑或地名有關，如都、郭、邕、郊、郡、鄂、鄒、鄧等。

甲骨文

金文

小篆

In the Oracle-Bone Inscriptions and Bronze Inscriptions, the character 邑 has a town part (口) and a man sitting on the ground, signalling a place to live. Hence the primary meaning of 邑 is a place where people live in a compact community, such as a town. In former times, big cities were known as 都 and small ones 邑. But it may also refer to the fief of a minister in the feudal society. Characters with 邑 (阝) as a component, which is written as 阝 when placed on the right, most have to do with towns or place names, e.g. 都 (capital), 郭 (the outer wall of a city), 邕 (the alternative name for Nanning, Guangxi), 郊 (suburbs), 郡 (a traditional Chinese administrative area, lager than a county), 鄂 (the alternative name for Hubei), 鄒 (a county in Shandong) and 鄧 (a place name).

guō

甲骨文的郭字，像一座城池的鳥瞰圖形：圖形中間的方框代表四方的城牆，而在四方城牆上各有一座建築——哨亭。後來字形簡化，四座哨亭省去其二，到小篆時另加"邑"旁，以表示城郭乃人口聚居的都邑。所以，郭的本義是指城牆，又特指外城，引申為指物體的四周或外部輪廓。

甲骨文　　　　金文　　　　小篆

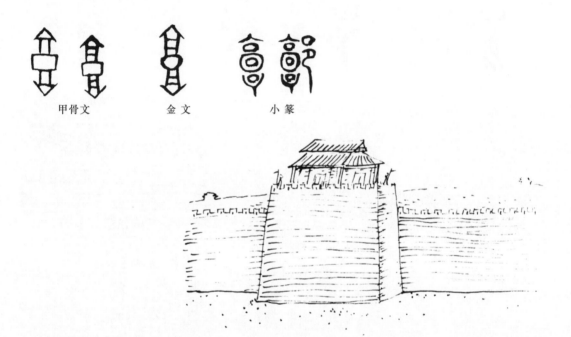

In the early Oracle-Bone Inscriptions, the character 郭 looks like a birds-eye view of a town: the square in the middle standing for the city walls and the parts on the four sides the sentry posts. In the late Oracle-Bone Inscriptions and Bronze Inscriptions, the form is simplified and there are only two sentry posts left. In the Later Seal Character, a town part (邑) is added to emphasize the point that it is a place where people live in compact community. The primary meaning of 郭 is "city wall", especially "the outer wall", but it may also refer to the four sides or outline of something.

bǐ

甲骨文的鄙字，下部為廩，上部的"口"則代表人口聚居的村邑；金文鄙字或從廩從邑，是指有糧草囤積的人口聚居地。所以，鄙的本義是指村邑，特指邊遠的小邑，與"都"相對。邊邑僻遠卑陋，不比都城，故鄙字又鄙陋、低下、粗野等義，又引申為小看、輕視的意思。

【鄙人】邊鄙之人。又指鄙陋之人，用作自謙之詞。

【鄙俚】粗俗。又指俗語、諺語。

【鄙薄】卑下，微薄。又指嫌惡、輕視。

甲骨文

金文

小篆

In the Oracle-Bone Inscriptions, the character 鄙 is made up of a town part (口) and a barn part (廩). In the Bronze Inscription, the character has either 廩 (barn) or 邑 (town) as the main component, but means the same. Hence鄙originally referred to a rural town, especially a remote town, opposite to都 (capital). As remote rural areas are less developed, the character鄙has taken on the senses of "ignorant", "vulgar" and "coarse". Used as a verb, it means "to despise" and "to look down upon".

【鄙人】(lit.) rustic; (self-depreciatory) me

【鄙俚】(1) vulgar (2) slang

【鄙薄】to despise

xiàng

甲骨文的向字,像在一座房屋的牆壁上開着一個窗口的形狀,它的本義是專指朝北的窗口。從這個本義又引申為方向、朝向、面對等義。此外,向字還有從前、往昔、舊時的意思。

【向壁虛造】比喻沒有根據事實而憑空虛構或捏造。

甲骨文　　　　　　金文　　　　　小篆

In the Oracle-Bone Inscriptions, the character 向 looks like a wall of a house with a window in it. It originally referred to a window facing the north. From this use have derived its other senses of "direction", "facing" and "turning towards". In addition, it may mean "in the past" and "all along".

【向壁虛造】to make up out of one's head

chuāng

小　篆

窗，即窗戶，指房屋牆壁上通氣透光的裝置。小篆的窗字，像一釘有窗櫺的窗戶形狀；或從穴，表示房屋之窗。

窗 means "window", a space in a wall of a house to let in light and air. In the Later Seal Character, the character 窗 looks like a traditional Chinese window with lattices on it; sometimes it has 穴 (house) as a component, signalling it is a part of a house.

mén

門，是指建築物的出入口。甲骨文的門字，有門框，有門楣，有一對門扇，是一座完整的門形。金文門字去掉門楣，但仍保留着兩扇門的原形。漢字中凡從"門"的字，大都與門有關，如閉、間、閑、閘、闖等。

【門戶】指門，引申為指出入的必經之地。又指家門、門第以及派別之義。

【門生】指學生、弟子。

【門可羅雀】大門前可以張網捕雀。形容賓客稀少，十分冷落。

【門庭若市】形容來往出入的人很多。

甲骨文	金文	小篆

門 means "door" or "gate', the entrance to a building. In the Oracle-Bone Inscriptions, the character 門 looks like a complete picture of a traditional Chinese door with its frame, lintel and a pair of leaves. In the Bronze Inscriptions, there are only the parts standing for the two leaves, the lintel is omitted. characters with 門 as a component most have to do with the entrance, e.g. 閉 (to close〔the door〕), 間 (gap), 閑 (fence gate), 閘 (floodgate) and 闖 (to break through a gate).

【門戶】(1) door (2) gateway (3) family status (4) faction

【門生】pupil; disciple

【門可羅雀】(Visitors are so few and far between that) one can catch sparrows on the doorstep.

【門庭若市】The courtyard is as crowded as a marketplace.

hù

戶，指單扇的門。一扇為戶，兩扇為門。甲骨文的戶字，正像一副門扇的形狀。它的本義指門扇；又泛指門窗，如門戶、窗戶；引申為指人家、住戶，一家人稱為一戶。漢字中凡從"戶"之字，都與門、窗和房屋有關，如啟、扉、扇、扁、所、房等。

【戶口】住戶和人口。計家為戶，計人為口。又指戶籍，即登記居民戶口的簿冊。

【戶牖（yǒu）】指門窗。

【戶樞不蠹】門的轉軸不會被蟲蛀蝕。比喻經常運動的東西不易腐蝕，可以經久不壞。

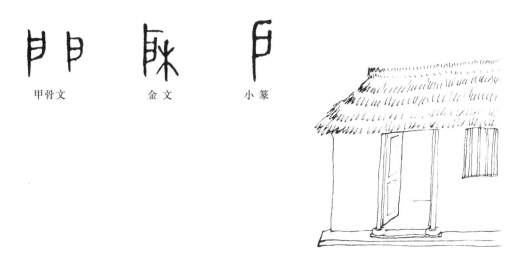

甲骨文　　　金文　　　小篆

戶 originally referred to a door with one leaf, and doors with two leaves were known as 門. In the Oracle-Bone Inscriptions, the character 戶 looks like a picture of such a door. But it is now used in the general senses of "door" or "window", e.g. 門戶 (door), 窗戶 (window). It is also used in its extended meanings of "household" and "family". Characters with 戶 as a component most have to do with the door, window and house, e.g. 啟 (to open〔the door〕), 扉 (door leaf), 扇 (door leaf), 扁 (a horizontal inscribed board), 所 (a classifier used of the house) and 房 (house).

【戶口】(1) number of households and total population (2) registered permanent residence

【戶牖】door and window

【戶樞不蠹】A door-hinge is never worm-eaten.

xián

閑字從木從門，是以木條編為門牆之意，其本義即指柵欄，又指馬廄，引申為指範圍，如《論語》："大德不逾閑，小德出入可也。"現在的閑字，多用為安靜、閑暇之義。

【閑雅】閑靜文雅。

【閑適】清閑安逸。

金文

小篆

The character 閑 consists of 木 (wood) and 門 (gate), signalling a gate made of wood sticks, i.e. fence gate. It may also refer to the stable and has an extended meaning of "limit". For example, the *Analects of Confucius* says, "大德不逾閑，小德出入可也。 (In matters of importance one should act in strict accordance with the rules while in trivial matters one may be allowed to act more freely)". Nowadays, however, 閑 is more usually used in the sense of "idle" and "unoccupied".

【閑雅】quiet and elegant

【閑適】idle and comfortable

shuān

　　古代沒有門鎖，而在門的內面安裝一條橫木來把兩扇門拴住。閂字從一從門，"一"代表橫木，門內的橫木即指門栓。所以閂字的本義指門栓。

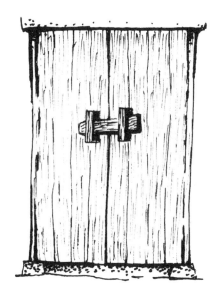

In ancient China, one of the ways to keep a door firmly closed was to run a wooden bar across the two leaves. The character 閂 consists of 一 and 門, the former standing for the wooden bar and the latter the door, hence its primary meaning: the wooden bar for closing a door, i.e. bolt.

jiān

古文字的間字從月從門，表示兩扇門中間有空隙可以透入月光，其本義指門縫，引申為指中間、空隙。間又讀為jiàn，用作動詞，有間隔、離間、干犯等義。

【間不容髮】比喻相距極近，兩者中間沒有能容一根頭髮的空隙。

【間架】本指房屋的結構形式，借指漢字書寫的筆畫結構，也指文章的佈局。

金 文

小 篆

In ancient writing systems, the character 間 consists of 月 (moon) and 門 (door), signalling that there is a gap between the two leaves of a door and the moonlight may come through it. Hence its primary meaning "gap between the two leaves of a door", from which have derived its meanings of "space in between" and "middle". Used as a verb and pronounced as jiàn, it means "to separate", "to sow discord" and "to interfere".

【間不容髮】Two objects are so close to each other that there is no space whatsoever in-between, not even for a hair.

【間架】framework

shǎn

閃字從人從門，像有人從門縫中探頭偷看的樣子，其本義為偷窺。由門中偷窺的動作，閃字可引申出忽隱忽現或驟然一現之義，如閃光、閃電、閃念等；又指突然迅速的動作，如躲閃、閃避、閃擊等。

【閃失】意外的損失、事故。

小篆

The character 閃, made up of 人 and 門, looks like a man trying to see the inside through the gap between the two leaves of a door. From this original meaning has derived its use for things which appear suddenly or appear at one moment but disappear at another, e.g. 閃光 (flash of light), 閃電 (lightning) and 閃念 (flash of an idea). It may also refer to actions which last a very short moment, e.g. 躲閃 (to dodge), 閃避 (to sidestep) and 閃擊 (to blitz).

【閃失】mishap

qǐ

啟

啟是一個會意字。甲骨文的啟字，像人用手（又）打開一扇門（戶）的樣子，表示開門、打開的意思，引申為開發、開拓、啟發等義。啟發別人要用言辭，金文的啟字加一個口旁表示說話，所以啟字又有說話、陳述之義，如"啟事"（指陳述的事情）。

甲骨文　　　　　　金文　　　　　　小篆

The character 啟 was an ideograph. In the Oracle-Bone Inscriptions, the character 啟 looks like a hand opening a door leaf. Hence it primarily means "to open a door", from which have derived its meanings "to develop", "to open up" and "to enlighten". As to enlighten someone one needs to use speech, the character 啟 in the Bronze Inscriptions has a mouth part (口) added. And it has taken on the meaning "to state" as well, e.g. 啟事 (notice).

kāi

金文和古文的開字，像用雙手把門打開的樣子，其本義即指開門，引申為打開、開通、開放、開發、開闢、分開等義，又引申為開創、開始、開展、張設、啟發等義。

【開門見山】比喻説話寫文章直截了當，開端就入本題。

【開誠佈公】待人處事，坦白無私。

【開源節流】比喻在財政經濟上增加收入，節省開支。

古 文

小 篆

In the Bronze Inscriptions and Ancient Script, the character 開 looks like two hands opening a door. Hence its primary meaning "to open a door", from which have derived the extended meanings "to unfold", "to remove obstacles from", "to lift a ban", "to hew out", "to separate", "to start", "to carry out", "to set up" and "to enlighten".

【開門見山】 to come straight to the point

【開誠佈公】 to speak frankly and sincerely

【開源節流】 to broaden sources of income and reduce expenditure

guān

古代沒有門鎖，而是在門的內面安裝一根可以活動的橫木來把兩扇門拴牢在一起。金文的關字，正像門內加栓之形，其本義即指門栓。門栓是用來閉門的，所以關字有關閉、閉合、封閉之義，又指關口、關隘、關卡。此外，關還可以引申為指事物中起轉折關聯作用的部份，如機關、關節、關鍵等；又含有關聯、牽連之義。

【關津】指水陸要道關卡。

【關涉】牽連、聯繫。

金文　　　　小篆

In ancient China, one of the ways to keep a door firmly closed was to run a wooden bar across the two leaves. In the Bronze Inscriptions, the character 關 looks like a door with a wooden bar, hence its original meaning: the wooden bar for closing a door, i.e. bolt. As the bolt is used to close a door, the character 關 is also used in the sense "to close". When used as a noun, it means "strategic pass". In addition, it may refer to things which function as linking points, e.g. 機關 (gear), 關節 (joint), 關鍵 (key point). And it may, as a verb, mean "to link".

【關津】strategic pass

【關涉】to relate

wǎ

瓦，是指鋪在屋頂上用來遮雨的建築材料。小篆的瓦字，像屋頂上兩塊瓦片俯蓋仰承相交接的樣子，其本義當指瓦片。因瓦片是由泥土燒成，故凡由泥土燒成的陶瓷器物皆稱"瓦器"。漢字中凡從"瓦"之字大都指陶瓷器具或與陶瓷製作有關，如甕、瓶、甌、甑、瓷、甄等。

【瓦合】比喻勉強湊合，又指臨時湊合。

【瓦解】比喻崩潰之勢如瓦片碎裂。

【瓦解冰消】比喻完全失敗或崩潰，如同瓦片碎裂、冰雪消溶一樣。

小篆

瓦 means "tile", a piece of baked clay for covering roofs. In the Later Seal Character, the character 瓦 looks like one concave tile and one convex tile linked together, hence its meaning "tile". As tiles are made of baked clay, any object made of baked clay is referred to as 瓦器 (earthenware). Characters with 瓦 as a component most have to do with earthenware, e.g. 甕 (urn), 瓶 (vase), 甌 (pot), 甑 (steamer), 瓷 (porcelain) and 甄 (potter's wheel).

【瓦合】to make do and mend

【瓦解】to disintegrate

【瓦解冰消】to break like tiles and melt like ice; to collapse completely

dān

丹是一種用作顏料的礦石。甲骨文丹字，像井中有一點，井為採石的礦井，其中一點表示從礦井中採挖出來的礦石。丹的本義為丹砂（或稱朱砂），即所謂的"朱石"。因丹砂為紅色顏料，所以丹字又含有紅色的意思，如丹唇（紅唇）、丹霞（紅霞）。

【丹青】丹砂和青臒，兩種可製顏料的礦石，泛指繪畫用的顏色，又指繪畫藝術。古代丹冊紀勳，青史紀事，所以丹青又是史籍的代稱。

【丹心】紅心，指忠實赤誠之心。

【丹田】道家稱人身臍下三寸為丹田。

甲骨文

金 文

小 篆

丹 refers to cinnabar, an element for colouring. In the Oracle-Bone Inscriptions, the character 丹 looks like a well part (井) with a dot in it, the former standing for the mine where the mineral is found and the latter the mineral excavated. As cinnabar is red in colour, it is known as 丹砂, 朱砂 or 朱石, literally "red sand" or "red stone". The character 丹 may also refer to other red things, e.g. 丹唇 (red lips), 丹霞 (rosy clouds).

【丹青】 (lit.) red and black pigments; painting; historical records

【丹心】 a loyal heart

【丹田】 (acupuncture) the point three cùn below the navel

jǐng

甲骨文井字，像井口用木石構成的井欄，其本義就是水井。而形似水井的物形皆可稱井，如天井、礦井等。古代制度，同一鄉里以八家共井，後來井引申為指鄉里、人口聚居地，如市井、井里等。井字還含有整齊、有條理之義，如"井井有條"、"秩序井然"等。

【井蛙】井底之蛙，比喻見識狹隘的人。

【井中視星】坐井觀天的意思，比喻見識狹隘。

| 甲骨文 | 金文 | 小篆 |

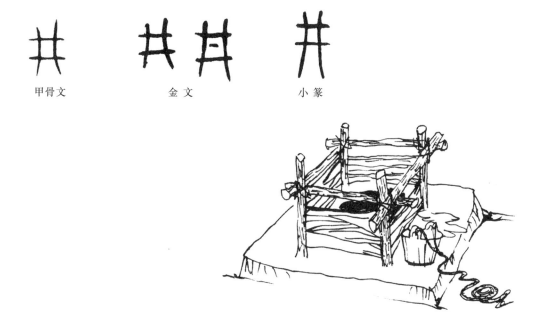

In the Oracle-Bone Inscriptions, the character 井 looks like the square railings on top of a well. It primarily refers to a water well, but other enclosed spaces similar to a well may also be referred to by 井, e.g. 天井 (courtyard), 礦井 (mine). In former times, eight house holds shared a well, and the character 井 has taken on the sense of "neighbour hood", e.g. 市井 (marketplace), 井里 (neighbourhood). 井 may also mean "neat" and "orderly", e.g. 井井有條 (in perfect order), 秩序井然 (in perfect arrangement).

【井蛙】 (lit.) a frog in a well; a person with a very limited outlook

【井中視星】 (lit.) to look at the sky from the bottom of a well; to have a very narrow view

動物類

Animal

niú

牛，是一種反芻類動物，力大性善，可用於載物或耕地，是人類最早馴養的六畜之一。古文字的牛字，是一顆牛頭的簡化圖形，而重點突出了牛角、牛耳的特徵。漢字中凡從"牛"之字都與牛、牛屬動物及其動作行為有關，如牝、牡、牟、牧、犀、犁、犢等。

【牛鬼蛇神】牛頭鬼、蛇身神，比喻虛幻荒誕，又比喻社會上的醜惡東西或形形色色的壞人。

【牛刀小試】比喻有很大的本領，先在小事情上施展一下。

甲骨文

金文

小篆

牛 means "ox", one of the earliest six domestic animals, used for pulling carts or ploughs. In ancient writing systems, the character 牛 looks like the sketch of an ox head, with the horns and ears especially prominent. Characters with 牛 as a component most have to do with oxen and their activities, e.g. 牝 (cow), 牡 (bull), 牟 (the sound made by an ox), 牧 (to herd), 犀 (rhinoceros), 犁 (to plough) and 犢 (calf).

【牛鬼蛇神】(lit.) ghost with an ox head and spirit with a snake body; anything ugly and evil

【牛刀小試】a master hand's first small display

móu

小篆的牟字，下從牛，上部像從牛口中出氣之形，表示牛在鳴叫的意思。所以牟的本義為牛叫。許慎《說文解字》說："牟，牛鳴也。從牛，像其聲氣從口出。"牟通"謀"，有謀取之義，其本義則由哞表達。

【牟利】謀取利益。

小篆

In the Later Seal Character, the character 牟 consists of ㄙ, standing for the breath coming out of an ox's mouth, and 牛 (ox), signalling an ox is making a sound. Hence its original meaning "the sound made by an ox". Xu Shen says in his *Origin of Chinese Characters,* "牟, with its shape of an ox making a sound, refers to the sound made by an ox". Nowadays, however, 牟 is mainly used, the same as 謀, in the sense of "trying to gain", and its original meaning is expressed by 哞.

【牟利】to seek profit

mǔ

甲骨文的牡字，左邊為牛，右邊的字形是雄性動物生殖器的形象，所以牡的本義指雄性的牛，即公牛。牡是雄性的統稱。在甲骨文中還有表示公羊、公鹿、公豬（豕）等雄性動物的字形，後世則通稱之為"牡"，如牡馬、牡羊等。

甲骨文

金文

小篆

In the Oracle-Bone Inscriptions, the character 牡 has an ox part (牛) on the left and a part standing for the male sexual organ on the right, hence the original meaning "bull". But nowadays 牡 may also refer to other male animals, e.g. 牡馬 (stallion), 牡羊 (ram), though there were different characters for these male animals in the Oracle-Bone Inscriptions.

láo

牢字的本義指關養在圈欄內的牲畜。甲骨文的牢字，像一頭牛（或羊、馬）被困在圈欄之中；小篆的牢字則在圈欄出口加一橫表示圈門。牢是關養在圈欄內的牲畜，也指關養牲畜的圈欄（如成語"亡羊補牢"），引申為指關押犯人的監獄（如監牢、牢獄等）。此外，牢字還可用作形容詞，有堅固之義（如牢靠、牢不可破等）。

甲骨文

金 文

小 篆

牢 originally referred to the domestic animals kept in a shed or stable. In the Oracle-Bone Inscriptions, the character 牢 looks like an ox (or a sheep, a horse) enclosed in a shed. In the Later Seal Character, there is a stroke standing for the gate added at the entrance of the shed. But it may also refer to the place to keep the domestic animals, e.g. 亡羊補牢 (to mend the fold immediately after sheep are lost); from which has derived its use for the place to lock up prisoners, e.g. 監牢 (prison). Used as an adjective, it means "firm", e.g. 牢靠 (firm; reliable) and 牢不可破 (unbreakable).

qiān

小篆

小篆的牽字，下從牛，上部的"玄"代表牽牛的繩子，中間的橫槓代表牛的鼻栓，表示用繩牽牛的意思。《說文解字》："牽，引前也。從牛，像引牛之縻也，玄聲。"則牽還是一個會意兼形聲的字。所以，牽的本義為牽引、挽、拉，引申為牽涉、關聯、牽制等義。

【牽連】互有關聯。

【牽強】勉強。

【牽掣】引曳、束縛。又指牽制。

【牽腸掛肚】比喻非常操心惦念。

In the Later Seal Character, the character 牽 has three parts: a string part (玄), a stroke through the middle of the string part standing for the nasal bolt, and an ox part (牛); signalling to lead an ox with a string through the nasal septum of an ox. Xu Shen says in his *Origin of Chinese Characters,* "牽, in the shape of a string to lead an ox, and with 牛 as the radical and 玄 as the phonetic, means to lead along". In this sense, 牽 is both an ideograph and phonetic compound. From its primary meaning "to lead along", "to pull", have derived the extended senses "to involve", "to implicate" and "to tie up".

【牽連】to involve

【牽強】farfetched

【牽掣】(1) to impede (2) (also 牽制) to tie up

【牽腸掛肚】to feel deep anxiety about

mù

牧字的形體，像人手持牧鞭（或樹枝）趕牛之狀，表示放牛吃草的意思。放牛為牧，同樣，放馬、放羊、放豬等均可稱"牧"，所以牧字的本義為放養牲畜。引申為名詞，指放養牲畜的人。在古代，統治者把老百姓視同牛馬，而以牧人自居，所以稱管理和統治老百姓為"牧民"。一些地方州郡的最高長官也被稱為"牧"或"牧伯"。

甲骨文

金文

小篆

The character 牧 looks like a man driving an ox with a whip in hand, signalling to herd cattle. But it may be used in the general sense of "herding", i.e. the animals looked after may be horses, sheep or pigs as well. As a noun, it refers to the herdsman. In the old days, the rulers saw themselves as herdsmen and the subjects as oxen and horses, so to rule was known as 牧民 (to herd people). The rulers of some local areas were known as 牧 or 牧伯 (herdsmen).

wù

甲骨文物字，從刀從牛，是以刀殺牛的意思，刀上的兩點是殺牛時沾在刀上的血滴。因此，物的本義是指殺牛，引申為指雜色牛，泛指一切物種或東西，和事物的內容實質，如萬物、言之有物等。

【物色】原指牲畜的毛色，又指形貌，引申為指按一定的標準去挑選、訪求。

【物議】指眾人的議論或批評。

甲骨文　　　　　　　小篆

In the Oracle-Bone Inscriptions, the character 物 consists of 刀 (knife) and 牛 (ox), signalling to slaughter an ox with a knife, and the two dots on the knife part stand for drops of blood. Hence its original meaning was "to slaughter an ox", from which has derived its reference to oxen of mixed colours, things in general, and content, e.g. 萬物 (all things on earth), 言之有物 (having substance in a speech).

【物色】 (lit.) the colour of domestic animals; to choose

【物議】 criticism from the people

mái

甲骨文的埋字，像把牛、羊或鹿、犬等牲畜掩埋於土坑中之形，其本義指埋牲。埋牲是古代祭祀活動中的一種儀式，引申而言之，則把任何東西藏於土中都可以叫做"埋"。此外，埋還有填塞、隱沒等義。

【埋名】隱藏姓名、不為人知。後稱故意不使人知為隱姓埋名。

【埋伏】潛伏，隱藏。多用於軍事行動。

【埋怨】抱怨，責備。

【埋頭】比喻專心不旁顧。

甲骨文　　　　　　　　　小篆

In the Oracle-Bone Inscriptions, the character 埋 looks like laying an animal sacrifice such as an ox or sheep into a hole, an important part of a sacrifice-offering ceremony. Hence its original meaning was to bury an animal, but it may also be used for the covering of anything with earth. In addition, 埋 may also mean "to fill" and "to hide".

【埋名】 to conceal one's name

【埋伏】 to lie in ambush

【埋怨】 to complain

【埋頭】 to immerse oneself in

gào

告字從牛從口，其本義為牛叫。牛叫為告；其造字方法與吠、鳴等字同（吠為狗叫，鳴為鳥叫）。告字後來引申為報告、告訴、告發、請求等義。

【告示】曉示、通知，又指舊時官府的佈告，如安民告示等。
【告密】揭發別人的祕密。
【告急】遇急難向人求救。

甲骨文

金文

小篆

The character 告 consists of 牛 (ox) and 口 (mouth), meaning originally the sound made by an ox. This character is structured in the same way as 吠 (with a mouth part and a dog part, signalling the sound made by a dog) and 鳴 (with a mouth part and a bird part, signalling the sound made by a bird). But it is now used in the senses of "reporting", "telling", "informing" and "asking for".

【告示】official notice
【告密】to inform against sb.
【告急】to ask for emergency help

bàn

古文字的半字從八從牛，八是分別的意思，表示把一條牛分開成兩部份。半的本義是指事物的二分之一（即一半）；引申為指在……中間，如半夜；又比喻很少的意思，如一星半點；還有不完全的意思，如半成品、半透明等。

【半斤八兩】舊制一斤合十六兩，半斤等於八兩。比喻彼此一樣，不分上下。

【半推半就】心裡願意，表面上卻假作推辭，不肯痛快答應。

金文

盟文

小篆

In ancient writing systems, the character 半 consists of 八 (to separate) and 牛 (ox), signalling to divide an ox into two parts. The primary meaning of 半 is "half", from which have derived its extended meanings: "in the middle of" as in 半夜 (midnight), "very little" as in 一星半點 (a tiny bit), and "semi" as in 半成品 (semi-manufactured goods) and 半透明 (semitransparent).

【半斤八兩】(in the traditional Chinese weight system, sixteen liǎng make a jīn, so half a jīn equals to eight liǎng) not much to choose between the two

【半推半就】to appear to be unwilling while only too willing at heart

chén

【沉】

沈和沉在古代原本是同一個字。甲骨文的沈字，像一頭牛沒於水中的形狀。這是古代祭禮的一種儀式，即把牲牛沉於河中以祭山林川澤之神。也有用人來作為祭品的。金文的沈字，即是把人沉於水中的意思。沈的本義為沉沒、沒於水中，引申為沉溺、深沉等義。近代沈多讀為 shěn，用作姓氏；而以"沉"來代表它的本義。以下各詞現均寫作"沉"。

【沉重】深沉莊重。
【沉湎】指沉溺於酒。
【沉冤】指積久不得昭雪的冤案。
【沉鬱頓挫】指文章深沉蘊藉，抑揚有致。

甲骨文　　　　　　　金文　　　　小篆

沈 and 沉 were originally variant forms of the same character. In the Oracle-Bone Inscriptions, the character 沈 looks like an ox sinking to the bottom of a river. It was an important part of a sacrifice-offering ceremony to offer an animal to the gods and spirits governing mountains and rivers by sinking it. Sometimes, man would be used

as a sacrifice as well. In the Bronze Inscriptions, the character 沈 looks like the sinking of a man to a river. The original meaning of 沈 was "to sink", but it may also mean "to indulge" and "deep". Nowadays, 沈 is pronounced as shěn, used as a surname, and its original meaning is expressed by 沉. 沈 in all the following words is written as 沉 now.

【沉重】(1) heavy　(2) serious
【沉湎】to be given to (drinking)
【沉冤】unrighted wrong
【沉鬱頓挫】(of writing) to rise and fall in proper tones

quǎn

犬即現在所說的狗。它是人類最早馴養的家畜之一，古人主要用它來作為打獵的助手。在甲骨文和金文中，犬和豕字的形體比較接近，區別只在於腹和尾：豕為肥腹、垂尾；犬則是瘦腹、翹尾。從犬之字大都與狗及其行為有關，如狩、狂、莽、猛、獵等。

【犬子】古人對自己兒子的謙稱。

【犬牙交錯】形容交界線很曲折，像狗牙那樣參差不齊，相互交錯。

【犬馬】古代臣子在君王面前的謙稱，又用作效忠之辭，指臣子要像犬馬順從主人一樣甘心情願效忠君王。

甲骨文

金文

小篆

犬 refers to the dog, one of the earliest domestic animals kept by man, used mainly for hunting. In the Oracle-Bone Inscriptions and Bronze Inscriptions, the characters 犬 and 豕 (pig) are very similar, except that the character for pig shows that it has a big belly and falling tail while that for dog shows that it has a small belly and rising tail. Characters with 犬 as a component most have to do with dogs and their actions, e.g. 狩 (hunting), 狂 ((a dog) going mad), 莽 ((a dog in) rank grass), 猛 (fierce) and 獵 (to hunt).

【犬子】(self-depreciatory) my son

【犬牙交錯】jigsaw-like

【犬馬】(to serve one's master like) a dog or a horse

fèi

吠字從犬口，是個會意字。《説文解字》："吠，犬鳴也。"它的本義即指狗叫。

【吠雪】嶺南不常下雪，故狗見之而吠，是少見多怪的意思。

【吠形吠聲】《潛夫論·賢難》："一犬吠形，百犬吠聲。"指一條狗叫，群犬聞聲跟着叫。比喻不明察事情的真偽而盲目附和。

小篆

The character 吠, consisting of 犬 (dog) and 口 (mouth), is an ideograph, signalling the sound made by a dog, i.e. bark. Xu Shen says in his *Origin of Chinese Characters*, " 吠 refers to the sound made by a dog".

【吠雪】(It seldom snows in the province of Guangdong and Guangxi, and a dog barks when seeing snow falling.) to be surprised at a common event out of ignorance

【吠形吠聲】to follow others blindly

xiù

臭的本義為嗅，即聞氣味的意思。臭字由自（鼻的本字）
和犬（狗）組成，指狗的鼻子。狗鼻子的嗅覺特別靈敏，故用
它來表示嗅味之義。有氣味才能用鼻子來嗅，故臭字又有氣味
之義，如"無聲無臭"（沒有聲音和氣味，比喻沒有名聲，不
被人知道）、"其臭如蘭"（表示某種東西的氣味像蘭花一樣
幽香宜人）等。現在，臭字讀chòu，由一般泛指的氣味引申
為專指一種腐爛難聞的氣味，如糞臭、腐臭等。加"口"旁的
"嗅"讀xiù，表示聞氣味。

甲骨文

小 篆

臭 originally meant the same as 嗅, i.e. to smell. The character 臭 consists of 自 (the original form of 鼻, nose)
and 犬 (dog), referring to the nose of a dog. As the dog has a very acute sense of smell, the character referring
to its nose has come to mean "to smell". The character 臭 may also refer to the quality in substances which the
nose senses, i. e. smell, e.g. 無聲無臭 ((lit.) without sound or smell; unknown), 其臭如蘭 (to have the smell
of an orchid). However, the character 臭, pronounced as chòu, now generally refers to foul smell, e.g. 糞臭 (to
odour of night soil) and 腐臭 (stinking). And its original meaning, to smell, is expressed by. 嗅, with a 口
added.

mǎng

古文字的莽字，像一隻狗（犬）在林木草莽中之形，表示獵犬在草木叢中追逐獵物的意思。莽的本義是指叢生的草木，也指草木叢生的地方，引申為粗率、不精細之義。

【莽蒼】形容原野景色迷茫。也指原野。
【莽原】草長得很茂盛的原野。
【莽撞】魯莽冒失。

小篆

In ancient writing systems, the character 莽 looks like a dog running among trees and grass, signalling the dog is chasing a game among plants. The primary meaning of 莽 is plants growing thickly, but it may also refer to the place where plants grow thickly. And it has an extended meaning of "crude and impetuous".

【莽蒼】(1) misty (2) open country
【莽原】wilderness overgrown with grass
【莽撞】rash

fú

　　金文的伏字，像一隻狗（犬）趴在人的腳邊，其本義為趴下、俯伏，引申為藏匿、埋伏，又引申為屈服、降服、制服之義。

【伏兵】埋伏待敵的部隊。

【伏擊】用埋伏的兵力突然襲擊敵人。

【伏罪】承認自己的罪過。又作"服罪"。

【伏筆】文章裡前段為後段埋伏的線索。

金 文

小 篆

In the Bronze Inscriptions, the character 伏 looks like a dog lying at the feet of a man. Its primary meaning is "to lie down", "to lie prone", from which have derived its extended meanings "to hide", "to lie in ambush", "to submit", "to tame" and "to subdue".

【伏兵】 troops in ambush

【伏擊】 to ambush

【伏罪】 (also 服罪) to plead guilty

【伏筆】 a hint foreshadowing later developments in writing

tū

突字從穴從犬，表示猛犬從洞孔中卒然衝出的意思。突的本義為急速外衝，引申為衝撞、穿掘之義，又引申為指凸出，與"凹"相對。由突的急速外衝之義，又可引申為指時間上的突然、卒然之義。

【突出】衝出、穿過。又指鼓凸出來或超過一般地顯露出來。

【突兀】指物體高高聳起。又指事情突然發生，出乎意外。

【突如其來】事情突然發生，出乎意外。

甲骨文　　　　　小篆

The character 突 consists of 穴 (hole) and 犬 (dog), signalling a dog rushing out from a hole suddenly. The primary meaning of 突 is "to rush out", and its extended meanings include "to collide" and "to break through". It may also mean "protruding", opposite to 凹 (hollow). From its sense of "rushing out suddenly" have also derived its senses of "suddenly" and "abruptly".

【突出】(1) to break out (2) protruding; outstanding

【突兀】(1) towering (2) suddenly

【突如其來】to come all of a sudden

shòu

獸的本義為狩，即打獵的意思。甲骨文的獸字，由單（一種杈形狩獵工具）和犬（追捕野獸的獵狗）組成，表示一種採用捕獵工具和由獵犬協助來捕獲野獸的活動，後被用來專指狩獵所獲的動物，又泛指所有野生的動物，即野獸，與馴養的家畜相對。而獸字的本義，則為狩字所代替。

甲骨文

金 文

小 篆

獸 was the original form of 狩, meaning "hunting". In the Oracle-Bone Inscriptions, the character 獸 consists of 單 (a forklike hunting weapon) and 犬 (dog), signalling to hunt with a fork and a dog. Nowadays, it refers to the animals captured or killed during hunting, or more generally to any wild animal, opposite to 家畜 (domestic animal). And its original meaning is expressed by 狩 instead.

mǎ

馬是一種哺乳動物，善跑耐重，是人類最早馴養的六畜之一。甲骨文的馬字，像一頭身足尾俱全的側視馬形。金文的馬字則主要突出馬眼和馬鬃。漢字中凡從"馬"的字大多與馬、馬屬動物及其動作、功能有關，如馳、駝、駒、駱、騰、驕、驢等。

【馬到成功】戰馬所至，立即成功。形容迅速地取得勝利。

【馬首是瞻】作戰時看主將馬頭所向以統一進退。比喻跟隨某人行動，聽從指揮。

【馬革裹屍】用馬皮把屍體包裹起來。指軍人戰死沙場。

甲骨文

金文

小篆

馬 refers to the horse, one of the six earliest animals tamed by man, good at running and carrying things. In the Oracle-Bone Inscriptions, the character 馬 looks like a horse seen from the side, with its head, body, feet and tail all represented. In the Bronze Inscriptions, however, only the eye and mane are emphasized. Characters with 馬 as a component most have to do with horses, other related animals and their uses, e.g. 馳 (to drive a horse forward), 駝 (camel), 駒 (foal), 駱 (a white horse with black mane), 騰 (to gallop), 驕 (〔of horses〕 tall and strong) and 驢 (donkey).

【馬到成功】to win success immediately upon arrival

【馬首是瞻】to take the head of the general's horse as guide

【馬革裹屍】(lit.) to be wrapped in a horse's hide after death; to die on the battlefield

qí

奇是"騎"的本字。甲骨文的奇字，像一個人跨在馬背上之形，其中的馬形極其簡略；或在馬下加一口形。小篆的奇字則訛變為從大從可。奇的本義為騎馬，後來多用為怪異、奇特之義，而其本義則為"騎"字所代替。

【奇觀】指雄偉美麗而又罕見的景象或出奇少見的事情。

【奇跡】想像不到的不平凡的事情。

| 甲骨文 | 金 文 | 小 篆 |

奇 was the original form of 騎. In the Oracle-Bone Inscriptions, the character 奇 looks like a man riding on a horse, though the part representing the horse is very simple, and sometimes there is a square part (口) underneath. In the Later Seal Character, it consists of 大 and 可 by mistake. The original meaning of 奇 was to ride a horse, but it is nowadays used mainly in the sense of "strange", and its original meaning is expressed by 騎.

【奇觀】marvellous spectacle

【奇跡】wonder

chuǎng

闖

小 篆

闖字從馬從門，表示馬從門中猛衝而過的意思，其本義為向前猛衝，兼有一往無前和無所顧忌之義。此外，闖字還有經歷、歷練之義。

【闖蕩】指離家在外謀生。即"闖蕩江湖"的意思。

【闖將】勇於衝鋒陷陣的將領。

The character 闖 consists of 馬 (horse) and 門 (gate), signalling a horse rushing through a gate. Its primary meaning is to rush forward fearlessly, suggesting there is nothing to stop it. In addition, it may mean "to experience" and "to go through".

【闖蕩】 to make a living wandering from place to place

【闖將】 daring general

yù

馭

金文的馭字，從馬從鞭，像人手持馬鞭驅馬前行狀。小篆馭字改為從馬從又（手），也是趕馬的意思。馭的本義為驅馬、駕駛馬車，引申為駕馭、控制、統治之義。

【馭宇】指帝王統治天下。同"御宇"。

甲骨文　　　　　　　金 文　　　　　　　小 篆

In the Bronze Inscriptions, the character 馭 consists of 馬 (horse) and 鞭 (whip), signalling a man driving a horse forward with a whip. In the Later Seal Character, it consists of 馬 (horse) and 又 (hand), but means the same. The primary meaning of 馭 is to drive a horse or a cart, from which have derived its senses of "controlling", "mastering" and "ruling".

【馭宇】 (also 御宇) (of a monarch) to rule over a land

yáng

羊是一種家畜，自古以來稱為六畜之一，有山羊、綿羊、羚羊等。羊字是一個象形字，但和牛一樣，它所像的不是羊的整體形象，而是局部特徵。甲骨文和金文的羊字，是簡化了的羊頭形象，而羊頭形象又特別突出了彎卷的羊角，使人一見便知是羊而不是別的動物。這種以局部替代整體的造型方法，是漢字象形的主要方式之一。

【羊車】羊拉的小車，又指宮內所乘小車。羊，通"祥"，吉祥之義。

【羊角】指曲旋而上升的旋風。

【羊酒】羊和酒。饋贈之禮物，也作祭品。

甲骨文

金文

小篆

羊 refers to one of the six domestic animals, such as sheep, goat and the like. The character 羊 is a pictograph. But, similar to the character 牛, it depicts only part of the animal, i.e. the head. In the Oracle-Bone Inscriptions and Bronze Inscriptions, it looks like the head of a sheep, and the curving horns are especially prominent so that it will not be mistaken for other animals. It is one of the important ways to create Chinese characters to use the picture of a part for the whole.

【羊車】 (1) a sheep-drawn cart (2) (羊 used in the sense of "lucky" like 祥) a palace cart

【羊角】 whirlwind

【羊酒】 (lit.) sheep and wine; presents; sacrifices

shàn

善為"膳"的本字。古人以羊為膳食的美味,故金文的善字從羊從二言,表示眾口誇讚的意思。善字由膳食之美引申為美好之義,故後世另造"膳"字來代替它的本義。又羊性溫和馴順,故善又有善良、慈善之義,與"惡"相對。善字用作動詞,則有喜好、愛惜、親善、擅長等義。

【善本】珍貴難得的古書刻本、寫本。

【善事】好事,慈善的事情。又指善於侍奉。

【善始善終】自始至終都完美,含有結局圓滿的意思。

金 文

小 篆

善 was the original form of 膳. Ancient people thought mutton was the best food, so the character 善 in the Bronze Inscriptions consists of one mutton part (羊) and two speech parts (言), signalling everybody praises mutton. After 善 took on the general sense of "good", another character 膳 was created to express its original meaning. As the sheep is tame and docile, the character 善 can also mean "kindhearted" and "loving", opposite to 惡 (evil). Used as a verb, it means "to love", "to cherish", "to be good to" and "to be good at".

【善本】rare copy

【善事】philanthropic act

【善始善終】to start well and end well

yǎng

甲骨文、金文的養本是個會意字,像手執鞭杖趕羊之形,表示放養羊群,意同牧字;小篆變為從羊從食,羊又代表讀音,所以養字又成為一個形聲字,表示以食物飼養之意。養字後來又引申為生養、培養、療養、教養等義。

【養生】攝養身心,以期保健延年,又指事養父母於其生時。

【養老】古禮,對老而賢者按時享以酒食以敬禮之,謂之養老。

【養志】涵養高尚的志趣、情操。

甲骨文 　　　　　　　　　金文　　　　　　　　　小篆

In the Oracle-Bone Inscriptions and Bronze Inscriptions, the character 養 is an ideograph, looking like a man driving a sheep with a stick in hand. Hence its primary meaning, like that of 牧, "to herd". In the Later Seal Character, it consists of 羊 (sheep) and 食 (food), signalling to give a sheep its feed. The part 羊 may be seen as a phonetic, in this sense 養 is also a phonetic compound. But the character 養 has also the extended meanings: "to give birth to", "to train", "to recuperate one's health" and "to educate".

【養生】 to preserve one's health

【養老】 to provide for the aged

【養志】 lofty aspirations

gāo

甲骨文羔字。從羊從火，像羊在火上，它的意思為用火烤羊。像烤乳豬一樣，烤羊一般也是整條地烤，而所烤的整羊往往都是小羊，所以羔字通常又指小羊。

【羔羊】指小羊，同時又比喻天真無知、缺少社會經歷的人或弱小者。

【羔裘】用小羊皮做的袍服。古代諸侯以羔裘作為朝服。

甲骨文

金文

小篆

In the Oracle-Bone Inscriptions, the character 羔 consists of 羊 (sheep) and 火 (fire), signalling to roast a lamb on a fire. As it is usually lambs that are roasted, the character 羔 has come to refer to the lamb as well.

【羔羊】(1) lamb (2) an inexperienced or feeble person

【羔裘】a garment made of lambskin

xiū

古文字的羞字，從羊從又，表示用手捧羊進獻的意思。羞字的本義為進獻食品，又指美味的食物，如珍羞、庶羞等。後來，用作食物的羞字多寫作饈，而原來的羞字則借用為恥辱、愧怍等義。

【羞（饈）膳】進食。又指美味的食物。

【羞澀】因羞愧而舉動拘束。

【羞花閉月】形容女子貌美，使鮮花和明月都自愧退縮。

甲骨文

金文

小篆

In ancient writing systems, the character 羞 consists of 羊 (sheep) and 又 (hand), signalling to present mutton with hands. The original meaning of 羞 was to present food, but it may also refer to something pleasant to the taste, e.g. 珍羞 (a rare delicacy). However, nowadays 羞 is more usually used in the sense of "shame" or "to feel ashamed", and its original meaning is expressed by 饈.

【羞（饈）膳】(1) to dine (2) delicious food

【羞澀】shy

【羞花閉月】(a woman who is so beautiful that) flowers feel themselves inferior and the moon shies away

shǐ

豕，就是我們現在所說的豬。它是人類最早飼養的家畜之一。甲骨文的豕字，長嘴短腳，肚腹肥圓，尾下垂，正是豬的形象描繪。不過在古代，豕和豬是略有區別的：豕指大豬，而豬則是指小豬。

【豕牢】養豕之處，或兼廁所。

【豕突】豕受驚則奔突難制，比喻人的橫衝直撞，流竄侵擾。

甲骨文　　　　　　金文　　　　　　小篆

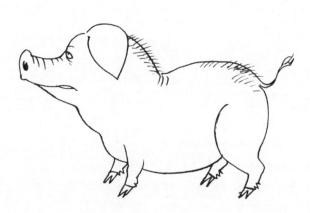

豕 refers to the pig, now called 豬, one of the earliest domestic animals kept by human beings. In the Oracle-Bone Inscriptions, the character 豕 looks like a pig with its long mouth, short legs, round belly and falling tail. In ancient times, however, there was a distinction between 豕 and 豬: the former referring to adult pigs and the latter young ones.

【豕牢】pigsty

【豕突】to dash around madly like frightened pigs

hùn

圂字從囗從豕，是個會意字。甲骨文的圂字，像把豬關養在欄舍中之形，它的本義即指豬圈。由於古代的豬圈和廁所通常是連在一起的，所以圂又可以引申為指廁所。

甲骨文

金文

小篆

The character 圂, consisting of 囗 (enclosure) and 豕 (pig), is an ideograph. In the Oracle-Bone Inscriptions, the character 圂 looks like a pig enclosed in a pigsty, hence its primary meaning "pigsty". As the pigsty and toilet were usually next to each other, 圂 may refer to the toilet as well.

zhì

甲骨文彘字，從矢從豕，像一支箭射中一頭大野豬的樣子。家豬馴善，只有野豬力大兇猛，不用弓矢是很難捕獲的。所以彘的本義是指野豬，後來代指一般的成年大豬。如《方言》："豬，關東西或謂之彘。"

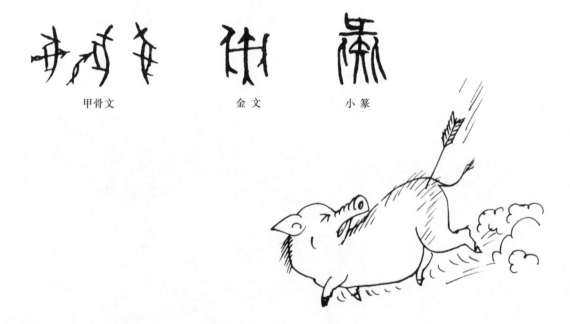

甲骨文　　　　金文　　　　小篆

In the Oracle-Bone Inscriptions, the character 彘 consists of 矢 (arrow) and 豕 (pig), signalling an arrow has hit a pig. As it is usually wild boars that are hunted, the character 彘 originally referred to wild boars. But nowadays it may refer to adult pigs in general. For example, the *Dialects* says, "豬 is known as 彘 in central China."

zhú

甲骨文逐字，像一隻豬（豕，或鹿、兔）在前奔逃，有人在後追趕之形，其本義為追趕。引申為驅逐、放逐，後有競爭、追求之義。

【逐北】追逐敗走之敵兵。

【逐客】戰國時指驅逐列國入境的遊說之士，後來又指被朝廷貶謫的人。

【逐鹿】指在國家分裂紛亂時，眾人爭奪天下政權。語出《史記·淮陰侯列傳》："秦失其鹿，天下共逐之，於是高材疾足者先得焉。"

甲骨文　　　　　金文　　　　　小篆

In the Oracle-Bone Inscriptions, the character 逐 looks like a man chasing a pig (or a deer, a rabbit). Hence its primary meaning "to chase", from which have derived its extended meanings "to drive", "to send into exile", "to compete" and "to seek".

【逐北】 to chase the defeated

【逐客】 to order sb. to leave; banished official

【逐鹿】 (lit.) to chase the deer; to fight for the throne (from the *Historical Records* "When the Qin Emperor lost his throne, everyone competed for it. But it fell into the hands of those who were more powerful and swifter.")

gǎn

　　甲骨文敢字，像人手持獵叉迎面刺擊野豬（豕）之形。金文敢字則簡省為以手（又）搏豕，而豕形也變得簡略難辨。持叉刺豕有進行之意，故《説文解字》稱："敢，進取也。"又因為野豬是一種兇猛的野獸，敢於搏取，需要有很大的膽量和勇氣，所以敢字又有大膽勇猛的意思。

金文　　　　　　　　小篆

In the Oracle-Bone Inscriptions, the character 敢 looks like a man attacking a wild boar face to face with a hunting fork in hand. In the Bronze Inscriptions, the part representing the hunting fork is left out, and the wild boar part is simplified so much that it no longer resembles a boar. To attack a wild boar one must forge ahead. Thus the *Origin of Chinese Characters* says, "敢 means to forge ahead". As wild boars are fierce animals, one fighting with them must be courageous and daring, the character 敢 has also taken on the senses of "courageous" and "daring".

sì

兕是一種類似犀牛的野獸。它的形狀像牛，頭上有一隻青黑色的獨角，又稱獨角獸。甲骨文的兕字，像一頭動物的形狀，而特別突出了它的大獨角；篆書的兕字，則主要強調其頭形的怪異。

【兕觥(gōng)】古代一種有帶角獸頭形器蓋的酒器。初用木頭製成，後用青銅鑄造。盛行於商代和西周前期。

甲骨文　　　　　　　　　小篆

兕 refers to a rhinoceros-like animal, which has a horn on its head, also known as single-horned animal. In the Oracle-Bone Inscriptions, the character 兕 looks like such an animal, with its single horn especially prominent. In the Later Seal Character, however, it is the strange shape of its head that is brought into focus.

【兕觥】a type of drinking vessel with a lid shaped like the head of a horned animal. It was made of wood at the beginning, but of bronze later, and was widely used in the Shang Dynasty and the early Zhou Dynasty.

xiàng

中國古代的中原地區，氣候溫濕，叢林茂密，曾經是大象出沒的地方。象是一種生活在熱帶、亞熱帶叢林地區的哺乳動物，身大力強，但性情溫順。甲骨文和早期金文的象字，是大象的側視圖形，主要突出了它長長的鼻子、寬厚的身軀，筆畫簡單而形態生動。象字後來多引申為指具體的形狀，又泛指事物的外表形態，如形象、景象、星象、氣象、現象等。

【象形】古代漢字構造方法的"六書"之一，指描述實物形狀的
　　　　一種造字方法。

甲骨文

金 文

小 篆

象 refers to the elephant, a large docile animal, which used to live in central China, a much hotter place then. In the Oracle-Bone Inscriptions and early Bronze Inscriptions, the character 象 is a vivid sketch of an elephant seen from the side, with its long nose and broad trunk especially prominent. However, it is also used in the sense of "likeness", it may also refer to the outside appearance in general, e.g. 形象 (image), 景象 (scene), 星象 (the appearance of stars), 氣象 (meteorological phenomena) and 現象 (phenomenon).

【象形】pictograph, one of the six basic types of Chinese characters

wéi

　　古代中原一帶氣候溫和，生活着許多熱帶和亞熱帶動物。大象就是其中之一。大象身強體壯，力大無比，而且性情溫和，是人類勞動的好幫手。人們在還沒有馴服牛馬之前，就先學會了馴服大象。甲骨文的為字，像一個人用手牽着大象的鼻子，其本義為馴象，即驅使大象幫人幹活，因此，為字有幹活、做、作等意思。這個字由甲骨文到金文，又由篆書變成隸書、楷，再由草書演變成今天的簡化字，原來的形象和意思一點也看不出來了。

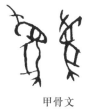

甲骨文

金 文

小 篆

In the Oracle-Bone Inscriptions, the character 為 looks like a man leading an elephant by the nose, signalling to domesticate an elephant. In ancient times, there were elephants living in central China, a much hotter place then. And people trained elephants to help them with their work. Hence the character 為 has the sense of "working" and "doing things". However, as a result of its evolution from the Oracle-Bone Inscriptions, to the Bronze Inscriptions, Later Seal Character and Regular Script, and especially through the modern simplification, there is no trace whatsoever of the original form left in the present-day 為.

néng

　　能是"熊"的本字。金文中的能字,巨口弓背,粗爪短尾,正是熊的形象特徵。所以,能的本義即指熊。因為熊以力大無窮著稱,故能字引申出能力、才能等義。後能字多用為引申義,於是在"能"下加"火"(楷書變為四點)另造一個"熊"字,來代替它的本義。

【能吏】有才能的官吏。又稱能臣、能士。

【能幹】有才能、會辦事。

【能者多勞】能幹的人多勞辛苦。後用為讚譽的話。

金 文

小 篆

能 was the original form of 熊, referring to the bear. In the Bronze Inscriptions, the character 能 looks like a bear with its big mouth, arched back, strong claws and short tail. As the bear is noted for its strength, the character 能 has taken on the extended senses of "ability" and "talent". Nowadays, 能 is only used in its extended senses, and its original meaning is expressed by a new creation, formed by adding a fire part (火) to 能, i.e. 熊.

【能吏】 (also 能臣 and 能士) able official

【能幹】 competent

【能者多勞】 (used to praise someone) It is duty-bound for the able to do more work.

hǔ

虎是一種猛獸，通稱老虎。甲骨文虎字，形象地勾畫出虎形的基本特徵：大口利齒、強健靈活的腰身，爪尾有力，毛色絢麗。金文、小篆字形，漸趨簡化和抽象，其象形意味也就逐漸消失。虎字古今詞義變化不大，都作老虎講；但因老虎特別兇猛，故取其猛意，引申為比喻勇猛、威武之義，如虎將、虎威、虎賁（bēn，指勇士）等。

甲骨文

金文

小篆

虎 refers to the tiger, a fierce animal. In the Oracle-Bone Inscriptions, the character 虎 looks like a tiger with its big mouth, sharp teeth, powerful back, strong claws and tail, and colourful fur. In the Bronze Inscriptions and Later Seal Character, its form is simplified and has lost much of its original picturelike flavour. But its meaning has little change throughout the years. As tigers are especially fierce, the character 虎 has also taken on the senses of "brave" and "vigorous", e.g. 虎將 (brave general), 虎威 (tiger's power) and 虎賁 (warrior).

nüè

小篆的虐字，像虎用爪傷人之形。虎傷人極其殘暴狠毒，故虐字有殘暴之義，又引申為指災害。

【虐政】暴政。
【虐待】以殘暴狠毒的手段對待人。
【虐疾】暴疾。

金文

小篆

In the Later Seal Inscriptions, the character 虐 looks like a tiger trying to capture a man with its claws. As the tiger is especially cruel and fierce, the character 虐 has taken on the sense of "cruel" and may refer to disasters as well.

【虐政】tyranny
【虐待】to maltreat
【虐疾】sudden attack of a serious illness

lù

鹿是鹿類動物的總稱，其特點是四肢細長，雄性生有枝角。甲骨文和金文的鹿字，生動地表現出鹿的這些特徵：枝叉狀的角、長頸細腿，身軀輕靈，正是雄鹿的形象。在漢字中，凡以鹿為形符的字大都與鹿類動物有關，如麟、麝、麋等。

【鹿死誰手】鹿，喻指政權。比喻群雄共爭，未知誰能取勝。後也泛指在競爭中勝利誰屬。

甲骨文

金文

小篆

鹿 refers to the deer, a fast four-footed animal, of which the males have wide branching horns. In the Oracle-Bone Inscriptions and Bronze Inscriptions, the character 鹿 looks like a male deer with its wide branching horns, long neck and thin legs. Characters with 鹿 as a component most have to do with deers and related animals, e.g. 麟 (〔Chinese〕unicorn), 麝 (musk deer) and 麋 (elk).

【鹿死誰手】(lit.) At whose hand will the deer die? Who will gain supremacy?

lì

甲骨文、金文的麗字，是一隻鹿的形象，而特別突出了鹿頭上一對漂亮的鹿角。所以，麗的本義是指一對、一雙。這個意思，後來多寫作"儷"。此外，麗字又含有漂亮、華麗的意思。

【麗人】指美人。
【麗質】美麗的姿質。

甲骨文

金 文

小 篆

In the Oracle-Bone Inscriptions and Bronze Inscriptions, the character 麗 looks like a deer, with its beautiful pair of branching horns especially prominent. Hence its original meaning "a pair" or "a couple". However this meaning is now expressed by 儷, and the character 麗 is used in the sense of "beautiful" and "magnificent".

【麗人】a beauty
【麗質】the looks of a beauty

lù

麓字是個會意兼形聲的字。鹿的生活習性，是喜歡陰涼潮濕的環境，最理想的活動場所是在山腳林間。甲骨文麓字從林從鹿，是個會意字，像鹿在林中之形，其本義是指山腳。同時，鹿與麓讀音相同，所以鹿又可以代表麓的讀音。從這個意義上來說，麓字又是一個從林鹿聲的形聲字。至於金文的麓字，從林錄聲，則是一個完完全全的形聲字。

甲骨文　　　　　金文　　　　　小篆

麓 is both an ideograph and phonetic compound. In the Oracle-Bone Inscriptions, the character 麓, an ideograph, consists of 林 (forest) and 鹿 (deer), signalling a deer in its favourite living environment, a forest at the foot of a hill. Hence its primary meaning the foot of a hill. On the other hand, 鹿 and 麓 sound the same, and the former may be seen as the phonetic of the latter. In this sense, the character 麓 is a phonetic compound with 林 as the radical and 鹿 as the phonetic. In the Bronze Inscriptions, it is a complete phonetic compound, with 林 as the radical and 錄 as the phonetic.

chén

　　古文字塵字，從土從三鹿，表示群鹿奔騰，沙土飛揚的意思。塵字的本義指飛揚的灰土，又泛指極細微的沙土。

【塵世】俗世，人間。

【塵垢】塵土和污垢，比喻微末卑污的事物。也指塵世。

【塵囂】世間的紛擾、喧囂。

甲骨文

小篆

In ancient writing systems, the character 塵 consists of a soil part (土) and three deer parts (鹿), signalling there is a group of deers running about and clouds of dust flying up. Hence 塵 primarily refers to the dust flying up. But it may also refer to the tiny particles of sandy soil.

【塵世】mortal life; the world

【塵垢】dust and dirt

【塵囂】hubbub

tù

兔，獸名，是一種長耳短尾，肢體短小的小動物。甲骨文的兔字形體，簡單而概括地表現了兔子的這些基本特徵。

【兔死狐悲】比喻物傷其類，因同類的死亡而感到悲傷。

【兔起鶻(hú)落】像兔子的躍起，像鶻鳥的俯衝，極言行動敏捷。也用來比喻書畫家用筆的矯健敏捷。

甲骨文

石鼓文

小篆

兔 refers to a small animal with long ears and a short tail, i.e. a hare or rabbit. In the Oracle-Bone Inscriptions, the character 兔 looks like a sketch of this animal, showing its characteristic ears and tail.

【兔死狐悲】(lit.) The fox mourns the death of the hare; Like grieves for the like.

【兔起鶻(hú)落】(lit.) like the springing up of a hare and the diving down of an eagle; (of writers and painters) quick in thought and imagination.

shǔ

鼠，俗稱老鼠，又叫耗子，是哺乳動物中的一科，身小尾長，門齒特別發達。小篆的鼠字，是一隻老鼠的形象，而特別突出了它的牙齒、腳爪和尾巴的特徵。從"鼠"之字，大都是指鼠類小動物而言，如鼴、鼬、鼯等。

【鼠竄】比喻像老鼠那樣地驚慌逃走。

【鼠目寸光】比喻眼光短，見識淺。

小篆

鼠 refers to the mouse or rat, a small animal with a long tail, whose front teeth are very strong. In the Later Seal Character, the character 鼠 looks like a picture of this animal, showing its characteristic teeth, claws and tail. Characters with 鼠 as a component most refer to animals like the mouse, e.g. 鼴 (mole), 鼬 (weasel) and 鼯 (flying squirrel).

【鼠竄】 to scamper off like a rat

【鼠目寸光】 to have the eyes of a mouse, which can see only an inch; (fig.) short-sighted

chóng

蟲是昆蟲類的通稱，指昆蟲和類似昆蟲的小動物。甲骨文、金文的虫（huǐ）字，像一種長身盤曲、三角頭形的蟲形，實際上是蛇的象形。蛇只是蟲類中的一種，所以小篆的蟲字用三個虫疊在一起來代表種類繁多的蟲類。蟲也可泛指昆蟲類之外的其他動物。漢字中凡從"蟲"的字，大都與昆蟲和動物有關，如蛇、蜀、蠶、蚊、蜂、蟬等。

【蟲豸】泛指蟲類小動物。又用作斥罵之詞，比喻下賤者。

【蟲雞】"雞蟲得失"省語，指不足輕重的瑣屑小事。

甲骨文

金文

小篆

蟲 is a general term for insects, worms and small creatures like them. In the Oracle-Bone Inscriptions and Bronze Inscriptions, the character 虫 (huǐ) looks like a worm with a pointed head and a curving body, in fact it is the shape of a snake. In the Later Seal Character, the character is made up of three snake parts, perhaps reflecting the fact that there are many different types of insects, worms and the like. Characters with 蟲 as a component most have to do with insects, worms and related creatures, e.g. 蛇 (snake), 蜀 (larva), 蠶 (silkworm), 蚊 (mosquito), 蜂 (bee) and 蟬 (cicada).

【蟲豸】 (lit.) insect or worm; mean fellow

【蟲雞】 (an abbreviation of 蟲雞得失) trivial things

gǔ

相傳古代有一種人工培養的毒蟲，可以放入飲食中毒人，使人神志惑亂，不能自主。甲骨文的蠱字，像器皿中有蟲子之形。它的本義當指這種人工培養的毒蟲，又指人腹中的寄生蟲；引申為指誘惑、迷惑。

【蠱毒】毒害。

【蠱惑】迷惑、毒害。

【蠱媚】以姿態美色惑人。

甲骨文

金文

小篆

According to legend there was a venomous worm known as 蠱, which, if eaten, would cause a man to lose consciousness. In the Oracle-Bone Inscriptions, the character 蠱 looks like a vessel with some worms in it. It primarily refers to this venomous worm, but may also refer to parasitic worms living in the human body. And it has the extended meanings: "to entice" and "to confuse".

【蠱毒】to poison

【蠱惑】to confuse

【蠱媚】to seduce

wàn

甲骨文的萬字，像一個巨螯屈尾的蠍子形狀，其本義是指蠍子。此字後來借用為數詞，十百為千，十千為萬；又極言其多，如萬物、萬象等；又引申為極其、非常、絕對等義，如萬全、萬無一失等。

【萬一】萬分之一，表示極微。又用作連詞，表示假設。

【萬般】各種各樣。又用作副詞：極其，非常。

【萬萬】數詞，萬萬為一億。或極言數量之多。又用為副詞：絕對，斷然。

甲骨文

金文

小篆

In the Oracle-Bone Inscriptions, the character 萬 looks like a scorpion with its big chela and curving tail, hence its original meaning "scorpion". Nowadays, however, it is used as a numeral, meaning "ten thousand". But it may also mean "numerous", e.g. 萬物 (all the things), 萬象 (every phenomenon on earth); and "absolutely", e.g. 萬全 (perfectly sound), 萬無一失 (no danger of anything going wrong).

【萬一】 (1) (lit.) one ten thousandth; a very small percentage (2) just in case

【萬般】 (1) all the different kinds (2) extremely

【萬萬】 (1) a hundred million (2) absolutely

zhū

蛛，即蜘蛛，是一種節肢動物。它的尾部能分泌出一種黏液，用來結網捕食昆蟲。軀體較小而四肢長大是蜘蛛的顯著特徵。金文的蛛字，像一隻四腳長大的蜘蛛形，上部從朱，代表蛛字的讀音。小篆蛛字從黽朱聲或從蟲朱聲，完全是個形聲字。

【蛛絲馬跡】比喻隱約可尋的線索，依稀可辨的跡象。

甲骨文

小篆

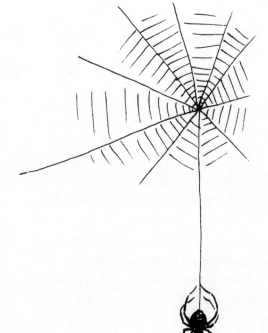

蛛 refers to the spider, a small creature with eight legs, which makes webs for catching insects to eat. In the Bronze Inscriptions, the character 蛛 looks like a spider with its long legs, on top of whose head there is a part 朱 representing its pronunciation. In the Later Seal Character, it is a complete phonetic compound with 黽 (frog) or 蟲 (insect) as the radical and 朱 as the phonetic.

【蛛絲馬跡】 (lit.) thread of a spider and trail of a horse; clues

tā

甲骨文的它字，像一條長身盤曲，頭呈三角形的毒蛇之形，其本義即指蛇。由於它字後來多借用為指稱事物的代詞，其本來的意義逐漸消失，於是新造"蛇"字來代替它的本義。

【它們】代詞，稱不止一個的事物。

甲骨文　　　　　　金　文　　　　　　小　篆

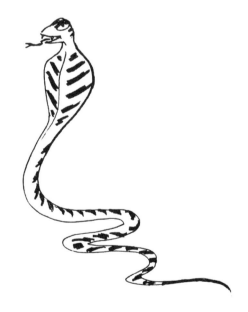

In the Oracle-Bone Inscriptions, the character 它 looks like a snake with its long winding body and pointed head, hence the original meaning "snake". As 它 has come to be used as a pronoun for inanimate things, a new character 蛇 was created for the original meaning.

【它們】they (inanimate)

lóng

龍是中國古代傳說中一種善於變化，能興雲佈雨的神異動物，為鱗蟲之長。甲骨文、金文中的龍字，巨口長身有角，正是人們想像中的神異動物的形象。古代以龍來作為皇帝及皇家的像徵，又喻指神異非常之人。

【龍行虎步】形容人昂首闊步氣勢威武的樣子。又喻指帝王儀態威武。

【龍蟠虎踞】形容地形雄偉險要。

【龍鳳】舊指帝王之相。又喻賢才。

【龍虎】形容帝王氣派。又喻英雄豪傑。

甲骨文

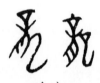
金文

小篆

龍 refers to a traditional Chinese legendary animal, capable of varying its forms and summoning wind and rain, i. e. dragon. In the Oracle-Bone Inscriptions and Bronze Inscriptions, the character 龍 looks like such a mythical animal with its horns, big mouth and long winding body. In the past, the dragon was a symbol of the emperor and his family, or a person with magical power.

【龍行虎步】 to stride ahead like a dragon or tiger; powerful and magnificent

【龍蟠虎踞】 like a coiling dragon and crouching tiger; a forbidding strategic point

【龍鳳】 (lit.)dragon and phoenix; emperor and empress; able and virtuous person

【龍虎】 (lit.)dragon and tiger; emperor and his ministers; hero

měng

甲骨文的黽字，像巨首、大腹、四足的蛙形。金文黽字字形訛省，漸失其形。黽是蛙類的總稱；又特指金線蛙，似青蛙，大腹，又稱"土鴨"。漢字中凡從"黽"之字，多屬蛙、蟲、龜類等四足爬行動物，如黿、鼇、鱉等。字又讀 mǐn，表示努力的意思。

【黽(mǐn)勉】努力，盡力。

甲骨文　　　　　　小篆

In the Oracle-Bone Inscriptions, the character 黽 looks like a frog with its big head, round belly and four legs. In the Bronze Inscriptions, the character is simplified in some way and no longer picturelike. 黽 is a general term for frogs but it may refer to a type of frog, known as 金線蛙 or 土鴨, in particular. Characters with 黽 as a component (in their original complicated forms) most refer to creatures like frog in a way, e.g. 黿 (〔infml.〕 soft-shelled turtle), 鱉 (soft-shelled turtle) and 鼇 (turtle). When 黽 pronounced as mǐn, it means "work hard".

【黽(mǐn)勉】 to try one's best

gū

　　龜是兩棲的爬行動物，俗稱烏龜和水龜。龜身圓而扁，腹背皆有硬甲，四肢和頭尾均能縮入甲內。甲骨文、金文的龜字，分別是烏龜正面和側視的形象，故其本義即指烏龜。

【龜玉】龜甲和寶玉，都是古代極其貴重的東西，皆為國家的重器。後因以龜玉指國運。

【龜齡】古人相傳龜壽百歲以上，故用來比喻高齡。

甲骨文

金 文

小 篆

龜 refers to the tortoise, an amphibian whose body is covered by a hard shell into which the legs, tail and head can be pulled for protection. In the Oracle-Bone Inscriptions, the character 龜 looks like a tortoise seen from the side while in the Bronze Inscriptions it looks like a tortoise seen from the top, hence its meaning "tortoise".

【龜玉】(lit.) tortoise-shell and jade; the prosperity of a nation

【龜齡】advanced age

yú

魚是一種水生的脊椎動物，有鱗有鰭，用鰓呼吸。它的種類極多。甲骨文、金文的魚字，完全是一條魚的形象，其本義即指魚類。漢字中凡從魚之字皆與魚類有關，如鯉、鯊、鮮等。

【魚水】比喻人與人之間關係融洽，像魚和水不可分離一樣。

【魚目混珠】拿魚的眼睛來冒充珍珠。比喻以假充真。

甲骨文　　　　　　金文　　　　　　小篆

魚 refers to the fish, an aquatic vertebrate with scales and fins, and breathing through gills. In the Oracle-Bone Inscriptions and Bronze Inscriptions, the character 魚 looks like a picture of a fish, hence its meaning "fish". Characters with 魚 as a component all have to do with fish and the like, e.g. 鯉 (carp), 鯊 (shark) and 鮮 (fresh fish).

【魚水】to be as close as fish and water

【魚目混珠】to pass off fish eyes as pearls

gòu

遘是一個會意字。甲骨文的遘字，像兩條魚在水中相遇，口嘴相交的形狀，表示相遇、相交的意思。此字後來加"彳"或"辵"，是特指人的行為動作。所以，遘的本義指相逢、遭遇。

【遘禍】遭受禍患。
【遘閔】遭遇父母之喪。

甲骨文

金 文

小 篆

遘 is an ideograph. In the Oracle-Bone Inscriptions, the character 遘 looks like two fishes getting together, mouth to mouth, signalling to meet. In other writing systems, a walk part (彳 or 辵) is added, to indicate that it is a human action. Hence 遘 means "to meet" and "to experience".

【遘禍】to suffer disaster
【遘閔】to have one's parents dead

yú

自古至今，人類捕魚的方法主要有三種：一是下水徒手捉魚，二是張網捕魚，三是垂竿而釣。這三種捕魚方法在甲骨文、金文漁字的字形中都有形象的反映。所以漁字的本義為捕魚，後引申為掠奪、騙取之義。

【漁獵】捕魚打獵。又比喻泛覽博涉。

【漁利】用不正當手段牟取利益。

甲骨文

金 文

小 篆

There are usually three ways of fishing: with one's hands, a net, or a fishing rod. In the Oracle-Bone Inscriptions, the character 漁 looks like fishing in one of these ways. Hence its primary meaning "fishing", from which have derived its meanings "to plunder" and "to gain by cheating".

【漁獵】fishing and hunting; to read widely

【漁利】to reap unfair gains

chēng

甲骨文、金文中的稱字，像人用手提起一條魚的樣子。它的本義為提、舉，引申為稱量之義，又引申為舉薦、頌揚、聲言之義。字又讀 chèn，表示相當、符合的意思。

【稱兵】舉兵、興兵。
【稱讚】稱譽讚揚。
【稱舉】舉薦、稱道。
【稱(chèn)心】符合心意。

甲骨文

金文

小篆

In the Oracle-Bone Inscriptions and Bronze Inscriptions, the character 稱 looks like a man lifting a fish with his hand. Its original meaning was "to lift", "to raise", from which have derived its extended meanings of "weighing", "recommending", "praising" and "stating". 稱 pronounced as chèn means "to be equal to" and "to correspond".

【稱兵】to send an army
【稱讚】to praise
【稱舉】to recommend
【稱(chèn)心】after one's own heart

lǔ

甲骨文、金文的魯字，從魚從口，像魚在器皿之中，表示把魚烹熟盛在盤碟之中，作為味道嘉美的菜餚。因此，魯字有嘉、美之義。後來，魯字被借用為表示莽撞、遲鈍等義，而當"嘉"講的本義反而罕為人知了。

【魯鈍】笨拙，遲鈍。

【魯國】春秋時諸侯國名。周武王封其弟周公旦於魯，戰國時為楚所滅。

【魯魚亥豕】在古文字中，魯和魚、亥和豕形體相近，容易寫錯，後世即以"魯魚亥豕"來代指文字傳抄因形近而產生的錯誤。

甲骨文

金文

小篆

In the Oracle-Bone Inscriptions and Bronze Inscriptions, the character 魯 consists of 魚 (fish) and 口 (vessel), signalling that the fish has been cooked and is ready to be served as a delicious dish on a plate. Hence 魯 meant originally "nice". Nowadays, however, it is mainly used in the senses of "rash" and "stupid", and its original meaning is lost.

【魯鈍】dull-witted

【魯國】a state in the Spring and Autumn Period, situated in present-day Shandong Province

【魯魚亥豕】In ancient writing systems, 魯 and 魚, 亥 and 豕, are two confusing pairs, so they together refer to the mistakes arising from the similarity of written forms in the process of copying.

niǎo

鳥是一種長尾禽，又是所有飛禽的總稱。甲骨文、金文的鳥字，正像一隻頭、尾、足、羽俱全的側面鳥形。在漢字中，凡以鳥為偏旁的字大都與禽類及其行為有關，如雞、鶯、鴨、鵝、鳴等。

【鳥瞰】 指在高處俯視下面的景物，引申為對事物的概括性看法。

【鳥道】 指險絕的山路，僅通飛鳥。如李白《蜀道難》：“西當太白有鳥道，可以橫絕峨眉巔。”

【鳥篆】 篆體古文字，形如鳥跡，故稱。

【鳥盡弓藏】 鳥盡則弓無所用，比喻事成而功臣被害。

甲骨文　　　　　　金 文　　　　　　小 篆

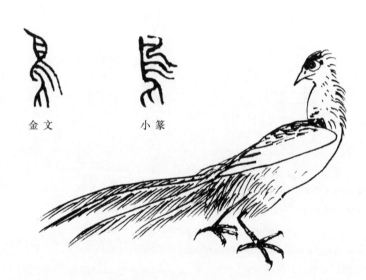

鳥 means "bird". In the Oracle-Bone Inscriptions and Bronze Inscriptions, the character 鳥 looks like a bird with its head, tail, legs and feathers all present seen from the side. Characters with 鳥 as a component most have to do with birds and their activities, e.g. 雞 (chicken), 鶯 (oriole), 鴨 (duck), 鵝 (goose) and 鳴 (to chirp).

【鳥瞰】 to get a bird's-eye view

【鳥道】 (lit.) areas in which nobody can pass except birds; dangerous mountain path

【鳥篆】 a type of ancient Seal Character, looking like birds' traces

【鳥盡弓藏】 (lit.) to cast aside the bow once the birds are gone; to kill a person when he has served his purpose

zhuī

　　甲骨文、金文的隹字，像一頭、身、翅、足俱全的鳥形，其特徵是尾部較短。按照《說文解字》的說法，"隹"就是短尾巴鳥的總稱，而"鳥"則是長尾巴鳥的總稱。在漢字中凡從"隹"的字都與鳥類有關，如焦、集、雉、雕、雀等。

甲骨文

金　文

小　篆

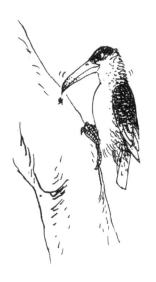

In the Oracle-Bone Inscriptions and Bronze Inscriptions, the character 隹 looks like a bird with its head, body, wings and legs, but its tail is short. According to Xu Shen's characterization in the *Origin of Chinese Characters*, 隹 refers to birds with short tails while 鳥 birds with long tails. Characters with 隹 as a component all have to do with birds, e.g. 焦 (to roast a bird), 集 (to perch), 雉 (pheasant), 雕 (eagle) and 雀 (sparrow).

wū

金文的烏字，像一隻大嘴朝天、有眼無睛的鳥形。烏為鳥名，指烏鴉。由於烏鴉性喜夜啼，所以特別突出它的嘴形；又因為它全身黑色，與眼珠的黑點渾同一色，故只見眼白不見睛黑，所以金文的烏字形有眼無睛。此外，烏又是黑色的代稱。

【烏衣】黑色衣，古時賤者之服。

【烏鳥情】指烏鳥反哺之情，比喻奉養父母的情懷。簡稱"烏鳥"。

【烏有先生】虛擬的人名，即本無其人之意。

【烏合之眾】像烏鴉一樣聚合的群眾，指無組織紀律的一群人。

【烏煙瘴氣】比喻環境嘈雜、秩序混亂或社會黑暗。

金文　　　　　　小篆

烏 refers to the crow. The crow likes to cry at night, and it is black all over so that the apple is not distinguishable. To reflect these features, the character 烏 in the Bronze Inscriptions looks like a bird with its bill upwards as if crying and there is no pupil in the eye. But 烏 may refer to other black things as well.

【烏衣】black clothes; the clothes of the underdogs

【烏鳥情】to support and wait on one's parents like a crow, abbreviated as 烏鳥

【烏有先生】an invented person

【烏合之眾】a disorderly band

【烏煙瘴氣】foul atmosphere

yàn

甲骨文燕字，像張開翅膀向上飛翔的燕子之形，其本義即指燕子，又稱玄鳥。古代燕與宴、晏讀音相同，故燕字可借用為宴，即宴飲之義；又可借用為晏，有安逸、和樂等義。

【燕雀】 燕和雀皆為小鳥，不善高飛遠翔。比喻胸無大志且不足輕重的小人物。

【燕遊】 宴飲遊樂。燕，通"宴"。

【燕爾新婚】 新婚和樂。燕，通"晏"。

甲骨文

小篆

In the Oracle-Bone Inscriptions, the character 燕 looks like a swallow spreading its wings and flying upwards, hence its primary meaning "swallow", which is also known as 玄鳥 in Chinese. As the three characters 燕, 宴 and 晏 sound the same, the character 燕 may also be used in the latters' senses of "feast", "easy" and "comfort".

【燕雀】 (lit.) swallow and sparrow; person of no ambition

【燕遊】 feasts and playing

【燕爾新婚】 happy newlyweds

què

雀字本為象形字。甲骨文的雀字，像一個鳥頭的樣子，鳥頭頂上有一撮羽毛，它的本義是指麻雀或山雀。由於這類鳥的體形都比較小，所以有時也泛稱雀形的小鳥為"雀"。而小篆的雀字也變成從小從佳，成為會意字，專指小鳥。

【雀息】雀的氣息。比喻氣力微弱。

【雀躍】高興得像雀兒一樣跳躍。

甲骨文

小篆

雀 was originally a pictograph. In the Oracle-Bone Inscriptions, the character 雀 looks like the head of a bird with a crest. It primarily refers to the sparrow or tit. As sparrows and tits are small, the character 雀 may also refer to small birds in general. In the Later Seal Character, however, the character consists of 小 (small) and 隹 (bird), resulting in an ideograph.

【雀息】(lit.) the breath of a sparrow; weak

【雀躍】to jump for joy

fèng

鳳是傳説中的瑞鳥，是鳥中之王。甲骨文的鳳字，像一隻長尾巴的鳥形。此鳥頭上有冠，尾羽上有彩色耀人的眼形，其實就是孔雀的形象；有的鳳字還在鳥形上加上聲符"凡"表示讀音，所以它又是一個從鳥凡聲的形聲字。因為鳳是人們心目中的神瑞之物，所以凡與鳳有關係的事物都具有美好、祥瑞的含義，如稱盛德為"鳳德"，稱美麗的文辭為"鳳藻"，稱文才薈萃之地為"鳳穴"，而皇帝或仙人所乘之車為"鳳車"，皇帝居住的京城叫"鳳城"等。

【鳳凰】傳説中的鳥名，雄曰鳳，雌曰凰，現在則渾稱不別。

甲骨文

小篆

鳳 refers to the imaginary lucky bird, the king of birds － phoenix. In the Oracle － Bone Inscriptions, the character 鳳 looks like a bird with a long tail. This bird has a crest on its head and eyes on its colourful tail feathers, which is in fact an image of a peacock. Sometimes there is a phonetic part 凡 added, so it is also a phonetic compound with 鳥 as its radical and 凡 as its phonetic. As the phoenix is a symbol of good luck, the character 鳳 is used to describe anything good and pleasing, e.g. 鳳德 (moral integrity), 鳳藻 (literary embellishment), 鳳穴 (a gathering of talents), 鳳車 (the royal carriage) and 鳳城 (capital).

【鳳凰】(male and female) phoenix

jī

【鷄】

雞,是一種家禽。甲骨文、金文的雞,是一個象形字,像一隻頭、冠、嘴、眼、身、翅、尾、足俱全的雞的形狀;小篆以後,雞字變成為一個從隹奚聲的形聲字。

【雞肋】雞的肋骨,吃起來肉不多,但扔了又可惜,以此喻指那些乏味又不忍捨棄之物。

【雞口牛後】比喻寧在局面小的地方自主,不願在局面大的地方受人支配。

【雞犬升天】相傳漢朝淮南王劉安修煉成仙後,剩下的丹藥散在庭院裡,雞和狗吃了也都升了天。後來比喻一個人做了大官,同他有關係的人也都跟着得勢。

甲骨文

金 文

小 篆

雞 refers to the chicken. In the Oracle-Bone Inscriptions and Bronze Inscriptions, the character 雞 is an ideograph, looking like a cock with its crest, bill, eyes, wings, legs and tail all represented. In the Later Seal Character, it becomes a phonetic compound, with 隹 as its radical and 奚 as its phonetic.

【雞肋】(lit.) chicken ribs; things of little value yet one is not willing to throw them away

【雞口牛後】(lit.) fowl's beak and ox's buttocks; preferable to lead in petty position than to follow behind a greater leader

【雞犬升天】(lit.) Even fowls and dogs ascend to the heaven with their master; When a man gets to the top, all his friends and relations get there with him.

jù

瞿字從隹從二目，像一隻鳥張大雙目的樣子，其本義在表現鷹隼一類鷙鳥眼大而明銳的特點。所以《說文解字》云："瞿，鷹隼之視也。"人受驚而瞪目，故瞿字可引申為指驚視貌，即人驚恐回顧的樣子，又引申為驚愕、驚悸的意思。後作姓氏，讀 qú。

小篆

The character 瞿 consists of a bird part (隹) and two eye parts (目), looking like a bird with its eyes wide open, signalling that fierce birds like the eagle and falcon have big and sharp eyes. Thus the *Origin of Chinese Characters* says, " 瞿 refers to the eye of birds like an eagle and falcon". When a man is frightened, he may open his eyes wide, hence the character 瞿 has taken on the sense of "frightened". Used as a surname, it is pronounced as qú.

dí

翟字本是一個象形字。金文翟字,像一隻頭上長着一撮雞冠形羽毛的鳥形。小篆從羽從佳,變成會意字。翟的本義指長尾巴的野雞;引申為指野雞的尾毛,古代用作服飾或舞具。翟又通"狄",是古代北方地區一個民族名稱。又作姓氏,音 zhái。

【翟茀】古代貴族婦女所乘車,飾雉羽作障蔽,稱翟茀。

金文

小篆

翟 was originally a pictograph. In the Bronze Inscriptions, the character 翟 looks like a bird with a tuft of feathers on its head. In the Later Seal Character, it becomes an ideograph, consisting of 羽 (feather) and 隹 (bird). 翟 primarily refers to pheasants with long tail feathers, and it may, in particular, refer to their tail feathers, used as ornaments by people in former times. 翟, meaning the same as 狄, is also a name of a national minority in the north. And it is a surname, pronounced as zhái.

【翟茀】a type of carriage, decorated with the tail feathers of pheasants, used by ladies of the aristocrat families

zhì

雉字從矢從隹，本來是個會意字，表示用箭射鳥的意思，而雉則指所獵取到的禽類。在古代射獵的禽類中以野雞為最多，所以到後來雉就專指野雞而言。此外，雉還借用為計算城牆面積的單位名稱，以長三丈高一丈為一雉；又引申為指城牆。

【雉堞】泛指城牆。

甲骨文

小篆

雉 was originally an ideograph, consisting of 矢 (arrow) and 隹 (bird), signalling to shoot a bird with an arrow. And 雉 referred to the bird captured or killed. As pheasants accounted for a greater part of the birds shot, the character 雉 has come to refer to pheasants in particular. In addition, 雉 may be used as a unit for measuring the area of city walls, and three zhàng (one zhàng equal to $3\frac{1}{3}$ metres) in length and one zhàng in height is a zhì (雉). From this sense has derived its use to refer to city walls.

【雉堞】 city walls.

jiù

舊本是一種鳥的名稱，又稱鴟鴞，即貓頭鷹。據說這種鳥在鳥類中非常兇猛，常常侵佔別的鳥類窩巢，獵食幼鳥。甲骨文、金文的舊字，像一隻鳥足踏鳥巢之形，正是鴟鴞（貓頭鷹）毀巢取子的形象。此字後來多用為陳舊之義，與"新"相對；其本義則逐漸消失。

【舊觀】原來的樣子。

【舊居】從前曾經住過的地方。

【舊調重彈】比喻把陳舊的理論、主張重新搬出來。又作"老調重彈"。

甲骨文

金文

小篆

舊 was originally a name of a bird, also known as 鴟鴞 or 貓頭鷹, i.e. owl. This bird is said to be very fierce and often occupies nests of other birds and eats their young. In the Oracle-Bone Inscriptions and Bronze Inscriptions, the character 舊 looks like a bird attacking a nest of other birds, depicting the characteristic behaviour of the owl. Nowadays, however, this character is used in the sense of "old", opposite to 新 (new), and its original meaning is lost.

【舊觀】former appearance

【舊居】old home

【舊調重彈】(also 老調重彈) to harp on the same old tune; to repeat the shop-worn stuff

míng

鳴字從口從鳥，本義為鳥叫；從鳥叫擴大到野獸、蟲類的叫，都可稱為"鳴"，如蟬鳴、驢鳴、鹿鳴等；後引申為敲響、發出響聲等義，如鳴鼓、鳴鐘、鳴槍、鳴炮、孤掌難鳴（一個巴掌拍不響，比喻一個人力量薄弱，難以成事）。

甲骨文

金 文

小 篆

The character 鳴 consists of 口 (mouth) and 鳥 (bird), referring to the cry of a bird. But its meaning has been extended. It can also refer to the sound made by animals or insects, e.g. 蟬鳴 (the noise made by a cicada), 驢鳴 (a donkey's bray), 鹿鳴 (the sound made by a deer). Used as a verb, it means to make a sound by striking something, e.g. 鳴鼓 (to beat a drum), 鳴鐘 (to toll a bell), 鳴槍 (to fire a shot), 鳴炮 (to open fire with artillery) and 孤掌難鳴 (It is impossible to clap with one hand)

ㄒㄧˊ

甲骨文習字從羽從日，羽即羽毛，代表鳥的翅膀，表示鳥兒在日光下練習飛翔的意思。《說文解字》："習，數飛也。"所以，習的本義是指鳥兒練習飛翔，泛指學習、練習、複習，引申為通曉、熟悉之義，又指慣常、習慣。

【習氣】長期以來逐漸形成的壞習慣或壞作風。

【習性】長期在某種自然條件或社會環境下所養成的特性。

【習用】經常用、慣用。

【習非成是】對於某些錯的事情習慣了，反認為是對的。

甲骨文

小篆

In the Oracle-Bone Inscriptions, the character 習 consists of 羽 (feather) and 日 (sun), signalling that birds are practising flying in the sun. Xu Shen says in his *Origin of Chinese Characters,* " 習 means to fly time and again". Hence its primary meaning birds' practising flying, from which have derived its more general meanings, "to learn", "to exercise", "to review", "to be familiar with" and "to be used to".

【習氣】 bad habit

【習性】 habits

【習用】 to habitually use

【習非成是】 to accept what is wrong as right as one grows accustomed to it

huò

霍字的形體，像眾鳥在雨中飛翔的樣子，其本義指鳥兒飛動的聲音；又可用作象聲詞使用，如磨刀霍霍等。由鳥在雨中飛翔，霍字又含有迅疾、渙散等義，如霍然而癒（指人的疾病迅速好轉）。電光霍霍（電光閃動迅疾）等。後來把輕散財物稱為“揮霍”，也即取其渙散之義。

甲骨文

金文

小篆

The character 霍 looks like many birds flying in the rain, referring to the sound made by the birds' fluttering of their wings. It may also be used as an onomatopeia for sounds similar to it, e.g. 磨刀霍霍 (to sharpen one's swords on a grindstone). As birds fly swiftly and in all directions in the rain, the character 霍 has taken on the senses of "quickly" and "freely", e.g. 霍然而癒 (to recover from an illness quickly), 電光霍霍 (the flashing of lightning) and 揮霍 (to spend freely).

fèn

金文的奮字，從隹從衣從母，其中的"衣"象徵鳥兒的羽毛翅膀，表示鳥兒在田間振翅飛翔的意思。奮的本義指鳥兒張開翅膀飛翔，引申為舉起、搖動、鼓動，又引申為振作、發揚之義。

【奮飛】鳥振翅高飛，比喻人的奮發有為。

【奮勇】鼓動勇氣。

【奮臂】高舉手臂，振臂而起。

【奮不顧身】勇往直前，不顧己身之安危。

金文

小篆

In the Bronze Inscriptions, the character 奮 consists of 隹 (bird), 衣 (feather) and 田 (field), signalling that birds are flying across fields with their wings spread. Hence its original meaning birds taking wings, from which have derived its senses of "raising", "exerting oneself" and "carrying on".

【奮飛】 to fly vigorously

【奮勇】 to summon up all one's courage and energy

【奮臂】 to raise one's hand

【奮不顧身】 to dash ahead regardless of one's safety

jìn

進字是個會意字。甲骨文的進字，從隹從止，隹即鳥，止即趾（腳），表示行走，所以進是鳥行走或飛行的意思。金文進字又增加一個表示行動的符號"彳"，就更能表明前進之意。進的本義為前行，即向前移動，與"退"相對；又指進入，與"出"相對。此外，進又有推薦、呈進之義。

【進退維谷】進退兩難。谷，比喻困難的境地。

甲骨文　　　　　金文　　　　　小篆

進 is an ideograph. In the Oracle-Bone Inscriptions, the character 進 consists of 隹 (bird) and 止 (foot), signalling that a bird is walking or flying. In the Bronze Inscriptions, a walking part (彳) is added to emphasize its meaning of moving forward. The character 進 primarily means to move forward, opposite to 退 (to retreat). It may also mean "to enter", opposite to 出 (to exit). In addition, it may mean "to recommend" and "to present".

【進退維谷】 to be caught in a dilemma

fēi

小篆的飛字，像鳥兒張開翅膀在空中飛翔的樣子，它的本義即指飛翔。引申言之，則凡物在天空飄蕩，都叫做"飛"，如飛蓬、飛雪。飛字還可用來形容快速、急促之意。

【飛揚】飛舞，飄揚。又比喻精神振奮，意志昂揚。

【飛揚跋扈】指驕橫恣肆，不守法度。

【飛短流長】指流言蜚語，說短道長，造謠中傷。

小篆

In the Later Seal Character, the character 飛 looks like a bird flying with its wings spread, hence its primary meaning "to fly". From this meaning has derived its use for anything floating in the air, e.g. 飛蓬 (fleabane), 飛雪 (fluttering snowflakes). 飛 may also be used in the sense of "swift".

【飛揚】 to fly upward

【飛揚跋扈】 arrogant and domineering

【飛短流長】 to spread embroidered stories and malicious gossip

fēi

甲骨文、金文的非字，像兩扇反向的鳥翅之形。鳥兒張翅飛翔則兩翅必相背，故非的本義指違背，引申為責難、詆毀之義。非又指過失、不對，引申為不、不是之義。

【非凡】不平凡，不尋常。

【非同小可】指事關重大，不可輕視。

金文

小篆

In the Oracle-Bone Inscriptions and Bronze Inscriptions, the character 非 looks like two wings opposite to each other. The primary meaning of 非 is "to run counter to", from which have derived its meanings "to blame", "to reproach", "wrong" and "not".

【非凡】extraordinary

【非同小可】no small matter

jí

甲骨文、金文的集字，像一隻鳥飛落在樹枝上，表示棲息的意思。鳥類棲息，大多成群結隊，故小篆的集字變成三隻鳥停在樹上，表示聚集、集合之義。

甲骨文

金 文

小 篆

In the Oracle-Bone Inscriptions and Bronze Inscriptions, the character 集 looks like a bird resting on a branch of a tree, hence its original meaning "to perch". As birds usually perch together, the character 集 in the Later Seal Character consists of three bird parts (隹), and it has taken on the sense of "gathering" and "assembling".

chóu

讎字是個會意字。金文讎字是面對面的兩隻鳥,中間的"言"表示雙鳥對言的意思。讎的本義為對答、應答,引申為相對、對等、相當之義,又引申為指對手、仇敵。此外,讎字還有應驗、校對之義。

【讎問】指辯駁問難。

【讎校】校對文字。

【讎隙】仇恨、嫌隙。

金文　　　　　　小篆

The character 讎 is an ideograph. In the Bronze Inscriptions, the character 讎 looks like two birds facing each other, and the speech part (言) in the middle signals that they are talking. The original meaning of 讎 was "to reply" and "to respond", from which have derived its meanings of "corresponding", "equal", "opponent" and "enemy". In addition, 讎 may mean "to come true" and "to proofread".

【讎問】to retort

【讎校】to proofread

【讎隙】hatred

zhī

【只】

作為單位量詞"一隻"、"兩隻"的隻字，在甲骨文、金文和小篆中，均像是用手抓住一隻鳥形，其本義為一隻鳥。後來引申為"單"，與"雙"的意思相對。如《宋史》："肅宗而下，咸隻日臨朝，雙日不坐。"（從唐肅宗李亨以下，都是單日上朝，雙日就不坐朝問政）。簡化字的只字，乃是借用了另外一個同音字的字形。它又有"僅僅"、"只有"等意，而這個意思卻是從繁體的"祇"字而來的。

甲骨文

金 文

小 篆

The character 隻 in the function of a classifier looks like a bird in the grasp of a hand in all ancient writing systems, the Oracle-Bone Inscriptions, Bronze Inscriptions and Later Seal Character, and its primary meaning is "a single bird". From this sense has derived its meaning of "odd number", opposite to 雙 (even number). For example, the *History of the Song Dynasty* records, "肅宗而下，咸隻日臨朝，雙日不坐。(After the reign of Suzong, every emperor meets his ministers on odd days only, not on even days.)" But the character 只 in the modern simplified form was originally the form of another character. In addition, 只 also means "only", which was originally expressed by 祇.

shuāng

　　用手捉住一隻鳥為一隻，捉住兩隻鳥為一雙，這就是古文字雙字的會意所在。所以，雙的本義是指兩個、一對，引申為指偶數，與“單”相對。

【雙關】用詞造句時表面上是一個意思，而暗中還隱藏着另一個意思。

【雙管齊下】原指畫畫時兩管筆同時並用，比喻兩方面同時進行。

【雙飛雙宿】比喻夫妻或情侶同居同行。

小篆

In ancient writing systems, the character 雙 looks like two birds in the grasp of a hand, hence its primary meaning "two" and "couple". From this sense has derived the extended meaning of "even number", opposite to 單 (odd number).

【雙關】pun

【雙管齊下】(lit.) to paint a picture with two brushes at the same time; to work along two lines

【雙飛雙宿】(of couples or lovers) to work and rest together

jiāo

金文焦字從隹從火，像鳥在火上之形，即用火烤鳥之意。小篆從三隹在火上，則表示烤了很多鳥的意思。焦的本義為烤鳥，引申為指物體經火烤而呈乾枯狀態，又泛指乾枯、乾燥，還可以用來表示人的心裡煩躁、煩憂之義。

【焦土】指焚燒後的土地。泛指乾枯的土地。

【焦心】心情憂急。

【焦渴】比喻心情急切。又指乾涸。

【焦金流石】金屬燒焦，石頭熔化，極言陽光的酷烈。

【焦頭爛額】本形容救火時燒焦頭、灼傷額。後比喻處境十分狼狽窘迫。

金文   小篆

In the Bronze Inscriptions, the character 焦 consists of 隹 (bird) and 火 (fire), signalling to roast a bird with fire. In the Later Seal Character, there are three bird parts on a fire, indicating many birds are being roasted. The primary meaning of 焦 is to roast a bird, from which have derived its use for anything that is dried by fire, the state of being dry and that of being worried.

【焦土】 scorched earth

【焦心】 worried

【焦渴】 terribly thirsty

【焦金流石】 (lit.) burnt metal and molten rock; the scorching sun

【焦頭爛額】 (of a person) badly burnt; in a terrible fix

yí

甲骨文、金文的彝字，像一個人雙手抓住一隻反縛雙翅的雞，雞頭旁兩點代表殺雞時濺出的血滴，表示殺雞取血用來祭祀的意思。彝的本義指殺雞以祭，引申為泛指祭器，又專指古代一種盛酒的器具。此外，彝還有法度、常規的意思。

【彝器】古代青銅祭器，如鍾鼎尊俎之類。
【彝倫】天地人之常道。

甲骨文　　　　　金　文　　　　　小　篆

In the Oracle-Bone Inscriptions and Bronze Inscriptions, the character 彝 looks like two hands holding a chicken whose wings are bound at the back, and there are two dots beside the chicken standing for drops of blood, signalling to kill a chicken and use its blood as an offering to spirits. Its original meaning was to offer a chicken as a sacrifice, from which has derived its reference to any sacrificial object, a type of wine vessel in particular. In addition, 彝 also means "regulations" and "norms".

【彝器】bronze vessels used in sacrifice-offering ceremonies

【彝倫】order of importance or seniority in human relationships

yǔ

甲骨文的羽字，像鳥類羽翼之形，其本義乃是指禽類翅膀上的毛，所以由"羽"字所組成的字大都與羽毛或翅有關，如習、翎、翔、翻、翼等。羽又是鳥類的代稱，如"奇禽異羽"。羽還可以代指箭矢。因為古代箭尾上部綁有羽毛以使箭在飛行時定向，稱為"鵰翎箭"，所以有時就用羽來代稱箭。如"負羽從軍"，就是揹負着箭矢去參軍打仗的意思，而不是揹着羽毛去作戰。

甲骨文　　　　　小篆

In the Oracle-Bone Inscriptions, the character 羽 looks like feathers, hence its primary meaning "feather". Characters with 羽 as a component most have to do with feathers and wings, e.g. 習 (to practise flying), 翎 (feather), 翔 (to fly), 翻 (the flying of birds) and 翼 (wing). 羽 may also be used as a substitute for bird, e.g. 奇禽異羽 (rare birds). As arrows usually have feathers at their ends, known as 鵰翎箭 (feathered arrow), the character 羽 may also refer to arrows, e.g. 負羽從軍 (to join the army with arrows on the back).

fān

番為"蹯"的本字。金文番字,上部像野獸的腳掌印,下部從田,表示野獸在田間留下的足跡。番的本義指獸足,引申為更替、輪值之義,又用作量詞,相當於次、種的意思。舊時漢族蔑視外族,稱少數民族或外國為"番邦",即禽獸野蠻之邦的意思。

【番地】舊時指我國西部邊遠地區。唐時多指吐蕃(bó)。

【番役】輪番服役。又指緝捕罪犯的差役,也稱"番子"。

金文

小篆

番 was the original form of 蹯. In the Bronze Inscriptions, the character 番 has a part like a foot print of beast on top of a field part, signalling the track left by beasts on the field. The original meaning of 番 was the foot or claw of a beast, from which have derived its meaning "to alternate" and its use as a classifier of actions. In the past, the Han nationality despised the national minorities and foreigners, and referred to them as 番邦, meaning "barbarous peoples".

【番地】the remote areas in the west

【番役】to do forced labour alternatively

pí

金文的皮字，像用手（又）剝取獸皮，其本義即為獸皮，又指經過加工脫去毛的獸皮，即"皮革"。皮字還可用來泛指一切物體的表面層，如人皮、樹皮、地皮等，引申為表面、膚淺等義，如皮相（指表面膚淺的認識或只看表面）、皮傅（指以膚淺的見解牽強附會）等。

【皮之不存，毛將焉附】連皮都沒有了，毛往哪兒依附呢？（焉：哪兒）比喻事物失去了藉以生存的基礎，就不能存在。

金文

小篆

In the Bronze Inscriptions, the character 皮 looks like a hand removing the skin of a beast. Hence its primary meaning "hide", or the skin that has been tanned, i.e. leather. But it may also refer to the surface layer of anything, e.g. 人皮 (human skin), 樹皮 (bark) and 地皮 (ground). Used as an adjective, it means "superficial" and "shallow", e.g. 皮相 (superficial understanding), 皮傅 (to infer on the basis of a superficial knowledge).

【皮之不存，毛將焉附】With the skin gone, what can the hair adhere to? A thing cannot exist without its basis.

ròu

古文字肉字，像一塊帶肋骨的牲肉，其本義即指動物的肌肉，如羊肉、豬肉等；由動物的肌肉又引申為指植物（如蔬菜瓜果等）去皮去核而中間可食的部份，如棗肉、筍肉、龍眼肉等。漢字中凡以"肉"（月）為偏旁的字都與人和動植物的肌體有關，如腸、股、腳、腰、臉等。

甲骨文　　　　　小篆

In ancient writing systems, the character 肉 looks like a piece of meat with ribs. It primarily refers to the flesh of animals, e.g. 羊肉 (mutton), 豬肉 (pork). From this use has derived its reference to the soft eatable part of a plant, e.g. 棗肉 (jujube), 筍肉 (bamboo shoot) and 龍眼肉 (longan pulp). Characters with 肉 or 月 as a component all have to do with the parts of a human being or animal, e.g. 腸 (intestine), 股 (thigh), 腳 (foot), 腰 (waist) and 臉 (face).

yǒu

　　古文字的有字，從又從肉（月），像人手持肉塊之形，表示持有之意。有的本義指佔有、取得，與"無"相對，引申為表示存在、發生之義。

【有口皆碑】人人滿口稱頌，像記載功德的石碑。

【有備無患】事先有準備，可以避免禍患。

甲骨文　　　　　　金 文　　　　　　小 篆

In ancient writing systems, the character 有 consists of 又 (hand) and 月 (meat), signalling a man with a piece of meat in hand. Hence its primary meaning is "to possess" and "to obtain", opposite to 無 (not to have); from which have derived its extended meanings "to exist" and "to take place".

【有口皆碑】 to win universal praise

【有備無患】 Where there is precaution, there is no danger.

zhì

小篆的炙字，從肉在火上，表示用火烤肉的意思。它的本義為燒烤，又指烤熟的肉。

【炙手可熱】火焰灼手。比喻權勢和氣焰之盛。

【炙冰使燥】比喻所行適與所求相反。

小篆

In the Later Seal Character, the character 炙 consists of 月 (meat) and 火 (fire), signalling to roast a piece of meat by fire. Its primary meaning is "to roast", but it may refer to the meat roasted as well.

【炙手可熱】 (lit.) If you stretch out your hand you feel the heat; the supreme arrogance of a person with great power

【炙冰使燥】 to dry ice by fire; to try in vain

gǔ

骨，即骨骼，指人或動物肢體中堅硬的組織部份。甲骨文的骨字，像一堆剔去肉的脛骨之形；小篆骨字加肉旁（月）則表示骨肉相連的意思。漢字中凡從"骨"的字都與人或動物的骨骼有關，如骷、骰、骼、髀、髓等。

【骨幹】支撐人或動物形體的骨架，比喻在整體中起主要作用的人或事物。

【骨肉】比喻緊密相連，不可分割的關係。又指至親，如父母兄弟子女等。

【骨格】指人的品質、風格。又指詩文的骨架和格式。

小篆

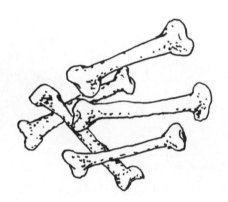

骨 refers to the hard parts of body, i.e. bones. In the Oracle-Bone Inscriptions, the character 骨 looks like bones with flesh cut off. In the Later Seal Character, a flesh part (月) is added to signal that flesh and bone are related to each other. Character with 骨 as a component all have to do with the bones of a human being or animal, e.g. 骷 (skeleton), 骰 (bone dice), 骼 (bone), 髀 (thigh bone) and 髓 (marrow).

【骨幹】backbone; the life and soul; mainstay

【骨肉】flesh and blood; kindred

【骨格】(of a person) character; (of writing) format

jiǎo

甲骨文和金文角字,像獸角之形,其本義即指獸角,如牛角、羊角、鹿角等。牛羊之類的角,是護身和比試體力的一種武器,所以把比武和決鬥勝負稱為"角力"。此外,角在上古時曾充當過飲酒的容器,後來用作計量單位,如"兩角酒"就相當於"兩杯酒",所以以角為偏旁的多與酒器和量器有關,如觚、觴、斛等。"角"用於競爭、戲角人物義,讀 jué。

【角(jué)逐】 爭奪,競爭取勝。
【角(jué)色】 傳統戲劇演員的類別。

甲骨文　　　　　金 文　　　　　小 篆

In both the Oracle-Bone Inscriptions and Bronze Inscriptions, the character 角 looks like the horn of an animal, such as an ox, sheep or deer. The horn in animals like oxen and sheep is a weapon to fight and protect themselves, so the character 角 has taken on the sense of "competition in physical strength" (角力). In former times, the horn was also used as a vessel for drinking, thus the character 角 is used as a unit of volume like 杯 (glass). As a result, characters with 角 as a component most refer to vessels, e.g. 觚 (a wine vessel), 觴 (a wine glass) and 斛 (a vessel for measuring). In the senses of "contend" and "dramatic role", it is pronounced as jué.

【角(jué)逐】 to contend
【角(jué)色】 dramatic role

jiě

甲骨文解字，像兩手解判牛角之形，其本義為剖開、分解肢體，如"庖丁解牛"；引申為解開、消散、分裂、脫去、排除等義；進一步引申，則還有分析、解釋、理解、曉悟等義。此外，解字又是一個多音多義詞：表示押送之意的解應讀為 **jiè**（音介）；而作為姓氏的解，則應讀為 **xiè**（音謝）。

【解人】見事高明能通曉人意者。

【解(jiè)元】科舉時，鄉試第一名稱為解元，也稱解首。因鄉試本稱解試，故名。

【解決】排難解紛而作出決斷。

【解放】除罪釋放。現在通指解除束縛，得到自由。

【解衣推食】贈人衣食，指關心別人生活。

甲骨文

金文

小篆

In the Oracle-Bone Inscriptions, the character 解 looks like two hands opening up an ox horn. Its primary meaning is to dismember, e.g. 庖丁解牛 (the skillful dismemberment of an ox by a cook). From this meaning have derived its senses "to divide", "to separate", "to untie", "to dispel", "to analyze", "to explain" and "to understand". Pronounced as jiè, it means "to send under guard". And as a surname, it is pronounced as xiè.

【解人】 person of great understanding

【解(jiè)元】 first prize winner in a local examination of the old system

【解決】 to solve

【解放】 to liberate

【解衣推食】 to help somebody by offering him food and clothing

máo

金文的毛字，像人或動物的毛髮之形。它的本義是指人和動物身上的毛髮，泛指動植物的皮上所生的叢狀物，引申為指粗糙的，未加工的。從"毛"之字大都與毛髮有關，如氈、毫、毯等。

【毛皮】帶毛的獸皮，可製衣、帽、褥子等。

【毛糙】粗糙，不細緻。

【毛茸茸】形容動植物細毛叢生的樣子。

【毛骨悚然】形容很害怕的樣子。

金文　　　　　　小篆

In the Bronze Inscriptions, the character 毛 looks like the hair of a man or animal, hence its primary meaning "hair". But it may also refer to other thread-like growth from the skin of an animal or plant, from which has derived its meaning "rough", "crude". Characters with 毛 as a component most have to do with hair, e.g. 氈 (felt), 毫 (fine long hair) and 毯 (blanket; carpet).

【毛皮】fur

【毛糙】crude; careless

【毛茸茸】hairy

【毛骨悚然】with one's hair standing on end; absolutely
　　　　　terrified

植物類

Plant

zhú

竹，即竹子，是一種多年生的禾本科木質常綠植物。金文竹字，像兩枝下垂的竹葉，以此代表竹子。在古書中，竹還可用來代指竹簡和竹製管樂器，如笙簫之類。

【竹帛】竹指竹簡，帛指白絹。古代還未使用紙張之前，多以竹簡和絹帛為書寫材料。後用以指書冊、史籍。

金 文

小 篆

竹 refers to an evergreen perennial plant of the grass family — bamboo. In the Bronze Inscriptions, the character 竹 looks like two hanging bamboo branches with leaves, signifying "bamboo". But the character 竹 may also refer to bamboo slips on which one writes, or musical instruments made of bamboo, such as flutes and pipes.

【竹帛】(lit.) bamboo and silk; writing material; books

mù

　　這是一個象形字，字形象一棵小樹的形狀，上有枝，下有根，中間是樹幹。所以，木的本義即指樹，是木本植物的通稱；現在多用於指木材、木料或某些木製的器物，如木馬、木工、木屐、木偶等。在漢字中，凡以木為偏旁的字，大都與樹木有關，如本、末、析、果等。

甲骨文

金　文

小　篆

This is a pictograph, looking like a small tree with its branches on top and roots underneath. Hence its primary meaning "tree" or "woody plant". Nowadays it mainly refers to wood, timber and objects made of wood, e.g. 木馬 (rocking horse), 木工 (wood work; carpenter), 木屐 (clogs) and 木偶 (puppet). Characters with 木 as a component most have to do with trees, e.g. 本 (root), 末 (treetop), 析 (to split logs) and 果 (fruit).

lín

　　林字由兩個木字組成，表示樹木眾多，其本義是指成片的樹木。引申為指人或事物的會聚叢集。如說船隻多為"帆檣林立"；而儒林、藝林、民族之林、書林等則是比喻人或事物之多。

【林泉】山林與泉石，指幽靜宜於隱居之地。
【林莽】指草木深邃平遠的境域。
【林林總總】林林：紛紛眾多貌。形容事物繁多。

甲骨文

金文

小篆

The character 林 consists of two tree parts (木), signalling there are many trees, hence its primary meaning "forest". But it can also refer to people or things gathered together, e.g. 帆檣林立 (a forest of masts), 儒林 (a society of scholars), 藝林 (art circles), 民族之林 (nationalities in the world) and 書林 (stack room).

【林泉】(lit.) forest and spring; quiet and secluded
　　　　area
【林莽】luxuriant vegetation
【林林總總】things of all kinds

sēn

森字由三個"木"組成，是樹木眾多、叢林茂密的意思。林木茂密，往往給人一種陰沉幽暗、肅穆之感，所以森字又有陰森、森嚴之義。

【森林】指叢生的群木，現在通常指大片生長的樹木。
【森羅萬象】指紛然羅列的各種事物或現象。

甲骨文　　　　　小篆

The character 森 consists of three tree parts (木), signalling that there is a luxuriant forest. In forests, one often feels something cloudy, gloomy, and solemn, so the character 森 also means "gloomy" and "stern".

【森林】forest
【森羅萬象】myriads of things

yì

甲骨文、金文的藝字，像一個人雙手捧着一棵樹苗，樹下有土，表示種樹於土之義。它的本義為栽樹，引申為泛指種植。種植在古代可以說是一種非常重要的生活技能，所以藝術又可以引申為指某種特殊的才能或技術，如藝術、工藝等。

【藝術】泛指各種技術技能。

甲骨文

金文

小篆

In the Oracle-Bone Inscriptions and Bronze Inscriptions, the character 藝 looks like a man holding a sapling in his two hands, signalling to plant a tree. From this primary meaning has derived its more general sense of cultivation. It was a very important skill to be able to grow things in former times, so the character 藝 has also come to mean "talent" or "skill", e.g. 藝術 (art), 工藝 (craft).

【藝術】art

xiū

休字從人從木，像一個人背靠大樹乘涼歇息的樣子，其本義即為歇息，又有停止之義。能夠自由自在地背靠大樹休息一下，對於在炎炎烈日下從事田間勞動的人來説，無疑是一種美好的享受了。因此，休字又有美好、吉利、喜樂等義。

【休養生息】 休養：休息調養。生息：人口繁殖。指在戰爭或社會大動盪後，減輕人民負擔，安定生活，恢復元氣。

【休戚相關】 休：喜悅，吉利。戚：憂愁，悲哀。憂喜、禍福彼此相關連。形容關係密切，利害相關。

甲骨文

金文

小篆

The character 休 consists of 人 (man) and 木 (tree), signalling a man is taking a rest against a tree. Hence its primary meaning "to rest" and "to stop". It is no doubt a great pleasure for a labourer in the sun to take a rest under a tree, so the character 休 also means "good", "lucky" and "happy".

【休養生息】 to rest and build up strength

【休戚相關】 to be linked together in common joys and sorrows

zhī

支為 "枝" 的本字。小篆支字，像人手持一條小樹枝（或竹枝）的形狀。支的本義指枝條，引申為指分支、支派、支流；用作動詞，有伸出、豎起、支撐、支持、分派、指使等義。

【支吾】抵拒，勉強撐持。又指言語牽強，有應付搪塞的意思。
【支使】唆使或指派別人做事。
【支配】調度。

金 文　　　　小 篆

支 was the original form of 枝, meaning "branch". In the Later Seal Character, the character 支 looks like a man with a branch of a tree (or a bamboo) in hand. But it may also refer to other things similar to the branches of a tree, e.g. 支流 (the tributary of a river). As a verb, it means "to protrude", "to raise", "to prop up", "to support" and "to order about."

【支吾】to equivocate
【支使】to order about
【支配】to arrange

zhū

古文字的朱字，像一棵樹木的形狀，中間的一點（或短橫）為指示符號，指明樹幹所在的位置。朱的本義指樹幹，是"株"的本字。後來朱字多借用來指顏色，即朱紅，指比較鮮艷的紅色，故另造"株"字來代替它的本義。

【朱門】紅漆門。古代王侯貴族的住宅大門漆成紅色，表示尊貴，故稱豪門大戶為朱門。

【朱批】清代皇帝在奏章上用紅筆所寫的批示叫"朱批"。

金文

小篆

朱 was the original form of 株, meaning "stem". In ancient writing systems, the character 朱 looks like a tree with a dot (or a short stroke) in the middle denoting the position of stem. Nowadays, however, 朱 is used to denote a colour of bright red, and its original meaning is expressed by 株.

【朱門】 (lit.) red-lacquered door; wealthy family

【朱批】 the emperor's comment on reports and suggestions by his ministers in the Qing Dynasty

běn

本的本義指樹木的根或莖幹。從本字的形體看,是在木的根部加上圓點或一短橫,以指明樹根的位置所在。由此引申出根本、基礎、本體、主體等意義。

【本末】樹木的根和梢,也用以比喻事物的始終、原委或主次、先後。

【本質】事物本來的形體,又指事物本來的性質。

【本末倒置】主次顛倒。本末,比喻事物的根本和枝節。

金 文

小 篆

本 originally referred to the root or stem of a tree. The character 本 is made up of a tree part (木) and a dot or short stroke at the bottom denoting the position of root. From this primary meaning have derived its senses of "foundation", "basis", "thing-in-itself" and "main part".

【本末】 (lit.) root and treetop; the beginning and end; the fundamental and incidental

【本質】 essence

【本末倒置】 to take the branch for the root; to put the cart before the horse

mò

末的本義指樹梢。從末字形體看，是在木上加一短畫，以指明樹梢所在的位置。由樹梢之義，末字又泛指事物的頂端、尾部，引申為指最終，最後和非根本的、不重要的事物。再進一步引申出細小的、渺小的、淺薄的等義。

【末流】河水的下游，也用來比喻事勢的後來發展狀態，又指衰亂時代的不良風習。

【末路】絕路，比喻沒有前途。

【末節】小節，小事。

【末學】膚淺、無本之學。

金文

小篆

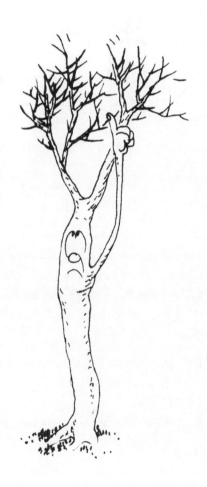

末 originally referred to the tip of a tree. The character 末 is made up of a tree part (木) and a short stroke on the top denoting the position of the tip of a tree. From this primary meaning have derived its meanings of "top", "end", "last", "incidental", "unimportant", "minor" and "shallow".

【末流】lower reaches

【末路】dead end

【末節】minor details

【末學】shallow knowledge

wèi

古文字的未字，像樹木枝葉重疊的樣子，表示枝葉茂盛的意思。此字後來多借用為干支名，是地支的第八位，其本義不再使用。此外未字又可以用作否定副詞，表示沒有、不曾、不等意義。

【未來】佛教語。泛指現在以後的時間。

【未然】還沒有成為事實。

【未遂】沒有達到（目的）。

【未雨綢繆】趁着天沒下雨，先修繕房屋門窗。比喻事前準備或預防。

甲骨文

金文

小篆

In ancient writing systems, the character 未 looks like a tree with leaves overlapping one another, signalling it is a luxuriant tree. But this character is now mainly used as a name of the eighth Earthly Branch, a traditional Chinese system of sequence, and its original meaning is lost. In addition 未 is used as a negative adverb, meaning "not".

【未來】future

【未然】unrealized

【未遂】not accomplished

【未雨綢繆】to repair the house before it rains; to take precautions

cì

　　朿是"刺"的本字。甲骨文、金文的朿字，像一棵長滿尖刺的樹木之形。它的本義是指長在樹木上的刺。許慎《説文解字》："朿，木芒也。"芒，即尖刺。漢字中凡從"朿"之字，都與帶刺的樹木有關，如棗、棘等。而刺字從朿從刀，又以朿為聲，屬於朿的後起字。

甲骨文

金文

小篆

朿 was the original form of 刺. In the Oracle-Bone Inscriptions and Bronze Inscriptions, the character 朿 looks like a tree with thorns all over it. Hence its original meaning "thorn". Xu Shen says in his *Origin of Chinese Characters,* "朿 refers to the thorns of a tree". Characters with 朿 as a component most refer to trees with thorns, e.g. 棗 (jujube tree), 棘 (thorn bushes). The character 刺, consisting of 朿, which also serves as the phonetic, and 刀 (knife), is a later development.

zǎo

棗，即棗樹，屬喬木，幼枝上有刺，結核果，味甜可食，木質堅硬，可供器具、雕版等材用。棗字由上下兩個"朿"重疊而成，表示它是帶刺的挺生喬木，而非低矮叢生的灌木。

【棗本】以棗木刻版印刷的書本。
【棗梨】即梨棗，指木刻書版。

金文

小篆

棗 refers to the jujube tree, which has thorns when young, produces sweet fruits with stones inside and supplies timber for furniture. The character 棗 consists of two thorn parts (朿) one on top of the other, signalling it is a tall tree, not a bush.

【棗本】 books printed in the past when the printing plate was made of jujube wood
【棗梨】 (also 梨棗) cut blocks for printing

jí

棘，是一種叢生的小棗樹，即酸棗樹。棘字由兩個"束"並列組成，表示它是一種低矮叢生的帶刺小灌木，而非挺生的喬木。此外，棘字還可用來泛指山野叢生的帶刺小灌木和帶刺的草本植物。

金文　　　　　小篆

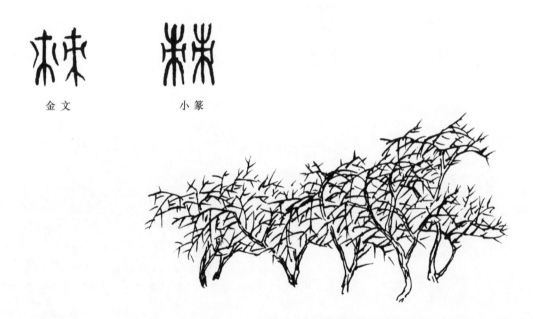

棘 refers to a sour jujube tree, short and bushlike. The character 棘 consists of two thorn parts (束) side by side, signalling it is short and bushlike. But 棘 may also refer to other thorny bushes and herbaceous plants as well.

jīng

荊，是一種帶刺的小灌木，枝條可用來編筐籃。金文的荊本是個會意字，像一個人的手腳扎滿荊刺之形；後來或加"井"作為聲符，成為形聲字。由於荊字的人形與"刀"極為接近，故金文荊字或訛變為從刀井聲，與"刑"字同。小篆荊字以刑為聲符而增加草頭，當是從金文的訛體演變而來。

【荊棘】泛指山野叢生的帶刺小灌木。又用來比喻環境困難，障礙極多。

金文

小篆

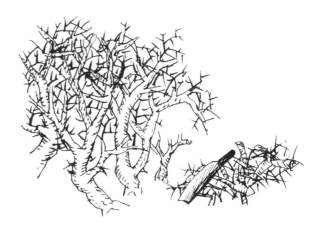

荊 refers to a thorny bush, whose branches may be made into baskets. In the early Bronze Inscriptions, the character 荊 is an ideograph, looking like a man whose hands and feet are full of thorns. In the late Bronze Inscriptions, a well part (井) is added to serve as the phonetic, resulting in a phonetic compound. As the man part in it is very similar to a knife part, sometimes the character has a knife part (刀) as the radical by mistake, and 井 as the phonetic, as if it were 刑 (punishment). In the Later Seal Character, a grass part (艹) is added on top of the mistaken variant in the Bronze Inscriptions (刑), resulting in the present form 荊.

【荊棘】thistles and thorns; difficulty

shù

　　古文字的束字，像是用繩索綑紮口袋兩端的形狀，有的形體則像綑綁木柴的樣子。所以，束字的本義為綑綁，後來又引申為管束，束縛等義。

甲骨文

金　文

小　篆

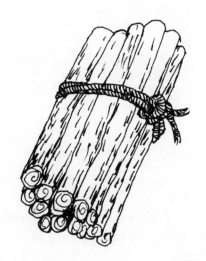

In ancient writing systems, the character 束 looks like a bag with its two ends tied up. Sometimes it looks like some firewood bound together. Hence its primary meaning "to tie", "to bind", from which have derived its senses of "restraining" and "checking".

cháo

小篆的巢字，下面是木，木上是鳥的窩巢形，巢上的三曲則像巢中幼鳥伸出來的頭嘴之形，表示鳥兒在樹上的窩巢中棲息的意思。所以巢字的本義是指鳥的窩，也泛指蜂窩、蟻窩等。

【巢穴】鳥獸藏身棲息的地方。穴指洞穴。

甲骨文

金 文

小 篆

In the Later Seal Character, the character 巢 looks like a bird nest on a tree, the three curving strokes on the top standing for the heads of young birds in the nest, signalling that birds are staying in the nest on a tree. Apart from bird nests, 巢 may refer to resting places of other creatures as well, e.g. 蜂巢 (honeycomb), 蟻巢 (ant nest).

【巢穴】nest; den; lair

Xī

甲骨文、金文的西字，像一個鳥巢之形。小篆西字，則更在鳥巢之上添一曲線以為鳥形，表示鳥在巢上之意。所以，西的本義指鳥巢，又有棲息之義。百鳥歸巢棲息，一般在黃昏太陽落山的時候，故西字又可用作方位名，指太陽落山的方向——西方，與"東"相對。

【西風】指秋風。又喻指日趨沒落的腐朽勢力。

【西天】中國佛教徒稱佛祖所在的古天竺為"西天"，即今印度。

甲骨文

金文

小篆

In the Oracle-Bone Inscriptions and Bronze Inscriptions, the character 西 looks like a bird nest. In the Later Seal Character, it has a curving line above the nest, signalling a bird is staying in the nest. Hence the character 西 originally meant "nest" or "to rest". As a bird comes back to its nest for a rest when the sun sets, the character 西 has come to be used as a locative, denoting the direction in which the sun sets, i.e. the west, opposite to 東 (east).

【西風】autumn wind; decadent and declining forces

【西天】(Buddhism) Western Paradise (the place where Sakyamuni, the founder of Buddhism, stays, which is to the southwest of China, i.e. the present-day India.)

guǒ

果是一個象形字。甲骨文的果字，像一棵樹上結滿果實的樣子；金文果字的果實減少為一個，但果形更大更突出；小篆果字則誤果形為田，意思就不明顯了。果字本義是指樹木所結之實，引申為指事物的結局（如"結果"），又有充實、飽滿以及決斷等義。

【果報】即因果報應，佛教語。通俗一點講，就是所謂的善有善報，惡有惡報。

【果腹】指肚子很飽或吃飽肚子。

【果斷】有決斷，不遲疑猶豫。

甲骨文

金文

小篆

果 is a pictograph. In the Oracle-Bone Inscriptions, the character 果 looks like a tree full of fruits on it. In the Bronze Inscriptions, the number of fruits is reduced to one but the size is increased. In the Later Seal Character, the fruit part becomes a field part (田) by mistake, losing its picturelike image. From its primary meaning of fruits of a tree have derived its extended meanings of "outcome", "substantial", "full" and "resolute".

【果報】 (Buddhism) Karma; Good will be rewarded with good, and evil with evil

【果腹】 to fill the stomach

【果斷】 resolute

mǒu

某為"梅"的本字。《說文解字》："某,酸果也。"古文字的某字,像樹上結果之形;又有人認為某字從木從甘,表示果實酸甜之意。總之,某的本義是指樹上結的酸果。此字後來多用為代詞,代指一定的或不定的人、地、事、物等;而另造"梅"字來代替它的本義。

金 文

小 篆

某 was the original form of 梅. The *Origin of Chinese Characters* says, "某 refers to the sour fruit". In ancient writing systems, the character 某 looks like a tree bearing fruits. Some people hold that 某 consists of 木 (tree) and 甘 (sweet), signalling its fruits are sour and sweet. Hence 某 originally referred to the sour fruit, now known as 梅 (plum). But this character is now used as a pronoun, referring to some particular person, place or thing, and its original meaning is expressed by 梅.

lì

甲骨文的栗字，像一棵樹的枝上結滿果實，果實的外殼長滿毛刺的樣子。這種長滿毛刺的果實就是栗子，俗稱"板栗"。栗的本義指栗子，又指栗樹。因栗子內殼堅硬，外皮毛刺繁密，故栗字又引申出堅硬、嚴密的意思。此外，栗又通"慄"，指因恐懼或寒冷而發抖。

【栗烈】猶溧冽，形容嚴寒。

【栗縮】戰栗畏縮。

甲骨文

金文

小篆

In the Oracle-Bone Inscriptions, the character 栗 looks like a tree full of prickly fruits — chestnuts, also known as 板栗. The character 栗 may refer to both the fruit and the tree. As the chestnut has a hard cover with dense prickles, the character 栗 has taken on the senses of "hard" and "tight". In addition 栗 may be used in the same sense of 慄, i.e. to tremble with cold or fear.

【栗烈】piercing cold

【栗縮】to shrink with fear

yè

葉是植物的營養器官之一，附生於莖、幹、枝條，多呈薄片狀。金文的葉字，上部的三點即像樹木枝上的葉片之形。小篆葉字增加草頭，表明葉子本身具有草本的特質。

【葉落歸根】比喻事物有了一定的歸宿，多指客居他鄉的人終究要回到本鄉。

金 文　　　　　小 篆

葉 refers to leaves, the usually flat and green parts of a plant that are joined to its stem or branches. In the Bronze Inscriptions, the character 葉 looks like a tree with three branches on top, on which there are three dots standing for leaves. In the Later Seal Character, a grass part is added on the top to signal that leaves are similar to grass in a way.

【葉落歸根】 (lit.) Falling leaves settle on their roots; A person residing elsewhere finally returns to his ancestral home.

sāng

桑即桑樹，是一種闊葉喬木，其葉可用來餵蠶。甲骨文的桑字是個象形字，像一棵枝葉繁茂的樹形。小篆的桑字，則樹葉與枝幹分離，葉形又訛變成三個"又"，已失去象形的意味。

【桑梓】桑樹和梓樹，代指家鄉。

【桑榆暮景】落日的餘輝照在桑榆樹梢上，比喻年老的時光。

甲骨文

小篆

桑 refers to the mulberry, a tall tree with broad leaves, which may serve as the food of silkworms. In the Oracle-Bone Inscriptions, the character 桑 is a pictograph, looking like a tree with luxuriant foliage. In the Later Seal Character, its leaf parts are separated from the branch parts and mistakenly changed into hand parts (又), destroying its picturelike image.

【桑梓】(lit.) mulberry and catalpa; hometown

【桑榆暮景】the evening of one's life

cǎi

【採】

采是一個會意字。甲骨文采字，像一個人用手去採摘樹上果實或樹葉的樣子，其本義為摘取，引申為搜羅、收集等義。金文、小篆的采字從爪從木，略有簡化；而繁體楷書增加手旁，則屬繁化。其實，采字上部的"爪"就是手形，增加手旁，是沒有必要的重複。

【采風】古代稱民歌為"風"，因稱搜集民間歌謠為"采風"。

甲骨文

金文

小篆

采 is an ideograph. In the Oracle-Bone Inscriptions, the character 采 looks like a hand picking fruits or leaves of a tree. Hence its primary meaning "to pick" and extended meaning "to gather". In the Bronze Inscriptions and Later Seal Character, the character 采 is somewhat simplified, made up of 爪 and 木. But the original complicated form in the Regular Script goes to the other direction by adding a hand part (扌) to it, which is in fact an unnecessary complication, since the part 爪 has already shown that hand is involved.

【采風】 to collect folk songs

huá

華為"花"的本字。甲骨文的華字，像一棵樹上繁花盛開的樣子。古代稱樹上開的花為"華"，稱草開的花為"榮"。所以，華的本義是指樹上開的花，後來泛指草木之花。鮮花盛開，表現出美麗光彩，象徵着繁榮茂盛，故華字又含有美觀、華麗和繁盛等義。

【華滋】茂盛。

【華瞻】指文章富麗多彩。

【華麗】美麗而有光彩。

【華而不實】只開花不結果。比喻外表好看，內容空虛；或言過其實。

甲骨文　　　　　　　金文　　　　　　　小篆

華 was the original form of 花. In the Oracle-Bone Inscriptions, the character 華 looks like a tree in full bloom. In former times, the flowers of a tree were known as 華 while those of a grass 榮. However, nowadays, 花 is used as a general term for any type of flower. As the trees and grasses in bloom look beautiful and luxuriant, the character 華 has also taken on the senses of "beautiful", "magnificent" and "prosperous".

【華滋】flourishing

【華瞻】flowery language

【華麗】magnificent

【華而不實】flashy and without substance

róng

　　金文榮字，像兩棵交相開放的花草形，上部的六個擴散的小點表示鮮花競放光艷照人的意思。榮的本義指草木開花。榮字是花開繁盛的樣子，含有茂盛、興盛的意思，又引申為光榮、榮耀之義。

【榮華】草木的花，又指興旺、茂盛，引申為富貴榮耀。

【榮枯】草木的盛衰，用來比喻政治上的得志和失意。

【榮譽】光榮的名譽。

金文

小篆

In the Bronze Inscriptions, the character 榮 looks like two grasses in blossom crossing each other, the three dots on each of them standing for flowers. Hence its original meaning "flower of a grass". As grasses in blossom look prosperous, the character 榮 has also taken on the senses of "prosperous" and "flourishing", from which have derived its senses of "glory" and "honour".

【榮華】glory; wealth and rank

【榮枯】(lit.) growth and withering of a plant; success and failure in a person's career

【榮譽】honour

bù

不為"胚"的本字。甲骨文的不字，上面的一橫表示地面，下面的鬚狀曲線表示種子萌發時首先向地下生長的胚根。所以，不字的本義乃指植物的胚種。不字後來多借用為否定詞，於是本義逐漸消失。

【不易之論】內容正確，不可改變的言論。

【不可救藥】病重到不可救治，比喻人或事物壞到無法挽救的地步。

【不一而足】不止一種或一次，而是很多。

甲骨文

金文

小篆

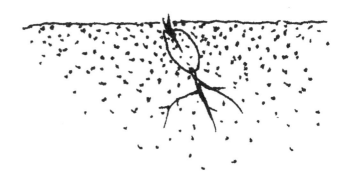

不 was the original form of 胚. In the Oracle-Bone Inscriptions, the character 不 has a horizontal stroke on top standing for the ground and some curving vertical lines beneath standing for the radicles. Hence its original meaning "the embryo of a plant". Nowadays, however, it is used as a negative adverb, meaning "no" or "not", and its original meaning is lost.

【不易之論】unalterable argument

【不可救藥】incurable; hopeless

【不一而足】by no means an isolated case; numerous

zhǔn

甲骨文、金文的屯字，像一顆植物種子剛剛發出來的小嫩芽，上面的圓圈（或圓點）是種子還未脫去的皮殼，所以屯字的本義當指草木初生的嫩芽。草木初生，需要破土脫殼，十分艱難，故屯字又有"艱難"之義。此外，屯又可讀為 tún，有聚集、駐守等義，如屯聚，屯戍（聚集兵力，駐守邊防）、屯兵（駐兵，又專指駐守邊疆、從事墾荒的軍隊）。

【屯(tún)落】指村莊。

甲骨文

金 文

小 篆

In the Oracle-Bone Inscriptions and Bronze Inscriptions, the character 屯 looks like a young plant newly grown from a seed, the small circle on the top standing for the seedcase that has not been detached yet. Hence its original meaning "seedling". At the beginning of its life, a seedling will have to break the ground, which is a hard job, so the character 屯 also has the meaning of "hard". In addition, 屯 pronounced as tún, means "to collect" and "to station", e.g. 屯聚 (to assemble), 屯戍 (to garrison the frontiers), 屯兵 (to station troops; troops stationed in the border).

【屯(tún)落】village

shēng

甲骨文生字，像地面上剛長出來的一株幼苗，其本義即指植物的生長、長出。後引申為泛指一切事物的產生和成長，如出生、生育、發生等；又引申為活的意思，與"死"相對；再引申為生命、生活、生年等義。總之，生字的引申義非常廣泛，可以組成的詞彙也非常之多。

【生氣】元氣，指使萬物生長發育之氣。

甲骨文

金文

小篆

In the Oracle-Bone Inscriptions, the character 生 looks like a young plant newly raised out of the ground. Hence its primary meaning is "the growth of a plant", from which have derived its more general use for the growth and development of anything, e.g. 出生 (to be born), 生育 (to give birth to), 發生 (to take place). It can also mean "alive", opposite to 死 (dead); and may be used in the senses of "life" and "living years". In short it can be used very extensively in many senses and form many words with other characters.

【生氣】vitality

cǎo

【艸】

小篆

草是草本植物的總稱。古文字的草是個會意字，像叢生的兩棵有稈有葉的小草之形。楷書草字為形聲字，實際上是借用"皂"的本字借用。漢字中凡從"草頭"的字大都與植物（特別是草本植物）有關，如芝、苗、荊、薪等。

【草莽】叢生的雜草，泛指荒野。又指草茅，喻指在野。

【草菅人命】把人命看得和野草一樣。

【草稿】指起草後未經改定膳正的文字。

草 means "grass". In ancient writing systems, the character 草 is an ideograph, looking like two young grasses with their stalks and leaves. The character 草 in the Regular Script is a phonetic compound, which was actually the original form of 皂 (Chinese honey locust). Characters with the top of 草, i.e. 艹, as a component most have to do with plants, especially herbaceous plants, e.g. 芝 (a fragrant herb, technically known as Dahurian angelica), 苗 (seedling), 荊 (thorn) and 薪 (firewood).

【草莽】 a rank growth of grass; (fig.) not in office

【草菅人命】 to treat human life as if it were not worth a straw

【草稿】 draft

huì

卉是各種草的總稱。一般多指供觀賞的草，如花卉、奇花異卉等。小篆的卉字，像叢生的三棵小草之形，表示草木眾多的意思。

【卉木】即草木。
【卉服】用草織的衣服。又稱"卉衣"。
【卉醴】指花蜜。

小篆

卉 is a general term for the different kinds of grass. Nowadays, it mainly refers to ornamental grasses, e.g. 花卉 (flowers and plants), 奇花異卉 (rare flowers and grasses). In the Later Seal Character, the character 卉 looks like three grasses, signalling there are many grasses.

【卉木】grasses and plants
【卉服】(also 卉衣) clothing made of grass
【卉醴】nectar

chú

甲骨文、金文的芻字，像一隻手抓住兩棵草木之形，表示用手拔草的意思。它的本義為拔草，又指割草。割草是為了餵牲口，所以芻專指餵牲口的草，又指用草料餵牲口，引申為指食草的牲口，如牛羊等。

【芻言】草野之人的言談。常用謙稱自己的言論，又作"芻議"。

【芻秣】飼養牛馬的草料。

【芻豢】指牛羊犬豕之類的家畜，牛羊食草為芻，犬豕食穀為豢。也指供祭祀的犧牲。

【芻靈】茅草紮成的人馬，古代殉葬用品。

甲骨文

小篆

In the Oracle-Bone Inscriptions and Bronze Inscriptions, the character 芻 looks like a hand taking hold of two grasses, signalling to pull up grasses with a hand. Hence its original meaning "to pull up grass", "to cut grass". The grass pulled up or cut will serve as food for cattle, so the character 芻 has come to refer to hay in particular, to the feeding of hay to cattle, and even to the cattle that take the hay.

【芻言】(also 芻議) rustic opinion; my humble opinion

【芻秣】fodder

【芻豢】(1) domestic animals like cattle, sheep, dogs and pigs (2) sacrifices

【芻靈】human figure or horse made of straw, used as funerary objects

miáo

苗字是個會意字。小篆的苗字，像草生於田中之形。它的本義是指莊稼，特指未揚花結實之禾，也可用來泛指所有初生的植物。苗字由初生之義，還可引申為泛指事物的預兆，又指後代。

【苗條】原指植物細長而多姿，現多用來指婦女身材細長柔美。

【苗頭】事物的預兆。

【苗裔】後代。

【苗而不秀】只長了苗而沒有結穗，比喻本身條件雖好，但沒有成就。

小篆

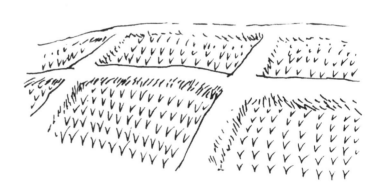

苗 is an ideograph. In the Later Seal Character, the character 苗 looks like grass growing in the fields. The primary use of 苗 is to refer to crops, especially the young ones, but it may also refer to other plants when they are young, i.e. seedlings. From its use to refer to young plants have derived its meanings of "symptom" and "offspring".

【苗條】 slender

【苗頭】 symptom of a trend

【苗裔】 offspring

【苗而不秀】 a crop that fails to pull forth ears; a failure in spite of favourable conditions

jiǔ

【韭】

小篆

韭，即韭菜，草本植物，葉子細長，是普遍的蔬菜。小篆的韭字，像一棵兩邊開葉整齊的韭菜之形，下面的一橫則代表地面。

韭 refers to the Chinese chive, a vegetable with narrow grasslike leaves. In the Later Seal Character, the character 韭 looks like a Chinese chive with its leaves growing on the two sides orderly, and the horizontal line at the bottom stands for the ground.

guā

瓜指的是蔓生植物所結的子實，有蔬瓜、果瓜之分。金文瓜字，像藤蔓分叉處懸結一瓜的形狀。由於瓜的形狀不易辨認，所以為了表示瓜，就連帶把瓜蔓也畫了出來。

【瓜分】比喻像剖瓜一樣分割國土或劃分疆界。

【瓜代】指瓜熟時赴戍，到來年瓜熟時派人接替。後因稱任職期滿，由別人接任為"瓜代"。

【瓜葛】瓜和葛都是蔓生植物，比喻互相牽連。多指親戚而言。

金 文

小 篆

瓜 refers to the fruit of any creeping or climbing plant with thin twisting stems, such as melon or gourd. In the Bronze Inscriptions, the character 瓜 looks like a large round fruit hanging from a node of two branching vines. Hence its primary meaning fruits like melons or gourds.

【瓜分】 to carve up

【瓜代】 to leave one's post to a successor on the expiration of the term

【瓜葛】 implication; connection

hé

我國的商代、周代社會已經全面進入了以農業為主的時代。在甲骨文和金文中出現了大量有關農作物的字，如禾、黍、來（麥）、粟、米等。其中的禾字，像一株有根有葉、穀穗下垂的植物形狀。禾是穀類植物的總稱，但在秦漢以前，禾多指粟，即今小米，後世則多稱稻為禾。在漢字中，凡以禾為義符的字，都與農作物或農業活動有關，如秉、秋、秀、種、租等。

甲骨文

金文

小篆

Agriculture has been a major industry in China ever since the Shang and Zhou Dynasties. In both the Oracle-Bone Inscriptions and Bronze Inscriptions, there are many characters referring to crops, e.g. 禾 (standing grain), 黍 (broomcorn millet), 來 (麥, wheat), 粟 (corn; millet) and 米 (rice). The character 禾 looks like a plant with its roots, leaves and hanging ears. 禾 is a general term for cereal crops. However, it referred, in particular, to millet before the Qin and Han Dynasties and to unhusked rice afterwards. Characters with 禾 as a component most have to do with crops or agriculture, e.g. 秉 (a handful of crop), 秋 (the time when crops are ripe, i.e. autumn), 秀 (earing), 種 (seed; to plant) and 租 (land tax).

lái

甲骨文的來字，像一株根葉稈穗俱全的麥苗形，它的本義是指小麥。此字後來多借用為來往之來，是由彼至此、由遠及近的意思，與"去"相對。而來的本義，則為後起的"麥"字所代替。

【來歷】人或事物的歷史或背景。

【來由】緣故，原因。

【來日方長】未來的日子還很長，表示事有可為。

【來龍去脈】比喻人、物的來歷或事情的前因後果。

甲骨文　　　　金　文　　　　小　篆

In the Oracle-Bone Inscriptions, the character 來 looks like a wheat plant with its roots, leaves, stalk and ears. It originally referred to wheat, but nowadays is more usually used in the sense of "coming", movement towards the speaker, opposite to 去 (go). And its original meaning is expressed by 麥, a later development.

【來歷】background

【來由】reason

【來日方長】There will be ample time.

【來龍去脈】origin and development

sù

甲骨文粟字，像一棵玉米禾稈，在稈葉交接的地方多結有
碩大的玉米棒球。它的本義，當指玉米，或玉米粒。古代以粟
為黍、稷、秫的總稱，又泛指糧食。今稱粟為穀子，去殼後稱
小米。此外，粟又泛指顆粒如粟之物，也用以比喻微小。

【粟米】玉米粒。又泛指穀類糧食。
【粟飯】粗米飯。
【粟錯】細微差錯。

甲骨文　　　　　小篆

In the Oracle-Bone Inscriptions, the character 粟
looks like a corn plant with its big ears. Hence its
primary meaning corn or its grains. But the character 粟 could also be used as a cover term in the past
for broomcorn millet, millet and sorghum, and even
for all the cereal crops. Nowadays, however, it refers to millet only. Besides, 粟 may refer to particles as small as millet grains.

【粟米】corn grains
【粟飯】coarse meal
【粟錯】slight mistake

mù

金文的穆字，像一棵成熟的稻禾，禾穗飽滿下垂，下面的三點表示穀粒成熟後簌簌下落的樣子。穆的本義為禾穀，指成熟了的莊稼，引申為溫和、和睦、肅穆、靜默等義。

【穆然】默然。又指整肅貌。

【穆穆】端莊盛美貌。又肅敬恭謹貌。

【穆如清風】像清風一樣和暢而美好。

金 文

小 篆

In the Bronze Inscriptions, the character 穆 looks like a ripe rice plant with its plump ears hanging down, the three dots below standing for the falling ripe grains. The original meaning of 穆 was grain, the ripe crop, from which have derived its extended meanings of "mild", "harmonious", "solemn" and "quiet".

【穆然】 silent

【穆穆】 dignified

【穆如清風】 gentle and pleasant as a breeze

qí

甲骨文的齊字，像吐穗的禾麥排列整齊的形狀。齊字的本義為平整、整齊，引申為指相等、同等、一致，又引申為完備、齊全之義。

【齊心】即同心。

【齊名】名望相等。

【齊驅】驅馬並進。又指才力相等。

【齊頭並進】並駕齊驅，形容步調一致，共同前進。

　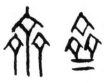　

甲骨文　　　　　　金文　　　　　小篆

In the Oracle-Bone Inscriptions, the character 齊 looks like a line of earing wheat crops in good order. The primary meaning of 齊 is "level" and "orderly", from which have derived its senses of "equal", "the same as", "in conformity with", "perfect" and "complete".

【齊心】of one mind

【齊名】to be equally famous

【齊驅】abreast of one another

【齊頭並進】to advance side by side

bǐng

古文字的秉字，像一隻手握住禾稈之形，表示執持、用手拿着的意思，引申為操持、主持、掌握等義，如《詩經》："秉國之鈞，四方是維。"（掌握國家政權，維護四方安定。）

【秉燭夜遊】夜晚看不見，要手持點燃的蠟燭出去遊玩，意思是提倡人們及時行樂。

甲骨文

金文

小篆

In ancient writing systems, the character 秉 looks like a hand holding the stalk of a grain plant, signalling to take hold of. From this primary meaning have derived its senses of "handling", "in charge of" and "controlling". Thus the *Classic of Poetry* has the lines, " 秉國之鈞，四方是維 (To take hold of the state power and maintain the stability throughout the land)".

【秉燭夜遊】to take an evening stroll with a lantern; not to waste any chance to seek amusement

jiān

古文字的兼字，像一隻手抓住兩棵禾的樣子。它的本義為併持，合併，即把兩個或兩個以上的事物或方面合併在一起；又專指兩倍。

【兼程】一天走兩天的路程。又指加倍趕路。

【兼備】同時具備兩個或許多方面，如"德才兼備"。

【兼聽】聽取多方面的意見。

【兼收並蓄】把不同的人或事物都吸收進來。

甲骨文

小篆

In ancient writing systems, the character 兼 looks like a hand holding two grain plants at once. Its primary meaning is "to hold together" and "to combine", and it may also mean "double".

【兼程】to travel at double speed

【兼備】to have both...and...

【兼聽】to hear both sides of the question

【兼收並蓄】to incorporate things of diverse nature

nián

年的本義指莊稼的收成。五穀熟曰年。如成語 "人壽年豐" 的年字，就是這個意思。甲骨文、金文的年字，像一個人揹負稻禾的形狀，表示收割稻禾的意思。因為古代稻禾一歲只有一次收成，故年字又引申出 "歲" 的意思，一年就是一歲，代表春夏秋冬四季十二個月份。由年歲之義，年字還可引申為指人的年齡、壽命等。

甲骨文　　　　　　　金文　　　　　　　小篆

年 originally meant the amount of crops gathered. When the crops are ripe, there is 年. Thus we may say 人壽年豐 (people enjoy good health and land yields bumper harvests). In the Oracle-Bone Inscriptions and Bronze Inscriptions, the character 年 looks like a man carrying a grain plant on his back, signalling the harvest of crops. As the crops were reaped once a year in former times, the character 年 has come to mean "year", in which there are twelve months, or four seasons of spring, summer, autumn and winter. From this meaning has also derived its use to refer to the age of a person.

shǔ

黍為穀物名，指黍米，性黏，可供食用或釀酒。《管子》："黍者，穀之美者也。"甲骨文黍字像禾上結着纍纍果實而下垂的樣子，有的禾下加水，表示可用黍米釀酒的意思。

【黍酒】用黍米釀造的酒。

【黍離】《詩經‧王風》有《黍離》篇，是周朝大夫路過舊的王室宗廟遺址，見宗室盡為禾黍，徬徨傷感之作。後多用為感慨亡國觸景傷情之詞。

甲骨文

金文

小篆

黍 refers to broomcorn millet, a glutinous grain used as food or for making Chinese wine. *Guan Zi* says, "黍 is one of the best grains". In the Oracle-Bone Inscriptions, the character 黍 looks like a grain plant with heavy ears hanging down. Sometimes there is a water part beneath the plant part, signalling that this crop may be used for making wine.

【黍酒】wine made from broomcorn millet

【黍離】the title of a sentimental poem in the *Classic of Poetry;* sentimental writing

shū

金文叔字，從又從尗(尗即豆菽之"菽"的本字)，像以手撿拾散落的豆菽之形，它的本義即為撿拾、拾取。此字後來多借用為叔伯之"叔"，作為對父親之弟的稱呼，也指與父平輩而年齡比父小的男子。而叔字的本義，反而不大為人所知了。

金文　　　　　小篆

In the Bronze Inscriptions, the character 叔 consists of 又 (hand) and 尗 (the original form of 菽, bean), signalling to pick up beans with one's hand. Hence its original meaning "to pick up". Nowadays, however, it is used in the sense of "uncle", referring to the younger brother of one's father in particular, and its original meaning is lost.

mǐ

米指的是去掉皮、殼的穀物,如大米、小米等。甲骨文的米字,像散落的米粒之形,中間加一橫主要是為了和沙粒、水滴相區別。米是人類經常食用的糧食,故漢字中凡從"米"的字大都與糧食有關,如籼、粒、粳、糠、粟等。現在的米字,還用作長度單位名稱(舊稱公尺),一米的長度相當於三市尺。

【米珠薪桂】米貴如珍珠,薪柴如桂,形容物價昂貴,生活困難。

甲骨文　　　　　　　小篆

米 refers to the husked seeds of cereal crops, especially those of rice, e.g. 大米 (rice), and 小米 (millet). In the Oracle-Bone Inscriptions, the character 米 looks like scattered grains of rice, and the horizontal stroke in the middle serves to distinguish them from grains of sand or drops of water. Rice is one of the common foods of human beings, so characters with 米 as a component most have to do with food, e.g. 籼 (long-grained rice), 粒 (a classifier of grains), 粳 (round-grained rice), 糠 (husk) and 粟 (millet). In addition, 米 is a transliteration of "metre", a measure of length.

【米珠薪桂】 Rice is as precious as pearls and firewood as costly as cassia bark; extraordinarily high cost of living

xiāng

小篆

甲骨文香字，像一高足器具中盛滿食物，並散發出氣味的形狀，它的本義是指食物散發的氣味，引申為指氣味好聞，與"臭"相對。小篆香字或從黍從甘，表示米飯香甜可口的意思，所以香又指食物味道好。此外，香又用作名詞，指香料。

【香澤】指潤髮用的香油。也指香氣。

【香艷】舊時形容詞藻艷麗或內容涉及閨閣的詩文，也形容色情的小説、電影等。

【香車寶馬】指裝飾華美的車馬。

In the Oracle-Bone Inscriptions, the character 香 looks like a high-legged vessel full of food, sending out some fragrance. It primarily refers to the smell of food, from which has derived its use for sweet smell, as against 臭 (foul smell). In the Later Seal Character, the character 香 sometimes consists of 黍 and 甘, signalling that the food is delicious, and this is another sense of 香. In addition, 香 may refer to perfume or spice.

【香澤】(1) a fragrant hair conditioner (2) fragrance

【香艷】love poem in a flowery style

【香車寶馬】beautifully decorated carriage

qín

秦是古代諸侯國名。它位於今陝西省境內，擁有八百里秦川的肥沃土地，自古以來就是有名的大糧倉。古文字的秦字，雙手持杵（用以春糧），下面從禾，其本義當與稻禾收成有關。用作地名和國名，大概也與它是農業最發達的地區有關。戰國末年，秦始皇統一中國，建立起中國歷史上第一個中央集權制的封建王朝，是為秦朝。此後，秦又成為外族對中國或中原地區的代稱，如漢朝時西域諸國就稱中國為秦。

甲骨文　　　　　　金 文　　　　　　小 篆

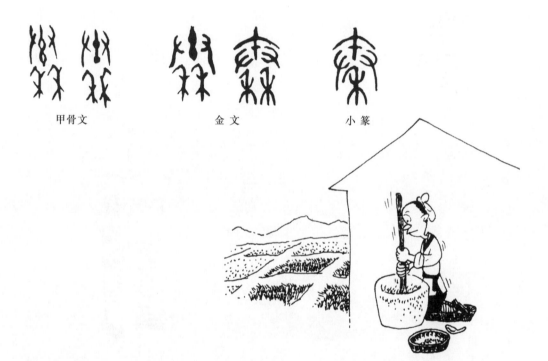

秦 was originally the name of a state in the Zhou Dynasty, situated in the present-day Shanxi Province, a land well-known for its abundance of grain. In ancient writing systems, the character 秦 consists of two parts: the upper part looks like two hands holding a pestle (for husking rice) and the lower part two grain plants. Hence it originally referred to the harvest of crops. Perhaps because this area was advanced in agriculture, the character 秦 was used as a name of the place and the state. At the end of the Warring States Period, the first emperor of the Qin Dynasty unified China, established the first centralized monarchy and named it Qin. Since then 秦 has also been used as a substitute for the name of China.

自 然 類

Nature

rì

太陽和月亮是我們最常見的天文景觀：月亮有時圓有時缺，而太陽則永遠是圓的。古人根據這一自然規律，造出了字形彎缺的月字和圓滿的日字。金文中的一些日字，就像是一輪圓圓的太陽。但在大多數情況下，日字寫成方形，這主要是與刻畫和書寫的習慣有關。總之，日字的本義就是指太陽。太陽出來是白天，所以日又有晝、白天的意思，與"夜"的意思相對。日還可以用來指時間，一日代表一個晝夜。此外，日字也可以用來泛指光陰、時間等。

【日子】指某日，古代紀日的一種方法，又指時光、生活。

【日月】太陽和月亮；又指一天和一月，每天每月；又指季節、光陰。

【日常】原指太陽永恆存在，現多用來指平日、平常。

【日程】每日的行程，又指逐日安排的工作程序。

甲骨文　　　　　金　文　　　　　小　篆

日 refers to the sun. The sun and moon are two of the most common celestial bodies. As the moon sometimes appears to be crescent while the sun is always circular, the characters referring to them are also crescent and circular respectively. The character 日 in the Bronze Inscriptions, for example, is sometimes circular. For the convenience of printing and writing, however, 日 is more usually square. When the sun rises in the sky it is daytime, so the character 日 also means "daytime", as against 夜 (night). 日 is also used as a unit of time, consisting of twenty-four hours, from which has derived its more general meaning of "time".

【日子】day; time; life

【日月】the sun and moon; day and month; time

【日常】daily

【日程】(lit.) the distance travelled in a day; work schedule

dàn

旦本來是個形聲字。甲骨文、金文的旦字，上面的部份是日，下面的方框或圓點乃是表示釘子的丁字（參見"丁"字條），代表這個字的讀音。小篆的旦字變成日下一橫，成為一個會意字，表示太陽剛剛從地平線上昇起，它的本義則是"天明"、"早晨"的意思。

【旦夕】朝暮，從早到晚；又指時間短促。

甲骨文

金 文

小 篆

旦 was originally a phonetic compound. In the Oracle-Bone Inscriptions and Bronze Inscriptions, the character 旦 has the radical part 日 (the sun) on the top and the phonetic part, a square or a dot, underneath. In the Later Seal Character, the second part becomes a horizontal line, resulting in an ideograph, signalling that the sun is rising above the horizon, hence its meaning "dawn".

【旦夕】(lit.) dawn and dusk; in a short while

yùn

　　甲骨文的暈是個會意字，中間是個太陽，周圍的四點代表光圈。小篆的暈從日軍聲，則變成為形聲字。暈的本義是指日月周圍由於雲氣折射而形成的模糊光圈，引申為眼花、昏眩之義。我們現在所説的頭暈、暈車、暈船等，都是從暈字的本義來的，但不讀作 yùn，而讀作 yūn。

甲骨文

小篆

In the Oracle-Bone Inscriptions, it is an ideograph. The middle part stands for the sun and the four dots around the halo. In the Later Seal Character, the character becomes a phonetic compound, with 日 as the radical and 軍 as the phonetic. The character 暈 primarily refers to the halo of the sun or moon, from which has derived its sense "to feel dizzy". Thus we may say 頭暈 (to have a dizzy spell), 暈車 (carsickness) 暈船 (seasickness), but in those condition 暈 pronounced as yūn.

zè

昃本來是個會意字。甲骨文的昃字，左側的日表示太陽，右側是一個斜的人形，像陽光斜照時所投射在地上的人影，表示太陽西斜之意。金文昃字從日從矢（歪頭人形），矢又可以表示讀音；而從小篆開始昃字從日仄聲，完全變成了形聲字。昃的本義是指太陽偏西的意思，如《易經》："日中則昃，月盈則食。"（太陽過了中午就會偏斜，月亮圓了之後還會殘缺。）但在商代甲骨文中，昃字用作紀時的專用字，約相當於現在下午的兩三點鐘。

【昃食】晚食。太陽偏西時才吃飯，表示勤於政事。

甲骨文　　　　金 文　　　　小 篆

昃 was originally an ideograph. In the Oracle-Bone Inscriptions, the character 昃 has a sun part on the left and a slant man figure on the right, signalling the shadow of a man when the sun is not directly on his head. In the Bronze Inscriptions, the character 昃 consists of 日 (the sun) and 矢 (a man whose head is tilted to one side), and the latter also serves as the phonetic. But in the Later Seal Character, it becomes a complete phonetic compound with 日 as the radical and 仄 as the phonetic. 昃 primarily refers to the sun approaching the west. Thus the *Book of Changes* says, "日中則昃，月盈則食 (The sun will approach the west after noon, and the crescent follows a full moon)". But in the written records of the Shang Dynasty, 昃 was used as a name of time referring to the period equivalent to the present two or three o'clock in the afternoon.

【昃食】to be late for one's meals; hardworking

bào

暴為"曝"的本字。小篆的暴字，從日從出從𰀀從米，表示在太陽下曝曬穀物的意思，所以暴的本義指曝曬，又指顯露。因曝曬時陽光猛烈，故暴字又含有猛烈之意；引申為兇狠、殘酷、急躁等義。

【暴行】兇惡殘酷的行為。

【暴利】用不正當手段在短時間內獲得的巨額利潤。

【暴露】露天而處，無所隱蔽。又指揭露、宣揚。

【暴風驟雨】來勢急遽而猛烈的風雨。

小篆

暴 was the original form of 曝. In the Later Seal Character, the character 暴 consists of 日, 出, 𰀀 and 米, signalling to dry grain in the scorching sun for a long time. Hence its primary meaning "to dry in the sun" and "to expose". As the rays of the scorching sun are strong and forceful, the character 暴 also means "violent", from which have derived its extended meanings of "cruel", "fierce" and "short-tempered".

【暴行】savage act

【暴利】sudden huge profits; staggering profits

【暴露】(1) in the open　(2) to expose

【暴風驟雨】violent storm

zhāo

朝本是一個會意字。金文朝字，右邊像一條河流的形狀，左邊上下是草木、中間是日（太陽），像早晨的太陽從河邊的草木間慢慢昇起，正是一幅河邊看日出的圖景。它的本義即指早晨。小篆以後，朝字的字形一再發生訛變，原來字形的會意蕩然無存。

【朝廷】古代宮廷聚眾議事都是在早晨進行，所以就把早晨聚眾議事的地方稱為“朝（cháo）”，代表整個宮廷。而大臣到朝廷觀見皇帝則稱為“朝見”。

【朝氣】早上清新的空氣，又指新銳振奮的士氣，相對暮氣而言。

金 文

小 篆

朝 was originally an ideograph. In the Bronze Inscriptions, the character 朝 is made up of two parts: the left side looks like a sun in between two plants and the right side a river, signalling the sun is rising from among plants on a riverside in the morning. Hence its primary meaning "morning". In the Later Seal Character, the character has undergone a series of changes in its form, and its original image is no longer there.

【朝廷】(朝 pronounced as cháo) imperial court
【朝氣】(1) morning air (2) youthful spirit

mò

古文字的莫字，由一"日"和四"木"（或草）組成，像太陽（日）落入草木叢中，表示日落時分，白晝行將結束，夜晚快要來臨，其本義指傍晚、黃昏，也就是日暮的"暮"（"暮"是"莫"的後起字）。莫由"日落"、"太陽已盡"之義，引申為無、沒有之義（如"溥天之下，莫非王土"），又用作副詞不、不要（如"高深莫測"，"莫愁"）。

【莫須有】未定之詞，猶言或許。北宋時奸臣秦檜誣陷岳飛謀反，韓世忠為抱不平，追問罪證，秦檜答以"莫須有"。韓世忠憤怒地説："莫須有三字何以服天下？"後世稱以不實之詞誣陷他人為莫須有。

甲骨文　　　　金　文　　　　小　篆

莫 was the original form of 暮. In ancient writing systems, the character 莫 consists of a sun part and four tree (or grass) parts, looking like a sun setting among plants, signalling the sun is setting. Hence its original meaning "sunset", which is now expressed by 暮. From this original meaning have derived its extended senses of "without", e.g. 溥天之下，莫非王土 (All the land under heaven belongs to the king without exception), and "no" or "not", e.g. 高深莫測 (too high and deep to be measured) and 莫愁 (not to worry).

【莫須有】unwarranted (charge)

chūn

春字是個會意兼形聲的字。甲骨文的春字,由一"日"三"木"(或二"草")和"屯"字組成,其中"屯"(zhūn)既代表春字的讀音,同時又是草木嫩芽的象形(詳見"屯"字條),整個字表達出來的意思是,陽光普照,草木萌生,一派生機勃勃的景象。如唐代劉禹錫詩:"沉舟側畔千帆過,病樹前頭萬木春。"而這種生機勃勃的景象只有在一年之首的春天才能看到,所以春字的本義就是指春季,為一年中春夏秋冬四季之首,相當於農曆的正、二、三月。

【春秋】春季和秋季。代指四季。一年只有一個春季和秋季,所以一個春秋也就是一年。引申為指年歲、歲月或人的年齡等。

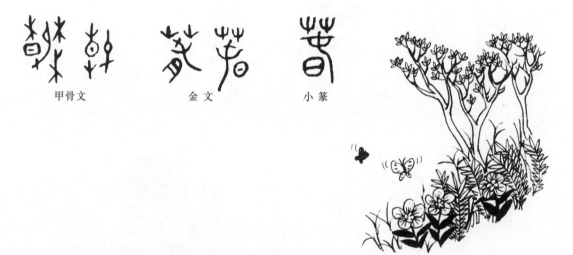

甲骨文　　　　金文　　　　小篆

春 is both an ideograph and phonetic compound. In the Oracle-Bone Inscriptions, the character 春 consists of a sun part, three tree parts (or two grass parts) and a seedling part (屯), signalling that plants are beginning to shoot forth in the sun and there is vigour and vitality everywhere. This is the picture of a scene one usually sees in the beginning of a year, i.e. the spring season. Hence its primary meaning "spring". Thus poet Liu Yuxi of the Tang Dynasty wrote, " 沉舟側畔千帆過, 病樹前頭萬木春 (A thousand boats sail past a sunk, and even more tress grow after one's sick)." But the seedling part (屯), pronounced as zhūn, may serve as a phonetic as well. In this sense 春 is a phonetic compound.

【春秋】spring and autumn; the four seasons; year; age

jīng

甲骨文的晶字，像夜空中錯落分佈的三顆小星星。星星的形狀有的圓，有的方（這是由於刀刻線條易方直不易圓曲的緣故），有的在圓圈中加點，近似日字。所以從小篆開始，晶字的星形均寫成日。晶的本義是指夜空眾星閃亮，表示明朗、明淨的意思。

【晶瑩】明亮透徹。

【晶輝】明亮的光彩。多指日月、星辰之光。

甲骨文

小篆

In the Oracle-Bone Inscriptions, the character 晶 looks like three stars, sometimes circular, sometimes square (for the convenience of printing), and sometimes with a dot in the centre making it like the character 日. That is why in the Later Seal Character, the star parts are all written like sun parts. The original meaning of 晶 was a clear night with the stars shining, from which have derived its meanings of "bright" and clear".

【晶瑩】 sparkling and crystal-clear

【晶輝】 brilliant rays

xīng

星通常是指夜間天空中發光的星斗天體。甲骨文的星字，像夜空中繁多的星星，即用五個方塊來表示星星，"生"代表讀音。我們用肉眼看，星星在天空中是細小的，所以星字又指細碎如星之物，如火星兒，一星半點等。

【星移斗轉】星斗變換位置，表示季節改變，比喻時間流逝。

【星羅棋佈】像天上的星星和棋盤中的棋子那樣分佈，形容數量多，分佈廣。

【星火燎原】星星之火，可以燎原。比喻小事可以釀成大變，現比喻為開始時弱小的新生事物有偉大的發展前途。

甲骨文　　　　　　　金文　　　　　　小篆

星 refers to stars, the shining bodies in the sky at night. In the Oracle-Bone Inscriptions, the character 星 has five little squares standing for stars and the part in the middle, i.e. 生, indicating its pronunciation. As the stars appear to be tiny in the sky, the character 星 can also refer to tiny particles, e.g. 火星兒 (spark), 一星半點 (a tiny bit).

【星移斗轉】change in the positions of the stars; change of the seasons; passage of time

【星羅棋佈】scattered all over like stars in the sky or men on the chessboard

【星火燎原】A single spark can start a prairie fire.

shēn

參，最初是星宿的名稱，為二十八宿之一。金文的參字，像人頭頂上三顆星星在閃爍的樣子，表示人在仰觀星象的意思。此字後來借用為數詞"三"（讀 **sān**），故在下面加上三道橫線寫作"叄"。字又讀 **cān,** 有參與、參拜等義。

【參（shēn）商】參和商都是二十八星宿之一，但兩者相隔遙遠，不能同時在天空中出現，故以參商比喻親友不能會面，或比喻感情不和睦，合不到一塊。

金文

小篆

參 was originally the name of a constellation, one of the lunar mansions. In the Bronze Inscriptions, the character 參 looks like three stars shining on top of a man, signalling a man is looking at stars. From this meaning has derived its use as a numeral meaning "three", pronounced as sān, and written as 叄. 參, pronounced as cān, also means "to participate in" and "to pay respects to".

【參(shēn)商】 two of the lunar mansions far away from each other; (of people) unable to see each other or get along

yuè

天上的月亮，時圓時缺，但圓的時候少，而缺的時候多。這種現象非常形象地反映在字形上。甲骨文的月字，缺而不圓，分明是一彎新月的形象。月亮平均每三十天左右圓滿一次，所以後來就拿月來計算時日，平均三十天為一個月份，於是一年就有了十二個月。

甲骨文   金 文   小 篆

月 refers to the moon. The moon appears to change its shape all the time, and most of the time it is not completely circular. This phenomenon is reflected in the form of the character. Thus in the Oracle-Bone Inscriptions, the character 月 looks like a crescent moon. As the full moon comes once thirty days on average, the character 月 has come to mean "thirty days", in other words, "a month". And twelve months constitute a year.

míng

甲骨文的明字有兩種寫法：一是由日月兩字組成，用來計時，表示月落日出、日月交替之際，即拂曉時分；另一種寫法是由月和一個窗形的結構組成，意思是月光照進窗內，表示光亮之意。金文、小篆的明字，均以後一種形體為準，只是到隸書、楷書以後，兩種形體並存，現在的明字則確定為日月之明了。不過現在的明字，一般用為光亮之義，反不表示拂曉的意思。

甲骨文　　　　　　金文　　　　　　小篆

In the Oracle-Bone Inscriptions, the character 明 has two forms. One consists of 日 and 月, referring to the time when the sun rises and the moon sets, i. e. daybreak. The other consists of a moon part and a window part, signalling that the moonlight has come into a room, and the room is bright. In both the Bronze Inscriptions and the Later Seal Character, the composition of the character 明 follows the second approach, while in the Regular Script the two forms coexist. The modern simplified form, however, consists of 日 and 月 again, but it means "bright" rather than "daybreak".

ㄒㄧ

夕的本義是指夜晚,又特指傍晚。夜晚有月亮,所以甲骨文的夕字,也是一彎新月的形象,即用月亮來代表夜晚。早期甲骨文夕字在月形的中間加一點,和月中無點的月字區分開來;後來月字和夕字的使用發生混淆和顛倒,月字中間有了一點,夕字反而變成了無點之月。

【夕陽】指傍晚的太陽,又比喻人的晚年。如唐代李商隱詩:
"夕陽無限好,只是近黃昏。"

甲骨文

金文

小篆

夕 refers to night, and dusk in particular. As the moon rises at night, the character 夕 in the Oracle-Bone Inscriptions also looks like a crescent moon. In other words, the moon represents night. In the early Oracle-Bone Inscriptions, the character 夕 has a dot in the middle, to differ from the character 月. In later developments, however, there was confusion between 月 and 夕. As a result, a dot is added to 月, and 夕 becomes 月 without a dot instead.

【夕陽】 the setting sun; old age (For example, Li Shangyin of the Tang Dynasty wrote, "夕陽無限好,只是近黃昏 " 〔The setting sun seems so sublime, O but' tis near its dying time!〕)

sù

甲骨文、金文的夙字，左上是一個月形，表示星月未落，天尚未亮；右下是一個跪着的人形，揚起雙手表示勞作，即天不亮就起來幹活的意思。所以，夙字的本義為早，又指早晨、凌晨。此外，夙又通"宿"，指舊日、平素。

【夙夜】早晚，朝夕。
【夙因】前世的因緣。同"宿因"。
【夙願】平素的志願。
【夙興夜寐】早起晚睡。指生活勤勞。

甲骨文　　　金文　　　小篆

In the Oracle-Bone Inscrptions and Bronze Inscriptions, the character 夙 looks like a man on his knees working in the moonlight, signalling that the man starts working before dawn. Hence 夙 means "the small hours". But it may, like 宿, mean "old" and "long-standing" as well.

【夙夜】morning and night
【夙因】(also 宿因) causes of the previous life
【夙願】long-cherished wish
【夙興夜寐】to rise early and retire late; hard at work night and day

hóng

虹本是一種自然現象，是由於太陽光線與水氣相映而出現在天空的彩色暈帶。而古人則認為它是天上的一種神奇動物，長身、兩首、巨口，常於雨後出現，橫跨天空，低頭吸飲東方的水氣。甲骨文的虹字，正是這種想象中的神物形象。小篆的虹從蟲工聲，則變成為形聲字。

【虹吸】自高處用拱形彎管。引水先升高而再下流。因管彎似虹，故名虹吸。

【虹橋】拱橋似虹，故名虹橋。

甲骨文

金文

小篆

虹 refers to the rainbow, and arch of different colours appearing in the sky opposite the sun after rain. However, ancient people, unable to understand this natural phenomenon, thought it was a mystical animal with a long body, two heads and a big mouth, appearing after rain in the sky to drink water. The character 虹 in the Oracle-Bone Inscriptions looks like a picture of this animal. In the Later Seal Character, the character becomes a phonetic compound with 蟲 as the radical and 工 as the phonetic.

【虹吸】siphonage

【虹橋】arch bridge

qì

甲骨文的氣字，為三條長短不一的橫線，表示雲氣橫漂的意思；金文、小篆的氣字，橫線曲環縈繞，更像雲氣飄流之狀。氣的本義指雲氣，引申為泛指一切氣體，如空氣、人或其他動物呼吸出入之氣（氣息）；同時，氣還用來指自然界冷熱陰晴等現象（氣候、氣像）；此外，氣還是一個抽象概念，用來指人的精神狀態或作風習氣（氣質、氣度）等。

【氣氛】指一定環境中給人某種強烈感覺的精神表現或景象。

【氣勢】指人或事物表現出來的某種力量或形勢。

【氣韻】指書畫、文章等的風格和意境。

甲骨文　　　　　金　文　　　　　小　篆

In the Oracle-Bone Inscriptions, the character 氣 looks like three horizontal lines of unequal length, signalling thin clouds floating about. In the Bronze Inscriptions and Later Seal Character, the horizontal lines are curved, presenting an even truer description of the floating clouds. From its primary meaning of "thin clouds" has derived its more general use for any gases, e.g. 空氣 (air), 氣息 (breath). 氣 may also refer to the weather conditions of wind, rain, sunshine, snow, etc. e.g. 氣候 (climate), 氣象 (meteorological phenomena). In addition, 氣 is also an abstract concept referring to the mood of a person, e.g. 氣質 (temperament) and 氣度 (tolerance).

【氣氛】atmosphere

【氣勢】momentum

【氣韻】the style and artistic appeal of a painting or article

hán

金文的寒字，像一個人住在一間堆滿乾草（用來保暖）的屋子裡以避寒冷的形狀，人腳下的兩點代表冰塊，所以寒的本義指寒冷。寒冷能使人顫抖，因此寒字有戰慄恐懼之義，如膽寒、心寒等。此外，寒字還有窮困之義，如貧寒、寒酸等。

【寒暄】指冬季和夏季，一寒一暄代表一年。又指相見互道天氣冷暖，作為應酬之詞。

金文

小篆

In the Bronze Inscriptions, the character 寒 looks like a man in a room full of straw (material for warming up), the two dots underneath the man standing for ice blocks, hence the primary meaning "cold". As cold weather may cause a man to tremble, the character 寒 can also mean "to tremble", even with fear, e.g. 膽寒 (terrified), 心寒 (bitterly disappointed). In addition, 寒 may be used in the sense of "poor", e.g. 貧寒 (poor), 寒酸 (miserable and shabby).

【寒暄】(lit.) cold and hot; exchange of conventional greetings

bīng

冰，是指水在攝氏零度以下凝結成的固體。甲骨文、金文的冰字，像兩塊凝結的棱狀冰塊。小篆則在冰塊旁加"水"字，表示冰塊是由水凝結而成的。

【冰心】比喻心地清明純潔，表裡如一。

【冰炭】冰冷炭熱，比喻性質相反，互不相容。

【冰清玉潔】比喻人品高潔。又比喻官吏辦事清明公正。

【冰消瓦解】比喻事物完全消釋或渙散、崩潰。

　　甲骨文　　　　　金　文　　　　　小　篆

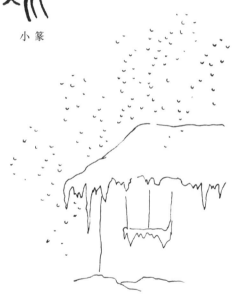

冰 refers to ice, water which has frozen to a solid at zero degree centigrade. In the Oracle-Bone Inscriptions and Bronze Inscriptions, the character 冰 looks like two ridged ice blocks. In the Later Seal Character, a water part (水) is added to indicate that ice is formed from water.

【冰心】(fig.) pure in mind

【冰炭】as incompatible as ice and hot coals

【冰清玉潔】clear as ice and pure as gem; pure and noble

【冰消瓦解】to melt like ice and break like tiles

shēn

申為"電"的本字。甲骨文、金文的申字，像天空閃電所發出的曲折光線。由於閃電多在雨天出現，故後來的電字即在"申"上增加"雨"。而申字則借用為干支名，為地支的第九位。此外，申字還有說明、引述之義。

【申時】舊式計時法指下午三點鐘到五點鐘的時間。

【申報】用書面向上級或有關部門報告。

【申請】向上級或有關部門說明理由，提出請求。

甲骨文

金文

小篆

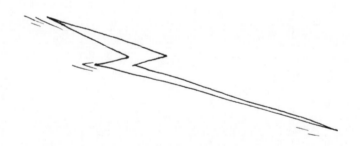

申 was the original form of 電. In the Oracle-Bone Inscriptions and Bronze Inscriptions, the character 申 looks like a curving light appearing in the sky when there is lightning. As lightning often occurs during a rain, the character has a rain part (雨) added in its later development, resulting in the original complicated form of 電. The character 申 on the other hand is used as a name of the ninth Earthly Branch, a traditional Chinese system of sequence. In addition 申 may mean "to state" and "to express".

【申時】 from 3:00 to 5:00 in the afternoon

【申報】 to report to a higher body

【申請】 to apply for

diàn

古文字的電字，從雨從申，申為閃電之形（參見"申"字條），表示雨中雷電閃耀的意思。電的本義指閃電，引申為迅疾之義。現在的電字，則多用來指電力。

【電光石火】像閃電的光和敲石所產生的火花一樣稍縱即逝。比喻人生短暫。

金文

小篆

In ancient writing systems, the character 電 consists of 雨 and 申, referring to the lightning in a rain. From this primary meaning has derived its meaning of "quick". Nowadays, however, it mainly refers to electricity.

【電光石火】as short-lived as lightning or a spark

léi

甲骨文，金文的雷字，中間彎曲的弧線代表閃電的光線，閃電周圍的圓形表示響雷所發出的巨大爆裂聲響；而小篆雷字增加雨頭，則表示雷電多發生在雨天。因此，雷的本義是指下雨時空中激電所發出來的響聲。

【雷霆】暴雷、霹靂。形容威力或發怒的樣子。

【雷同】打雷時很多東西會引起共鳴，同時響應。喻指隨聲附和，又指不該相同而相同。

【雷屬風行】像打雷那樣猛烈，像颱風那樣迅速，比喻行動快，聲勢猛烈。

甲骨文

金文

小篆

In the Oracle-Bone Inscriptions and Bronze Inscriptions, the character 雷 consists of curving lines and small circles, respectively standing for the light and sound perceptible during a thunderstorm. In the Later Seal Character, a rain part (雨) is added to indicate that thunder and lightning occur in rainy days. Hence its meaning "thunder", the loud explosive noise caused by the discharge of electricity in the sky.

【雷霆】(1) thunderclap (2) thunder-like power or rage

【雷同】echoing what others have said; to duplicate

【雷屬風行】with the power of a thunderbolt and the speed of a wind; vigorously and speedily

yún

　　甲骨文、金文的雲字,像雲氣回旋飄動的樣子,其本義即指雲氣。雲是由空中水氣凝聚而成,積久則變生為雨,所以小篆的雲字增加雨頭,表示它與雨有關。

【雲集】比喻許多人從各處來聚集在一起。

【雲遊】到處遨遊,行蹤不定。

【雲泥之別】相差像天空的雲和地下的泥。比喻地位、才能高下懸殊。

【雲蒸霞蔚】形容景物絢爛美麗、異彩紛呈。

| 甲骨文 | 金文 | 小篆 |

In the Oracle-Bone Inscriptions and Bronze Inscriptions, the character 雲 looks like clouds floating about, hence its primary meaning "cloud". As clouds are in fact light drops of water, which will fall as rain when heavy enough, the character 雲 in the Later Seal Character has a rain part (雨) added, to indicate its relation with rain.

【雲集】to come together in crowds

【雲遊】to travel about aimlessly

【雲泥之別】as different as clouds and mud; nide gap in social status and capacity

【雲蒸霞蔚】as colourful and gorgeous as morning clouds

yǔ

甲骨文、金文的雨字，像從天空中降落水滴的形狀，其本義指雨水，又作動詞指降雨，引申為從天空中散落之義，如雨雪、雨粟等。漢字中凡從雨的字大都與雲、雨等天文現象有關，如雷、霧、霜、雪等。

【雨露】雨和露。又喻指恩澤。

【雨散雲飛】比喻離散分別。

甲骨文

金文

小篆

In the Oracle-Bone Inscriptions and Bronze Inscriptions, the character 雨 looks like drops of water falling from the sky, hence its primary meaning "rain". Used as a verb, it may refer to not only the falling of rain but also the falling of anything from the sky, e.g. 雨雪 (to snow), 雨粟 (to drop millet grains). Characters with 雨 as a component most have to do with weather conditions like clouds and rain, e.g. 雷 (thunder), 霧 (fog), 霜 (frost) and 雪 (snow).

【雨露】(lit.) rain and dew; favour

【雨散雲飛】to separate from each other as rain drops or floating clouds

líng

甲骨文的零字，上從雨，下面三個點像大水滴之形。後來水滴形訛變成口形，但其會意仍然不變。而零作為從雨令聲的形聲字，則是後起的字形。零的本義指連續不斷地下雨，又指雨滴；引申為掉落、凋落之義，又引申為指零碎，即細碎散亂之物。

【零雨】徐雨。斷續不止之雨。
【零落】凋謝。又指喪敗，衰亡。

甲骨文

金文

小篆

In the Oracle-Bone Inscriptions, the character 零 consists of a rain part and three big drops of water, hence its original meaning "to rain continuously" or "rain drop". Sometimes the drops of water are square in shape, but the character is still ideographic. The phonetic compound form with 雨 as the radical and 令 as the phonetic is a later development. From its original meaning have derived its extended meanings of "falling", "withering" and "fragments".

【零雨】a steady drizzle
【零落】(1) withered and fallen (2) decayed

xū

　　金文需字，像雨下一個站立的人形（天），表示人遇雨不行，等待雨停的意思。小篆人形（天）訛變為"而"，需字則由會意變而成為從雨而聲的形聲字。需的本義為等待，通"頦"，引申為遲疑之義，後來則多用為需要、給用的意思。

【需次】舊時候補官吏，等待依次補缺，稱為"需次"。
【需索】指勒索。

金文

小篆

In the Bronze Inscriptions, the character 需 consists of a part like a man on his feet (天) and a rain part (雨), signalling a man at a standstill waiting for the rain to stop. In the Later Seal Character, the man part (天) changes into 而 by mistake, resulting in a phonetic compound with 雨 as the redical and 而 as the phonetic. The original meaning of 需 was, the same as 頦 , "to wait", from which has derived its extended meaning of "hesitation". Nowadays, however, it means more usually "to need" and "to require".

【需次】(arch.) to wait for one's turn to fill a vacancy
【需索】to extort

shuǐ

水是一種無色無味的透明液體。甲骨文、金文中的水字，像一條彎曲的水流。中間的彎曲斜線代表河道主流，兩旁的點是水珠水花。所以水的本義當指水流或流水；泛指水域，如江河湖海，與"陸"對稱；後來引申為指所有的汁液，如藥水、淚水、橘子水等。

【水火不容】指互不相容、勢不兩立。
【水乳交融】水和乳極易融合，比喻意氣相投，感情融洽。
【水清無魚】水太清了魚就無法生存，比喻人太精明細察，就不能容人。
【水滴石穿】水經常不斷地滴在石頭上，能使石頭穿孔，比喻只要堅持不懈，事情就能成功。

甲骨文　　　　金文　　　　小篆

水 refers to water, a transparent liquid without colour, taste or smell. In the Oracle-Bone Inscriptions and Bronze Inscriptions, the character 水 looks like a river turning here and there, the curving line in the middle standing for the main course and the dots on the sides the spray. Hence the character 水 originally referred to the river, or more generally, the water area, including lakes and seas, opposite to 陸 (land). From this meaning has derived its use for liquid in general, e.g. 藥水 (medicinal liquid), 淚水 (tears) and 橘子水 (orange juice).

【水火不容】 as incompatible as fire and water
【水乳交融】 as well blended as milk and water
【水清無魚】 When the water is too clear, there is no fish; One who is too clever has no friends.
【水滴石穿】 Dripping water wears through rock; Constant effort brings success.

quán

甲骨文中的泉字，像泉水從泉眼中涓涓流出的樣子。其本義指泉水，即從地下流出來的水；又泛指地下水。在古代，泉字還可作為錢幣的代稱。

【泉下】黃泉之下。指人死後埋葬的墓穴。舊時迷信也指陰間。

【泉布】古代錢幣的別稱。

甲骨文

小篆

In the Oracle-Bone Inscriptions, the character 泉 looks like water trickling from a spring. Hence 泉 primarily refers to spring water coming up from the ground, or more generally any ground water. In former times, it was also used as a substitute for money.

【泉下】 the nether world

【泉布】 (arch.) money

yuán

原為"源"的本字。金文的原字從厂從泉,表示岩下有泉的意思。小篆原字或從三泉,則表示眾泉匯聚成流之意。原的本義即指水源,引申為指最初的(如原始)、本來的(如原地)和未加工的(如原料)等義。此外,原亦可用作動詞,是推究根源的意思;又有原諒、寬恕之義。

【原因】造成某種結果或引起某件事情發生的條件。

【原宥】諒情而寬赦其罪。

【原形畢露】本來面目徹底暴露,多用為貶義。

【原始要終】探究事物發展的起源和歸宿。

金文

小篆

原 was the original form of 源. In the Bronze Inscriptions, the character 原 consists of 厂 (rock) and 泉 (spring), signalling there is a spring under the rock. In the Later Seal Character, the character 原 sometimes has three spring parts, signalling many springs are coming together to form a river, The original meaning of 原 was "the source of a river", from which have derived its senses of "earliest", e.g. 原始 (primitive); "original", e.g. 原地 (original place); and "unprocessed", e.g. 原料 (raw material). Used as a verb, it means "to trace to the source". But it may also mean "to forgive".

【原因】cause

【原宥】to pardon

【原形畢露】(derog.) to be revealed for what it is

【原始要終】to find out the original cause and the final result

gǔ

　　谷，指的是兩山間的夾道或流水道。甲骨文、金文的谷字，上部像溪流出自山澗之形，下部的"口"表示谷口，所以谷的本義指山谷。

【谷口】山谷出口。

【谷地】地面上向一定方向傾斜的低凹地，如山谷、河谷。

甲骨文	金文	小篆

谷 means "valley", the land lying between two lines of mountains, often with a river running through it. In the Oracle-Bone Inscriptions and Bronze Inscriptions, the character 谷 consists of two parts: the upper part looks like streams running out of a valley and the lower part the entrance of a valley.

【谷口】the entrance of a valley

【谷地】a valley and its surrounding area

chuān

甲骨文川字像一條彎彎曲曲的河流的形狀，兩邊的彎線代表河岸，中間三點是流水。金文、小篆的川字乾脆寫成三條流動的曲線，也可以表示河流的意思。川字的本義為河流，引申為指山間或高原間的平坦而低的地帶。

【川流不息】水流不停。比喻行人、車船等來往不斷。

甲骨文　　　　　　　金文　　　　　　　小篆

In the Oracle-Bone Inscriptions, the character 川 looks like a river turning here and there, the two lines on the sides standing for river banks and the three dots in the middle the flowing water. In the Bronze Inscriptions and Later Seal Character, the character simply consists of three curving lines, still signalling a river. The primary meaning of 川 is "river", from which has derived its reference to a large stretch of flat land between mountains, i.e. plain.

【川流不息】to flow past endlessly like a river

pài

古文字的派字，像河水分流之形。它的本義即指河流的分支、支流，引申為指事物的流別，如學派、黨派、宗派等。派字還可用作動詞，有差遣、委派的意思。

【派別】學術、宗教、政黨等內部因主張不同而形成的分支或小團體。

【派生】從主要事物發展中分化出來。

【派遣】差遣，即把人委派到某地從事某項工作。

甲骨文

金文

小篆

In ancient writing systems, the character 派 looks like a river branching off. Hence its original meaning "a branch of a river", from which has derived its extended meaning of "division", e.g. 學派 (school of thought), 黨派 (political parties and groups) and 宗派 (sect; faction). Used as a verb, it means "to send" and "to appoint".

【派別】divisions

【派生】to derive

【派遣】to send

yǎn

　　古文字的衍字，從水（或川）從行（或彳），表示水在江中流行的意思。它的本義指水流貌，引申為流行、推演、擴大、發展、衍生等義。

【衍溢】氾濫、滿佈。

【衍曼】連綿不絕貌。

【衍義】推演發明的義理。

【衍變】演變。

金文

小篆

In ancient writing systems, the character 衍 consists of a river part (水 or 川) and a movement part (行 or 彳), signalling water flowing in a river. It originally refers to the flowing of water, from which use has derived its senses "to spread", "to broaden", "to develop", "to evolve" and "to derive".

【衍溢】 to spread all over

【衍曼】 to flow endlessly

【衍義】 inference

【衍變】 to evolve

liú

小篆的流字，兩邊為水，中間一個倒"子"形，子的頭部是飄散的頭髮，表示一個人順水漂流的意思。流的本義為流動，即水向下游移動，引申為移動、流傳、傳佈、傳遞、放逐等義；又指水流、河道，引申為指流派、支流及品級之義。

【流行】傳佈，盛行。

【流毒】傳播毒害。

【流弊】滋生的或相沿而成的弊端。

【流水不腐】流動的水，污濁自去，不會腐臭，比喻人經常運動
　　　　　　 則不容易得病。

【流芳百世】美名永久流傳於後世。

甲骨文

石鼓文

小篆

In the Later Seal Character, the character 流 looks like an upside-down man whose hair is loose and drifting with the current in between two river parts, signalling a man driven along by currents. The primary meaning of 流 is "to flow", from which have derived its senses "to move", "to spread", "to circulate", "to pass on" and "to send into exile". Used as a noun, it may refer to a river, a branch , a school of thought, or a grade.

【流行】popular, prevalent; in vogue

【流毒】to exert a pernicious influence

【流弊】corrupt practices

【流水不腐】Running water is never stale.

【流芳百世】to leave a good name for a hundred generations

zhōu

州為"洲"的本字。甲骨文、金文的州字,像一條河流,中間的小圓圈代表河中的小沙洲。州字的本義是指水中的陸地,即河流中高出水面的土地。相傳上古時洪水氾濫,後來大禹治水,把天下劃分為九州。於是州字成為古代行政區域的專字,而另造了一個"洲"字來代替它的本義。現在作為地名,州、洲用法有別:一般國內地名用州字,如廣州、徐州等;世界地名則用洲,如亞洲、歐洲等。國內地名特指水中陸地義仍用"洲",如株洲、橘子洲(均在湖南)、沙洲(在江蘇)、鸚鵡洲(在湖北)、桂洲(在廣東)等。

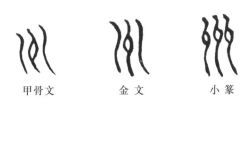

甲骨文　　　　金　文　　　　小　篆

州 was the original form of 洲. In the Oracle-Bone Inscriptions and Bronze Inscriptions, the character 州 has a river part with a small circle in the middle, signalling there is an islet in the river. Hence its original sense "islet", a piece of land in a river rising above the water level. According to legend, when Yu, the last of the three wise leaders in the primitive society of China, conquered the floods, he divided the country into nine administrative areas known as 州. Since then 州 has become a special term for administrative areas, and another character 洲 was created to express its original meaning. Nowadays, as a place name, 洲 is used for continents, such as 亞洲 (Asia), 歐洲 (Europe), while 州 is used for cities, such as 廣州 (Guangzhou), 徐州 (Xuzhou). Some exceptions are 株洲 (Zhuzhou, in Hunan), 橘子洲 (Juzizhou, In Hunan), 沙洲 (Shazhou, in Jiangsu), 鸚鵡洲 (Yingwuzhou, in Hubei) and 桂洲 (Guizhou, in Guangdong).

huí

【迴】

古文字的回字，像淵水回旋之形，其本義為環繞、旋轉，後來多用為掉轉、返回之義，又引申為違背、邪僻等義。

【回味】食後感覺到的餘味。後也指對往事的回憶或體會。

【回春】冬去春來，草木重生。後多比喻醫術高明，能治好嚴重的病症。

【回風】旋風。

【回僻】邪僻不正。又稱回邪。

【回避】避忌，躲避。

【回護】委曲袒護。

【回腸蕩氣】腸為之直，氣為之舒，常用來比喻音樂或文章感人至深。

甲骨文　　　金文　　　小篆

In ancient writing systems, the character 回 looks like a whirl in a pool. Hence its original meaning "to whirl" and "to circle", from which have derived its present-day senses "to turn about", "to go back", "to run counter to" and "to be perverse".

【回味】(1) aftertaste (2) to call sth. to mind and ponder over it

【回春】(lit.) the return of spring; to bring a dying person back to life

【回風】whirl

【回僻】perverse

【回避】to evade

【回護】to be partial to

【回腸蕩氣】(of music, poems, etc.) soulstirring

yuān

甲骨文、金文的淵字，像一個水流回旋的深水潭；有的在水潭外再加一個水旁，則為小篆體的淵字所沿用。淵的本義指深潭，引申為深邃、深遠、深沉等義。

【淵博】指學識精深廣博。

【淵源】指事物的本源。

【淵默】深沉不言。

【淵藪】淵為魚所居之處，藪為獸所居之處。比喻人或事物會聚的地方。

甲骨文　　　　　金文　　　　　小篆

In the Oracle-Bone Inscriptions and Bronze Inscriptions, the character 淵 looks like a deep pool with whirling water. Sometimes there is a river part added, which is the source of the form in the Later Seal Character. The primary meaning of 淵 is "deep pool", from which have derived its senses of "deep", "profound" and "far-reaching".

【淵博】broad and profound

【淵源】origin

【淵默】reticent

【淵藪】(lit.) pool and den; a gathering place

miǎo

　　淼字由三個"水"組成，是個會意字，表示水面遼闊、浩無邊際的意思。許慎《説文解字》："淼，大水也。"淼的本義是形容水大，即大水茫無邊際的樣子，意與"渺"同。

【淼茫】水廣闊遼遠貌。又作"渺茫"。

小篆

The character 淼, consisting of three river parts, is an ideograph, signalling there is a vast, boundless expanse of water. Xu Shen says in his *Origin of Chinese Characters*, "淼 means a vast area of water". In other words, 淼 means the same as 渺, that is, the space covered by water is so vast that one can hardly see its bounds.

【淼茫】 (also 渺茫) (of water) to stretch as far as the eye can see

XĪ

昔字的本義是從前、往日、過去，和今的意思相對。甲骨文的昔字，像太陽（日）漂浮在波浪之上，有的則在水波之下，像是被波浪所淹沒，表示洪水滔天的意思。相傳上古時期，曾經一度洪水氾濫，陸地大多被淹沒，人們只好居住在山上，靠吃野菜樹葉為生，到大禹治水，才使洪水消退。後來人們提起過去，總是會想起那一段洪水成災的日子，於是就造了這麼個昔字。

甲骨文　　　　　　金 文　　　　　　小 篆

昔 means "former times", "the past", opposite to 今 (the present). In the Oracle-Bone Inscriptions, the character 昔 consists of a wave part and a sun part, sometimes the sun part is above the waves and sometimes the waves are above the sun, signalling that there is water everywhere. According to legend, there were once serious floods in ancient times and people had to stay on top of mountains living on tree barks and edible wild herbs until Yu, One of the three legendary, wise leaders in ancient China, conquered them. After the floods were gone, people would still call to mind those old miserable days, which they invented the character 昔 to refer to.

mò

金文沒字從水從回，像水流漩渦之形；小篆加"又"（手形），表示人沉沒入水的意思。所以沒的本義為沉下，又指淹沒；引申為隱沒、隱藏、淪落等義，進一步引申為盡、無之義，讀méi。又特指死亡。

【沒人】潛水的人。

【沒世】死。又指終身，永久。

【沒落】衰敗，趨向死亡。

【沒齒不忘】終身不能忘記。

【沒（méi）精打采】精神萎靡不振。

金 文 　　　　　　　小 篆

In the Bronze Inscriptions, the character 沒 consists of 水 and 回, signalling whirling water. In the Later Seal Character, a hand part (又) is added to indicate that a man is sinking into the whirling water. Hence its primary meaning "to sink", "to submerge", from which have derived its extended meanings "to disappear", "to hide", "to decline", "without" (pronounced as méi) and "till the end (esp. the end of one's life)".

【沒人】(arch.) diver

【沒世】till the end of one's life

【沒落】to decline

【沒齒不忘】never to forget to the end of one's days

【沒（méi）精打采】in low spirits

yù

　　甲骨文浴字，像一個人站在一個大盆子裡面，周圍水滴四濺，表示人在洗澡的意思。小篆浴字則從水谷聲，變成了形聲字。浴的本義為洗澡；引申為修養德性，使身心整潔，如"浴德"。

【浴血】全身浸於血泊之中。形容戰鬥激烈，血染全身。

甲骨文

小篆

In the Oracle-Bone Inscriptions, the character 浴 looks like a man in a bathtub with drops of water around, signalling a man is taking a bath. In the Later Seal Character, the character becomes a phonetic compound with 水 as the radical and 谷 as the phonetic. The primary meaning of 浴 is "to take a bath", but it is also used metaphorically to refer to one's mental hygiene, e.g. 浴德 (to cultivate one's moral character).

【浴血】 bathed in blood; (the fight is so fierce that one is) bloodied all over

shā

沙指的是土石的細小微粒。沙字從水從少，其中"少"字就是細小沙粒的形象；而金文沙字更像河流水邊眾多沙粒的形狀。所以沙字的本義當指水邊或水底的細小石粒，引申為指細碎鬆散的物質，如豆沙、沙糖等。

【沙汰】淘汰。

【沙漠】地面全被沙礫所覆蓋、乾旱缺水的地區。

【沙場】平沙曠野。後來多指戰場。

金 文

小 篆

沙 means "sand", extremely small pieces of stone. In the Bronze Inscriptions, the character 沙 consists of 水 and 少, the former looking like a river and the latter particles of sand. Hence it primarily refers to the extremely small pieces of stone on the riverside or riverbed, from which use has derived its reference to loose material of very small fine grains, e.g. 豆沙 (bean paste), 沙糖 (granulated sugar).

【沙汰】 to sift out

【沙漠】 desert

【沙場】 battlefield

xiǎo

小，是一個比較抽象的概念。甲骨文、金文的小字，以散落細微的小點來象徵細小的沙粒，表示微小；小篆的"小"字形體則有所訛變，像用一豎把一物體一分為二，也含有變小之義。"小"的本義是指物積上的細微；引申為指在體積、面積、數量、力量、強度等方面不及一般或不及所比較的對象。其用法與"大"字的用法正好相對。

甲骨文　　　　　金文　　　　　小篆

小 means "small". In the Oracle-Bone Inscriptions and Bronze Inscriptions, the character 小 consists of three dots, signalling very small fine grains of sand. In the Later Seal Character, it looks like the dividing of something into two by a vertical line in the middle, signalling to make smaller. The primary meaning of 小 is "small in size", from which has derived its use for things small in quantity, force, importance, etc., opposite to 大 (big).

tǔ

甲骨文的土字，像地面上隆突起來的一個小土堆，其本義指土壤，引申為指土地、田地，又引申為指國土、領土。漢字中凡從土之字都與土壤或土地有關，如城、埋、垣、塞等。

【土木】指房屋、道路、橋樑等建築工程。

【土產】指某地出產的富有地方色彩的物品。

【土著】世代居住本地的人。

【土崩瓦解】像土倒塌、瓦破碎，比喻潰敗不可收拾。

甲骨文　　　　　　金文　　　　　　小篆

In the Oracle-Bene Inscriptions, the character 土 looks like a heap of earth raised above the ground. Its primary meaning is "soil", from which have derived its senses of "field", "land" and "territory". Characters with 土 as a component most have to do with soil and land, e.g. 城 (town), 埋 (to bury), 垣 (wall) and 塞 (fortress).

【土木】building; construction

【土產】local speciality

【土著】aboriginal

【土崩瓦解】to fall apart like the collapse of an earth wall or the breakup of a tile

qiū

甲骨文丘字的造形與山字非常接近，區別只在於："山"有三個山峰，而"丘"則只有兩個。丘字的本義指小山，通常指土質的、小而低矮的山峰；引申為指高出平地的土堆，如墳丘、丘墓等。

【丘陵】連綿成片的小山。

甲骨文

金文

小篆

In the Oracle-Bone Inscriptions, the character 丘 looks very similar to 山, except that the former has two peaks while the latter has three. 丘 primarily refers to hills, not so high as mountains, from which use has derived its reference to any heap of earth raised above the ground, e.g. 墳丘 (grave mound), 丘墓 (grave).

【丘陵】hills

yáo

古文字的堯字，從土（或一土，或二土、三土不等）在人上，表示土堆高出人頭之意。所以，堯字的本義是指高大的土丘，引申為高的意思。此字後來成為傳說中的古帝陶唐氏的專用名號，又用作姓氏名，其本義則改用"嶢"字來代替。

【堯舜】唐堯和虞舜，遠古部落聯盟時代的兩位首領，古史相傳為聖明之君。堯、舜並舉，後來成為稱頌帝王的套語。

【堯天】即"堯天舜日"。相傳堯、舜時天下太平，因以堯天舜日比喻太平盛世。

甲骨文　　　　　　小 篆

In ancient writing systems, the character 堯 has a soil part (土; sometimes two or three soil parts) above a man part, signalling a heap of earth raised higher than a man. The original meaning of 堯 was "high heaps of earth", or simply "high", Nowadays, however, it is used as proper name for the first of the three legendary wise leaders of ancient China, or as a surname, and its original meaning is expressed by 嶢.

【堯舜】(lit.) Yao and Shun (two legendary wise leaders in ancient China); ancient sages

【堯天】(also 堯天舜日) the reign of Yao (and Shun); piping times of peace

fù

　　阜，指土山、丘陵。甲骨文的阜字，像陡坡上的腳登、階梯之形，表示山體高大，須有腳登階梯方能便於登降之意。阜的本義為高大的土丘，引申為高大、肥大之義，又引申為多的意思，特指財物殷盛。

【阜陵】高大的土丘，山崗，丘陵。

【阜康】富足康樂。

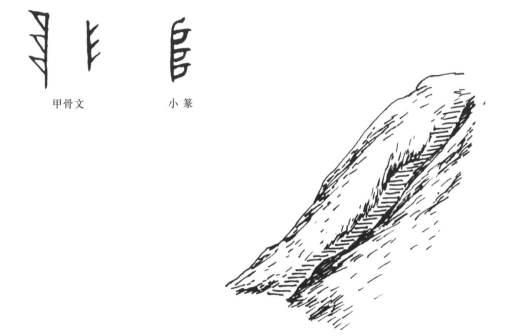

甲骨文　　　　　小篆

阜 means "mound", "hill". In the Oracle-Bone Inscriptions, the character 阜 looks like the steps on a cliff, signalling that the hill is high and one has to climb it through steps. The primary meaning of 阜 is "a high mound", from which have derived its senses of "high", "large" and "many (esp. of treasures)".

【阜陵】 high mound, hill

【阜康】 rich and happy

yáng

古文字的陽字，從阜易聲，是個形聲字。陽的本義是指山之南面，水之北岸，即日光經常能普照的地方；引申為指太陽、日光；又引申為指凸出的、表面的、外露的等義，與"陰"相對。

【陽光】日光。

【陽奉陰違】表面順從而暗中違背。

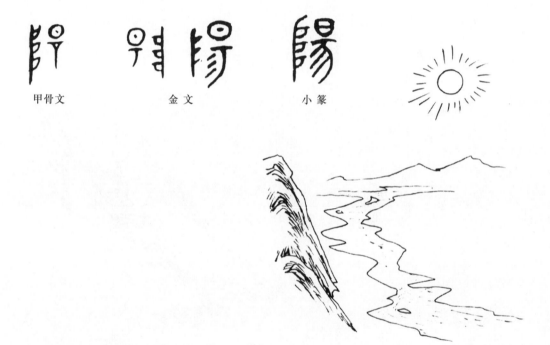

甲骨文　　　　　金文　　　　　小篆

In ancient writing systems, the character 陽 is a phonetic compound with 阜 as the radical and 易 as the phonetic. 陽 originally refers to the south of a mountain or the north of a river, i.e. the side sunlight reaches. From this use has derived its reference to the sun, sunlight, or anything standing out, on the surface or in the open, opposite to 陰 (dark; hidden).

【陽光】 sunlight

【陽奉陰違】 to overtly agree but covertly oppose

shān

所謂山，是指陸地上隆起高聳的部份。甲骨文的山字，正像一座由多個高聳山峰組成的山嶺的形狀。在漢字中凡由"山"組成的字大都與山嶺及其形態有關，如嵩、崇、峻、巍等。

【山河】高山大河，指地區形勝。又是疆域、國土的代稱。

【山明水秀】形容風景優美。

【山高水長】喻人品節操高潔，影響深遠。

【山盟海誓】盟誓堅定，如山海之長久。多指男女真誠相愛。

甲骨文

金文

小篆

山 means "mountain", the natural elevation of earth's surface. In the Oracle-Bone Inscriptions, the character 山 looks like a mountain range consisting of several peaks. Characters with 山 as a component most have to do with mountains, e.g. 嵩, 崇, 峻 and 巍 used of mountains all mean "high".

【山河】 mountains and rivers; the land of a country

【山明水秀】 green hills and clear water

【山高水長】 (of nobility of character) as high as mountains and as long as rivers; of lasting influence

【山盟海誓】 a solemn pledge, usu. of love

dǎo

島，指的是海洋中被水環繞、面積比大陸小的陸地，也指江河湖泊中被水環繞的陸地。島字從山從鳥，是個會意字，表示海中有山可供海鳥棲止的意思；同時鳥又代表島字的讀音，故島字又是一個從山鳥聲的形聲字。

【島嶼】島的總稱。

【島國】全部領土由島嶼組成的國家。

小篆

島 means "island", a piece of land surrounded by water. The character 島 consisting of 山 and 鳥, is an ideograph, signalling there is a hill in the sea where birds may stay as their resting place. Meanwhile 鳥 may serve to indicate its pronunciation, in this sence, 島 is a phonetic compound with 山 as the radical and 鳥 as the phonetic.

【島嶼】islands and islets

【島國】island country

sōng

小篆

嵩字從山從高，是個會意字。它的本義指高山，泛指高大的樣子。後來這個意思常為"崇"字所代替，而"嵩"則成為嵩山的專名。嵩山在今河南省境內，又稱嵩岳、嵩高，是五岳中的中岳。

【嵩巒】高聳的峰巒。

【嵩華】中岳嵩山與西岳華山，合稱"嵩華"。

【嵩呼】相傳漢元封元年春，漢武帝登嵩山，吏卒聽到三次高呼萬歲的聲音。後用以指舊時臣下祝頌皇帝高呼萬歲的意思。

The character 嵩, consisting of 山 and 高, is an ideograph. It primarily refers to high mountains, and may refer to other high things as well, a use which is often assumed by 崇 now. 嵩 is also a proper name for a mountain is Henan Province, i.e. Mount Song (嵩山), also known as 中岳 (the Central Mountain), one of the five famous mountains in China.

【嵩巒】high mountains

【嵩華】Mount Song and Mount Hua

【嵩呼】loud wishes for the emperor to live for ever

shí

古文字的石字，像山崖下一塊石狀，它的本義即指崖石、石頭，泛指各種各類的石料。因石性堅硬，所以凡從石的字大都與石質及其堅硬的屬性有關，如礦、硬、研、確、碑等。

【石破天驚】極言震動之甚。後常用於指文章議論出人意表。

【石沉大海】比喻杳無音信，事情沒有一點下文。

甲骨文　　　　　金 文　　　　　小 篆

In ancient writing systems, the character 石 looks like a stone underneath a cliff. Hence its primary meaning "stone" or "rock". Characters with 石 as a component most have to do with stones and their qualities, e.g. 礦 (mineral deposit), 硬 (hard), 研 (to grind), 確 (firm) and 碑 (stele).

【石破天驚】earth-shattering and heaven-battering; remarkably original and forceful

【石沉大海】like a stone dropping into the sea; to disappear for ever; to have never been heard of since

lěi

磊字由三個石字組成，像眾多石塊壘積之形，其本義為眾石壘積貌，又引申為指高大貌。

【磊塊】石塊。又指壘石高低水平，比喻心中阻梗或不平。

【磊落】高大貌。也比喻人的俊偉。又指石塊錯落分明，引申為指人灑脫不拘，直率開朗。

小篆

The character 磊 consists of three stone parts, looking like many stones piled up. Its primary meaning is "stones piled up", from which has derived its sense of "high".

【磊塊】 uneven; indignant

【磊落】 high; open and upright

zhuó

斫字從石從斤，是個會意字。甲骨文的斫字，像人手持斧斤砍擊岩石的形狀。斫字的本義為砍擊，引申為泛指削、切等義，又引申為指攻擊。斫字還可用作名詞，指斧刃。

【斫營】偷襲敵營。

【斫膾】薄切魚片。

甲骨文

小篆

The character 斫, consisting of 石 and 斤, is an ideograph. In the Oracle-Bone Inscriptions, the character 斫 looks like a man cutting a rock with an axe in hand. The primary meaning of 斫 is "to cut", "to chop", from which has derived its sense "to attack". Used as a noun, it refers to the axe.

【斫營】 to make a surprise attack on an enemy camp

【斫膾】 slices of fish meat

duàn

金文的段字，像手持錐鑿在山岩下捶打石塊之形，兩小點代表打碎的石屑。它的本義為打石，引申為捶擊之義，所以凡以段為偏旁的字，如鍛，大多有捶打之義。作為姓氏的段氏，估計其祖先最早也是以打石（或打鐵）為職業的。現在的段字，多借用來指布帛的一截，泛指長度或事物、時間的一部份，如片段、段落、分段等。

金 文

小 篆

In the Bronze Inscriptions, the character 段 looks like a man extracting stones by striking at a cliff, the two dots standing for the broken pieces. Its primary meaning is "to extract stones", from which has derived its sense "to strike". Character with 段 as a component most have to do with striking, e.g. 鍛 (to forge). 段 is also a surname, started perhaps by people who extracted stones or forged iron. But the more usual meaning of 段 now is "section", whether of cloth, time or other things, e.g. 片段 (fragment), 段落 (paragraph) and 分段 (to divide into sections).

tián

田字的形體古今變化不大，均像一片阡陌縱橫的田地的形狀，其本義指農田，即供耕種的土地，如稻田、麥田等。在有的地區，則稱水田為田，旱田為地。漢字中凡從田的字大都與田地或耕種有關，如疇、畛、畔、畦等。

【田父】老農。

【田舍】田地和房舍。又泛指村舍、農家。

甲骨文

金文

小篆

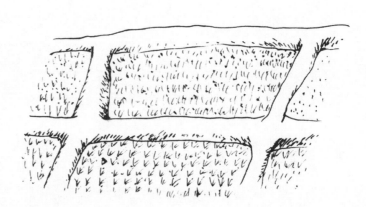

The character 田 has not changed much in its form over the years. It looks like fields with crisscross footpaths in between in any writing systems. Its primary meaning is "farmland", e.g. 稻田 (rice field), 麥田 (wheat field). In some areas, however, only the paddy field is known as 田 while the dry land is referred to as 地. Characters with 田 as a component most have to do with field and cultivation, e.g. 疇 (farmland), 畛 (raised paths between fields), 畔 (the border of a field) and 畦 (plot of land).

【田父】old farmer

【田舍】field and house; farmhouse

zhōu

甲骨文周字，像田地形，中間四點代表田中密植的農作物，其本義應指農田。因周朝發源於今陝西岐山一帶，是當時農田種作、農業生產最發達的地區，周代又是以農業立國，所以就以"周"作為其國名。在實際語言運用中，周字的意義很多，但基本的含義為周圍、環繞、曲折等。而這些基本含義，又都是從農田疆界的意義引申出來的。

甲骨文

金 文

小 篆

In the Oracle-Bone Inscriptions, the character 周 has a field part (田) with four dots in each section standing for crops. Hence its original meaning "farmland". 周 is also the name of a dynasty after Shang. The choice of this name reflects a fact that the Zhou Dynasty started from a place, the present-day Qishan of Shanxi Province, where agriculture was at an advanced stage of development. Nowadays, the character 周 may be used in many senses, but the most important ones are "circumference", "to surround" and "to twist", all deriving from the sense of "border of a field".

xíng

甲骨文、金文的行字，像兩條縱橫交叉的大路，有的加人形，表示有人在路上行走的意思，所以行的本義指道路，又指行走、步行。由道路這個本義，行（háng）字可引申出行列、行業等義；而由行走之義，行（xíng）字又可引申出流動、傳佈、經歷、行為、使用等義。

【行李】出行時隨身攜帶的衣裝及用品。又指使者。

【行（háng）當】行業。特指職業、工作。

【行政】執掌政權，管理政務。

【行雲流水】比喻純任自然，毫無拘束。

甲骨文　　　　金文　　　　小篆

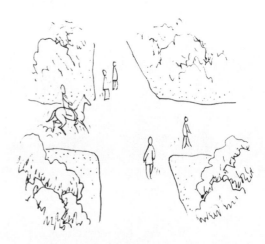

In the Oracle-Bone Inscriptions and Bronze Inscriptions, the character 行 looks like two roads crossing each other. Sometimes there is an additional man part in the middle, signalling that a man is walking on the road. Hence the primary meaning of 行 is "road" and "to walk". From its meaning of "road" have derived its senses of "a row of people" and "a line of business", pronounced as háng. From its sense "to walk" have derived its meanings "to move about", "to circulate", "to perform" and "to experience".

【行李】luggage

【行（háng）當】line of business

【行政】administration

【行雲流水】like floating clouds and flowing water; natural and smooth

fēng

甲骨文、金文的封字，像植樹於土堆之上或用手培土植樹的樣子，其本義為培土植樹，又有聚土成墳的意思，引申為堆、冢之義。古人封土植樹的目的是為了劃分田界和疆域，所以封字還有疆界、界域之義。古代帝王把土地或爵位賜給臣子就叫做封，而諸侯或大夫所分得的土地就稱為封地、封邑。封字由疆界之義又可引申為密閉、拘限之義，如封閉、封鎖、查封等。

【封建】古代帝王把爵位、土地賜給諸侯，在封定的區域內建立邦國，是為封建。現代所言"封建"，指封建主義社會形態。

【封疆】指疆界。又明清時稱總督、巡撫等地方軍政長官為封疆大吏、封疆大臣。

【封疆畫界】築土為台，以表識（zhì）疆境，叫封疆；在二封之間又建牆垣，以劃分界域，叫畫界。

甲骨文　　　金文　　　小篆

In the Oracle-Bone Inscriptions and Bronze Inscriptions, the character 封 looks like (a man) planting a tree or earthing up a tree with his hands. Its original meaning is "to earth up a tree" or "to bank up earth into a grave", from which have derived its senses of "a heap of earth" or "a grave". One of the purposes of planting trees was to draw lines of demarcation between different families or states, so the character 封 has taken on the sense of "boundary". Thus the granting of land or titles of nobility to his ministers by a monarch is known as 封, and the land granted to them 封地. From its sense of boundary have also derived its meanings "to close" and "to limit", e.g. 封閉 (to close), 封鎖 (to blockade) and 查封 (to seal off).

【封建】(1) the system of enfeoffment (2) feudalism

【封疆】(1) boundary (2) highest local officer

【封疆畫界】to draw demarcation lines

jiāng

甲骨文、金文的疆字，像兩塊相連的田地，有的中間有界線，左邊的弓是用來丈量土地的。因此，疆字的本義為丈量土地，劃分田界，又指田界，引申為指國界、邊界。

【疆界】國界、地界。

【疆場】戰場。

【疆域】國家領土。

甲骨文　　　　　金文　　　　　小篆

In the Oracle-Bone Inscriptions and Bronze Inscriptions, the character 疆 looks like two fields one above the other with a measuring instrument (弓) on the left. Sometimes there is a line between the two fields standing for a boundary. Hence 疆 means "to measure land", "to delimit a boundary", "field boundary" and "national boundaries".

【疆界】 national boundaries

【疆場】 battlefield

【疆域】 territory

里字是個會意字。里字從田從土，田指水田，土指旱地。古代農業社會，有田有地才能生產，才能生活居住。所以里的本義指居民所聚居的地方，即鄉里；引申為指居民單位，如先秦時以"五家為鄰，五鄰為里"，也就是說二十五家為一"里"。此外，里又用作長度單位，古代以一百五十丈為一里。

【里正】古時鄉里的小吏。

【里居】指辭官居於鄉里。

【里閭】里巷、鄉里。

【里落】村落。

金 文

小 篆

里 is an ideograph, consisting of 田 and 土, the former referring to paddy field and the latter dry land. In the agricultural society, one has to have land to produce things and support one's life. The original meaning of 里 was the place where a community inhabit, i.e. village. Hence it has come to be used as an administrative unit. For example, in the Qin Dynasty, five families formed a neighbourhood (鄰) and five neighbourhoods a village (里). In other words, there were twenty-five families in a village. In addition, 里 is a measure of length, equal to 150 zhàng in the Chinese System and 500 metres in the Metric System.

【里正】head of a village

【里居】to resign from office and live in the country

【里閭】lane

【里落】village

yě

【埜】

甲骨文、金文的野字，從土從林，本指山林曠野之地；小篆從里予聲，變為形聲字，但含義不變。野字的本義指郊原、田野，又指邊邑、邊鄙；引申為指民間，與"朝廷"相對。野又指野生的動物或植物，與"家養"、"人工種植"相對；引申為指人行為的野蠻、粗魯，與"文明"相對。

【野史】舊時指私家編撰的史書。又作稗史。

【野性】放縱不拘，難於馴服的生性。又指樂居田野的性情。

甲骨文

金文　　　　　　小篆

In the Oracle-Bone Inscriptions and Bronze Inscriptions, the character 野 has a soil part (土) in the middle of a forest part (林), signalling the open field and forest. In the Later Seal Character, the character becomes a phonetic compound with 里 as the radical and 予 as the phonetic, but the meaning is not changed. 野 originally refers to the outskirts of a town, or remote areas, from which has derived its sense of "nongovernmental", as against 朝廷 (royal government). 野 may also refer to wild animals or natural plants as against 家養 (domesticated) or 人工種植 (cultivated), from which has derived its sense of "barbarous", as against 文明 (civilized).

【野史】 (also 稗史) unofficial history

【野性】 unruliness

yòu

囿本來是個會意字。從甲骨文和石鼓文的形體看，囿字像是一個四周有圍牆、內面栽種草木的園林。由於書寫繁難，從金文開始，這個字就變成了從口有聲的形聲字。囿的本義是指有圍牆的園林，後來專指古代帝王放養禽獸的林苑（漢代以後多稱為"苑"）。由囿的"有圍牆"義，囿字又可引申為局限、見識不廣等義。

甲骨文

金 文

小 篆

囿 was originally an ideograph. In the Oracle-Bone Inscriptions and Stone-Drum Inscriptions, the character 囿 looks like a garden of flowers with walls on the four·sides. In the Bronze Inscriptions, however, it becomes a phonetic compound with 口 (enclosure) as the radical and 有 as the phonetic, for the convenience of writing. From its original meaning of "walled garden" has derived its use to refer to the royal garden in particular, which is now known as 苑. From this original meaning has also derived its use to refer to a person's knowledge which is limited one way or another.

huǒ

火是物體燃燒時所發出的光和焰。甲骨文的火字,像火苗正在燃燒的樣子,其本義即指火焰。漢字中凡由火所組成的字大都與火及其作用有關,如炎、炙、焚、然、焦、烹、煮等。

【火候】指燒火的火力大小和時間長短,又比喻修養程度的深淺。

【火急】非常緊急。

【火氣】中醫指引起發炎、紅腫、煩躁等症狀的病因。現多指怒氣,暴躁的脾氣。

【火上加油】比喻使人更加憤怒或使事態更加嚴重。

【火樹銀花】形容燦爛的燈火或煙火。

甲骨文

小篆

火 means "fire", the light and flame given out from a burning substance. In the Oracle-Bone Inscriptions, the character 火 looks like the flames of something burning, hence it primarily refers to fire. Characters with 火 as a component most have to do with fire and its uses, e.g. 炎 (a big fire), 炙 (to roast), 焚 (to burn a forest), 然 (to burn), 焦 (burned), 烹 (to cook), and 煮 (to boil).

【火候】(1) duration and degree of heating (2) level of attainment

【火急】urgent

【火氣】(1) (Chinese medicine) internal heat (2) temper

【火上加油】to pour oil on the fire; to add fuel to the flames

【火樹銀花】fiery trees and silver flowers; a display of fireworks and a sea of lanterns

yán

　　古文字炎字，像上下兩把大火，火光沖天，表示火勢旺盛。因此，炎的本義是火盛，引申為熱、極熱（指天氣）。

【炎荒】指南方炎熱荒遠之地。

【炎炎】形寫陽光強烈。

【炎涼】熱和冷，用天氣的變化比喻人情的變化無常，對待不同地位的人或親熱攀附，或冷淡疏遠。

甲骨文　　　　　　金文　　　　　　小篆

In ancient writing systems, the character 炎 has two fire parts one upon the other, signalling there is a big fire. From this primary meaning of "big fire" have derived it senses of "scorching" and "burning hot", used of weather.

【炎荒】 the hot, remote areas in the south

【炎炎】 the blazing sun

【炎涼】 (1) (lit.) hot and cold (2) snobbishness

liáo

　　燎是古代的一種祭祀方法，即焚柴以祭天地山川。甲骨文、金文的燎字，像木柴交積之形，或從火，四周加點表示火星爆裂狀。燎的本義為焚燒，引申為指烘烤，又指火炬、火燭等。

【燎祭】燃火以祭天地山川。

【燎原】火燒原野。比喻勢盛不可阻擋。

【燎炬】火把，火炬。

甲骨文

金文

小篆

燎 refers to an ancient sacrificial ceremony in which wood is burned as an offering to Heaven. In the Oracle-Bone Inscriptions and Bronze Inscriptions, the character 燎 looks like pieces of wood crossing each other, with dots around standing for sparks from the fire. Sometimes there is even a fire part beneath. The primary meaning of 燎 is "to burn", from which have derived its meanings of "drying by fire", "torch" and "flammable things".

【燎祭】to offer burning wood as a sacrifice to Heaven

【燎原】to set the prairie ablaze; irresistible

【燎炬】torch

fén

原始社會時代，農業落後，實行刀耕火種，開墾田地時往往採取用火燒山林的辦法。甲骨文中的焚字，上面是林，下面是熊熊燃燒的火焰，又像一個人手持火把在引火燒林之形。所以，焚字的本義為火燒山林，引申為引火燃燒、燒毀等義。

甲骨文

小篆

In the primitive society, agriculture was at a low stage of development and people used some primitive methods known as slash-and-burn cultivation, which is to some extent reflected in the form of the character 焚. In the Oracle-Bone Inscriptions, 焚 has a forest part above a fire part, and sometimes the lower part looks like a man holding a torch in hand. Hence 焚 meant originally "to burn a forest", from which have derived its present-day meanings of "burning" and "destruction by fire".

zāi

　　人類所遭受的苦難，莫大於水、火和戰亂所造成的禍害，人們稱之為"災"，如水災、火災、兵災。除此之外，當還有其他的災害，如蟲災、風災等。甲骨文的災字，有的從宀從火，表示房屋失火；有的從水，表示洪水為患；有的從戈，表示戰爭之亂。所以災的本義是指人類所遭受的禍害、苦難。這個意義，從古至今都沒有多大的改變。

【災荒】指自然變化給人帶來的損害（多指荒年）。
【災難】天災人禍所造成的嚴重損害和痛苦。又作"災殃"。

甲骨文

金文

小篆

The disasters man suffers are known as 災 in Chinese, e.g. 水災 (flood), 火災 (fire), 兵災 (war), 蟲災 (plague of insects) and 風災 (disaster caused by windstorm). In the Oracle-Bone Inscriptions, the character 災 consists of 宀 (house) and 火 (fire), signalling the house is on fire. Sometimes it has a water part (水) instead of a fire part, signalling there is a flood. And there may also be a weapon part (戈) as a substitute, signalling there is war. Hence 災 refers to the different kinds of disaster man suffers, and this meaning has remained unchanged over the years.

【災荒】 famine due to crop failure
【災難】 (also 災殃) disaster

shù

在古代炊具還沒有發明之前，人們為了吃到熟食，除一般性地用火直接燒烤外，還採用燒熱的石塊來烙熟食物，或把燒熱的石塊投入盛水的器皿中而煮熟食物。甲骨文、金文的庶字，從石從火，表示以火燒石而煮的意思。因此，庶的本義為煮。後來庶字多用為眾庶之庶，指庶民、老百姓，又有眾多之義。而庶的本義，則為"煮"字所代替。

【庶民】老百姓、平民、眾人。
【庶務】煩雜瑣碎的各種事務。
【庶類】眾多的物類。

甲骨文

金 文

小 篆

Before the invention of cooking utensils people would burn some stones and then use them to heat food directly or by putting them in a vessel containing water, apart from roasting the food on an open fire. In the Oracle-Bone Inscriptions and Bronze Inscriptions, the character 庶 consists of 石 (stone) and 火 (fire), signalling to burn stones by fire. Hence its original meaning was "to cook". Nowadays, however, 庶 is more usually used in the senses of "the common people" and "numerous", and its original meaning is expressed by 煮.

【庶民】the common people
【庶務】general affairs
【庶類】numerous types

tàn

小篆的炭字，上面是山崖形，下部從火，表示在山中燒木成炭的意思。炭的本義指木炭；又指石炭，即煤。

【炭敬】舊時外地官員對京官冬季饋送銀兩，稱為"炭敬"。

小篆

In the Later Seal Character, the character 炭 has a cliff part above a fire part, signalling to burn wood and make charcoal in the mountains. 炭 primarily refers to charcoal, but in former times it may also refer to coal, known as 石炭.

【炭敬】(arch.) presents sent by local officials to the officials in the capital in winter

huī

灰，指的是物質經燃燒後剩下的粉末狀的東西。甲骨文灰字，像人手持木棍撥弄火灰之形。它的本義是指火灰，如木灰、石灰等；引申為指塵土；又用作顏色，介於白色和黑色之間，是一種比較暗淡的顏色。

【灰塵】塵土。

【灰燼】物品燃燒後的灰和燒剩的東西。

【灰暗】暗淡，不鮮明。

【灰飛煙滅】像灰土和輕煙一樣地消失。

甲骨文

小篆

灰 means "ash", powder that remains after a substance has been burnt. In the Oracle-Bone Inscriptions, the character 灰 looks like a man stirring ashes with a stick. Its primary meaning is "ash", e.g. 木灰 (plant ash), 石灰 (lime), from which has derived its use to refer to dust. It may also refer to a colour like black mixed with wihte, namely, grey.

【灰塵】dust

【灰燼】ashes

【灰暗】murkey grey

【灰飛煙滅】to disappear completely like ash or smoke

chì

古代有焚人牲而求雨的習俗。古文字赤字，從大在火上，像把人置於火上焚燒之形，正是這種習俗的形象反映。赤本是一種祭祀名稱，指的是以火焚人；又指被火烤紅的意思。引申為泛指紅色；又含有空淨、赤裸等義。

【赤子】指初生的嬰兒，比喻心地純潔。

【赤貧】極貧，家無一物。

【赤條條】形容光着身體，一絲不掛，毫無遮掩。

【赤膽忠心】形容十分忠誠。

甲骨文

金 文

小 篆

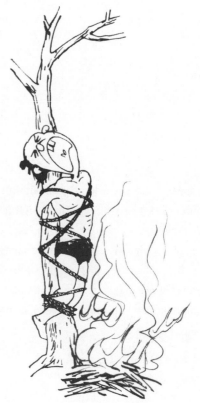

There was a practice among ancient people to burn a man or animal as an offering to Heaven when they preyed for rain. And this practice is reflected in the form of the character 赤, which in ancient writing systems has a man part (大) on a fire part (火), signalling to burn a man. From this original meaning have derived its meanings of "being redden by fire", "red" and "bare".

【赤子】a newborn bady; utter innocence

【赤貧】in extreme poverty

【赤條條】stark-naked

【赤膽忠心】a noble loyalty of heart

zhǔ

主即"炷"的本字。小篆的主字,像一盞油燈之形,上面的一點代表燈心上燃燒的火苗。所以,主的本義即指燈心。主字後來多用為主人、家長以及主持、掌管等義,故另造"炷"代替它的本義。

【主上】臣下對國君或帝王的稱呼。

【主宰】主管、支配。

【主張】見解、主意。

【主顧】顧客。

小 篆

主 was the original form of 炷. In the Later Seal Character, the character 主 looks like an oil lamp, the dot on top standing for the flame of the lampwick. Hence its original meaning "lampwick". Nowadays, however, 主 is mainly used in the senses of "host", "master", "in charge of" and "to manage", and its original meaning is expressed by 炷.

【主上】Your Majesty

【主宰】to dominate

【主張】view; advocate

【主顧】customer

guāng

光通常是指照耀在物體上，使人能看見物體的那種物質，如太陽光、燈光等，引申為指明亮、光滑的意思。古文字光字，像人頭頂上有一團火的樣子，表示火種常在、光明永存的意思。

【光芒】向四面放射的強烈光線。

【光景】時光景物。又指境況、狀況、情景。

【光風霽月】雨過天晴時風清月朗的景象，比喻開闊的胸襟和坦白的心地。

【光怪陸離】形容現象奇異、色彩繁雜。

甲骨文	金文	小篆

光 means "light", the natural agent that stimulates the sense of sight, e.g. 太陽光 (sunlight), 燈光 (lamplight), from which have derived its senses of "bright" and "smooth". In ancient writing systems, the character 光 looks like a fire on top of a man, signalling that there is kindling material so that it will be bright for ever.

【光芒】rays of light

【光景】(1) scene (2) circumstances

【光風霽月】(lit.) refreshing breeze and bright moon; broadminded and openhearted

【光怪陸離】grotesque in shape and gaudy in colour

sǒu

　　叟為"搜"的本字。甲骨文的叟字，像人在室內手持火把照明，表示搜索、尋找的意思。所以，叟的本義為搜索、尋找。此字後來借用為指老人，故另造"搜"字表示它的本義。

甲骨文　　　　　　小篆

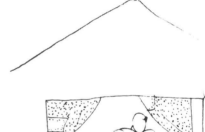

叟 was the original form of 搜. In the Oracle-Bone Inscriptions, the character 叟 looks like a man holding a torch in a room, signalling "to search", "to look for". However, it is now used in the sense of "old man", and its original meaning is expressed by 搜.

其他
Miscellanea

yī

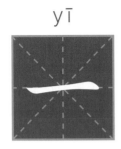

一像一積畫形。上古先民迫於生活上的需要所發生的數字觀念，畫一橫代表一樁事物，二橫代表兩樁，如此積畫，可至三、四。就像結繩記數一樣，一個結代表一十，兩個結代表二十。一字用法很多，主要有兩種：一種是當最小的整數用，如一人、一馬、一槍等；另一種則是當"專一"講，如"一心一意"。

甲骨文　　　　　金 文　　　　　小 篆

一 is a numeral, meaning "one". In Chinese, the simplest numerals are picturelike: one is represented by one horizontal stroke, two by two horizontal strokes, three by three, and four by four. The idea behind it is the same as that behind counting with knots in ropes: one knot represents ten, and two knots twenty. The character 一 may be used in many senses, but the most important two are: as the smallest integer, e.g. 一人 (one man), 一馬 (one horse), 一槍 (one gun); and meaning "wholehearted", e.g. 一心一意 (heart and soul).

shàng

上是一個指事字。甲骨文、金文的上字,是在一長橫(或弧線)的上方加一短畫,以表示位置在上的意思。所以,上的本義指高處、上面;引申為指等級或品質在上的(即上等),如上級、上品;又次序或時間在前的,如上冊、上半年。上還可用作動詞,有由低處向高處升登的意思,如上山、上樓;有由此處向彼處前進的意思,如上街等。

甲骨文　　　　　金文　　　　　小篆

The character 上 is an indicative. In the Oracle-Bone Inscriptions and Bronze Inscriptions, it consists of a short horizontal stroke on top of a longer one (or a concave curve), signifying "on top of". hence its primary meaning "the higher", "the upper"; from which have derived the meanings of "higher in rank" or "better in quality", e.g. 上級 (higher authorities), 上品 (top grade product); and the meanings of "before in sequence" or "before in time", e.g. 上冊 (first volume), 上半年 (the first half of the year). Used as a verb, it means "to ascend", e.g. 上山 (to go up a hill), 上樓 (to go upstairs); from which has further derived its more general sense "to go", e.g. 上街 (to go into the street).

xià

下和上一樣是個指事字。甲骨文、金文的下字，是在長橫（或弧線）下加一短畫，以表示位置在下的意思。下的本義指低處、下面，與"上"相對；引申為指等級或品質在下的、次序或時間在後的等義。下也可用作動詞，有由高處向低處下降等意義。

甲骨文　　　　　　金　文　　　　　　小　篆

The character 下, like 上, is also an indicative. In the Oracle-Bone Inscriptions and Bronze Inscriptions, it consists of a short horizontal stroke underneath a longer one (or a convex curve), signifying "underneath". The primary meaning of 下 is, opposite to 上, "the lower", "underneath"; from which has derived its use for things which are lower in rank, worse in quality, or after in sequence or time. Used as a verb, it means "to descend".

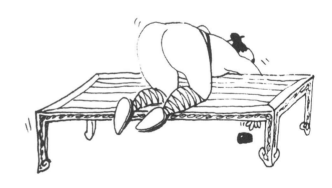

shí

古代計數，最初是採用實物和結繩的辦法：凡單數一二三四等，可以用實物（如小木棍）累積而成；而整數則用結繩來表示，即在一根繩上打一個結表示一十，兩個結為二十（廿），三個結是三十（卅）。金文的十字為一直畫，中間作一圓點（或加肥筆），正是結繩計數的形象描繪。十為數詞，是一個整數，大寫作"拾"。

【十分】是"完全"、"已達極度"的意思。如孔平仲詩："庭下金齡菊，花開已十分。"（庭院中的金菊花已完全開放。）

【十九】是"十分之九"的意思，也泛指絕大多數。

【十全十美】指一個人或一件事物十分完美，毫無欠缺。

甲骨文

金 文

小 篆

十 is a numeral, meaning "ten", the unchangeable variant being 拾. In ancient times, people used to calculate through counting objects or tying knots in ropes. When the number was smaller than ten, they would use objects like sticks. For round numbers, they would tie knots in ropes, one knot stood for ten, two for twenty, three for thirty, and so on. In the Bronze Inscriptions, the character 十 consists of a vertical line with a circular dot in the middle (or an enlarged middle part), a vivid descriptions of calculating through knotting.

【十分】fully; extremely

【十九】(lit.) nine tenths; the overwhelming majority

【十全十美】perfect in every way

niàn

金文的廿字，像一根彎曲的繩子，上面的兩個圓點（或肥筆）代表兩個繩結，表示記數二十的意思。《説文解字》：“廿，二十並也。”（廿是二十的合文。）甲骨文由於受契刻的限制，只刻出一根曲繩的形狀，而無法刻出圓點表示繩結；小篆則連二點為一橫，原字的象形意味就大大減弱了。廿作為“二十”的意思，多用於文言文中，一般不用於白話文和口語。以舊曆（農曆）紀時可用“廿”，如廿六年（二十六年），廿九日（二十九日）；而以公曆紀時則不能用“廿”，一律改稱“二十”。

甲骨文　　　　金文　　　　小篆

In the Bronze Inscriptions, the character 廿 looks like a U-shaped rope with two circular dots on the shafts (or two enlarged shafts) standing for knots, signifying "twenty". The *Origin of Chinese Characters* says, " 廿 means two tens put together". In the Oracle-Bone Inscriptions, the character has a U-stroke only, there are no circular dots, which are difficult to engrave. In the Later Seal Character, there is a horizontal stroke linking the two shafts, which are no longer dotted, losing much of its original picturelike image. In the sense of twenty, 廿 is usually used in classical Chinese, not in the vernacular or the colloquial style. Thus it is used in the lunar calendar, e.g. 廿六年 (the twenty-sixth year), 廿九日 (the twenty-ninth day); but not in the solar calendar, where 二十 would be used in its stead.

sà

"卅"也是結繩記數的反映。金文的卅字，像一根繩上的三個繩結，表示"三十"的意思。如"五卅運動"，其中的"五卅"就是指"五月三十日"。

甲骨文　　　　　　金文　　　　　　小篆

The character 卅 also results from the practice to tie knots in a rope to facilitate counting. In the Bronze Inscriptions, it looks like an almost W-shaped rope with three knots on the shafts, signifying "thirty". For example, the character 卅 in 五卅運動 (the May 30th Movement) refers to the thirtieth day.